THE SERMONS AND

OF THE RIGHT REVEREND

FATHER IN GOD

JOSEPH BUTLER D.C.L.

LATE LORD BISHOP OF DURHAM

NEWLY EDITED WITH A MEMOIR AND INDICES BY

THE REV. E. STEERE LL.D.

LONDON
BELL AND DALDY 186 FLEET STREET
1862

GENERAL PREFACE.

IN giving to the public a new edition of Bishop Butler's Sermons, it has been the wish of the publishers to put forth such a volume as with their previous edition of the "Analogy" might embrace the whole of his recoverable works, together with a summary of what is known concerning his personal history. I have been greatly indebted, in editing this volume, to the kindness of many friends; among whom I must particularise, in the first place, the Rev. John E. B. Mayor, of St. John's College, Cambridge, who procured me a copy of the unpublished "Fragment of the Charge at Bristol," which is the gem of our edition, as well as furnishing several valuable hints and notices; and in the second, the Rev. M. Benson, who most kindly allowed me the use of a MS. biography of his great namesake the Bishop of Gloucester, from which I have drawn such notices of his life as are worked into my Memoir. I would gladly mention other friends also, but space would fail me to do them all justice, so that I trust they will accept this general acknowledgment of their great and spontaneous kindness.

With the exception of what refers to Bp. Benson, I have done little more than re-arrange the materials already collected by Mr. Bartlett and by the Bishop of Cork, in his admirable edition of the " Analogy," so that I have thought it unnecessary to burden my pages with frequent references to authorities. I believe the series of Letters is much more complete than any hitherto published ; the " Fragment of the Bristol Charge" I have already referred to. The only other new features are the small Remains I first published in 1853, the attempt to follow Dr. Whewell in marking out the " Fifteen Sermons" into paragraphs, and the Index, for which I must ask the indulgence of the learned, who will allow for the difficulty of the work in judging of the manner of its performance.

EDWARD STEERE.

Little Steeping,
Aug. 1861.

TABLE OF CONTENTS.

A MEMOIR OF BISHOP BUTLER.

HE Church of England has had many prelates of whose wisdom, piety, and learning she might be justly proud, yet few of these have exhibited at the same time so much wisdom and so much piety as the subject of our present memoir. Modesty and sober truthfulness were among the chief features of his character. He left the dissenting community in which he was brought up, without any of a convert's rancour. He was a Whig in politics, and yet he stood forward manfully on behalf of comely old Church usages. Without any display or boast of asceticism, he spent most liberally upon Church works, while he was a pattern of moderation in his own style of living.

Very much of the same sobriety and truthfulness mark his published works. There is no display, no showy theorizing. It was said of him that he read every book he could meet with, and the fruits of this extended reading are to be found not in margins overloaded with citations, but in that clear fulness of thought which large and well-digested reading alone can give. The avoidance of some common word, or the mere turn of a phrase will

often show, not only that the author has read and
considered the theories of others, but also that his
aim is something so much higher than the display
of knowledge, that he does not care to exhibit to
the multitude how much he knows. His learning
enables him to avoid the many sunken rocks that lie
around, and thus warned and guided he looks into
men's hearts and examines the course of nature,
and what he finds there he describes and uses in
a manner that would seem cold were it not for its
extreme truthfulness. He did not wish to cover
those with confusion who were in error, but rather
to make the truth so clear that no one should be
able to doubt of it.[1] He always speaks with great
respect of *à priori* reasoning, in which, however, he
never indulges, thinking it, though a higher and
better style of argument, one not so level to the
capacities of men in general.

In private life his friends describe him as a most
delightful companion, from " a delicacy of thinking,
an extreme politeness, a vast knowledge of the
world, and a peculiar something to be met with in
no one else." His retiring modesty, which allowed
him to come forward only when he had something
really of value to impart, while it gives an additional
charm to what we know, almost prevents the com-

[1] The same calmness seems to have distinguished him in
spoken controversy. John Byrom, after relating a discussion
he had with him on the respect due to authority in matters of
faith, says :—" I wished I had Dr. Butler's temper and calmness, yet not quite, because I thought him a little too little
vigorous." Byrom had maintained the absolute supremacy of
authority in all conceivable cases, and perhaps Butler felt that
to be equally " vigorous" on the other side would only have
been to be equally mistaken. See " John Byrom's Diary,"
March 27th, 1737. Butler afterwards invited him to come and
see him when in London.

pilation of anything like a complete biography,—
we know so little, where we desire to know so
much.

JOSEPH BUTLER was born at Wantage, in Berk-
shire, on the 18th of May, in the year 1692. He
was the youngest of eight children. Thomas
Butler, his father, had been a linendraper in the
town, but had for some time retired from business,
and then lived in a house, now still standing, called
the Priory, where Joseph Butler was born. As a
boy he was sent to the grammar-school at Wantage,
of which the Rev. Philip Barton was then master.
It is a pleasing evidence of the respect with which
this teacher impressed his pupil, that some forty
years afterwards, when Dean of St. Paul's, Butler
presented Mr. Barton to the living of Hutton, in
Essex, where he survived his patron by ten years,
dying there in 1762.

Thomas Butler was a Presbyterian, and finding
that his son made good progress in learning he removed him to a Dissenting Academy at Gloucester,
under the charge of Mr. Samuel Jones, that he
might be trained for the ministry. Jones was a
man of considerable learning, and had amongst his
pupils many who were afterwards famous for their
attainments and success. Among these Nathaniel
Lardner, whose ponderous defence of the New Testament has been the common storehouse whence
Paley and so many others have drawn their chief
arguments, Jeremiah Jones, who distinguished himself in the same department of controversy, and
Samuel Chandler, an acute and copious theological
writer, were all celebrated as Dissenting Ministers.
Lardner was two years, the others but one year,
younger than Butler. There were besides Lord

Bowes, Chancellor of Ireland, and Thomas Secker,
ever after a firm friend of Butler's, who died Archbishop of Canterbury in the year 1768.

The state of religion in England was at this time
one to call forth all the powers of those who were
capable of forming an opinion upon the subject.
The controversy with the Non-jurors was not over,
the Bangorian controversy was beginning, infidelity
was making rapid strides among the higher classes
of society, while in the Church Arianism and So-
cinianism were gathering proselytes, and among
Dissenters the Presbyterians, as we know, became,
not long after, completely Unitarian. Nathaniel
Lardner, who did such good service against infidelity, was a Socinian, and Dr. Samuel Clarke, who
distinguished himself in another branch of the
defence of Christianity, was almost, if not quite, an
Arian.

Dr. Clarke was born in 1673, and in the years
1704 and 1705 he preached, and afterwards published, a series of lectures, containing his Demonstration of the Being and Attributes of God. This
work was intended to crush all the atheistical notions which were beginning to show themselves in
society, and to many minds it seemed thoroughly
well fitted to do so. Amongst other careful readers,
Butler, who had in the meantime followed his
master to Tewkesbury, examined every link in the
" Demonstration," and found two which seemed to
him defective, and they are the two which have since
been generally considered the most faulty, although
Butler afterwards confessed himself satisfied. The
first turns upon the assertion that necessary existence implies omnipresence, and the second relates
to the deduction of the unity of God from the one-
ness of space and time. These objections were

communicated to Dr. Clarke in a letter carried by
Secker to Gloucester, and a correspondence ensued,
which was appended to after editions of the " Demonstration," as the correspondence with a gentleman in Gloucestershire, so much did the learned
author value the acuteness of his young opponent.
Thus began an acquaintance which led to very important results.

In one of the letters from Gloucester, Butler had
said, that he designed to make the pursuit of truth
the business of his life, and soon he began to feel
that he could not remain in the ranks of the Presbyterians. His father was very anxious to remove
his scruples, and several Presbyterian Ministers
were called in to confer with him, but in vain. It
seems to have been in the agitation of this time of
controversy that he wrote the despairing letter to
Dr. Clarke, in which he says that he had left
Gloucester three weeks before, and was saddened
by the thought that he must give up those studies
which had a direct tendency to divinity. No such
fate, however, befell him, for on the 17th of March,
1714, he was entered as a commoner of Oriel College, Oxford.

While there he won the friendship and esteem
of Mr. Edward Talbot, and was by him introduced to
his father, Bishop Talbot, who left the See of Oxford
to succeed Bishop Burnet in that of Salisbury in the
year 1715, and was seven years afterwards translated to Durham.

The group of young men which gathered round
Bishop Talbot at this time, and continued through life
closely united, is one too remarkable to be passed over
without notice. The eldest of the party was Martin
Benson, at that time a Student of Christ Church, of
whom it was afterwards said :—" His piety, though

awfully strict, was inexpressibly amiable. It diffused
such a sweetness through his temper and such a
benevolence over his countenance, as none who
were acquainted with him can forget. Bad nerves,
bad health, and naturally bad spirits, were so totally
subdued by it, that he not only seemed, but really
was the happiest of men. He looked upon all that
the world calls important, its pleasures, its riches,
its various competitions, with a playful and good-
humoured kind of contempt ; and could make persons ashamed of their follies, by a raillery that
never gave pain to any human being. Of vice he
always spoke with severity and detestation, but looked
on the vicious with the tenderness of a pitying
angel." Benson was descended from a clerical family, his father having been Rector of Cradley and
his grandfather Dean of Hereford. At Oxford he
was noted for his application to mathematics, and
his good taste and love for the fine arts. In the
year 1717, he went into Italy as tutor to Lord
Pomfret, and at Florence became acquainted with
George Berkeley, afterwards the famous Bishop of
Cloyne, and thus Butler was introduced on their return to his great philosophical contemporary. On
his way home Benson met at Paris with Thomas
Secker, who, having shared Butler's dislike of Pres-
byterianism, without feeling so ready to conform to
the Church, had applied himself to the study of
medicine, and for that purpose was then visiting the
great medical schools on the Continent. Secker was
a man of considerable learning, especially as a
Hebrew scholar, prudent, amiable, and devout, not
perhaps so saintly as some, or so able as others of
the group, but with a clear attractive style and a
winning manner, that told more quickly in his favour
with most men than their deeper merits. Secker

had all along kept up a correspondence with Butler,
who prevailed upon him, about the time Benson
made his acquaintance, to conform to the Church
and look forward to ordination.   Another member of
the party was Rundle, afterwards Bishop of Derry,
whose chief points seem to have been his social
qualities and his appreciation of the superior characters of his friends.   However, though he went
to Derry excessively unpopular and suspected of
Arianism, he had won before his death the universal
esteem of his adopted country.   It is curious that
Butler's close personal acquaintance should thus include the Bishops singled out by Pope for his
grudging commendation :—

> " Even in a Bishop, I can spy desert,
> Secker is decent, Rundle has a heart,
> Candour with manners are to Benson given,
> To Berkeley, every virtue under heaven."

Edward Talbot, the Bishop's younger son, who
was the link which bound them all together, was at
this time a Fellow of Oriel College ; his early death
leaves us nothing by which to estimate his character,
save the ardent affection he inspired in the minds
of so many of the best men of his time.

While Butler was at Oxford, Rundle and Edward
Talbot joined a society for the restoration of Primitive Christianity, formed on the model of the *quasi*
brotherhoods, then so numerous in England, by the
learned and eccentric William Whiston ; who united
to express Arianism a perfect faith in the Apostolic
Constitutions, as though they were part of Scripture.   They both, however, soon quitted it—to
Whiston's intense disgust.

In the year 1717 we find another correspondence
going on with Dr. Clarke, who thought so much of
its philosophical value, that he proposed to print it

with the letters which had passed between himself
and Leibnitz. From these letters we learn that
Butler, besides having little relish for the ordinary
course·of study at his University, wished to migrate
to Cambridge, and to take his degree there; and
Dr. Clarke had actually written to his friend Mr.
Laughton, then one of the Tutors at Clare Hall,
about his going. However, he abandoned his intention on finding that the terms he had already
kept would probably not be allowed him at Cambridge, and took his B.A. degree at Oxford on the
11th of October, 1718. Possibly it was owing to
this preference for Cambridge, which may have
originated in his admiration of Dr. Clarke, that
Butler afterwards wrote his degrees in Laws (the
first of which was taken in June, 1721) after the
Cambridge manner, and not as Oxford men generally do. About a fortnight after taking his degree,
Bishop Talbot ordained him Deacon at Salisbury;
and the Parish Registers show that he officiated
occasionally for his friend Edward Talbot, who had
just been collated to the living of Hendred, near
Wantage. Butler was ordained Priest on the 21st
of December in the same year.

In 1719, being then 26 years old, by the joint
interest of Mr. Talbot and Dr. Clarke, he was appointed Preacher at the Rolls, and apparently went
to reside in London. He continued to preach in
the Rolls Chapel for about eight years.

Meanwhile Edward Talbot had married (in the
year 1715) Mary the daughter of the Rev. G.
Martin, a near relative of Benson's, and an inseparable companion of Benson's sister Catherine. He
died prematurely of the small pox in the winter of
the year 1720. On his death-bed he recommended
his friends to his father's patronage.

The effect of this recommendation was that when, in the year 1722, Bishop Talbot went to Durham, he immediately collated Butler to the Rectory of Haughton, near Darlington ; Rundle became his Domestic Chaplain ; Benson was, two years after, chosen to succeed Sir G. Wheeler in one of the rich prebends of Durham, and about the same time Secker was made Rector of Houghton-le-Spring. Thus the Bishop again gathered round him the whole party at Durham.

The parsonage house at Haughton was very much out of repair, and though the emoluments of the benefice were not then reckoned large, Butler determined to rebuild it. His friends thought this a rash undertaking, as he had no private means, and persuaded the Bishop to remove him to Stanhope, a well-endowed Rectory, where there was no need of any great expenditure. He therefore handed over the materials he had collected to his successor at Haughton, and resigned the preachership at the Rolls, after publishing his famous Fifteen Sermons, which he dedicated to Sir Joseph Jekyll, in whose chapel they had been preached. His last act there seems to have been the celebration of the Holy Communion on July 12, 1726.

There is no appearance that these Fifteen Sermons caused at first any great sensation. It was four years before a second edition came out ; and then it appeared with a long preface, defending them from contempt on account of the difficulty of their style, and giving a sort of conspectus of the subjects, that their nature and object might be better understood. Secker is said to have revised this preface, and he was exactly the man to suggest its necessity. It is impossible that they could generally have been effective in delivery, and with

one or two exceptions, no ordinary sermon reader
would be able to make them out. And yet the first
three are perhaps, in their department, the three
most valuable essays that were ever published.
Without appealing to anything but experience, the
preacher establishes, by reasons too solid to be
gainsaid, that the nature of man is not *merely*
selfish, and then that conscience differs from all
other faculties and sentiments in possessing a necessary supremacy over them.

It is this doctrine of conscience which is the great
thing that has made their author famous. Gradually
and surely the influence of sober truth has grown
up and prevailed, and doctrines which, in the hands
of sentimental writers under the appellations of the
moral sense and *following nature,* could make but
little way, when explained according to the strict
truth of our mental constitution are irresistible.
But he was more than a philosopher, who could
have penned the prayer at the end of the sermon
upon loving our neighbour, when, after observing
how all our affections are complete in the love of
God, he thus concludes :—" O Almighty God, inspire us with this divine principle ; kill in us all the
seeds of envy and ill-will, and help us by cultivating
within ourselves the love of our neighbour to improve in the love of Thee. Thou hast placed us in
various kindreds, friendships, and relations, as the
school of discipline for our affections. Help us by
the due exercise of them to improve to perfection,
till all partial affection be lost in that entire and
universal one, and Thou, O God, shalt be all in
all."

It is not to be wondered at that he who could so
think should leave a good name behind him in
Stanhope ; so that when eighty years afterwards the

present Bishop of Exeter made inquiries there, it was well remembered that he had won the love and respect of his parishioners, though, as to personal details, there was nothing to be learnt except that he generally rode a black pony, and rode very fast, and that he was sorely plagued by the importunities of beggars, whom he was too kind-hearted very firmly to resist.

Seven years were spent at Stanhope, in the society of his college friends and the quiet performance of his parish duties. Meanwhile Secker had married Miss Benson, and Edward Talbot's widow and his posthumous daughter Catherine from thenceforth made Secker's house their home. It seemed that the affection Edward Talbot had inspired was now transferred to his widow and daughter, for they were always on terms of the closest friendship with his old companions, and were often staying in Butler's house, as well at Stanhope as afterwards in London. It was in 1731 that Butler's father died at Wantage, leaving his sons Robert and Joseph co-executors and residuary legatees.

While at Stanhope he was engaged in a correspondence with Henry Home, better known as Lord Kames, upon the evidences of natural and revealed religion. Butler declined a personal interview, on the ground that being unaccustomed to *vivâ voce* controversy he feared the cause of truth might suffer by his want of skill. Possibly this correspondence may have suggested the thought of publishing the "Analogy." The Letters are now lost, but Lord Kames always expressed a very high respect for his correspondent; a respect which was shared by his more famous relative David Hume, far as he was from any true sympathy with such a man as Butler.

The death of Bishop Talbot, in the year 1730, did much toward the breaking up of the little circle at Durham, which had indeed commenced two years before, when Benson consented, at the earnest solicitation of Browne Willis, the antiquary, to accept the living of Bletchley, in Buckinghamshire; and in the year 1733 Secker also was called away, when he became Rector of St. James'. Both, however, retained their stalls at Durham; so that, living as he had done among his old college friends, there was more wit than justice in Archbishop Blackburne's reply when Queen Caroline asked if Butler were dead,—" No, Madam, he is not *dead,* but he is *buried.*"

In the same year that Secker removed to St. James', Bishop Talbot's eldest son was made Lord Chancellor. He at once nominated Butler as his Chaplain, and three years after appointed him to a prebend in Rochester Cathedral. These dignities he would only accept on the understanding that he was not to be too much drawn away from his parochial charge at Stanhope. On accepting the Chaplaincy he went to Oxford and took his degree of D.C.L.

Secker and Benson were both raised to the Episcopate in the year 1734; the former as Bishop of Bristol, the latter, much against his own wish, as Bishop of Gloucester: and it is curious that, in the same year, Berkeley became Bishop of Cloyne, and Rundle, Bishop of Derry, so that Butler alone remained a simple Priest.

In 1736 the Queen made him her Clerk of the Closet, and in the same year he published the " Analogy," dedicating it to Lord Talbot, who only survived until February 14 in the following year.

It is probable that the Sermons at the Rolls,

from which we are tantalizingly told that the published fifteen were chosen almost at random, may
have furnished much of the material for this great
work, as indeed parts of it are anticipated by parts
of those Sermons, especially that on the " Ignorance
of Man."

Perhaps no other controversial work was ever so
free from bitterness against the persons assailed by
it.   Butler felt that he was secure in his own position, and that if those who doubted would but think
more deeply, they would see the folly of their
doubts.   In the "Analogy," as in the Sermons, he
strives to lay a firm foundation, rather than to set
up a showy superstructure.   The natural effect of
this has been, that, to those who never look below
the surface, he seems to have done nothing.   It is
a terrible reflection upon the age, that it was necessary to write an elaborate work to prove that it was
not clear that there was nothing in Christianity;
but, sorely tried as our faith then was, its strength
only showed itself the greater; and the closer its
enemies had pressed on, the more complete was
their overthrow.   It was not that the argument of
the "Analogy" was new.   The passage from Origen,
on the title-page, gave it in a few words, and not long
before, Berkeley, in his " Alciphron," had stated the
substance of it very clearly.   But for completeness,
and that thorough recurrence to first principles and
total absence of local and personal allusions which
prevent a book from growing old, none of the other
writings of the period could be compared with it.

No answer to the whole work was ever published; but a tract in defence of Locke's notion
of personal identity was soon issued by the Rev.
Vincent Perronet, Vicar of Shoreham, in Kent, and
the Essay on Virtue was attacked by a clergyman

named Bott, who thought that the chief rewards of virtue would be of a temporal nature. In the main, however, the "Analogy" was, and is, unanswerable.

In the year 1737 Secker was translated to the See of Oxford, and Dr. Gooch succeeded him at Bristol.

In the same year Butler lost his patron, Queen Caroline, a woman remarkable for her strength of mind and her many charities—she loved to gather round her all the most able theologians and philosophers of the time; and at her decease the king continued charitable pensions to the amount of 13,000*l.* a year, which she had been accustomed to pay out of her own private purse. She received the Holy Communion from Butler's hands at Hampton Court shortly before her death, and recommended him strongly to the king's patronage. She died on the 20th of November, 1737.

The king soon after summoned Butler to preach before him. "He took for his subject the being bettered by affliction; and his majesty was so much moved that he desired to have the sermon, and said he would do something very good for him."[2]

It was a curious fulfilment of this magnificent promise, that when, about a year afterwards, the Bishop of Norwich died, Dr. Gooch was translated from Bristol, and that See, the poorest in England, worth only about 400*l.* a year, was given to him. Butler felt strongly that he should gain little by this promotion, as it would not enable him to leave Stanhope, and was at a most inconvenient distance from it. He told Sir Robert Walpole, in acknowledging the letter informing him of the king's

---

[2] From the Diary of Dr. Thomas Wilson, son of the Bishop of Sodor and Man, 23rd December, 1737. It is much to be wished that this Sermon could be recovered.

pleasure, that while he felt very grateful for his Majesty's kindness, he did not think the Bishopric of Bristol very suitable, either to the condition of his fortune, or the circumstances of his preferment, neither was it exactly what might have been expected from the Queen's recommendation. However, a better provision was made for the new Bishop about eighteen months afterwards, when he was nominated Dean of St. Paul's. He then at once resigned his Rectory of Stanhope and his Prebend at Rochester, where he had just been elected Vice-Dean.

Not only was the endowment of the See of Bristol very small, but the palace was in an exceedingly dilapidated condition, so much so that during the first eight years of Butler's episcopate he spent nearly the whole of his income upon the restoration of it. When that indefatigable antiquary, the Rev. Wm. Cole, visited Bristol, in 1746, he remarked with especial praise how careful the Bishop had been in preserving whatever could be retained of the old buildings, and especially the old chapel, which had in the east window a representation of the Crucifixion in ancient stained glass, and below it the Bishop had set up a new altar-piece, inlaid with a plain milk-white marble cross.[3] This altar-piece

---

[3] " Having done with what is in the Cathedral, let us just step into the Bishop's Palace on the south side of it : and here we cannot help observing the generous Temper of the present worthy prelate; who in a poor Bishoprick of about 500*l.* per ann. has already laid out on building an entire new Palace in the room of the old one which was gone to decay, above 3,000*l.* The small Chapel belonging to the old one is standing ; but entirely new fitted up, furnished in an elegant Taste and newly wainscoted and a Tribune from one of his Lordship's rooms to look into it at the west end, over the door which is entirely new. The altar piece is of black marble

rather shocked the narrow taste of the age; and
when Dr. Young was Bishop of Bristol, Lord Chancellor Hardwicke urged him to have it taken down.

inlaid with a milk-white cross of white marble; which is
plain and has a good effect.   In the East window over it is a
small Crucifix with the B. Virgin and St. John under the
Cross weeping, of old glass; and not very curious.   Over the
new Door into the Chapel from the Hall, in a void space made
on purpose, is a very old Coat of Glass of the Arms of Berkly
ensigned with a mitre : and this is another reason to make one
think that the old Abbey of Bristol gave these arms to their
Founder, for their own Coat.   I was pleased to find the present
Bishop paid such a regard to the memory of the ancient Abbey
and its Founders, as to preserve this old memorial of them
with so much care and precaution.   A pattern worthy to be
imitated in an age, that to my knowledge, in certain places,
has not only had such marks of their benefactors taken away
in order to get up modern crown glass; but has also given away
and destroyed such memorials of them, as the care of their
predecessors for three or four hundred years have with the
utmost gratitude and veneration preserved.

"Over the Hall chimney-piece, which is preserved with
equal care by his Lordship, are the arms of Bishop Wright
impaled by his See, and a mitre over them, and R. W. on
each side of them ; as also Wright impaling per Pale undé
six martlets counterchanged for Fleetwood.

"I don't see his Lordship's Arms in any part of the Palace,
which has so just a title to have them in every part of it ; but,
however, I shall give them a place here in gratitude to his
memory who so well deserves of this place, which, though I
have no concern in, nor no acquaintance with his Lordship,
yet one always has a value for a grateful and benevolent mind.

"The arms of Joseph Butler, Lord Bishop of Bristol and
Dean of St. Paul's, are :—A. three covered Cups on Bend S,
inter two Bendlets engrailed G.

"His Lordship was, on the decease of the late Lord Bishop
of Hereford, by his Majesty appointed Clerk of the Royal
Closet; and it is said that he has also a promise, on the next
vacancy, of a translation to the rich See of Durham, which
will be well bestowed on a person of his Lordship's large and
universal benevolence."—*From the MS. Collections of the Rev.
W. Cole, now in the British Museum,* vol. x. p. 92, *taken at
Bristol* A. D. 1746.

He replied, however, that he would never have it
said that Bishop Young had pulled down what
Bishop Butler had set up,[*] and so the cross retained
its place until the palace was burnt in the great
Bristol riots in 1831, when the marble was so shat-
tered by the heat that it could not be recovered.
The cross itself was about three feet high and
eighteen inches wide, let into a large slab of black
marble surrounded by wood carving.

The merchants of Bristol assisted in the restoration of their Bishop's palace by presenting him with
a large quantity of cedar; so much indeed, that he
afterwards carried some to Durham with him, to
help in the works there.

Butler, like almost all great thinkers and great
saints, seems to have delighted in silent meditation.
It was his custom when in Bristol to walk in his
garden there after nightfall. On one occasion, when
Dr. Tucker his domestic chaplain was with him, he
stopped suddenly and asked—" What security is
there against the insanity of individuals? the phy-
sicians know of none!"—and then, after a pause—
" Why may not whole communities be seized with
fits of insanity, as well as individuals? Nothing but
this can account for a great part of what we read in
history." " I thought little," says Tucker, in relating
this, " of that odd conceit of the Bishop's at the
time, but I own I could not avoid thinking of it a
great deal since, and applying it to many cases."

Another and a different specimen of his medita-
tions we have in a note, in his own handwriting,
which strongly illustrates the manner in which he
realized his own saying, that resignation to the will
of God is the whole of piety. It runs thus:—" Shall
I not be faithful to God? If He puts a part upon

[*] Cole MSS.

me to do, shall I neglect or refuse it? A part to
suffer, and shall I say, I would not if I could help
it? Can words more ill-sorted, more shocking be
put together? And is not the thing expressed by
them more so, tho' not expressed in words? What
then shall I prefer to the sovereign Good, supreme
Excellence, absolute Perfection? To whom shall I
apply for direction in opposition to Infinite Wisdom?
To whom for protection against Almighty Power?"
This beautiful fragment is dated, "Sunday Evening, June 17, 1742." A word in it has been sub-
sequently altered in a different ink, and beneath it
was written:—" Hunger and thirst after righteousness, till filled with it by being made partaker of the
Divine Nature." Such were the fervid thoughts
which stirred the heart of the most dispassionate of
theological writers. Butler was a true Englishman,
calm and sober in his language, deep and strong in
his inner nature.

In the year that Butler was consecrated, John
Wesley returned to England from Georgia, and
soon began his wonderful career as a preacher.
He first preached in the open air at Kingswood,
near Bristol, a strangely savage place, inhabited by
a lawless population of miners. The Bishop could
not fail to have a great interest in what followed;
and it is said that Wesley, who was an admirer of
the "Analogy," had an interview with him, in which
Butler expressed his pleasure at the seriousness
which his preaching awakened, but blamed him for
sanctioning the violent physical excitement that was
considered almost a necessary part of the so-called
new birth.

Kingswood was not forgotten by its Bishop, who
set himself to procure the erection of a church in
its neighbourhood. At first it was to have been a

Chapel of Ease to St. Philip and Jacob; but at the
desire of the inhabitants an Act of Parliament was
procured, constituting it the New Parish of St.
George. To its endowment Butler gave 400*l.* (a
whole year's income, be it remembered, of his
Bishopric), and he procured a further gift of 200*l.*
from a lady of his acquaintance. He evidently took
a warm interest in the welfare of the hospital at
Bristol, which had been opened the year before his
consecration, as well as sharing in the establishment of the London Hospital, for which he preached
in 1748, taking occasion to dwell upon the religious
character it might enjoy.

He was, we are told, most careful in the disposal
of his patronage, seeking out worthy men wherever
they were to be found. Thus Dr. Tucker, afterwards
Dean of Gloucester, owed his first rise to Butler's
notice of his diligence as Curate of St. Stephen's, in
Bristol; and there is a monument in Bath Abbey-
Church to the Rev. Daniel Watson, recording his
obligations to the Bishop, to whom he had no recommendation except his own merits. At the same
time he refused to do anything for one of his own
nephews, who did not quite come up to his standard
of what a clergyman should be. Here, as afterwards at Durham, Butler endeavoured to make
himself personally acquainted with his clergy in
their own parishes. But one small fragment of
his Episcopal Charges has been preserved; it is
enough, however, to show their solid practical character.

His appointment as Dean of St. Paul's, as well as
his parliamentary duties, called him frequently to
London, where he had a house at Hampstead,
praised very highly in the letters of his friends as
an enchanting place. He adorned it, amongst other

things, with a series of scriptural pieces, in old
stained glass, which some liked as little as his
Bristol altar-piece. Secker, and Benson, and Miss
Talbot were his constant guests, frequently dining
with him every day. There is a journal of the
parliamentary proceedings of this period, now in
the British Museum, which was kept by Secker,
from which we learn that Butler attended very
regularly, and voted with the Government, though
he does not appear to have spoken. The three
Bishops of Oxford, Gloucester, and Bristol seem almost always to have attended and voted and retired
together.

These three true friends were all of them much
interested in the Society for the Propagation of the
Gospel in Foreign Parts. They all had preached
for it, all left it large legacies, and all took an active
part in the design for planting bishops in America,
which was so long laboured for by good church-
men, and for which the Society had already received
donations. Butler drew up a paper on the subject,
which is interesting, as showing the sort of objections he had to meet, and as it became afterwards
a kind of text-paper in the discussion, it deserves
to be preserved at length. It consisted only of the
following four short articles :—

" 1. That no coercive power is desired over the
laity in any case, but only a power to regulate the
behaviour of the clergy who are in episcopal orders ;
and to correct and punish them according to the
laws of the Church of England, in case of misbehaviour or neglect of duty, with such power as the
Commissaries abroad have exercised.

" 2. That nothing is desired for such Bishops
that may in the least interfere with the dignity, or
authority, or interest of the Governor, or any other

office of State. Probates of wills, licence for marriages, &c. to be left in the hands where they are: and no share in the temporal government is desired for the Bishops.

" 3. The maintenance of such Bishops not to be at the charge of the colonies.

" 4. No Bishops are intended to be settled in places where the government is left in the hands of Dissenters, as in New England, &c. But authority to be given, only to ordain clergy for such Church of England congregations as are among them, and to confirm the members thereof."

It was a great sign of the real weakness of the Church that even so extremely moderate a scheme as this could be frustrated by the vehemence of the New England Puritans. Butler's efforts were all in vain. Benson showed his interest in the cause by leaving a large legacy, which he directed, in his own words, " to be added to the fund for settling Bishops in our plantations in America, hoping that a design so necessary, and so unexceptionable, cannot but at last be put in execution." Secker, when both his friends were dead, revived the subject as Archbishop, but in vain ; and it was reserved for Archbishop Moore, whom Benson had noticed when a poor boy in Gloucester, and himself supported at College, to consecrate the first of those American Bishops that now exceed our own in numbers.

Already, in 1746, Butler had been made Clerk of the Closet to the King, and it was understood that the rich See of Durham had been promised to him on its next avoidance. He is said to have refused the Archbishopric of Canterbury in 1747, saying that it was too late for him to try to support a falling Church. Perhaps this refusal, if the story be true, may have arisen from an inward consciousness that his strength was already failing, for, when in 1750 he was at length translated to Durham, though no more than 58, he seemed to every one not to have many years to live.

The Court wished to make several arrangements as conditions of his translation. It was intended to separate the Lieutenancy of the County from the Bishopric, to which it had been customarily attached, and he was asked to promise Secker's stall at Durham to Dr. Chapman, if Secker were named to succeed him at St. Paul's. Butler replied that he was quite content where he was, and did not wish to be translated; but that if he were to be Bishop of Durham he would make no bargains about his patronage, or consent to any diminution of the privileges of the See. He was accordingly translated without any concession, or conditions.

At Durham he had many old friends, and was received with a most flattering welcome. The Sub-Dean delivered a highly complimentary address, to which he replied with characteristic modesty. His was not the nature to rejoice in merely worldly wealth and station. " I should be ashamed of myself," he said once to his private secretary, " if I could leave ten thousand pounds behind me." " It would be a melancholy thing," he wrote, in answer to a letter of congratulation, " to have no reflections to entertain oneself with in the close of life, but that one had spent the revenues of the Bishopric of Durham in a sumptuous course of living, and enriched one's friends with the promotions of it, instead of having really set one's self to do good and to promote worthy men. Yet this right use of fortune and power is more difficult than the generality of even good people think, and requires both a guard upon oneself and a strength of mind to withstand solicitations, greater, I wish I may not find it, than I am master of."

Accordingly he proceeded to dispense his revenues with princely liberality. He immediately put down his name as an annual subscriber of 400*l.* to the County Hospital, and set about repairing and adorning the buildings belonging to the See. On one occasion a gentleman having waited upon him to explain some pious scheme he greatly approved of, he sent for his house-steward and inquired how much money he had in his hands. It happened to be 500*l.* " Five hundred pounds !" said he, " what a shame for a Bishop to have so much money, give it away, give it all to this gentleman for his charitable plan." He kept open house three days in the week at Durham, or at Auckland, as it might be, when the poorest of his clergy were as welcome as the great men of the county.

How he contrived to spare so much may be learnt from an anecdote told by John Newton of a friend of his, a man of fortune, who, dining once by appointment with the Bishop, found on the table only a plain joint of meat and a pudding. Butler observed, by way of apology, that he had long been disgusted with the fashionable expense of time and money in entertainments, and was determined it should receive no countenance from his example. If the Bishops of our own day would have the courage to follow this pattern, they would find their influence for good in no small degree the greater.

" During the short time," says Surtees, in his " History of Durham," " that Butler held the See, he conciliated all hearts. In advanced years, and on the episcopal throne, he retained the same genuine modesty and native sweetness of disposition which had distinguished him in youth, and in retirement. During the ministerial performance of the sacred office, a divine animation seemed to pervade his whole manner, and lighted up his pale wan countenance, already marked with the progress of disease, like a torch glimmering in its socket, yet bright and useful to the last." Another writer says of him, " He was of a most reverend aspect; his face thin and pale; but there was a divine placidness in his countenance which inspired veneration, and expressed the most benevolent mind. His white hair hung gracefully on his shoulders, and his whole figure was patriarchal."

The only remarkable incident of his episcopate at Durham was the delivery of the well-known Charge upon the Use and Importance of External Religion, which speaks so much the language of our own day, that perhaps we ought not to wonder it should excite surprise and question a hundred years ago. It is interesting to remark how Butler, who began his career in close friendship with some of the leaders of the Latitudinarian party, should have severed from them so decidedly, and in the end have become the object of their fiercest attacks. It could not be that a soul penetrated with really holy principles could see, unmoved, the wretched carelessness so prevalent in the churches and the services of a century ago. His taste for architecture showed itself in new buildings wherever he went; and his fondness for solemn music may be seen in his taking into his house an under-secretary, named Emm, who had been a chorister of St. Paul's, on purpose that he might play for him upon the organ.

Soon, too soon, his bodily powers began to give way. In June 1752 he was carried in a very

weak condition to Bath, in the hope that he might
be benefited by the waters. It was with difficulty
that he could even walk to the door of his house.
The bad symptoms rapidly increased. On the
12th, Bishop Benson visited him, and found him
scarcely able to speak, and unable to take any
nourishment except now and then a few drops of
milk. Later in the day he had a little sleep, after
which his speech and power of attention revived so
much that he was able to take a last farewell of his
old friend; and, says Benson, writing to Secker,
who was kept at home by sickness, " he said kind
and affecting things more than I could bear." On
June 16th, at eleven o'clock, he died.

His chaplain, Nathaniel Forster, and his nephews,
had been in constant attendance upon him; and
Forster wrote day by day to Secker, giving an
account of the progress of the complaint, which seems
to have been a disease of the liver.

" On the 20th of June his remains were interred,'
amid much sorrow, but with little pomp, unostenta-
tiously, as he had lived, in his former Cathedral at
Bristol." Of his old friends, Rundle was already
dead; and in less than a year Benson and Berkeley
had both followed him to the grave.

It is fortunate that we have letters from Dr.
Forster, giving so minute an account of these few
last days; for, like the bodies of the Greek heroes,
the fiercest battles have been fought over the
death-bed of Bishop Butler. A few years after,
the Arians, who hated him for his Catholicity,
invented a story of his dying a Papist, with a view
to destroy the credit of his opinions; and this tale
the Romanists have since revived that they might
claim his great authority for themselves, while some

c

who mislike his works as *unevangelical,* tell how he
then for the first time felt the force of those gracious words of Christ,—"Him that cometh unto
Me, I will in no wise cast out." Neither tale has
any authority : the first was immediately proved to
be a miserable slander ; and the second seems to
be nothing more than a distorted version of the
pious words in which the dying Bishop spoke of
his hope in Christ, which the near approach of
death made doubly precious. The Estate left by
Bishop Butler did not quite reach 10,000*l.* ; his
Will and Codicil, which were administered under
the direction of the Court of Chancery, will be found
in the Appendix.

It only remains to take some notice of the works
that have been ascribed to Bishop Butler, but cannot be positively shown to be his. The most famous
of these is the "Letter of Thanks from a Young
Clergyman to the Rev. Dr. Hare, Dean of Worcester,
for his Visitation Sermon at Putney," published in
the year 1719. The authority for the authorship of
this pamphlet is a MS. note upon it by an uncertain
hand. The controversy in which it played its part
has long been forgotten, and there is nothing which
can either mark it as Butler's, or make its republi-
cation desirable.
There is another pamphlet, published by Knaptons
in 1744, with the title, "An Enquiry concerning
Faith," intended as a reply to a tract by the younger
Dodwell, which has in several copies a MS. note
ascribing it to Bishop Butler. The work itself is
for the most part not altogether unworthy of its
supposed author, but the evidence is too slight to
enable us to attribute it to him with any confidence.
It is most probable that many sermons and

papers escaped the general destruction which Butler
ordered by his Will. Some of these were probably
in the hands of his nephew Joseph, who also
directed by his Will that all his papers should be
destroyed unexamined. Mr. Bartlett has printed,
at the end of his Memoir, a Sermon on John iii. 8,
which is in no way remarkable, and by no means
clearly connected with the Bishop. There are five
MS. Sermons, apparently in Butler's handwriting,
now in the possession of a member of the family.
Among them are two which were preached, the one
on the Fast-day before, the other on the Thanks-
giving-day after the battle of Culloden; probably
before different audiences, as they are in substance
the same sermon; dwelling upon the advantages to
Church and State which flowed from the Hanoverian
succession, very much in the terms in which we
may suppose that Butler would have spoken. These
Sermons, if they are ever given to the public, will
require careful editing, as the first of the five is not
original, but a copy of one of Isaac Barrow's.

The Rev. J. Todd, of North Cowton in Yorkshire,
has lately printed a Sermon, which he supposes,
with a number of others in his possession, to have
been composed by Bishop Butler; beyond a certain
similarity of style and matter, however, there seems
nothing to connect them with the Bishop.

APPENDIX.

BISHOP BUTLER'S LETTERS AND WILL.

(For the Correspondence with Dr. Clarke, see p. 346.)

(For the Correspondence with Dr. Clarke, see p. 346.)

I.—TO SIR ROBERT WALPOLE.

Stanhope, August 28, 1738.

SIR,

I RECEIVED yesterday, from your own hand (an honour which I ought very particularly to acknowledge) the information that the King had nominated me to the Bishopric of Bristol. I most truly think myself very highly obliged to his Majesty, as much, all things considered, as any subject in his dominions; for I know no greater obligation, than to find the Queen's condescending goodness and kind intentions towards me transferred to his Majesty. Nor is it possible, while I live, to be without the most grateful sense of his favour to me, whether the effects of it be greater or less; for, this must in some measure depend upon accidents. Indeed, the Bishopric of Bristol is not very

suitable either to the condition of my fortune or the
circumstances of my preferment; nor, as I should
have thought, answerable to the recommendation
with which I was honoured. But you will excuse
me, Sir, if I think of this last with greater sensibility
than the conduct of affairs will admit of.

But without entering further into detail, I desire,
Sir, you will please let His Majesty know, that I
humbly accept this instance of his favour with the
utmost possible gratitude.

I beg leave, also, Sir, to return you my humble
thanks for your good offices upon this and all occasions; and for your very obliging expressions of
regard to,

Sir,

Your most obedient, most faithful, and most

humble Servant,

J. BUTLER.

By means of my distance from Durham, I had not
yours, Sir, till yesterday, so that this is the first
post I could answer it.

II.—ON THE POSSESSION OF ABBEY
LANDS.

MADAM,   *London, December 22, 1747.*

YOUR letter of the 14th current, which did not
come to hand till the 18th, cannot, indeed,
require any sort of apology. I know not how to
refuse my judgment, such as it is, to any person

that asks it; but I think myself strictly bound to give it to good persons of my own diocese. For I mention only this demand you have upon me, because, upon such an occasion as the present, I do not choose to speak of your rank, Madam, nor of the great civilities I have received from you.

The corruption and disorder of human affairs is such as has perplexed the rule of right, and made it hard in some cases to say how one ought to act. But I apprehend there is no such difficulty in the case you put. Property in general is, and must be, regulated by the laws of the community. This, in general, I say, is allowed on all hands. If, therefore, there be any sort of property exempt from these regulations, or any exception to the general method of regulating it, such exception must appear, either from the light of nature, or from revelation. But neither of these do, I think, show any such exception, and therefore we may with a good conscience retain any possessions, church lands, or tithes, which the laws of the state we live under give us a property in. And there seems less ground for scruple here in England than in some other countries; because our ecclesiastical laws agree with our civil ones in this matter. Under the Mosaic dispensation, indeed, God Himself assigned to the Priests and Levites, tithes, and other possessions; and in those possessions they had a Divine right; a property quite superior to all human laws, ecclesiastical as well as civil. But every donation to the Christian Church is a human donation, and no more; and therefore cannot give a Divine right, but such a right only as must be subject in common with all other property to the regulation of human laws. I would not carry you, Madam, into abstruse speculations; but think it might be clearly shown, that no one can have a right of perpetuity in any lands, except it be given by God; as the land of Canaan was to Abraham. There is no other means by which such a kind of property or right can be acquired; and plain absurdities would follow from the supposition of it. The persons then who gave these lands to the Church had themselves no right of perpetuity in them, consequently, could convey no such right to the Church. But all scruples concerning the lawfulness of laymen's possessing these lands go upon supposition that the Church has such a right of perpetuity in them: and therefore, all those scruples must be groundless, as going upon a false supposition.

As you do not mention, Madam, in what particular light you consider this matter, I chose to put it in different ones. And having said thus much concerning the strict justice of the case, I think myself obliged to add, that great disorders having been committed at the Reformation, and a multitude of parochial cures left scandalously poor, and become yet poorer by accidental circumstances, I think a man's possession of one of those impoverished cures is not, indeed, an obligation in justice, but a providential admonition, to do somewhat according to his abilities, towards settling some competent maintenance upon it, in one way or another. In like manner, as a person in distress, being my neighbour, dependant, or even acquaintance, is a providential admonition to me in particular, to assist him, over and above the general obligation to charity, which would call upon me to assist such a person, in common with all others who were informed of his case. But I think I ought to say, since I can say it with great truth, that I mention this, not, Madam, as thinking that you want to be reminded of it, but as the subject itself I write upon requires it should be mentioned.

You need not, Madam, have given yourself the trouble of desiring secresy, since the thing itself so plainly demands it.

> I am, with the truest esteem, Madam,
>
> Your most obedient, most faithful, and most
>
> humble Servant,
>
> Jo. Bristol.

I have considered tithes and church lands as the same, because I see no sort of proof, that tithes under the Gospel are of Divine right; and if they are not, they must come under the same consideration with lands.

III. & IV.—ON HIS TRANSLATION TO DURHAM.

Good Sir,

WHEN or where this will find you, I know not; but I would not defer thanking you for the obliging satisfaction you express, in my translation to the See of Durham. I wish my behaviour in it, may be such as to justify his Majesty's choice, and the approbation of it, which you (much too kindly I suppose) think to be general. If one is enabled to do a little good, and to prefer worthy men, this indeed is a valuable of life, and will afford satisfaction at the close of it; but the change of station in itself, will in no wise answer the trouble of it, and of getting into new forms of living: I mean in respect to the peace and happiness of one's own mind, for in fortune, to be sure it will.

I am, &c.

Bristol, Aug. 13, 1750

MY GOOD FRIEND,

I SHOULD have been mighty glad of the favour of a visit from you, when you were in town. I thank you for your kind congratulations, though I am not without my doubts and fears, how far the occasion of them is a real subject of congratulation to me. Increase of fortune is insignificant to one who thought he had enough before; and I foresee many difficulties in the station I am coming into, and no advantage worth thinking of, except some greater power of being serviceable to others; and whether this be an advantage, entirely depends on the use one shall make of it; I pray God it may be a good one. It would be a melancholy thing in the close of life, to have no reflections to entertain one's self with, but that one had spent the revenues of the Bishopric of Durham, in a sumptuous course of living, and enriched one's friends with the promotions of it, instead of having really set one's self to do good, and promote worthy men; yet this right use of fortune and power is more difficult than the generality of even good people think, and requires both a guard upon one's self, and a strength of mind to withstand solicitations, greater (I wish I may not find it) than I am master of. I pray God preserve your health, and am always, Dear Sir,

Your affectionate Brother and Servant,

JOSEPH DUNELM.

V.—FRAGMENT OF A LETTER TO THE DUCHESS OF SOMERSET,

[1751.]

I HAD a mind to see Auckland before I wrote to
your Grace, and, as you take so kind a part in
everything which contributes to my satisfaction, I
am sure you will be pleased to hear that the place
is a very agreeable one, and fully answering expectations, except that one of the chief prospects, which
is very pretty (the river Wear with hills, much di-
versified, rising above it) is too bare of wood ; the
park, not much amiss as to that, but I am obliged
to pale it anew all round, the old pale being quite
decayed. This will give an opportunity, with which
I am much pleased, to take in forty or fifty acres
competently wooded, though with that enlargement
it will scarce be sufficient for the hospitality of the
country. These, with some little improvements
and very great repairs, take up my leisure time.

Thus, Madam, I seem to have laid out a very
long life for myself; yet, in reality, everything I
see puts me in mind of the shortness and uncertainty of it : the arms and inscriptions of my predecessors, what they did, and what they neglected,
and (from accidental circumstances) the very place
itself, and the rooms I walk through and sit in.
And when I consider, in one view, the many things
of the kind I have just mentioned, which I have
upon my hands, I feel the burlesque of being employed in this manner at my time of life. But, in
another view, and taking in all circumstances, these
things, as trifling as they may appear, no less than

things of greater importance, seem to be put upon me to do, or at least to begin; whether I am to live to complete any or all of them, is not my concern.

REPLY TO THE ADDRESS FROM THE CHAPTER OF DURHAM.

I AM much obliged to you, Gentlemen, for your congratulations. 'Tis with a very real sense of my little merits and abilities, that I come to preside over a church of such distinction as this of Durham: and the more, from the great learning and abilities of my predecessors. But I shall endeavour, by acting suitably to our profession and my station, to answer what, I am sure, was his Majesty's intention in placing me here. And from my knowledge and particular acquaintance among you, I promise myself, that I shall have your advice and assistance upon all occasions, as the exigence of cases may require.

As for your kind manner of expressing yourselves concerning my character and behaviour, this I shall make use of to remind myself of my duty, and you must give me leave to consider it, too, as a declaration (of which, however, I had no doubt) that I shall have your concurrence, and your assistance in any good design, which may offer, for the benefit of the diocese or country.

WILL AND CODICIL.

I, JOSEPH BUTLER, Bishop of Durham, mindful of my mortality, and hoping for the mercy of God unto eternal life through Jesus Christ, do make this my last Will and Testament in manner following :—

1. I order my house and ground at Hampstead, and all other real estate or estates, which I may die possessed of elsewhere, to be sold, and the money arising from such sale to be employed in the payment of all my lawful debts; and the remainder, if any, to be divided into equal shares, and distributed equally amongst all my nephews and nieces by consanguinity.

2. My personal estate I intend to dispose of by a Codicil to be annexed to this my will; and I appoint my worthy Chaplain, Dr. Nathaniel Forster, to be sole executor of this my Will and Codicil to be annexed, and doubt not that he will take the trouble of it at this my particular desire. This I sign, seal, publish and declare to be my last Will, in the presence of the subscribing witnesses.

O   Jo. Duresme.

April 22, 1752.

O   Tho: Norwich.

O   Langhorne Warren.

O   Richard Gill.

CODICIL, APRIL 25, 1752.

1. TO my sister Hall, and to my sister Butler, widow of my brother, I give one hundred pounds apiece.

2. To each of the three sons of my late nephew, Thomas Cope, I give five hundred pounds, and to their mother twenty pounds per annum, during her widowhood.

3. To my niece Allright, daughter of my late sister Rigburg, I bequeath the interest of twelve hundred pounds, during her life, and the principal to her children, to be distributed to them equally after her death; unless she chooses to let them have any part of it during her life, and my executor consent to it.

4. To Dr. Forster, my executor, I give the sum of two hundred pounds.

5. I desire Mrs. Catherine Talbot, daughter of my ever honoured friend, Mr. Edward Talbot, to accept of one hundred pounds, as a small testimony of my perfect respect for her father and herself.

6. And in testimony of the like respect, I desire Mrs. Talbot her mother, the Lord Bishop of Gloucester, and the Lord Bishop of Oxford to accept of twenty guineas each of them, to buy themselves rings.

7. To my servant, Isaac Fawcett, I give two hundred pounds with all my clothes and wearing linen.

8. Whereas my under-secretary, William Emm, is altogether unprovided for, and cannot now provide for himself in the plain way he might easily

have done, had I not taken him into my family, I give to the said William Emm five hundred pounds.

9. To my servants Samuel Brooke and Launc[t] Westgarth, I give one hundred pounds apiece; and to my housekeeper Herbert fifty pounds.

10. To Andrew my coachman, I give forty pounds; to Phil. the postilion, John Woolley the helper, Will the underbutler, and Tom the groom, I give twenty pounds apiece. But if any of my servants, above mentioned, leave my service, or are turned away before my death, I revoke and cancel his legacy.

11. The residue of my estate, after these legacies are paid and discharged, I give to the governors of the Infirmary at Newcastle, for the use of the Infirmary, either for the fabrick, or relief of the sick, as they shall judge most proper, as far as five hundred pounds. And the residue after this, I give to the Society for the Propagation of the Gospel in Foreign Parts, as far as five hundred pounds. And the residue after this, I desire may be divided into equal shares, and distributed equally amongst all my nephews and nieces, by consanguinity, and their children.

Lastly, it is my positive and express will, that all my sermons, letters and papers, whatever, which are in a deal box, locked, directed to Dr. Forster, and now standing in the little room within my library at Hampstead, be burnt without being read by any one, as soon as may be after my decease.

Jo. DURESME.

PREFACE.

THOUGH it is scarce possible to avoid judging, in some way or other, of almost everything which offers itself to one's thoughts, yet it is certain that many persons, from different causes, never exercise their judgment upon what comes before them, in the way of determining whether it be conclusive and holds. They are, perhaps, entertained with some things, not so with others, they like and they dislike ; but whether that which is proposed to be made out be really made out or not, whether a matter be stated according to the real truth of the case, seems to the generality of people merely a circumstance of no consideration at all. Arguments are often wanted for some accidental purpose, but proof, as such, is what they never want for themselves, for their own satisfaction of mind or conduct in life. Not to mention the multitudes who read merely for the sake of talking, or to qualify themselves for the world, or some such kind of reasons, there are, even of the few who read for their own entertainment and have a real curiosity to see what is said, several, which is prodigious, who have no sort of curiosity to see what

is true : I say curiosity, because it is too obvious to
be mentioned, how much that religious and sacred
attention which is due to truth and to the important
question, What is the rule of life ? is lost out of the
world.

For the sake of this whole class of readers, for
they are of different capacities, different kinds, and
get into this way from different occasions, I have
often wished that it had been the custom to lay
before people nothing in matters of argument but
premises, and leave them to draw conclusions themselves; which, though it could not be done in all
cases, might in many. The great number of books
and papers of amusement, which of one kind or
another daily come in one's way, has in part occasioned and most perfectly falls in with and humours
this idle way of reading and considering things. By
this means time even in solitude is happily got rid
of without the pain of attention; neither is any part
of it more put to the account of idleness (one can
scarce forbear saying, is spent with less thought),
than great part of that which is spent in reading.
Thus people habituate themselves to let things pass
through their minds, as one may speak, rather than
to think of them. Thus by use they become satisfied merely with seeing what is said, without going
any further. Review and attention, and even forming
a judgment, become fatigue ; and to lay anything
before them that requires it, is putting them quite
out of their way.

There are also persons, and there are at least more
of them than have a right to claim such superiority,

who take for granted that they are acquainted with everything, and that no subject, if treated in the manner it should be, can be treated in any manner but what is familiar and easy to them.

It is true indeed, that few persons have a right to demand attention, but it is also true, that nothing can be understood without that degree of it which the very nature of the thing requires.   Now morals, considered as a science concerning which speculative difficulties are daily raised, and treated with regard to those difficulties, plainly require a very peculiar attention.   For here ideas never are in themselves determinate, but become so by the train of reasoning and the place they stand in ; since it is impossible that words can always stand for the same ideas, even in the same author, much less in different ones. Hence an argument may not readily be apprehended, which is different from its being mistaken ; and even caution to avoid being mistaken may, in some cases, render it less readily apprehended.   It is very un-allowable for a work of imagination or entertainment not to be of easy comprehension, but may be un-avoidable in a work of another kind, where a man is not to form or accommodate, but to state things as he finds them.

It must be acknowledged that some of the follow-ing Discourses are very abstruse and difficult, or, if you please, obscure ; but I must take leave to add, that those alone are judges whether or no and how far this is a fault, who are judges whether or no and how far it might have been avoided—those only who will be at the trouble to understand what is here said,

and to see how far the things here insisted upon, and
not other things, might have been put in a plainer
manner, which yet I am very far from asserting that
they could not.

Thus much, however, will be allowed, that general
criticisms concerning obscurity considered as a distinct thing from confusion and perplexity of thought,
as in some cases there may be ground for them, so
in others there may be nothing more at the bottom
than complaints, that everything is not to be understood with the same ease that some things are.
Confusion and perplexity in writing are indeed without excuse, because any one may, if he pleases,
know whether he understands and sees through what
he is about, and it is unpardonable for a man to lay
his thoughts before others, when he is conscious
that he himself does not know whereabouts he is, or
how the matter before him stands. It is coming
abroad in disorder, which he ought to be dissatisfied
to find himself in at home.

But even obscurities arising from other causes
than the abstruseness of the argument may not be
always inexcusable. Thus a subject may be treated
in a manner which all along supposes the reader
acquainted with what has been said upon it both by
ancient and modern writers, and with what is the
present state of opinion in the world concerning such
subject. This will create a difficulty of a very peculiar kind, and even throw an obscurity over the
whole before those who are not thus informed; but
those who are will be disposed to excuse such a
manner, and other things of the like kind, as a saving
of their patience.

However, upon the whole, as the title of Sermons gives some right to expect what is plain and of easy comprehension, and as the best auditories are mixed, I shall not set about to justify the propriety of preaching, or under that title publishing, Discourses so abstruse as some of these are; neither is it worth while to trouble the reader with the account of my doing either. Whether he will think he has any amends made him by the following illustrations of what seemed most to require them, I myself am by no means a proper judge.

THERE are two ways in which the subject of morals may be treated. One begins from inquiring into the abstract relations of *things;* the other from a matter of fact, namely, what the particular nature of *man* is, its several parts, their economy or constitution, from whence it proceeds to determine what course of life it is, which is correspondent to this whole nature. In the former method the conclusion is expressed thus, that vice is contrary to the nature and reason of things; in the latter, that it is a violation or breaking in upon our own nature. Thus they both lead us to the same thing, our obligations to the practice of virtue, and thus they exceedingly strengthen and enforce each other. The first seems the most direct formal proof, and in some respects the least liable to cavil and dispute; the latter is in a peculiar manner adapted to satisfy a fair mind, and is more easily applicable to the several particular relations and circumstances in life.

The following Discourses proceed chiefly in this latter method; the three first wholly. They were

intended to explain what is meant by the nature of
man, when it is said that virtue consists in following,
and vice in deviating from it; and by explaining to
show that the assertion is true. That the ancient
moralists had some inward feeling or other which
they chose to express in this manner, that man is
born to virtue, that it consists in following nature,
and that vice is more contrary to this nature than
tortures or death, their works in our hands are instances. Now a person who found no mystery in
this way of speaking of the ancients; who, without
being very explicit with himself, kept to his natural
feeling, went along with them, and found within
himself a full conviction, that what they laid down
was just and true; such a one would probably wonder
to see a point, in which he never perceived any difficulty, so laboured as this is in the second and third
Sermons, insomuch perhaps as to be at a loss for the
occasion, scope, and drift of them. But it need not
be thought strange that this manner of expression,
though familiar with them and if not usually carried
so far yet not uncommon amongst ourselves, should
want explaining; since there are several perceptions
daily felt and spoken of, which yet it may not be
very easy at first view to explicate, to distinguish
from all others, and ascertain exactly what the idea
or perception is. The many treatises upon the passions are a proof of this; since so many would never
have undertaken to unfold their several complications,
and trace and resolve them into their principles, if
they had thought what they were endeavouring to
show was obvious to every one who felt and

talked of those passions. Thus, though there seems
no ground to doubt but that the generality of mankind have the inward perception expressed so commonly in that matter by the ancient moralists, more
than to doubt whether they have those passions;
yet it appeared of use to unfold that inward conviction, and lay it open in a more explicit manner,
than I had seen done, especially when there were
not wanting persons who manifestly mistook the
whole thing, and so had great reason to express
themselves dissatisfied with it. A late author [1] of great
and deserved reputation says, that to place virtue in
following nature is at best a loose way of talk. And
he has reason to say this, if what I think he intends
to express, though with great decency, be true, that
scarce any other sense can be put upon those words,
but acting as any of the several parts, without distinction, of a man's nature happened most to incline him.

Whoever thinks it worth while to consider this
matter thoroughly, should begin with stating to himself exactly the idea of a system, economy, or constitution of any particular nature, or particular anything; and he will, I suppose, find, that it is one or
a whole, made up of several parts, but yet, that the
several parts even considered as a whole do not
complete the idea, unless in the notion of a whole
you include the relations and respects which those
parts have to each other. Every work both of nature
and of art is a system; and as every particular thing,
both natural and artificial, is for some use or purpose

[1] "Religion of Nature Delineated," ed. 1724, pp. 22, 23.

out of and beyond itself, one may add to what has been
already brought into the idea of a system, its condu-
civeness to this one or more ends.　Let us instance in
a watch.—Suppose the several parts of it taken to
pieces, and placed apart from each other; let a man
have ever so exact a notion of these several parts,
unless he considers the respects and relations which
they have to each other, he will not have anything
like the idea of a watch.　Suppose these several
parts brought together and any how united : neither
will he yet, be the union ever so close, have an idea
which will bear any resemblance to that of a watch.
But let him view those several parts put together, or
consider them as to be put together in the manner
of a watch; let him form a notion of the relations
which those several parts have to each other—all
conducive in their respective ways to this purpose,
showing the hour of the day; and then he has the
idea of a watch.　Thus it is with regard to the inward
frame of man.　Appetites, passions, affections, and
the principle of reflection, considered merely as the
several parts of our inward nature, do not at all give
us an idea of the system or constitution of this nature;
because the constitution is formed by somewhat not
yet taken into consideration, namely, by the relations
which these several parts have to each other, the
chief of which is the authority of reflection or conscience.　It is from considering the relations which
the several appetites and passions in the inward
frame have to each other, and, above all, the supremacy of reflection or conscience, that we get the
idea of the system or constitution of human nature.

And from the idea itself it will as fully appear, that
this our nature, *i.e.* constitution, is adapted to virtue,
as from the idea of a watch it appears, that its nature,
·*i. e.* constitution or system, is adapted to measure
time. What in fact or event commonly happens is
nothing to this question. ‒ Every work of art is apt
to be out of order, but this is so far from being according to its system, that let the disorder increase,
and it will totally destroy it. This is merely by way
of explanation what an economy, system, or constitution is. And thus far the cases are perfectly
parallel. If we go further there is indeed a difference, nothing to the present purpose, but too important a one ever to be omitted. A machine is
inanimate and passive, but we are agents. Our
constitution is put in our own power. We are
charged with it, and therefore are accountable for
any disorder or violation of it.

Thus nothing can possibly be more contrary to
nature than vice ; meaning by nature not only the
several parts of our internal frame, but also the *constitution* of it. Poverty and disgrace, tortures and
·death, are not so contrary to it. Misery and injustice
are indeed equally contrary to some different parts of
our nature taken singly, but injustice is moreover
contrary to the whole constitution of the nature.

If it be asked whether this constitution be really
what those philosophers meant, and whether they
would have explained themselves in this manner, the
answer is the same as if it should be asked, whether
a person, who had often used the word *resentment*,
and felt the thing, would have explained this passion

exactly in the same manner in which it is done in one of these Discourses. As I have no doubt but that this is a true account of that passion, which he referred to and intended to express as the word *resentment;* so I have no doubt, but that this is the true account of the ground of that conviction which they referred to, when they said vice was contrary to nature. And though it should be thought that they meant no more than that vice was contrary to the higher and better part of our nature, even this implies such a constitution as I have endeavoured to explain. For the very terms *higher* and *better* imply a relation or respect of parts to each other; and these relative parts, being in one and the same nature, form a constitution and are the very idea of it. They had a perception that injustice was contrary to their nature, and that pain was so also. They observed these two perceptions totally different, not in degree but in kind; and the reflecting upon each of them, as they thus stood in their nature, wrought a full intuitive conviction, that more was due and of right belonged to one of these inward perceptions than to the other, that it demanded in all cases to govern such a creature as man. So that, upon the whole, this is a fair and true account of what was the ground of their conviction, of what they intended to refer to, when they said virtue consisted in following nature, a manner of speaking not loose and undeterminate, but clear and distinct, strictly just and true.

Though I am persuaded the force of this conviction is felt by almost every one, yet since, considered as an argument and put in words, it appears somewhat abstruse, and since the connection of it is broken in the first three Sermons, it may not be amiss to give the reader the whole argument here in one view.

Mankind has various instincts and principles of action as brute creatures have, some leading most directly and immediately to the good of the community and some most directly to private good. Man has several which brutes have not, particularly reflection or conscience, an approbation of some principles or actions and disapprobation of others.

Brutes obey their instincts or principles of action, according to certain rules, suppose the constitution of their body and the objects around them. The generality of mankind also obey their instincts and principles, all of them, those propensions we call good, as well as the bad, according to the same rules, namely, the constitution of their body and the external circumstances which they are in. [Therefore it is not a true representation of mankind to affirm, that they are wholly governed by self-love, the love of power, and sensual appetites; since, as on the one hand they are often actuated by these, without any regard to right or wrong, so on the other it is manifest fact, that the same persons, the generality, are frequently influenced by friendship, compassion, gratitude; and even a general abhorrence of what is base, and liking of what is fair and just, take their turn amongst the other motives of action. This is the partial inadequate notion of human nature treated of in the first Discourse: and it is by this nature, if one may speak so, that the world is in fact influenced, and kept in that tolerable order in which it is.]

Brutes, in acting according to the rules before mentioned, their bodily constitution and circumstances, act suitably to their whole nature. [It is, however, to be distinctly noted, that the reason why we affirm this is not merely that brutes in fact act so; for this alone, however universal, does not at all determine, whether such course of action be correspondent to their whole nature: but the reason of the assertion is, that as in acting thus they plainly act conformably to somewhat in their nature, so, from all observations we are able to make upon them, there does not appear the least ground to imagine them to have anything else in their nature, which requires a different rule or course of action.]

Mankind also in acting thus would act suitably to their whole nature, if no more were to be said of man's nature than what has been now said; if that, as it is a true, were also a complete, adequate account of our nature.

But that is not a complete account of man's nature. Somewhat further must be brought in to give us an adequate notion of it, namely, that one of those principles of action, conscience, or reflection, compared with the rest as they all stand together in the nature of man, plainly bears upon it marks of authority over all the rest, and claims the absolute direction of them all, to allow or forbid their gratification; a disapprobation of reflection being in itself a principle manifestly superior to a mere propension. And the conclusion is—that to allow no more to this

superior principle or part of our nature, than to other
parts; to let it govern and guide only occasionally in
common with the rest, as its turn happens to come,
from the temper and circumstances one happens to
be in—this is not to act conformably to the constitution of man, neither can any human creature be
said to act conformably to his constitution or nature,
unless he allows to that superior principle the absolute
authority which is due to it. And this conclusion is
abundantly confirmed from hence, that one may determine what course of action the economy of man's
nature requires, without so much as knowing in what
degrees of *strength* the several principles prevail, or
which of them have actually the greatest influence.

The practical reason of insisting so much upon
this natural authority of the principle of reflection or
conscience is, that it seems in great measure overlooked by many who are by no means the worst sort
of men. It is thought sufficient to abstain from
gross wickedness, and to be humane and kind to such
as happen to come in their way. Whereas in reality
the very constitution of our nature requires that we
bring our whole conduct before this superior faculty,
wait its determination, enforce upon ourselves its
authority, and make it the business of our lives, as
it is absolutely the whole business of a moral agent,
to conform ourselves to it. This is the true meaning of that ancient precept, *Reverence thyself.*

The not taking into consideration this authority,
which is implied in the idea of reflex approbation or
disapprobation, seems a material deficiency or omis-
sion in Lord Shaftesbury's "Inquiry concerning

Virtue." He has shown beyond all contradiction
that virtue is naturally the interest or happiness and
vice the misery of such a creature as man, placed
in the circumstances in which we are in this world.
But suppose there are particular exceptions, a case
which this author was unwilling to put, and yet
surely it is to be put; or suppose a case which he
has put and determined, that of a sceptic not convinced of this happy tendency of virtue, or being of
a contrary opinion. His determination is, that it
would be *without remedy*.[1] One may say more
explicitly, that, leaving out the authority of reflex
approbation or disapprobation, such a one would be
under an obligation to act viciously, since interest,
one's own happiness, is a manifest obligation, and
there is not supposed to be any other obligation in
the case. "But does it much mend the matter to
take in that natural authority of reflection? There
indeed would be an obligation to virtue; but would
not the obligation from supposed interest on the side
of vice remain?" If it should, yet to be under two
contrary obligations, *i. e.* under none at all, would
not be exactly the same as to be under a formal obligation to be vicious, or to be in circumstances in
which the constitution of man's nature plainly required that vice should be preferred. But the
obligation on the side of interest really does not
remain. For the natural authority of the principle
of reflection is an obligation the most near and intimate, the most certain and known, whereas the

[1] "Characteristics," vol. ii. p. 69.

contrary obligation can at the utmost appear no more than probable, since no man can be *certain* in any circumstances that vice is his interest in the present world, much less can he be certain against another ; and thus the certain obligation would entirely supersede and destroy the uncertain one, which yet would have been of real force without the former.

In truth, the taking in this consideration totally changes the whole state of the case, and shows what this author does not seem to have been aware of, that the greatest degree of scepticism which he thought possible will still leave men under the strictest moral obligations, whatever their opinion be concerning the happiness of virtue. For that mankind upon reflection felt an approbation of what was good and disapprobation of the contrary, he thought a plain matter of fact, as it undoubtedly is, which none could deny, but from mere affectation. Take in then that authority and obligation, which is a constituent part of this reflex approbation, and it will undeniably follow, though a man should doubt of everything else, yet that he would still remain under the nearest and most certain obligation to the practice of virtue, an obligation implied in the very idea of virtue, in the very idea of reflex approbation.

And how little influence soever this obligation alone can be expected to have in fact upon mankind, yet one may appeal even to interest and self-love, and ask,—since from man's nature, condition, and the shortness of life, so little, so very little indeed, can possibly in any case be gained by vice—whether it be so prodigious a thing to sacrifice that little to

the most intimate of all obligations, and which a
man cannot transgress without being self-condemned,
and unless he has corrupted his nature, without real
self-dislike ; this question, I say, may be asked, even
upon supposition that the prospect of a future life
were ever so uncertain.

The observation that man is thus by his very
nature a law to himself, pursued to its just consequences, is of the utmost importance ; because,
from it, it will follow, that though men should,
through stupidity or speculative scepticism, be ignorant of, or disbelieve, any authority in the universe
to punish the violation of this law, yet, if there
should be such authority, they would be as really liable
to punishment as though they had been beforehand
convinced that such punishment would follow. For
in whatever sense we understand justice, even supposing, what I think would be very presumptuous to
assert, that the end of divine punishment is no other
than that of civil punishment, namely, to prevent
future mischief, – upon this bold supposition, ignorance or disbelief of the sanction would by no means
exempt even from this justice ; because it is not fore-
knowledge of the punishment which renders us ob-
noxious to it, but merely violating a known obligation.

And here it comes in one's way to take notice of a
manifest error or mistake in the author now cited,
unless perhaps he has incautiously expressed himself
so as to be misunderstood ; namely, that *it is malice
only, and not goodness, which can make us afraid.*[1]
Whereas, in reality, goodness is the natural and just

---

[1] " Characteristics," vol. i. p. 39.

object of the greatest fear to an ill man.   Malice
may be appeased or satiated, humour may change,
but goodness is a fixed, steady, immoveable principle
of action.   If either of the former hold the sword of
justice, there is plainly ground for the greatest of
crimes to hope for impunity ; but if it be goodness,
there can be no possible hope, whilst the reasons of
things or the ends of government call for punishment.   Thus every one sees how much greater
chance of impunity an ill man has in a partial administration than in a just and upright one.   It is
said that *the interest or good of the whole must be
the interest of the universal Being, and that he can
have no other.*   Be it so.   This author has proved
that vice is naturally the misery of mankind in this
world.   Consequently it was for the good of the
whole that it should be so.   What shadow of reason,
then, is there to assert that this may not be the case
hereafter?   Danger of future punishment (and if
there be danger, there is ground of fear) no more
supposes malice than the present feeling of punishment does.

The Sermon " Upon the Character of Balaam,"
and that " Upon Self-Deceit," both relate to one
subject.   I am persuaded, that a very great part of
the wickedness of the world is, one way or other,
owing to the self-partiality, self-flattery, and self-
deceit, endeavoured there to be laid open and explained.   It is to be observed amongst persons of
the lowest rank, in proportion to their compass of
thought, as much as amongst men of education and
improvement.   It seems that people are capable of

being thus artful with themselves in proportion as
they are capable of being so with others. Those
who have taken notice that there is really such a
thing, namely, plain falseness and insincerity in men
with regard to themselves, will readily see the drift
and design of these Discourses ; and nothing that I
can add will explain the design of them to him who
has not beforehand remarked at least somewhat of
the character.   And yet the admonitions they contain may be as much wanted by such a person as by
others, for it is to be noted, that a man may be entirely possessed by this unfairness of mind, without
having the least speculative notion what the thing is.

The account given of *Resentment* in the eighth
Sermon is introductory to the following one " Upon
Forgiveness of Injuries." It may possibly have
appeared to some, at first sight, a strange assertion,
that injury is the only natural object of settled resentment, or that men do not in fact resent deliberately anything but under this appearance of injury.
But I must desire the reader not to take any assertion alone by itself, but to consider the whole of what
is said upon it : because this is necessary, not only
in order to judge of the truth of it, but often, such
is the nature of language, to see the very meaning of the assertion.   Particularly as to this, injury
and injustice is, in the Sermon itself, explained to
mean, not only the more gross and shocking instances of wickedness, but also contempt, scorn,
neglect, any sort of disagreeable behaviour towards
a person, which he thinks other than what is due
to him.   And the general notion of injury or wrong

plainly comprehends this, though the words are mostly confined to the higher degrees of it.

Forgiveness of injuries is one of the very few moral obligations which have been disputed. But the proof, that it is really an obligation, what our nature and condition require, seems very obvious, were it only from the consideration, that revenge is doing harm merely for harm's sake. And as to the love of our enemies: resentment cannot supersede the obligation to universal benevolence, unless they are in the nature of the thing inconsistent, which they plainly are not.[1]

This divine precept, to forgive injuries and love our enemies, though to be met with in the Gentile moralists, yet is in a peculiar sense a precept of Christianity; as our Saviour has insisted more upon it than upon any other single virtue. One reason of this doubtless is, that it so peculiarly becomes an imperfect, faulty creature. But it may be observed also, that a virtuous temper of mind, consciousness of innocence, and good meaning towards everybody, and a strong feeling of injustice and injury, may itself, such is the imperfection of our virtue, lead a person to violate this obligation, if he be not upon his guard. And it may well be supposed, that this is another reason why it is so much insisted upon by him, who *knew what was in man.*

The chief design of the eleventh Discourse is to state the notion of self-love and disinterestedness, in order to show that benevolence is not more unfriendly to self-love, than any other particular affec-

[1] Page 108.

tion whatever. There is a strange affectation in many
people of explaining away all particular affections,
and representing the whole of life as nothing but
one continued exercise of self-love. Hence arises
that surprising confusion and perplexity in the Epicureans of old, Hobbes, the author of *Réflexions,
Sentences, et Maximes Morales,* and this whole set
of writers;[1] the confusion of calling actions interested which are done in contradiction to the most
manifest known interest, merely for the gratification
of a present passion.   Now all this confusion might
easily be avoided, by stating to ourselves wherein
the idea of self-love in general consists, as distin-

---

[1] One need only look into Torquatus' account of the Epicurean system, in Cicero's first book, "De Finibus," to see in what
a surprising manner this was done by them.   Thus the desire of
praise, and of being beloved, he explains to be no other than
desire of safety: regard to our country, even in the most
virtuous character, to be nothing but regard to ourselves.[a] The
author of "Réflexions, &c., Morales," says, Curiosity proceeds
from interest or pride; which pride also would doubtless have
been explained to be self-love.—Page 85, ed. 1725.   As if
there were no such passions in mankind as desire of esteem, or
of being beloved, or of knowledge.   Hobbes' account of the
affections of goodwill and pity are instances of the same kind.

---

[a] [Tu tam egregios viros censes tantas res gessisse sine causa?
Quæ fuerit causa, mox videro: interea hoc tenebo: si ob
aliquam causam ista, quæ sine dubio præclara sunt, fecerint,
virtutem his ipsam per se causam non fuisse.   Torquem detraxit
hosti: et quidem se texit, ne interiret.   At magnum periculum
adiit: in oculis quidem exercitus.   Quid ex eo est consecutus?
*Laudem et caritatem: quæ sunt vitæ sine metu degendæ præsidia
firmissima.*   Filium morte mulctavit: si sine causa, nollem me
ab eo ortum, tam importuno, tamque crudeli.   Sin ut dolore
suo sanciret militaris imperii disciplinam, exercitumque in gra-
vissimo bello animadversionis metu contineret; *saluti prospexit
civium, qua intelligebat contineri suam.*—De Finibus, i. 10.]

guished from all particular movements towards particular external objects : the appetites of sense, resentment, compassion, curiosity, ambition, and the rest.[1] When this is done, if the words *selfish* and *interested* cannot be parted with, but must be applied to everything, yet, to avoid such total confusion of all language, let the distinction be made by epithets : and the first may be called cool or settled selfishness, and the other, passionate or sensual selfishness. But the most natural way of speaking plainly is, to call the first only self-love, and the actions proceeding from it, interested : and to say of the latter, that they are not love to ourselves, but movements towards somewhat external, honour, power, the harm or good of another : and that the pursuit of these external objects, so far as it proceeds from these movements (for it may proceed from self-love),[2] is no otherwise interested, than as every action of every creature must, from the nature of the thing, be ; for no one can act but from a desire, or choice, or preference of his own.

Self-love and any particular passion may be joined together ; and from this complication it becomes impossible in numberless instances to determine precisely how far an action, perhaps even of one's own, has for its principle general self-love, or some particular passion. But this need create no confusion in the ideas themselves of self-love and particular passions. We distinctly discern what one is, and what the other are : though we may be uncertain how far one or the other influences us. And

[1] Page 135. [2] Note, p. 7.

though, from this uncertainty, it cannot but be that
there will be different opinions concerning mankind,
as more or less governed by interest, and some will
ascribe actions to self-love, which others will ascribe
to particular passions; yet, it is absurd to say that
mankind are wholly actuated by either, since it is
manifest that both have their influence.   For as, on
the one hand, men form a general notion of interest,
some placing it in one thing, and some in another,
and have a considerable regard to it throughout the
course of their life, which is owing to self-love ; so,
on the other hand, they are often set on work by
the particular passions themselves, and a considerable
part of life is spent in the actual gratification of
them, *i. e.* is employed, not by self-love, but by the
passions.

Besides, the very idea of an interested pursuit
necessarily presupposes particular passions or appetites ; since the very idea of interest or happiness
consists in this, that an appetite or affection enjoys
its object.   It is not because we love ourselves that
we find delight in such and such objects, but because we have particular affections towards them.
Take away these affections, and you leave self-love
absolutely nothing at all to employ itself about,[1] no
end or object for it to pursue, excepting only that of
avoiding pain.   Indeed the Epicureans, who maintained that absence of pain was the highest happiness, might, consistently with themselves, deny all
affection, and, if they had so pleased, every sensual
appetite too: but the very idea of interest or happi-

[1] Page 137.

ness other than absence of pain implies particular
appetites or passions, these being necessary to constitute that interest or happiness.

The observation, that benevolence is no more disinterested than any of the common particular passions,[1] seems in itself worth being taken notice of;
but is insisted upon to obviate that scorn, which one
sees rising upon the faces of people who are said to
know the world, when mention is made of a disinterested, generous, or public-spirited action.   The
truth of that observation might be made appear in
a more formal manner of proof : for whoever will
consider all the possible respects and relations which
any particular affection can have to self-love and
private interest, will, I think, see demonstrably, that
benevolence is not in any respect more at variance
with self-love, than any other particular affection
whatever, but that it is in every respect at least as
friendly to it.

If the observation be true, it follows, that self-love
and benevolence, virtue and interest, are not to be
opposed, but only to be distinguished from each
other ; in the same way as virtue and any other
particular affection, love of arts, suppose, are to be
distinguished.   Everything is what it is, and not
another thing.   The goodness or badness of actions
does not arise from hence, that the epithet, interested
or disinterested, may be applied to them, any more
than any other indifferent epithet, suppose inquisitive
or jealous, may or may not be applied to them ; nor
from their being attended with present or future

[1] Page 140.

pleasure or pain; but from their being what they
are, namely, what becomes such creatures as we
are, what the state of the case requires, or the contrary. Or, in other words, we may judge and determine, that an action is morally good or evil,
before we so much as consider, whether it be interested or disinterested. This consideration no more
comes in to determine whether an action be virtuous,
than to determine whether it be resentful. Self-love
in its due degree is as just and morally good, as any
affection whatever. Benevolence towards particular
persons may be to a degree of weakness, and so be
blamable: and disinterestedness is so far from being
in itself commendable, that the utmost possible depravity which we can in imagination conceive is that
of disinterested cruelty.

Neither does there appear any reason to wish
self-love were weaker in the generality of the world
than it is. The influence which it has seems plainly
owing to its being constant and habitual, which it
cannot but be, and not to the degree or strength of
it. Every caprice of the imagination, every curiosity of the understanding, every affection of the
heart, is perpetually showing its weakness, by prevailing over it. Men daily, hourly sacrifice the
greatest known interest, to fancy, inquisitiveness,
love or hatred, any vagrant inclination. The thing
to be lamented is, not that men have so great regard
to their own good or interest in the present world,
for they have not enough;[1] but that they have so
little to the good of others. And this seems plainly

[1] Page 14.

owing to their being so much engaged in the gratification of particular passions unfriendly to benevolence, and which happen to be most prevalent in
them, much more than to self-love. As a proof of
this it may be observed, that there is no character
more void of friendship, gratitude, natural affection,
love to their country, common justice, or more
equally and uniformly hard-hearted, than the *abandoned* in, what is called, the way of pleasure—hard-
hearted and totally without feeling in behalf of
others, except when they cannot escape the sight of
distress, and so are interrupted by it in their pleasures. And yet it is ridiculous to call such an
abandoned course of pleasure interested, when the
person engaged in it knows beforehand, goes on
under the feeling and apprehension, that it will be
as ruinous to himself, as to those who depend upon
him.

Upon the whole,—if the generality of mankind
were to cultivate within themselves the principle of
self-love; if they were to accustom themselves often
to set down and consider, what was the greatest happiness they were capable of attaining for themselves
in this life, and if self-love were so strong and prevalent, as that they would uniformly pursue this their
supposed chief temporal good, without being diverted
from it by any particular passion,—it would manifestly prevent numberless follies and vices. This
was in a great measure the Epicurean system of
philosophy. It is indeed by no means the religious
or even moral institution of life. Yet, with all the
mistakes men would fall into about interest, it would

to expect to find any other connection between
them, than that uniformity of thought and design,
which will always be found in the writings of the
same person, when he writes with simplicity and in
earnest.

STANHOPE, *Sept.* 16, 1729.

CONTENTS OF THE SERMONS AT

THE ROLLS.

SERMONS I. II. III.

SERMONS II. III.—UPON THE NATURAL SUPREMACY OF CONSCIENCE.

Rom. ii. 14.—*For when the Gentiles, which have not the law, do by nature the things contained in the law, these having not the law, are a law unto themselves.*

SERMON III.

SERMON IV.

Upon the Government of the Tongue.

James i. 26.—*If any man among you seem to be religious, and bridleth not his tongue, but deceiveth his own heart, this man's religion is vain.*

Contents. lxxix

SERMONS V. VI.

UPON COMPASSION.

Rom. xii. 15.—*Rejoice with them that do rejoice, and weep with them that weep.*

SERMON VI.

SERMON VII.

UPON THE CHARACTER OF BALAAM.

Numb. xxiii. 10.—*Let me die the death of the righteous, and let my last end be like his.*

f

Contents.

SERMONS VIII. IX.

Upon Resentment and Forgiveness of Injuries.

Matt. v. 43, 44.—Ye have heard that it hath been said, Thou shalt love thy neighbour and hate thine enemy: but I say unto you, Love your enemies, bless them that curse you, do good to them that hate you, and pray for them that despitefully use you and persecute you.

[Sermon VIII.—Upon resentment.

SERMON X.

Upon Self-Deceit.

2 Sam. xii. 7.—*And Nathan said to David, Thou art the man.*

SERMONS XI. XII.

Upon the Love of our Neighbour.

Rom. xiii. 9.—*And if there be any other command-ment it is briefly comprehended in this saying, namely, Thou shalt love thy neighbour as thyself.*

SERMONS XIII. XIV.

Upon Piety, or the Love of God.

Matt. xxii. 37.—*Thou shalt love the Lord thy God with all thy heart, and with all thy soul, and with all thy mind.*

[1. We must not refuse a truth because it has been made a shelter for enthusiasm, 171.

SERMON XIV.

SERMON XV.

UPON THE IGNORANCE OF MAN.

Eccles. viii. 16, 17.—*When I applied mine heart to know wisdom, and to see the business that is done upon the earth : then I beheld all the work of God, that a man cannot find out the work that is done under the sun : because though a man labour to seek it out, yet he shall not find it ; yea farther, though a wise man think to know it, yet shall he not be able to find it.*

xcii   **Contents.**

SERMON I.

UPON HUMAN NATURE.

" For as we have many members in one body, and all members have not the same office ; so we, being many, are one body in Christ, and every one members one of another."—ROM. xii. 4, 5.

THE Epistles in the New Testament have all of them a particular reference to the condition and usages of the Christian world at the time they were written. Therefore, as they cannot be thoroughly understood, unless that condition and those usages are known and attended to, so further, though they be known, yet if they be discontinued or changed, exhortations, precepts, and illustrations of things, which refer to such circumstances now ceased or altered, cannot at this time be urged in that manner and with that force which they were to the primitive Christians. Thus the text now before us, in its first intent and design, relates to the decent management of those extraordinary gifts which were then in the Church,[1] but

---

[1] I Cor. xii.

B

which are now totally ceased. And even as to the
allusion that *we are one body in Christ*, though what
the Apostle here intends is equally true of Christians in all circumstances, and the consideration
of it is plainly still an additional motive, over and
above moral considerations, to the discharge of the
several duties and offices of a Christian—yet it is
manifest this allusion must have appeared with much
greater force to those who, by the many difficulties
they went through for the sake of their religion,
were led to keep always in view the relation they
stood in to their Saviour, who had undergone the
same ; to those who, from the idolatries of all around
them, and their ill-treatment, were taught to consider themselves as not of the world in which they
lived, but as a distinct society of themselves, with
laws and ends, and principles of life and action,
quite contrary to those which the world professed
themselves at that time influenced by.   Hence the
relation of a Christian was by them considered as
nearer than that of affinity and blood, and they almost literally esteemed themselves as members one
of another.

It cannot indeed possibly be denied, that our
being God's creatures, and virtue being the natural
law we are born under, and the whole constitution
of man being plainly adapted to it, are prior obligations to piety and virtue, than the consideration that
God sent his Son into the world to save it, and the
motives which arise from the peculiar relation of
Christians, as members one of another under Christ
our head.   However, though all this be allowed, as
it expressly is by the inspired writers, yet it is manifest that Christians, at the time of the revelation
and immediately after, could not but insist mostly
upon considerations of this latter kind.

These observations show the original particular reference of the text; and the peculiar force with which the thing intended by the allusion in it must have been felt by the primitive Christian world. They likewise afford a reason for treating it at this time in a more general way.

[2] The relation which the several parts or members of the natural body have to each other and to the whole body is here compared to the relation which each particular person in society has to other particular persons and to the whole society; and the latter is intended to be illustrated by the former. And if there be a likeness between these two relations, the consequence is obvious: that the latter shows us we were intended to do good to others, as the former shows us that the several members of the natural body were intended to be instruments of good to each other and to the whole body. But as there is scarce any ground for a comparison between society and the mere material body, this without the mind being a dead unactive thing, much less can the comparison be carried to any length. And since the Apostle speaks of the several members as having distinct offices, which implies the mind, it cannot be thought an unallowable liberty, instead of the *body* and *its members*, to substitute the *whole nature of man,* and *all the variety of internal principles which belong to it.* And then the comparison will be between the nature of man as respecting self, and tending to private good, his own preservation and happiness, and the nature of man as having respect to society, and tending to promote public good, the happiness of that society. These ends do indeed perfectly coincide; and to aim at public and private good are so far from being inconsistent, that they mutually promote each other:

yet in the following discourse they must be considered as entirely distinct, otherwise the nature of man as tending to one, or as tending to the other, cannot be compared. There can no comparison be made without considering the things compared as distinct and different.

[3] From this review and comparison of the nature of man as respecting self, and as respecting society, it will plainly appear, that *there are as real and the same kind of indications in human nature, that we were made for society and to do good to our fellow-creatures, as that we were intended to take care of our own life and health and private good: and that the same objections lie against one of these assertions, as against the other.* For—

[4] First. There is a natural principle of *benevolence*[2] in man; which is in some degree to *society*,

² Suppose a man of learning to be writing a grave book upon *human nature*, and to show in several parts of it that he had an insight into the subject he was considering; amongst other things, the following one would require to be accounted for,— the appearance of benevolence or good-will in men towards each other in the instance of natural relation, and in others. Cautious of being deceived with outward show, he retires within himself to see exactly what that is in the mind of man from whence this appearance proceeds; and, upon deep reflection, asserts the principle in the mind to be only the *love of power, and delight in the exercise of it.** Would not everybody think here was a mistake of one word for another?—that the philosopher was contemplating and accounting for some other human actions, some other behaviour of man to man? And could any one be thoroughly satisfied, that what is commonly called benevolence or good-will was really the affection meant, but only by being made

* ["There is yet another passion, sometimes called *love*, but more properly *good-will* or *charity*. There can be no greater argument to a man of *his own power* than to find himself able not only to accomplish his own desires, but also to assist other men in theirs; and this is that conception wherein consisteth charity."]—HOBBES, *On Human Nature*, chap. ix. sect. 17.

what *self-love* is to the *individual*. And if there
be in mankind any disposition to friendship; if there

to understand that this learned person had a general hypothesis,
to which the appearance of good-will could no otherwise be
reconciled ?   (*b*) That what has this appearance is often nothing
but ambition ; that delight in superiority often (suppose always) mixes itself with benevolence, only makes it more specious to call it ambition than hunger, of the two : but in reality
that passion does no more account for the whole appearances
of good-will than this appetite does.   (*c*) Is there not often the
appearance of one man's wishing that good to another which
he knows himself unable to procure him, and rejoicing in it,
though bestowed by a third person ?   And can love of power
any way possibly come in to account for this desire or delight ?
Is there not often the appearance of men's distinguishing between two or more persons, preferring one before another, to
do good to, in cases where love of power cannot in the least
account for the distinction and preference, for this principle
can no otherwise distinguish between objects, than as it is a
greater instance and exertion of power to do good to one rather
than to another ?   (*d*) Again, suppose good-will in the mind of
man to be nothing but delight in the exercise of power : men
might indeed be restrained by distant and accidental considerations; but these restraints being removed, they would have a
disposition to, and delight in mischief, as an exercise and proof
of power, and this disposition and delight would arise from, or
be the same principle in the mind, as a disposition to and delight in charity.   Thus cruelty, as distinct from envy and resentment, would be exactly the same in the mind of man as
good-will : that one tends to the happiness, the other to the
misery of our fellow-creatures, is, it seems, merely an accidental
circumstance, which the mind has not the least regard to.
These are the absurdities which even men of capacity run into,
when they have occasion to belie their nature, and will per-
versely disclaim that image of God which was originally stam-
ped upon it, the traces of which, however faint, are plainly
discernible upon the mind of man.
   (*e*) If any person can in earnest doubt whether there be such
a thing as good-will in one man towards another (for the
question is not concerning either the degree or extensiveness
of it, but concerning the affection itself), let it be observed,
that *whether man be thus or otherwise constituted, what is the inward frame in this particular* is a mere question of fact or natural

be any such thing as compassion, for compassion is
momentary love ; if there be any such thing as the
paternal or filial affections ; if there be any affection
in human nature, the object and end of which is
the good of another,—this is itself benevolence, or
the love of another. Be it ever so short, be it in ever
so low a degree, or ever so unhappily confined, it
proves the assertion, and points out what we were
designed for, as really as though it were in a higher
degree and more extensive. [5] I must, however,
remind you that though benevolence and self-love
are different ; though the former tends most directly
to public good, and the latter to private,—yet they
are so perfectly coincident, that the greatest satisfactions to ourselves depend upon our having benevolence in a due degree ; and that self-love is one
chief security of our right behaviour towards society.

history, not proveable immediately by reason. It is therefore
to be judged of and determined in the same way as other facts
or matters of natural history are: by appealing to the external
senses, or inward perceptions, respectively, as the matter under
consideration is cognisable by one or the other: by arguing from acknowledged facts and actions ; for a great number
of actions of the same kind, in different circumstances, and
respecting different objects, will prove to a certainty what principles they do not, and, to the greatest probability, what principles they do proceed from: and lastly, by the testimony of
mankind. (*f*) Now that there is some degree of benevolence
amongst men, may be as strongly and plainly proved in all these
ways as it could possibly be proved, supposing there was this
affection in our nature. And should any one think fit to assert,
that resentment in the mind of man was absolutely nothing
but reasonable concern for our own safety, the falsity of this,
and what is the real nature of that passion, could be shown in
no other way than those in which it may be shown, that there
is such a thing in *some degree* as *real* good-will in man towards
man. It is sufficient that the seeds of it be implanted in our
nature by God. There is, it is owned, much left for us to do
upon our own heart and temper: to cultivate, to improve, to
call it forth, to exercise it in a steady, uniform manner. This
is our work ; this is virtue and religion.

It may be added, that their mutual coinciding, so that we can scarce promote one without the other, is equally a proof that we were made for both.

[6] Secondly. This will further appear from observing that the *several passions* and *affections*, which are distinct,[2] both from benevolence and self-

[2] Everybody makes a distinction between self-love and the several particular passions, appetites, and affections; and yet they are often confounded again. That they are totally different will be seen by any one who will distinguish between the passions and appetites *themselves*, and *endeavouring* after the means of their gratification. Consider the Appetite of hunger, and the Desire of esteem : these being the occasion both of pleasure and pain, the coolest *self-love*, as well as the appetites and passions themselves, may put us upon making use of the *proper methods of obtaining* that pleasure, and avoiding that pain; but the *feelings themselves*, the pain of hunger and shame, and the delight from esteem, are no more self-love than they are anything in the world. Though a man hated himself, he would as much feel the pain of hunger as he would that of the gout; and it is plainly supposable there may be creatures with self-love in them to the highest degree, who may be quite insensible and indifferent (as men in some cases are) to the contempt and esteem of those upon whom their happiness does not in some further respects depend. And as self-love and the several particular passions and appetites are in themselves totally different, so that some actions proceed from one, and some from the other, will be manifest to any who will observe the two following very supposable cases. One man rushes upon certain ruin for the gratification of a present desire : nobody will call the principle of this action self-love. Suppose another man to go through some laborious work upon promise of a great reward, without any distinct knowledge what the reward will be: this course of action cannot be ascribed to any particular passion. The former of these actions is plainly to be imputed to some particular passion or affection, the latter as plainly to the general affection or principle of self-love. That there are some particular pursuits or actions concerning which we cannot determine how far they are owing to one, and how far to the other, proceeds from this, that the two principles are frequently mixed together, and run up into each other. This distinction is further explained in the eleventh Sermon.

love, do in general contribute and lead us to *public*
good as really as to *private*. It might be thought
too minute and particular, and would carry us too
great a length, to distinguish between and compare
together the several passions or appetites distinct
from benevolence, whose primary use and intention
are the security and good of society, and the passions
distinct from self-love, whose primary intention and
design are the security and good of the individual.[4]
It is enough to the present argument, that desire of
esteem from others, contempt and esteem of them,
love of society as distinct from affection to the good
of it, indignation against successful vice, that these
are public affections or passions, have an immediate
respect to others, naturally lead us to regulate our
behaviour in such a manner as will be of service to
our fellow-creatures. If any or all of these may be
considered likewise as private affections, as tending
to private good, this does not hinder them from
being public affections too, or destroy the good influence of them upon society, and their tendency to
public good. It may be added, that as persons
without any conviction from reason of the desirable-
ness of life, would yet of course preserve it merely

[4] If any desire to see this distinction and comparison made
in a particular instance, the appetite and passion now mentioned may serve for one. *Hunger* is to be considered as a
private appetite; because the end for which it was given us
is the preservation of the individual. *Desire of esteem* is a
public passion; because the end for which it was given us
is to regulate our behaviour towards society. The respect
which this has to private good is as remote as the respect that
has to public good : and the appetite is no more self-love, than
the passion is benevolence. The object and end of the former
is merely food; the object and end of the latter is merely
esteem ; but the latter can no more be gratified, without contributing to the good of society, than the former can be gratified, without contributing to the preservation of the individual.

from the appetite of hunger, so by acting merely
from regard (suppose) to reputation, without any
consideration of the good of others, men often contribute to public good.. In both these instances they
are plainly instruments in the hands of another, in
the hands of Providence, to carry on ends, the preservation of the individual and good of society, which
they themselves have not in their view or intention.
The sum is, men have various appetites, passions,
and particular affections, quite distinct both from
self-love and from benevolence : all of these have a
tendency to promote both public and private good,
and may be considered as respecting others and
ourselves equally and in common, but some of them
seem most immediately to respect others, or tend
to public good, others of them most immediately to
respect self, or tend to private good : as the former
are not benevolence, so the latter are not self-love :
neither sort are instances of our love either to ourselves or others, but only instances of our Maker's
care and love both of the individual and the species,
and proofs that he intended we should be instruments of good to each other, as well as that we
should be so to ourselves.

[7] Thirdly. There is a principle of reflection
in men, by which they distinguish between, approve,
and disapprove, their own actions. We are plainly
constituted such sort of creatures as to reflect upon
our own nature. The mind can take a view of what
passes within itself, its propensions, aversions, passions, affections, as respecting such objects, and in
such degrees, and of the several actions consequent thereupon. In this survey it approves of one,
disapproves of another, and towards a third is affected in neither of these ways, but is quite indifferent.
This principle in man, by which he approves or dis-

approves his heart, temper, and actions, is conscience; for this is the strict sense of the word,
though sometimes it is used so as to take in more.
And that this faculty tends to restrain men from
doing mischief to each other, and leads them to
do good, is too manifest to need being insisted upon.
Thus a parent has the affection of love to his children: this leads him to take care of, to educate, to
make due provision for them; the natural affection
leads to this: but the reflection that it is his proper
business, what belongs to him, that it is right and
commendable so to do; this added to the affection
becomes a much more settled principle, and carries
him on through more labour and difficulties for the
sake of his children, than he would undergo from
that affection alone, if he thought it, and the course
of action it led to, either indifferent or criminal.
This indeed is impossible, to do that which is good
and not to approve of it; for which reason they are
frequently not considered as distinct, though they
really are, for men often approve of the actions of.
others, which they will not imitate, and likewise do
that which they approve not. [8] It cannot possibly
be denied, that there is this principle of reflection or
conscience in human nature. Suppose a man to relieve an innocent person in great distress; suppose
the same man afterwards, in the fury of anger, to
do the greatest mischief to a person who had given
no just cause of offence; to aggravate the injury,
add the circumstances of former friendship, and obligation from the injured person; let the man who
is supposed to have done these two different actions
coolly reflect upon them afterwards, without regard
to their consequences to himself: to assert that any
common man would be affected in the same way towards these different actions, that he would make no

distinction between them, but approve or disapprove
them equally, is too glaring a falsity to need being
confuted. There is therefore this principle of reflection or conscience in mankind. It is needless to
compare the respect it has to private good, with the
respect it has to public, since it plainly tends as much
to the latter as to the former, and is commonly
thought to tend chiefly to the latter. This faculty
is now mentioned merely as another part in the inward frame of man, pointing out to us in some degree what we are intended for, and as what will
naturally and of course have some influence. The
particular place assigned to it by nature, what authority it has, and how great influence it ought to have,
shall be hereafter considered.

[9] From this comparison of benevolence and self-
love, of our public and private affections, of the
courses of life they lead to, and of the principle of
reflection or conscience as respecting each of them,
it is as manifest, that *we were made for society, and
to promote the happiness of it, as that we were intended to take care of our own life, and health, and
private good.*

[10] And from this whole review must be given a
different draught of human nature from what we are
often presented with. Mankind are by nature so
closely united, there is such a correspondence between the inward sensations of one man and those
of another, that disgrace is as much avoided as
bodily pain, and to be the object of esteem and love
as much desired as any external goods; and in many
particular cases, persons are carried on to do good
to others, as the end their affection tends to and rests
in, and manifest that they find real satisfaction and
enjoyment in this course of behaviour. There is
such a natural principle of attraction in man towards

man, that having trod the same tract of land, having
breathed in the same climate, barely having been
in the same artificial district or division, becomes
the occasion of contracting acquaintances and familiarities many years after, for anything may serve
the purpose. Thus relations merely nominal are
sought and invented, not by governors, but by the
lowest of the people, which are found sufficient to
hold mankind together in little fraternities and co-
partnerships; weak ties indeed, and what may afford
fund enough for ridicule, if they are absurdly considered as the real principles of that union, but they
are in truth merely the occasions, as anything may
be of anything, upon which our nature carries us on
according to its own previous bent and bias, which
occasions therefore would be nothing at all, were there
not this prior disposition and bias of nature. Men
are so much one body, that in a peculiar manner
they feel for each other, shame, sudden danger,
resentment, honour, prosperity, distress; one or
another, or all of these, from the social nature in
general, from benevolence, upon the occasion of
natural relation, acquaintance, protection, dependence ; each of these being distinct cements of society.
[11] And therefore to have no restraint from, no
regard to, others in our behaviour, is the speculative
absurdity of considering ourselves as single, and independent, as having nothing in our nature which
has respect to our fellow-creatures, reduced to
action and practice. And this is the same absurdity,
as to suppose a hand, or any part, to have no natural
respect to any other, or to the whole body.

[12] But allowing all this, it may be asked,
"Has not man dispositions and principles within,
which lead him to do evil to others, as well as to do
good? Whence come the many miseries else, which

men are the authors and instruments of to each
other?" [13] These questions, so far as they relate to the foregoing discourse, may be answered by
asking, "Has not man also dispositions and principles within, which lead him to do evil to himself as
well as good? Whence come the many miseries
else, sickness, pain, and death, which men are instruments and authors of to themselves?"

[14] It may be thought more easy to answer one
of these questions than the other, but the answer to
both is really the same—that mankind have un-
governed passions which they will gratify at any rate,
as well to the injury of others, as in contradiction
to known private interest; but that as there is no
such thing as self-hatred, so neither is there any
such thing as ill-will in one man towards another,
emulation and resentment being away, whereas there
is plainly benevolence or good will; there is no
such thing as love of injustice, oppression, treachery, ingratitude, but only eager desires after such
and such external goods, which, according to a very
ancient observation, the most abandoned would choose
to obtain by innocent means, if they were as easy,
. and as effectual to their end; that even emulation and
resentment, by any one who will consider what these
passions really are in nature[5] will be found nothing
to the purpose of this objection; and that the principles and passions·in the mind of man, which are

[5] Emulation is merely the desire and hope of equality with,
or superiority over, others, with whom we compare ourselves.
There does not appear to be any *other grief* in the natural
passion, but only *that want* which is implied in desire. However, this may be so strong as to be the occasion of great *grief*.
To desire the attainment of this equality or superiority by the
particular means of others being brought down to our own level,
or below it, is, I think, the distinct notion of envy. From
whence it is easy to see, that the real end, which the natural
passion, emulation, and which the unlawful one, envy, aims

distinct both from self-love and benevolence, primarily and most directly lead to right behaviour with regard to others as well as himself, and only secondarily and accidentally to what is evil. Thus, though men, to avoid the shame of one villany, are sometimes guilty of a greater, yet it is easy to see, that the original tendency of shame is to prevent the doing of shameful actions, and its leading men to conceal such actions when done, is only in consequence of their being done, *i.e.*, of the passion's not having answered its first end.

[15] If it be said, that there are persons in the world, who are in great measure without the natural affections towards their fellow-creatures; there are likewise instances of persons without the common natural affections to themselves: but the nature of man is not to be judged of by either of these, but by what appears in the common world, in the bulk of mankind.

[16] I am afraid it would be thought very strange, if to confirm the truth of this account of human nature and make out the justness of the foregoing comparison, it should be added, that from what appears, men in fact as much and as often contradict that *part* of their nature which respects *self* and which leads them to their *own private* good and happiness, as they contradict that *part* of it which respects *society*, and tends to *public* good; that there are as few persons who attain the greatest satisfaction and enjoyment which they might attain in the present world, as who do the greatest good to others which they might do; nay, that there are as few

at, is exactly the same, namely, equality or superiority; and consequently, that to do mischief is not the end of envy, but merely the means it makes use of to attain its end. As to *Resentment*, see the eighth Sermon.

who can be said really and in earnest to aim at one,
as at the other. Take a survey of mankind : the
world in general, the good and bad, almost without
exception, equally are agreed, that were religion out
of the case, the happiness of the present life would
consist in a manner wholly in riches, honours, sensual
gratifications, insomuch that one scarce hears a reflection made upon prudence, life, conduct, but upon
this supposition. Yet, on the contrary, that persons
in the greatest affluence of fortune are no happier
than such as have only a competency, that the
cares and disappointments of ambition for the most
part far exceed the satisfactions of it, as also the
miserable intervals of intemperance and excess, and
the many untimely deaths occasioned by a dissolute course of life; these things are all seen, acknowledged, by every one acknowledged, but are
thought no objections against, though they expressly
contradict, this universal principle, that the happiness of the present life consists in one or other of
them. Whence is all this absurdity and contradiction? Is not the middle way obvious? Can anything be more manifest, than that the happiness of
life consists in these possessed and enjoyed only to
a certain degree ; that to pursue them beyond this
degree is always attended with more inconvenience
than advantage to a man's self, and often with extreme misery and unhappiness? Whence then, I
say, is all this absurdity and contradiction? Is it
really the result of consideration in mankind, how
they may become most easy to themselves, most
free from care, and enjoy the chief happiness attainable in this world? Or is it not manifestly owing
either to this, that they have not cool and reasonable
concern enough for themselves to consider wherein
their chief happiness in the present life consists ;

or else, if they do consider it, that they will not act conformably to what is the result of that consideration, *i. e.*, reasonable concern for themselves, or cool self-love, is prevailed over by passion and appetite ? So that from what appears, there is no ground to assert that those principles in the nature of man, which most directly lead to promote the good of our fellow-creatures, are more generally, or in a greater degree violated, than those which most directly lead us to promote our own private good and happiness.

[17] The sum of the whole is plainly this. The nature of man considered in his single capacity, and with respect only to the present world, is adapted and leads him to attain the greatest happiness he can for himself in the present world. The nature of man, considered in his public or social capacity, leads him to a right behaviour in society to that course of life which we call virtue. Men follow or obey their nature in both these capacities and respects to a certain degree, but not entirely ; their actions do not come up to the whole of what their nature leads them to in either of these capacities or respects, and they often violate their nature in both, *i. e.*, as they neglect the duties they owe to their fellow-creatures, to which their nature leads them, and are injurious, to which their nature is abhorrent ; so there is a manifest negligence in men of their real happiness or interest in the present world, when that interest is inconsistent with a present gratification, for the sake of which they negligently, nay, even knowingly, are the authors and instruments of their own misery and ruin. Thus they are as often un-just to themselves as to others, and for the most part are equally so to both by the same actions.

SERMON II.

" For when the Gentiles, which have not the law, do
by nature the things contained in the law, these,
having not the law, are a law unto themselves."
Rom. ii. 14.

A S speculative truth admits of different kinds of proof, so likewise moral obligations may be shown by different methods. If the real nature of any creature leads him and is adapted to such and such purposes only, or more than to any other, this is a reason to believe the Author of that nature intended it for those purposes. Thus there is no doubt the eye was intended for us to see with. And the more complex any constitution is, and the greater variety of parts there are which thus tend to some one end, the stronger is the proof that such end was designed. [2] However, when the inward frame of man is considered as any guide in morals, the utmost caution must be used that none make peculiarities in their own temper, or anything which is the effect of particular customs, though observable in several, the standard of what is common to the species, and above all, that the highest principle be not forgot or excluded, that to which belongs the

c

adjustment and correction of all other inward movements and affections, which principle will of course
have some influence, but which, being in nature
supreme, as shall now be shown, ought to preside
over and govern all the rest. The difficulty of rightly
observing the two former cautions, the appearance
there is of some small diversity amongst mankind
with respect to this faculty, with respect to their
natural sense of moral good and evil, and the attention necessary to survey with any exactness what
passes within, have occasioned that it is not so much
agreed what is the standard of the internal nature
of man, as of his external form. Neither is this
last exactly settled. [3] Yet we understand one
another when we speak of the shape of a human
body ; so likewise we do when we speak of the heart
and inward principles, how far soever the standard
is from being exact or precisely fixed. There is,
therefore, ground for an attempt of showing men to
themselves, of showing them what course of life and
behaviour their real nature points out and would
lead them to. Now obligations of virtue shown and
motives to the practice of it enforced from a review
of the nature of man, are to be considered as an
appeal to each particular person's heart and natural
conscience, as the external senses are appealed to for
the proof of things cognizable by them. [4] Since,
then, our inward feelings, and the perceptions we
receive from our external senses, are equally real,
to argue from the former to life and conduct is as
little liable to exception, as to argue from the latter
to absolute speculative truth. A man can as little
doubt whether his eyes were given him to see with,
as he can doubt of the truth of the science of optics
deduced from ocular experiments. And, allowing
the inward feeling, shame, a man can as little doubt

whether it was given him to prevent his doing shameful actions, as he can doubt whether his eyes were given him to guide his steps. And as to these inward feelings themselves, that they are real, that man has in his nature passions and affections, can no more be questioned, than that he has external senses. Neither can the former be wholly mistaken, though to a certain degree liable to greater mistakes than the latter.

[5] There can be no doubt but that several propensions or instincts, several principles in the heart of man, carry him to society, and to contribute to the happiness of it, in a sense and a manner in which no inward principle leads him to evil. These principles, propensions, or instincts, which lead him to do good, are approved of by a certain faculty within, quite distinct from these propensions themselves. All this hath been fully made out in the foregoing discourse.

[6] But it may be said, " What is all this, though true, to the purpose of virtue and religion? these require, not only that we do good to others when we are led this way, by benevolence or reflection, happening to be stronger than other principles, passions, or appetites, but likewise that the *whole* character be formed upon thought and reflection, that *every* action be directed by some determinate rule, some other rule than the strength and prevalency of any principle or passion. What sign is there in our nature (for the inquiry is only about what is to be collected from thence) that this was intended by its Author? Or how does so various and fickle a temper as that of man appear adapted thereto? It may indeed be absurd and unnatural for men to act without any reflection, nay, without regard to that particular kind of reflection which you

call conscience, because this does belong to our nature. For as there never was a man but who approved one place, prospect, building, before another, so it does not appear that there ever was a man who would not have approved an action of humility rather than of cruelty, interest and passion being quite out of the case. But interest and passion do come in, and are often too strong for and prevail over reflection and conscience. Now as brutes have various instincts, by which they are carried on to the end the Author of their nature intended them for, is not man in the same condition, with this difference only, that to his instincts (*i. e.*, appetites and passions) is added the principle of reflection or conscience? And as brutes act agreeably to their nature, in following that principle or particular instinct which for the present is strongest in them, does not man likewise act agreeably to his nature, or obey the law of his creation, by following that principle, be it passion or conscience, which for the present happens to be strongest in him? Thus, different men are by their particular nature hurried on to pursue honour, or riches, or pleasure, there are also persons whose temper leads them in an uncommon degree to kindness, compassion, doing good to their fellow-creatures, as there are others who are given to suspend their judgment, to weigh and consider things, and to act upon thought and reflection. Let every one, then, quietly follow his nature, as passion, reflection, appetite, the several parts of it, happen to be strongest; but let not the man of virtue take upon him to blame the ambitious, the covetous, the dissolute, since these equally with him obey and follow their nature. Thus, as in some cases we follow our nature in doing the works *contained in the law*, so in other cases we follow nature in doing contrary."

[7] Now all this licentious talk entirely goes upon a supposition, that men follow their nature in the same sense, in violating the known rules of justice and honesty for the sake of a present gratification, as they do in following those rules when they have no temptation to the contrary. And if this were true, that could not be so which St. Paul asserts, that men are *by nature a law to themselves.* If by following nature were meant only acting as we please, it would indeed be ridiculous to speak of nature as any guide in morals; nay, the very mention of deviating from nature would be absurd, and the mention of following it, when spoken by way of distinction, would absolutely have no meaning. For did ever any one act otherwise than as he pleased? And yet the ancients speak of deviating from nature as vice; and of following nature so much as a distinction that according to them the perfection of virtue consists therein. So that language itself should teach people another sense to the words *following nature,* than barely acting as we please. Let it, however, be observed, that though the words *human nature* are to be explained, yet the real question of this discourse is not concerning the meaning of words, any other than as the explanation of them may be needful to make out and explain the assertion, that *every man is naturally a law to himself,* that *every one may find within himself the rule of right, and obligations to follow it.* This St. Paul affirms in the words of the text, and this the foregoing objection really denies by seeming to allow it. And the objection will be fully answered, and the text before us explained, by observing that *nature* is considered in different views, and the word used in different senses, and by showing in what view it is considered, and in what sense the word is used, when

intended to express and signify that which is the
guide of life, that by which men are a law to themselves. I say, the explanation of the term will be
sufficient, because from thence it will appear, that
in some senses of the word *nature* cannot be, but
that in another sense it manifestly is, a law to us.

I. [8] By nature is often meant no more than
some principle in man, without regard either to the
kind or degree of it. Thus, the passion of anger,
and the affection of parents to their children, would
be called equally *natural*. And as the same person
hath often contrary principles, which at the same
time draw contrary ways, he may, by the same
action, both follow and contradict his nature in this
sense of the word; he may follow one passion and
contradict another.

II. [9] *Nature* is frequently spoken of as consisting
in those passions which are strongest, and most influence the actions, which being vicious ones, mankind is in this sense naturally vicious, or vicious by
nature. Thus St. Paul says of the Gentiles, who
were *dead in trespasses and sins, and walked according to the spirit of disobedience,* that they were
by nature the children of wrath.[1] They could be
no otherwise *children of wrath* by nature, than they
were vicious by nature.

Here, then, are two different senses of the word
nature, in neither of which men can at all be said to
be a law to themselves. They are mentioned only
to be excluded, to prevent their being confounded,
as the latter is in the objection, with another sense of
it, which is now to be inquired after and explained.

III. [10] The Apostle asserts, that the Gentiles
do by nature the things contained in the law. Nature is indeed here put by way of distinction from

[1] Ephes. ii. 3.

revelation, but yet it is not a mere negative. He intends to express more than that by which they *did not*, that by which they *did* the works of the law, namely, by *nature*. It is plain the meaning of the word is not the same in this passage as in the former, where it is spoken of as evil, for in this latter it is spoken of as good, as that by which they acted, or might have acted virtuously. What that is in man by which he is *naturally a law to himself*, is explained in the following words: *Which show the work of the law written in their hearts, their consciences also bearing witness, and their thoughts the mean while accusing or else excusing one another.* [11] If there be a distinction to be made between the *works written in their hearts* and the *witness of conscience*, by the former must be meant the natural disposition to kindness and compassion, to do what is of good report, to which this Apostle often refers, that part of the nature of man, treated of in the foregoing discourse, which with very little reflection and of course leads him to society, and by means of which he naturally acts a just and good part in it, unless other passions and interests lead him astray. Yet, since other passions, and regards to private interest which lead us (though indirectly, yet they lead us) astray, are themselves in a degree equally natural, and often most prevalent, and since we have no method of seeing the particular degrees in which one or the other is placed in us by nature, it is plain the former, considered merely as natural, good and right as they are, can no more be a law to us than the latter. [12] But there is a superior principle of reflection or conscience in every man, which distinguishes between the internal principles of his heart as well as his external actions, which passes judgment upon himself and them, pronounces

determinately some actions to be in themselves just,
right, good, others to be in themselves evil, wrong,
unjust, which, without being consulted, without
being advised with, magisterially exerts itself, and
approves or condemns him the doer of them accordingly, and which, if not forcibly stopped, naturally
and always of course goes on to anticipate a higher
and more effectual sentence, which shall hereafter
second and affirm its own. But this part of the office
of conscience is beyond my present design explicitly
to consider. It is by this faculty, natural to man,
that he is a moral agent, that he is a law to himself;
by this faculty, I say, not to be considered merely
as a principle in his heart, which is to have some
influence as well as others, but considered as a
faculty in kind and in nature supreme over all others,
and which bears its own authority of being so.

[13] This *prerogative*, this *natural supremacy*,
of the faculty which surveys, approves, or disapproves, the several affections of our mind and actions of our lives, being that by which men *are a
law to themselves*, their conformity or disobedience
to which law of our nature renders their actions, in
the highest and most proper sense, natural or unnatural, it is fit it be further explained to you, and
I hope it will be so, if you will attend to the following
reflections.

[14] Man may act according to that principle or
inclination which for the present happens to be
strongest, and yet act in a way disproportionate
to, and violate his real proper nature. Suppose a
brute creature by any bait to be allured into a
snare, by which he is destroyed. He plainly followed the bent of his nature leading him to gratify
his appetite, there is an entire correspondence between his whole nature and such an action, such

action therefore is natural. But suppose a man, foreseeing the same danger of certain ruin, should rush into it for the sake of a present gratification, he in this instance would follow his strongest desire, as did the brute creature, but there would be as manifest a disproportion between the nature of a man and such an action, as between the meanest work of art and the skill of the greatest master in that art, which disproportion arises, not from considering the action singly in *itself* or in its *consequences*, but from *comparison* of it with the nature of the agent. And since such an action is utterly disproportionate to the nature of man, it is in the strictest and most proper sense unnatural, this word expressing that disproportion. Therefore, instead of the words *disproportionate to his nature*, the word *unnatural* may now be put, this being more familiar to us, but, let it be observed, that it stands for the same thing precisely.

[15] Now, what is it which renders such a rash action unnatural? Is it that he went against the principle of reasonable and cool self-love, considered *merely* as a part of his nature? No, for if he had acted the contrary way, he would equally have gone against a principle, or part of his nature, namely, passion or appetite. But to deny a present appetite, from foresight that the gratification of it would end in immediate ruin or extreme misery, is by no means an unnatural action, whereas to contradict or go against cool self-love for the sake of such gratification is so in the instance before us. Such an action then being unnatural, and its being so not arising from a man's going against a principle or desire barely, nor in going against that principle or desire which happens for the present to be strongest, it necessarily follows, that there must be some other difference

or distinction to be made between these two principles, passion and cool self-love, than what I have
yet taken notice of. And this difference, not being
a difference in strength or degree, I call a difference
in *nature* and in *kind*. And since, in the instance
still before us, if passion prevails over self-love, the
consequent action is unnatural, but if self-love prevails over passion, the action is natural, it is manifest that self-love is in human nature a superior
principle to passion. This may be contradicted
without violating that nature, but the former cannot.
So that, if we will act conformably to the economy
of man's nature, reasonable self-love must govern.
Thus, without particular consideration of conscience,
we may have a clear conception of the *superior
nature* of one inward principle to another, and see
that there really is this natural superiority, quite
distinct from degrees of strength and prevalency.

[16] Let us now take a view of the nature of man,
as consisting partly of various appetites, passions,
affections, and partly of the principle of reflection
or conscience, leaving quite out all consideration of
the different degrees of strength, in which either of
them prevails, and it will further appear that there
is this natural superiority of one inward principle
to another, and that it is even part of the idea of
reflection or conscience.

Passion or appetite implies a direct simple tendency towards such and such objects, without distinction of the means by which they are to be
obtained. Consequently it will often happen there
will be a desire of particular objects, in cases where
they cannot be obtained without manifest injury to
others. Reflection or conscience comes in, and
disapproves the pursuit of them in these circumstances, but the desire remains. Which is to be

obeyed, appetite or reflection? Cannot this question be answered, from the economy and constitution of human nature merely, without saying which is strongest? Or need this at all come into consideration? Would not the question be *intelligibly* and fully answered by saying, that the principle of reflection or conscience being compared with the various appetites, passions, and affections in men, the former is manifestly superior and chief, without regard to strength? And how often soever the latter happens to prevail, it is mere *usurpation*, the former remains in nature and in kind its superior, and every instance of such prevalence of the latter is an instance of breaking in upon and violation of the constitution of man.

[17] All this is no more than the distinction, which everybody is acquainted with, between mere *power* and *authority*, only instead of being intended to express the difference between what is possible, and what is lawful in civil government, here it has been shown applicable to the several principles in the mind of man. Thus that principle, by which we survey, and either approve or disapprove our own heart, temper, and actions, is not only to be considered as what is in its turn to have some influence, which may be said of every passion, of the lowest appetites, but likewise as being superior; as from its very nature manifestly claiming superiority over all others, insomuch that you cannot form a notion of this faculty, conscience, without taking in judgment, direction, superintendency. This is a constituent part of the idea, that is, of the faculty itself, and to preside and govern, from the very economy and constitution of man, belongs to it. Had it strength, as it has right, had it power, as it has manifest authority, it would absolutely govern the world.

[18] This gives us a further view of the nature of man, shows us what course of life we were made for; not only that our real nature leads us to be influenced in some degree by reflection and conscience, but likewise in what degree we are to be influenced by it, if we will fall in with, and act agreeably to, the constitution of our nature; that this faculty was placed within to be our proper governor, to direct and regulate all under principles, passions, and motives of action. This is its right and office, thus sacred is its authority. And how often soever men violate and rebelliously refuse to submit to it, for supposed interest which they cannot otherwise obtain, or for the sake of passion which they cannot otherwise gratify, this makes no alteration as to the *natural right* and *office* of conscience.

[19] Let us now turn this whole matter another way, and suppose there was no such thing at all as this natural supremacy of conscience, that there was no distinction to be made between one inward principle and another but only that of strength, and see what would be the consequence.

Consider, then, what is the latitude and compass of the actions of man with regard to himself, his fellow-creatures, and the Supreme Being? What are their bounds, besides that of our natural power? With respect to the two first, they are plainly no other than these; no man seeks misery as such for himself, and no one unprovoked does mischief to another for its own sake. For in every degree within these bounds, mankind knowingly, from passion or wantonness, bring ruin and misery upon themselves and others. And impiety and profaneness, I mean, what every one would call so who believes the being of God, have absolutely no bounds at all. Men blaspheme the Author of Nature, formally and in words

renounce their allegiance to their Creator. Put an
instance, then, with respect to any one of these three.
Though we should suppose profane swearing, and in
general that kind of impiety now mentioned, to mean
nothing, yet it implies wanton disregard and irreve-
rence towards an infinite Being, our Creator; and
is this as suitable to the nature of man, as reverence
and dutiful submission of heart towards that Almighty Being? Or, suppose a man guilty of parri-
cide, with all the circumstances of cruelty which
such an action can admit of. This action is done in
consequence of its principle being for the present
strongest, and if there be no difference between
inward principles, but only that of strength, the
strength being given, you have the whole nature of
the man given, so far as it relates to this matter.
The action plainly corresponds to the principle, the
principle being in that degree of strength it was;
it therefore corresponds to the whole nature of the
man. Upon comparing the action and the whole
nature, there arises no disproportion, there appears
no unsuitableness between them. Thus the *murder
of a father* and the *nature of man* correspond to
each other, as the same nature and an act of filial
duty. If there be no difference between inward
principles, but only that of strength, we can make
no distinction between these two actions, considered
as the actions of such a creature, but in our coolest
hours must approve or disapprove them equally,
than which nothing can be reduced to a greater
absurdity.

SERMON III.

THE natural supremacy of reflection or conscience being thus established, we may from it form a distinct notion of what is meant by *human nature*, when virtue is said to consist in following it, and vice in deviating from it.

[20] As the idea of a civil constitution implies in it united strength, various subordinations under one direction, that of the supreme authority, the different strength of each particular member of the society not coming into the idea; whereas, if you leave out the subordination, the union, and the one direction, you destroy and lose it: so reason, several appetites, passions, and affections, prevailing in different degrees of strength, is not *that* idea or notion of *human nature*, but *that nature* consists in these several principles considered as having a natural respect to each other, in the several passions being naturally subordinate to the one superior principle of reflection or conscience. Every bias, instinct, propension within, is a natural part of our nature, but not the whole; add to these the superior faculty, whose office it is to adjust, manage, and preside over them, and take in this its natural superiority, and you complete the idea of human nature. And, as in civil government, the constitution is broken in upon, and violated by power and strength prevailing over authority, so the constitution of man is broken in upon and violated by the lower faculties or principles within prevailing over that which is in its nature supreme over

them all.   Thus, when it is said by ancient writers,
that tortures and death are not so contrary to human
nature as injustice, by this to be sure is not meant,
that the aversion to the former in mankind is less
strong and prevalent than their aversion to the latter,
but that the former is only contrary to our nature
considered in a partial view, and which takes in only
the lowest part of it, that which we have in common
with the brutes, whereas the latter is contrary to
our nature considered in a higher sense as a system
and constitution, contrary to the whole economy of
man.[1]

[1] Every man in his physical nature is one individual single
agent.   He has likewise properties and principles, each of
which may be considered separately, and without regard to the
respects which they have to each other. ·Neither of these is
the nature we are taking a view of.   But it is the inward frame
of man considered as a *system* or *constitution*, whose several parts
are united, not by a physical principle of individuation, but by
the respects they have to each other, the chief of which is the
subjection which the appetites, passions, and particular affections have to the one supreme principle of reflection or conscience.   The system or constitution is formed by and consists
in these respects and this subjection.   Thus the body is a *system*
or *constitution*, so is a tree, so is every machine.   Consider all
the several parts of a tree without the natural respects they
have to each other, and you have not at all the idea of a tree,
but add these respects, and this gives you the idea.   The body
may be impaired by sickness, a tree may decay, a machine be
out of order, and yet the system and constitution of them
not totally dissolved.   There is plainly somewhat which answers
to all this in the moral constitution of man.   (*b*) Whoever
will consider his own nature, will see that the several appetites,
passions, and particular affections, have different respects amongst
themselves.   They are restraints upon, and are in proportion to
each other.   This proportion is just and perfect, when all those
under principles are perfectly coincident with conscience, so
far as their nature permits, and in all cases under its absolute
and entire direction.   The least excess or defect, the least
alteration of the due proportions amongst themselves, or of
their coincidence with conscience, though not proceeding into

[21] And from all these things put together, nothing can be more evident, than that, exclusive of revelation, man cannot be considered as a creature left by his Maker to act at random, and live at large up to the extent of his natural power, as passion, humour, wilfulness, happen to carry him, which is the condition brute creatures are in; but that *from his make, constitution, or nature, he is in the strictest and most proper sense a law to himself.* He hath the rule of right within: what is wanting is only that he honestly attend to it.

[22] The inquiries which have been made by men of leisure after some general rule, the conformity to, or disagreement from which, should denominate our actions good or evil, are in many respects of great service. Yet let any plain honest man, before he engages in any course of action, ask himself, Is this I am going about right, or is it wrong? Is it good, or is it evil? I do not in the least doubt but that this question would be answered agreeably to truth and virtue, by almost any fair man in almost any circumstance. Neither do there appear any cases which look like exceptions to this, but those of superstition, and of partiality to ourselves. Superstition may perhaps be somewhat of an exception, but partiality to ourselves is not, this being

action, is some degree of disorder in the moral constitution. (c) But perfection, though plainly intelligible and supposable, was never attained by any man. If the higher principle of reflection maintains its place, and as much as it can corrects that disorder, and hinders it from breaking out into action, this is all that can be expected from such a creature as man. And though the appetites and passions have not their exact due proportion to each other, though they often strive for mastery with judgment or reflection; yet since the superiority of this principle to all others is the chief respect which forms the constitution, so far as this superiority is maintained, the character, the man, is good, worthy, virtuous.

itself dishonesty. For a man to judge that to be
the equitable, the moderate, the right part for him
to act, which he would see to be hard, unjust,
oppressive in another, this is plain vice, and can
proceed only from great unfairness of mind.

[23] But allowing that mankind hath the rule of
right within himself, yet it may be asked, "What
obligations are we under to attend to and follow it?"
I answer, it has been proved that man by his nature
is a law to himself, without the particular distinct
consideration of the positive sanctions of that law,
the rewards and punishments which we feel, and
those which from the light of reason we have ground
to believe are annexed to it. The question then
carries its own answer along with it. Your obligation
to obey this law, is its being the law of your nature.
That your conscience approves of and attests to such
a course of action, is itself alone an obligation. Conscience does not only offer itself to show us the way
we should walk in, but it likewise carries its own
authority with it, that it is our natural guide, the
guide assigned to us by the Author of our nature;
it therefore belongs to our condition of being, it is
our duty to walk in that path and follow this guide,
without looking about to see whether we may not
possibly forsake them with impunity.

[24] However, let us hear what is to be said
against obeying this law of our nature. And the
sum is no more than this. "Why should we be
concerned about anything out of and beyond ourselves? If we do find within ourselves regards to
others, and restraints of we know not how many
different kinds; yet these being embarrassments,
and hindering us from going the nearest way to our
own good, why should we not endeavour to suppress
and get over them?"

D

[25] Thus people go on with words, which, when applied to human nature, and the condition in which it is placed in this world, have really no meaning. For does not all this kind of talk go upon supposition, that our happiness in this world consists in somewhat quite distinct from regard to others, and that it is the privilege of vice to be without restraint or confinement? Whereas, on the contrary, the enjoyments, in a manner all the common enjoyments of life, even the pleasures of vice, depend upon these regards of one kind or another to our fellow-creatures. Throw off all regards to others, and we should be quite indifferent to infamy and to honour; there could be no such thing at all as ambition, and scarce any such thing as covetousness, for we should be equally indifferent to the disgrace of poverty, the several neglects and kinds of contempt which accompany this state, and to the reputation of riches, the regard and respect they usually procure. Neither is restraint by any means peculiar to one course of life, but our very nature, exclusive of conscience and our condition, lays us under an absolute necessity of it. We cannot gain any end whatever without being confined to the proper means, which is often the most painful and uneasy confinement. And in numberless instances a present appetite cannot be gratified without such apparent and immediate ruin and misery, that the most dissolute man in the world chooses to forego the pleasure, rather than endure the pain.

[26] Is the meaning, then, to indulge those regards to our fellow-creatures and submit to those restraints, which upon the whole are attended with more satisfaction than uneasiness, and get over only those which bring more uneasiness and inconvenience than satisfaction? "Doubtless this was our meaning." You

have changed sides then.   Keep to this; be consistent with yourselves; and you and the men of
virtue are *in general* perfectly agreed.   But let us
take care and avoid mistakes.   Let it not be taken
for granted that the temper of envy, rage, resentment, yields greater delight than meekness, forgiveness, compassion, and goodwill—especially when it
is acknowledged that rage, envy, resentment, are
in themselves mere misery, and the satisfaction
arising from the indulgence of them is little more
than relief from that misery—whereas the temper
of compassion and benevolence is itself delightful,
and the indulgence of it, by doing good, affords
new positive delight and enjoyment.   Let it not
be taken for granted, that the satisfaction arising
from the reputation of riches and power, however
obtained, and from the respect paid to them, is
greater than the satisfaction arising from the reputation of justice, honesty, charity, and the esteem
which is universally acknowledged to be their due.
And if it be doubtful which of these satisfactions is
the greater, as there are persons who think neither
of them very considerable, yet there can be no doubt
concerning ambition and covetousness, virtue and a
good mind, considered in themselves, and as leading
to different courses of life; there can, I say, be no
doubt, which temper and which course is attended
with more peace and tranquillity of mind, which with
more perplexity, vexation and inconvenience.   And
both the virtues and vices which have been now mentioned do, in a manner, equally imply in them regards
of one kind or another to our fellow-creatures.   And
with respect to restraint and confinement; whoever
will consider the restraints from fear and shame,
the dissimulation, mean arts of concealment, servile
compliances, one or other of which belong to almost

every course of vice, will soon be convinced that
the man of virtue is by no means upon a disadvantage in this respect. How many instances are
there in which men feel and own and cry aloud
under the chains of vice with which they are en-
thralled, and which yet they will not shake off!
How many instances, in which persons manifestly
go through more pains and self-denial to gratify a
vicious passion, than would have been necessary to
the conquest of it! To this is to be added, that
when virtue is become habitual, when the temper
of it is acquired, what was before confinement ceases
to be so, by becoming choice and delight. Whatever restraint and guard upon ourselves may be
needful to unlearn any unnatural distortion or odd
gesture, yet, in all propriety of speech, natural
behaviour must be the most easy and unrestrained.
It is manifest that, in the common course of life,
there is seldom any inconsistency between our duty
and what is *called* interest: it is much seldomer that
there is any inconsistency between duty and what
is *really* our present interest, meaning by interest,
happiness and satisfaction. Self-love, then, though
confined to the interest of the present world, does in
general perfectly coincide with virtue, and leads us
to one and the same course of life. But, whatever
exceptions there are to this, which are much fewer
than they are commonly thought, all shall be set right
at the final distribution of things. It is a manifest absurdity to suppose evil prevailing finally over good, under the conduct and administration of a perfect mind.

[27] The whole argument, which I have been
now insisting upon, may be thus summed up, and
given you in one view. The nature of man is adapted
to some course of action or other. Upon comparing
some actions with this nature, they appear suitable

and correspondent to it, from comparison of other
actions with the same nature, there arises to our view
some unsuitableness or disproportion. The correspondence of actions to the nature of the agent
renders them natural, their disproportion to it, unnatural. That an action is correspondent to the
nature of the agent, does not arise from its being
agreeable to the principle which happens to be the
strongest, for it may be so and yet be quite disproportionate to the nature of the agent. The correspondence, therefore, or disproportion, arises from somewhat else. This can be nothing but a difference in
nature and kind, altogether distinct from strength,
between the inward principles. Some, then, are in
nature and kind superior to others. And the correspondence arises from the action being conform-
able to the higher principle, and the unsuitableness
from its being contrary to it. Reasonable self-love
and conscience are the chief or superior principles
in the nature of man, because an action may be suitable to this nature, though all other principles be
violated, but becomes unsuitable, if either of those
is. Conscience and self-love, if we understand our
true happiness, always lead us the same way. Duty
and interest are perfectly coincident : for the most
part in this world, but entirely and in every instance
if we take in the future, and the whole ; this being
implied in the notion of a good and perfect administration of things. Thus they who have been so
wise in their generation as to regard only their own
supposed interest, at the expense and to the injury
of others, shall at last find, that he who has given
up all the advantages of the present world, rather
than violate his conscience and the relations of life,
has infinitely better provided for himself, and secured
his own interest and happiness.

SERMON IV.

UPON THE GOVERNMENT OF THE TONGUE.

" If any man among you seem to be religious, and bridleth not his tongue, but deceiveth his own heart, this man's religion is vain."—JAMES i. 26.

THE translation of this text would be more determinate by being more literal, thus: *If any man among you seemeth to be religious, not bridling his tongue but deceiving his own heart, this man's religion is vain.* This determines that the words, *but deceiveth his own heart*, are not put in opposition to, *seemeth to be religious*, but to, *bridleth not his tongue.* The certain determinate meaning of the text then being, that he who seemeth to be religious, and bridleth not his tongue, but in that particular deceiveth his own heart, this man's religion is vain, we may observe somewhat very forcible and expressive in these words of St. James. As if the Apostle had said, No man surely can make any pretences to religion, who does not at least believe that he bridleth his tongue: if he puts on any appearance or face of religion, and yet does not govern his tongue, he must surely deceive himself in that particular, and think he does: and whoever

is so unhappy as to deceive himself in this, to imagine he keeps that unruly faculty in due subjection,
when indeed he does not, whatever the other part of
his life be, his religion is vain, the government of the
tongue being a most material restraint which virtue
lays us under ; without it no man can be truly religious.

[2] In treating upon this subject, I will consider—
First, What is the general vice or fault here referred to, or what disposition in men is supposed
in moral reflections and precepts concerning *bridling
the tongue.*

Secondly, When it may be said of any one, that he
has a due government over himself in this respect.

I. [3] Now the fault referred to, and the disposition supposed, in precepts and reflections concerning the government of the tongue, is not evil-
speaking from malice, nor lying or bearing false
witness from indirect selfish designs. The disposition to these, and the actual vices themselves, all
come under other subjects. The tongue may be
employed about, and made to serve all the purposes
of vice, in tempting and deceiving, in perjury and
injustice. But the thing here supposed and referred to, is talkativeness : a disposition to be talking,
abstracted from the consideration of what is to be
said, with very little or no regard to, or thought of
doing either good or harm. [4] And let not any
imagine this to be a slight matter, and that it deserves not to have so great weight laid upon it, till
he has considered what evil is implied in it, and the
bad effects which follow from it. It is perhaps
true that they who are addicted to this folly would
choose to confine themselves to trifles and indifferent subjects, and so intend only to be guilty of
being impertinent ; but as they cannot go on for

ever talking of nothing, as common matters will not
afford a sufficient fund for perpetual continued discourse, when subjects of this kind are exhausted,
they will go on to defamation, scandal, divulging of
secrets, their own secrets as well as those of others,
anything rather than be silent. They are plainly
hurried on in the heat of their talk to say quite
different things from what they first intended and
which they afterwards wish unsaid, or improper
things, which they had no end in saying, but only to
afford employment to their tongue. [5] And if these
people expect to be heard and regarded (for there
are some content merely with talking), they will
invent to engage your attention, and, when they
have heard the least imperfect hint of an affair, they
will out of their own head add the circumstances of
time and place and other matters to make out their
story, and give the appearance of probability to it,
not that they have any concern about being believed,
otherwise than as a means of being heard. The thing
is, to engage your attention, to take you up wholly
for the present time; what reflections will be made
afterwards, is in truth the least of their thoughts.
[6] And further, when persons, who indulge themselves in these liberties of the tongue, are in any
degree offended with another, as little disgusts and
misunderstandings will be, they allow themselves to
defame and revile such a one without any moderation or bounds, though the offence is so very slight,
that they themselves would not do, nor perhaps
wish him an injury in any other way. And in this
case the scandal and revilings are chiefly owing to
talkativeness and not bridling their tongue, and so
come under our present subject. The least occasion in the world will make the humour break out
in this particular way or in another. It is like a

torrent, which must and will flow, but the least thing imaginable will first of all give it either this or another direction, turn it into this or that channel; or like a fire, the nature of which, when in a heap of combustible matter, is to spread and lay waste all around, but any one of a thousand little accidents will occasion it to break out first either in this or another particular part.

[7] The subject then before us, though it does run up into, and can scarce be treated as entirely distinct from all others, yet it needs not to be so much mixed or blended with them as it often is. Every faculty and power may be used as the instrument of premeditated vice and wickedness, merely as the most proper and effectual means of executing such designs. But if a man, from deep malice and desire of revenge, should meditate a falsehood with a settled design to ruin his neighbour's reputation and should with great coolness and deliberation spread it, nobody would choose to say of such a one, that he had no government of his tongue. A man may use the faculty of speech as an instrument of false witness, who yet has so entire a command over that faculty as never to speak but from forethought and cool design. Here the crime is injustice and perjury, and, strictly speaking, no more belongs to the present subject than perjury and injustice in any other way. [8] But there is such a thing as a disposition to be talking for its own sake, from which persons often say anything good or bad of others, merely as a subject of discourse, according to the particular temper they themselves happen to be in, and to pass away the present time. There is likewise to be observed in persons such a strong and eager desire of engaging attention to what they say, that they will speak good or evil, truth or other-

wise, merely as one or the other seems to be most
hearkened to: and this, though it is sometimes
joined, is not the same with the desire of being
thought important and men of consequence. There
is in some such a disposition to be talking, that an
offence of the slightest kind, and such as would not
raise any other resentment, yet raises, if I may so
speak, the resentment of the tongue, puts it into a
flame, into the most ungovernable motions. This
outrage, when the person it respects is present, we
distinguish in the lower rank of people by a peculiar
term: and let it be observed, that though the decencies of behaviour are a little kept, the same outrage and virulence, indulged when he is absent, is
an offence of the same kind. But not to distinguish
any farther in this manner: men run into faults and
follies, which cannot so properly be referred to any
one general head as this, that they have not a due
government over their tongue.

[9] And this unrestrained volubility and wantonness of speech is the occasion of numberless evils
and vexations in life. It begets resentment in him
who is the subject of it; sows the seed of strife
and dissension amongst others, and inflames little
disgusts and offences, which if let alone would wear
away of themselves; it is often of as bad effect upon
the good name of others, as deep envy or malice;
and to say the least of it in this respect, it destroys
and perverts a certain equity of the utmost importance to society to be observed, namely, that praise
and dispraise, a good or bad character, should always be bestowed according to desert. The tongue
used in such a licentious manner is like a sword in
the hand of a madman; it is employed at random,
it can scarce possibly do any good, and for the most
part does a world of mischief, and implies not only

great folly and a trifling spirit, but great viciousness
of mind, great indifference to truth and falsity, and
to the reputation, welfare, and good of others.   So
much reason is there for what St. James says of
the tongue.   *It is a fire, a world of iniquity, it
defileth the whole body, setteth on fire the course
of nature, and is itself set on fire of hell.*[1] This
is the faculty or disposition which we are required
to keep a guard upon, these are the vices and
follies it runs into, when not kept under due restraint.

II. [10] Wherein the due government of the
tongue consists, or when it may be said of any one
in a moral and religious sense that he *bridleth his
tongue,* I come now to consider.

The due and proper use of any natural faculty
or power, is to be judged of by the end and design
for which it was given us.   The chief purpose for
which the faculty of speech was given to man is
plainly that we might communicate our thoughts
to each other, in order to carry on the affairs of the
world, for business, and for our improvement in
knowledge and learning.   But the good Author of
our nature designed us not only necessaries, but
likewise enjoyment and satisfaction, in that being
he hath graciously given, and in that condition of
life he hath placed us in.   There are secondary uses
of our faculties, they administer to delight, as well
as to necessity, and as they are equally adapted to
both, there is no doubt but he intended them for
our gratification, as well as for the support and
continuance of our being.   The secondary use of
speech is to please and be entertaining to each
other in conversation.   This is in every respect
allowable and right; it unites men closer in alliances

---

[1] Chap. III. v. 6.

and friendships, gives us a fellow feeling of the prosperity and unhappiness of each other, and is in several respects serviceable to virtue, and to promote good behaviour in the world. And provided there be not too much time spent in it, if it were considered only in the way of gratification and delight, men must have strange notions of God and of religion to think that he can be offended with it, or that it is in any way inconsistent with the strictest virtue. But the truth is, such sort of conversation, though it has no particular good tendency, yet it has a general good one, it is social and friendly, and tends to promote humanity, good nature, and civility.

[11] As the end and use, so likewise the abuse of speech, relates to the one or other of these, either to business, or to conversation. As to the former: deceit in the management of business and affairs does not properly belong to the subject now before us, though one may just mention that multitude, that endless number of words, with which business is perplexed, when a much fewer should, as it would seem, better serve the purpose; but this must be left to those who understand the matter. The government of the tongue, considered as a subject of itself, relates chiefly to conversation, to that kind of discourse which usually fills up the time spent in friendly meetings and visits of civility. And the danger is lest persons entertain themselves and others at the expense of their wisdom and their virtue, and to the injury or offence of their neighbour. If they will observe and keep clear of these, they may be as free and easy and unreserved as they can desire. [12] The cautions to be given for avoiding these dangers and to render conversation innocent and agreeable, fall under the following particulars: silence; talking of indifferent

things; and (which makes up too great a part of conversation) giving of characters, speaking well or evil of others.

[13] The Wise Man observes that *there is a time to speak and a time to keep silence.* One meets with people in the world, who seem never to have made the last of these observations. And yet these great talkers do not at all speak from their having anything to say, as every sentence shows, but only from their inclination to be talking. Their conversation is merely an exercise of the tongue, no other human faculty has any share in it. It is strange these persons can help reflecting, that unless they have in truth a superior capacity, and are in an extraordinary manner furnished for conversation, if they are entertaining, it is at their own expense. Is it possible that it should never come into people's thoughts to suspect, whether or no it be to their advantage to show so very much of themselves? *Oh! that you would altogether hold your peace, and it should be your wisdom.*[2] Remember likewise there are persons who love fewer words, an inoffensive sort of people, and who deserve some regard, though of too still and composed tempers for you. Of this number was the son of Sirach, for he plainly speaks from experience when he says, *As hills of sand are to the steps of the aged, so is one of many words to a quiet man.* But one would think it should be obvious to every one, that when they are in company with their superiors of any kind, in years, knowledge, and experience, when proper and useful subjects are discoursed of, which they cannot bear a part in; that these are times for silence, when they should learn to hear, and be attentive, at least in their turn. It is indeed a very unhappy way these

[2] Job xiii.

people are in: they in a manner cut themselves out
from all advantage of conversation, except that of
being entertained with their own talk; their business in coming into company not being at all to be
informed, to hear, to learn, but to display themselves,
or rather to exert their faculty, and talk without any
design at all.   And if we consider conversation as
an entertainment, as somewhat to unbend the mind,
as a diversion from the cares, the business, and the
sorrows of life; it is of the very nature of it, that
the discourse be mutual.   This, I say, is implied in
the very notion of what we distinguish by conversation or being in company.   Attention to the continued discourse of one alone grows more painful
often than the cares and business we come to be
diverted from.   He therefore who imposes this
upon us is guilty of a double offence, arbitrarily en-
joining silence upon all the rest, and likewise obliging
them to this painful attention.

[14] I am sensible these things are apt to be
passed over as too little to come into a serious discourse, but in reality men are obliged, even in point
of morality and virtue, to observe all the decencies
of behaviour.   The greatest evils in life have had
their rise from somewhat which was thought of too
little importance to be attended to.   And as to the
matter we are now upon, it is absolutely necessary
to be considered.   For if people will not maintain
a due government over themselves, in regarding
proper times and seasons for silence, but *will* be
talking, they certainly, whether they design it or not
at first, will go on to scandal and evil-speaking, and
divulging secrets.

[15] If it were needful to say anything further
to persuade men to learn this lesson of silence, one
might put them in mind, how insignificant they

render themselves by this excessive talkativeness :
insomuch that, if they do chance to say anything
which deserves to be attended to and regarded, it is
lost in the variety and abundance which they utter
of another sort.

[16] The occasions of silence, then, are obvious,
and one would think should be easily distinguished
by everybody; namely, when a man has nothing to
say, or nothing but what is better unsaid; better
either in regard to particular persons he is present
with, or from its being an interruption to conversation itself or to conversation of a more agreeable
kind, or better, lastly, with regard to himself. I
will end this particular with two reflections of the
Wise Man, one of which in the strongest manner
exposes the ridiculous part of this licentiousness of
the tongue, and the other the great danger and
viciousness of it. *When he that is a fool walketh
by the way side, his wisdom faileth him, and he
saith to every one that he is a fool.*[3] The other is,
In the multitude of words there wanteth not sin.[4]

[17] As to the government of the tongue in
respect to talking upon indifferent subjects, after what
has been said concerning the due government of it
in respect to the occasions and times for silence,
there is little more necessary than only to caution
men to be fully satisfied that the subjects are indeed
of an indifferent nature, and not to spend too much
time in conversation of this kind. But persons must
be sure to take heed that the subject of their discourse be at least of an indifferent nature, that it
be no way offensive to virtue, religion, or good
manners, that it be not of a licentious dissolute
sort (this leaving always ill impressions upon the
mind), that it be no way injurious or vexatious to

[3] Eccles. x. 3.   [4] Prov. x. 19.

others, and that too much time be not spent this
way, to the neglect·of those duties and offices of
life which belong to their station and condition in
the world.   However, though there is not any
necessity that men should aim at being important
and weighty in every sentence they speak, yet
since useful subjects, at least of some kinds, are as
entertaining as others, a wise man, even when he
desires to unbend his mind from business, would
choose that the conversation might turn upon somewhat instructive.

[18] The last thing is the government•of the
tongue as relating to discourse of the affairs of
others and giving of characters.   These are in a
manner the same, and one can scarce call it an indifferent subject, because discourse upon it almost
perpetually runs into somewhat criminal.

And first of all, it were very much to be wished
that this did not take up so great a part of conversation, because it is indeed a subject of a dangerous
nature.   Let any one consider the various interests,
competitions, and little misunderstandings which
arise amongst men, and he will soon see that he is
not unprejudiced and impartial, that he is not, as I
may speak, neutral enough, to trust himself with
talking of the character and concerns of his neighbour in a free, careless, and unreserved manner.
There is perpetually, and often it is not attended to,
a rivalship amongst people of one kind or another,
in respect to wit, beauty, learning, fortune, and
that one thing will insensibly influence them to
speak to the disadvantage of others, even where
there is no formal malice or ill design.   Since
therefore, it is so hard to enter into this subject
without offending, the first thing to be observed is,
that people should learn to decline it, to get over

that strong inclination most have to be talking of the concerns and behaviour of their neighbour.

[19] But since it is impossible that this subject should be wholly excluded conversation, and since it is necessary that the characters of men should be known, the next thing is, that it is a matter of importance what is said; and therefore that we should be religiously scrupulous and exact to say nothing, either good *or* bad, but what is true. I put it thus, because it is in reality of as great importance to the good of society that the characters of bad men should be known, as that the characters of good men should. People who are given to scandal and detraction may indeed make an ill use of this observation, but truths which are of service towards regulating our conduct are not to be disowned, or even concealed, because a bad use may be made of them. This, however, would be effectually prevented, if these two things were attended to. [20] First, That though it is equally of bad consequence to society that men should have either good or ill characters which they do not deserve, yet, when you say somewhat good of a man which he does not deserve, there is no wrong done him in particular, whereas, when you say evil of a man, which he does not deserve, here is a direct formal injury, a real piece of injustice done him. This therefore makes a wide difference, and gives us, in point of virtue, much greater latitude in speaking well than ill of others. [21] Secondly, a good man is friendly to his fellow-creatures and a lover of mankind, and so will upon every occasion, and often without any, say all the good he can of everybody; but so far as he is a good man, will never be disposed to speak evil of any, unless there be some other reason for it besides barely that it is true. If he be charged with having

E

given an ill character, he will scarce think it a sufficient justification of himself to say it was a true one,
unless he can also give some further account how
he came to do so, a just indignation against particular instances of villany, where they are great and
scandalous, or to prevent an innocent man from
being deceived and betrayed when he has great
trust and confidence in one who does not deserve
it. Justice must be done to every part of a subject
when we are considering it. If there be a man who
bears a fair character in the world, whom yet we
know to be without faith or honesty, to be really
an ill man; it must be allowed in general, that we
shall do a piece of service to society by letting
such a one's true character be known. This is no
more than what we have an instance of in our
Saviour himself, though he was mild and gentle
beyond example.[5] However, no words can express
too strongly the caution which should be used in
such a case as this.

[22] Upon the whole matter, if people would
observe the obvious occasions of silence, if they
would subdue the inclinations to tale-bearing, and
that eager desire to engage attention, which is an
original disease in some minds, they would be in
little danger of offending with their tongue, and
would in a moral and religious sense have due
government over it.

I will conclude with some precepts and reflections
of the son of Sirach upon this subject. *Be swift to
hear ; and if thou hast understanding, answer thy
neighbour ; if not, lay thy hand upon thy mouth.
Honour and shame is in talk. A man of an ill
tongue is dangerous in his city, and he that is rash
in his talk shall be hated. A wise man will hold*

[5] Mark, xii. 38, 40.

*his tongue till he see opportunity ; but a babbler
and a fool will regard no time. He that useth
many words shall be abhorred ; and he that taketh
to himself authority therein shall be hated. A back-
biting tongue hath disquieted many ; strong cities
hath it pulled down, and overthrown the houses of
great men. The tongue of a man is his fall ; but
if thou love to hear, thou shalt receive understanding.*

SERMON V.

UPON COMPASSION.

" Rejoice with them that do rejoice, and weep with them that weep."—Rom. xii. 15.

VERY man is to be considered in two capacities, the private and public; as designed to pursue his own interest, and likewise to contribute to the good of others. Whoever will consider may see that in general there is no contrariety between these, but that, from the original constitution of man and the circumstances he is placed in, they perfectly coincide and mutually carry on each other. But, amongst the great variety of affections or principles of action in our nature, some in their primary intention and design seem to belong to the single or private, others to the public or social capacity. The affections required in the text are of the latter sort. When we rejoice in the prosperity of others and compassionate their distresses, we, as it were, substitute them for ourselves, their interest for our own, and have the same kind of pleasure in their prosperity, and sorrow in their distress, as we have from reflection upon our own. Now there is nothing strange or unaccountable in our

being thus carried out, and affected towards the
interests of others. For, if there be any appetite,
or any inward principle besides self-love, why may
there not be an affection to the good of our fellow-
creatures, and delight from that affection's being
gratified, and uneasiness from things going contrary to it?[1]

[1] There being manifestly this appearance of men's substituting others for themselves and being carried out and affected
towards them as towards themselves, some persons who have a
system which excludes every affection of this sort have taken
a pleasant method to solve it, and tell you it is *not another* you
are at all concerned about, but your *self only*, when you feel
the affection called compassion, *i. e.* Here is a plain matter of
fact, which men cannot reconcile with the general account
they think fit to give of things ; they, therefore, instead of *that*
manifest fact, substitute *another*, which is reconcileable to their
own scheme. For does not everybody by compassion mean an
affection the object of which is another in distress ? Instead
of this, but designing to have it mistaken for this, they speak
of an affection or passion, the object of which is ourselves, or
danger to ourselves. Hobbes defines *pity*, " *imagination, or fiction of future calamity to ourselves, proceeding from the sense* [he
means sight or knowledge] *of another man's calamity.*" (*b*) Thus
fear and compassion would be the same idea, and a fearful and
a compassionate man the same character, which every man
immediately sees are totally different. Further, to those who
give any scope to their affections, there is no perception or inward feeling more universal than this : that one who has been
merciful and compassionate throughout the course of his behaviour, should himself be treated with kindness, if he happen to
fall into circumstances of distress. Is fear, then, or cowardice,
so great a recommendation to the favour of the bulk of mankind ? Or is it not plain, that mere fearlessness (and therefore
not the contrary) is one of the most popular qualifications ?
This shows that mankind are not affected towards compassion
as fear, but as somewhat totally different.

(*c*) Nothing would more expose such accounts as these of
the affections which are favourable and friendly to our fellow-
creatures, than to substitute the definitions which this author
and others who follow his steps, give of such affections, instead
of the words by which they are commonly expressed. Hobbes,

[2] Of these two, delight in the prosperity of others, and compassion for their distresses, the last

after having laid down that pity or compassion is only fear for ourselves, goes on to explain the reason " why we pity our friends in distress more than others." Now substitute the *definition* instead of the word *pity* in this place, and the inquiry will be, why we *fear* our friends, &c., which words (since he really does not mean why we are afraid of them) make no question or sentence at all. So that common language, the words *to compassionate, to pity*, cannot be accommodated to his account of compassion. The very joining of the words to *pity our friends*, is a direct contradiction to his definition of pity, because those words, so joined, necessarily express that our friends are the objects of the passion, whereas his definition of it asserts that ourselves (or danger to ourselves) are the only objects of it. (*d*) He might indeed have avoided this absurdity, by plainly saying what he is going to account for, namely, " why the sight of the innocent, or of our friends in distress, raises greater fear for ourselves than the sight of other persons in distress." But had he put the thing thus plainly, the fact itself would have been doubted ; that the sight of our friends in distress raises in us greater fear for ourselves, than the sight of others in distress. And in the next place it would immediately have occurred to every one, that the fact now mentioned, which at least is doubtful, whether true or false, was not the same with this fact, which nobody ever doubted, that the sight of our friends in distress raises in us greater compassion than the sight of others in distress : every one, I say, would have seen that these are not the *same*, but *two different* inquiries, and consequently, that fear and compassion are not the same. (*e*) Suppose a person to be in real danger, and by some means or other to have forgot it, any trifling accident, any sound, might alarm him, recall the danger to his remembrance, and renew his fear ; but it is almost too grossly ridiculous (though it is to show an absurdity) to speak of that sound or accident as an object of compassion ; and yet, according to Mr. Hobbes, our greatest friend in distress is no more to us, no more the object of compassion, or of any affection in our heart ; neither the one nor the other raises any emotion in our mind, but only the thought of our liableness to calamity, and the fear of it ; and both equally do this. It is fit such sort of accounts of human nature should be shown to be what they really are, because there is raised upon them a general scheme which undermines

is felt much more generally than the former. Though
men do not universally rejoice with all whom they

the whole foundation of common justice and honesty. *See*
Hobbes " *On Human Nature*," chap. ix. § 10.[a]

(*f*) There are often three distinct perceptions or inward
feelings upon sight of persons in distress : real sorrow and concern for the misery of our fellow-creatures ; some degree of
satisfaction from a consciousness of our freedom from that
misery ; and as the mind passes on from one thing to another,
it is not unnatural from such an occasion to reflect upon our liableness to the same or other calamities. The two last frequently
accompany the first, but it is the first *only* which is properly
compassion, of which the distressed are objects, and which
directly carries us with calmness and thought to their assistance.
Any one of these, from various and complicated reasons, may
in particular cases prevail over the other two ; and there are,
I suppose, instances, where the bare *sight* of distress, without
our feeling any compassion for it, may be the occasion of either
or both of the two latter perceptions. (*g*) One might add, that
if there be really any such thing as the fiction or imagination of
danger to ourselves from the sight of the misery of others,
which Hobbes speaks of, and which he has absurdly mistaken
for the whole of compassion ; if there be anything of this sort
common to mankind, distinct from the reflection of reason, it
would be a most remarkable instance of what was furthest from
his thoughts, namely, of a mutual *sympathy* between each particular of the species, a fellow-*feeling* common to mankind.
It would not indeed be an example of our substituting others
for ourselves, but it would be an example of substituting ourselves for others.   And as it would not be an instance of benevolence, so neither would it be an instance of self-love : for this

* " Pity is imagination or fiction of future calamity to ourselves, proceeding from the sense of another man's calamity.
But when it lighteth on such as we think have not deserved
the same, the compassion is greater, because then there appear-
eth more probability that the same may happen to us ; for the
evil that happeneth to an innocent man may happen to every
man.   But when we see a man suffer for great crimes, which
we cannot easily think will fall upon ourselves, the pity is the
less.   And therefore men are apt to pity those whom they love ;
for, whom they love they think worthy of good, and therefore
not worthy of calamity."

see rejoice, yet, accidental obstacles removed, they
naturally compassionate all, in some degree, whom
they see in distress, so far as they have any real perception or sense of that distress; insomuch that words
expressing this latter, pity, compassion, frequently
occur, whereas we have scarce any single one, by
which the former is distinctly expressed. Congratulation indeed answers condolence, but both these
words are intended to signify certain forms of civility rather than any inward sensation or feeling.
This difference or inequality is so remarkable that
we plainly consider compassion as itself an original,
distinct, particular affection in human nature, whereas to rejoice in the good of others is only a consequence of the general affection of love and good-
will to them. [3] The reason and account of which
matter is this: when a man has obtained any particular advantage or felicity, his end is gained, and
he does not in that particular want the assistance of
another; there was, therefore, no need of a distinct
affection towards that felicity of another already obtained, neither would such affection directly carry
him on to do good to that person; whereas men in
distress want assistance, and compassion leads us
directly to assist them. The object of the former
is the present felicity of another, the object of the
latter is the present misery of another. It is easy
to see that the latter wants a particular affection for
its relief, and that the former does not want one,
because it does not want assistance. And upon supposition of a distinct affection in both cases, the one
must rest in the exercise of itself, having nothing
further to gain; the other does not rest in itself, but
carries us on to assist the distressed.

phantom of danger to ourselves, naturally rising to view upon
sight of the distresses of others, would be no more an instance
of love to ourselves, than the pain of hunger is.

[4] But, supposing these affections natural to the mind, particularly the last,—" Has not each man troubles enough of his own? must he indulge an affection which appropriates to himself those of others? which leads him to contract the least desirable of all friendships, friendships with the unfortunate? Must we invert the known rule of prudence, and choose to associate ourselves with the distressed? Or, allowing that we ought, so far as it is in our power to relieve them, yet is it not better to do this from reason and duty? Do not passion and affection of every kind perpetually mislead us? Nay, are not passion and affection themselves a weakness, and what a perfect being must be entirely free from?" [5] Perhaps so, but it is mankind I am speaking of, imperfect creatures, and who naturally and from the condition we are placed in, necessarily depend upon each other. With respect to such creatures it would be found of as bad consequence to eradicate all natural affections as to be entirely governed by them. This would almost sink us to the condition of brutes, and that would leave us without a sufficient principle of action. Reason alone, whatever any one may wish, is not in reality a sufficient motive of virtue in such a creature as man; but this reason joined with those affections which God has impressed upon his heart: and, when these are allowed scope to exercise themselves, but under strict government and direction of reason, then it is we act suitably to our nature, and to the circumstances God has placed us in. [6] Neither is affection itself at all a weakness, nor does it argue defect, any otherwise than as our senses and appetites do; they belong to our condition of nature, and are what we cannot do without. God Almighty is, to be sure, unmoved by passion or

appetite, unchanged by affection; but then it is to
be added, that he neither sees, nor hears, nor per-
ceives things by any senses like ours, but in a manner infinitely more perfect.   Now as it is an absurdity almost too gross to be mentioned, for a man
to endeavour to get rid of his senses, because the
Supreme Being discerns things more perfectly without them; it is a real, though not so obvious an
absurdity, to endeavour to eradicate the passions
he has given us, because he is without them.   [7]
For, since our passions are as really a part of our
constitution as our senses, since the former as really
belong to our condition of nature as the latter, to
get rid of either is equally a violation of, and breaking in upon, that nature and constitution he has
given us.   Both our senses and our passions are a
supply to the imperfection of our nature; thus they
show that we are such sort of creatures, as to stand
in need of those helps which higher orders of creatures do not.   But it is not the supply, but the
deficiency, as it is not a remedy, but a disease,
which is the imperfection.   However, our appetites,
passions, senses, no way imply disease; nor indeed
do they imply deficiency or imperfection of any sort,
but only this, that the constitution of nature according to which God has made us is such as to require them.   [8] And it is so far from being true that
a wise man must entirely suppress compassion and
all fellow-feeling for others, as a weakness, and trust
to reason alone to teach and enforce upon him the
practice of the several charities we owe to our kind;
that, on the contrary, even the bare exercise of such
affections would itself be for the good and happiness
of the world, and the imperfection of the higher principles of reason and religion in man, the little influence they have upon our practice, and the strength

and prevalency of contrary ones, plainly require those affections to be a restraint upon these latter, and a supply to the deficiencies of the former.

[9] First. The very exercise itself of these affections in a just and reasonable manner and degree, would upon the whole increase the satisfactions and lessen the miseries of life.

It is the tendency and business of virtue and religion to procure, as much as may be, universal good-will, trust, and friendship amongst mankind. If this could be brought to obtain, and each man enjoyed the happiness of others, as every one does that of a friend, and looked upon the success and prosperity of his neighbour, as every one does upon that of his children and fami y, it is too manifest to be insisted upon how much the enjoyments of life would be increased. There would be so much happiness introduced into the world, without any deduction or inconvenience from it, in proportion as the precept of *rejoicing with those who do rejoice* was universally obeyed. Our Saviour has owned this good affection as belonging to our nature, in the parable of The Lost Sheep, and does not think it to the disadvantage of a perfect state to represent its happiness as capable of increase from reflection upon that of others.

[10] But since, in such a creature as man, compassion or sorrow for the distress of others seems so far necessarily connected with joy in their prosperity, as that whoever rejoices in one must unavoidably compassionate the other, there cannot be that delight or satisfaction which appears to be so considerable, without the inconveniences, whatever they are, of compassion.

[11] However, without considering this connection, there is no doubt but that more good than evil,

more delight than sorrow, arises from compassion
itself; there being so many things which balance
the sorrow of it. [12] There is first the relief which
the distressed feel from this affection in others towards them. There is likewise the additional misery
which they would feel from the reflection, that no
one commiserated their case. It is indeed true,
that any disposition, prevailing beyond a certain
degree, becomes somewhat wrong; and we have
ways of speaking, which, though they do not
directly express that excess, yet always lead our
thoughts to it and give us the notion of it. Thus,
when mention is made of delight in being pitied,
this always conveys to our mind the notion of somewhat which is really a weakness; the manner of
speaking, I say, implies a certain weakness and
feebleness of mind, which is and ought to be disapproved. But men of the greatest fortitude would
in distress feel uneasiness from knowing that no
person in the world had any sort of compassion or
real concern for them, and in some cases, especially when the temper is enfeebled by sickness or
any long and great distress, doubtless would feel a
kind of relief even from the helpless good-will and
ineffectual assistances of those about them. [13]
Over against the sorrow of compassion is likewise
to be set a peculiar calm kind of satisfaction which
accompanies it, unless in cases where the distress
of another is by some means so brought home to
ourselves as to become in a manner our own, or
when from weakness of mind the affection rises
too high, which ought to be corrected. This tranquillity or calm satisfaction proceeds partly from
consciousness of a right affection and temper of
mind, and partly from a sense of our own freedom
from the misery we compassionate. This last may

possibly appear to some at first sight faulty, but it
really is not so.   It is the same with that positive
enjoyment which sudden ease from pain for the
present affords, arising from a real sense of misery,
joined with a sense of our freedom from it; which
in all cases must afford some degree of satisfaction.

[14] To these things must be added the observation which respects both the affections we are considering; that they who have got over all fellow-
feeling for others have withal contracted a certain
callousness of heart, which renders them insensible
to most other satisfactions but those of the grossest
kind.

[15] Secondly. Without the exercise of these
affections, men would certainly be much more wanting in the offices of charity they owe to each other,
and likewise more cruel and injurious, than they are
at present.

[16] The private interest of the individual would
not be sufficiently provided for by reasonable and
cool self-love alone, therefore the appetites and
passions are placed within as a guard and further
security, without which it would not be taken due
care of. It is manifest our life would be neglected,
were it not for the calls of hunger and thirst and
weariness, notwithstanding that without them reason
would assure us, that the recruits of food and sleep
are the necessary means of our preservation.   It is
therefore absurd to imagine that, without affection,
the same reason alone would be more effectual to
engage us to perform the duties we, owe to our
fellow-creatures.   One of this make would be as
defective, as much wanting, considered with respect
to society, as one of the former make would be defective or wanting, considered as an individual, or
in his private capacity.   Is it possible any can in

earnest think, that a public spirit, *i. e.* a settled reasonable principle of benevolence to mankind, is so
prevalent and strong in the species, as that we may
venture to throw off the under affections, which are
its assistants, carry it forward, and mark out particular courses for it—family, friends, neighbourhood,
the distressed, our country? The common joys and
the common sorrows, which belong to these relations and circumstances, are as plainly useful to
society as the pain and pleasure belonging to hunger,
thirst, and weariness, are of service to the individual.
In defect of that higher principle of reason, compassion is often the only way by which the indigent can
have access to us; and, therefore, to eradicate this,
though it is not indeed formally to deny them that
assistance which is their due, yet it is to cut them
off from that which is too frequently their only way
of obtaining it. And as for those who have shut up
this door against the complaints of the miserable, and
conquered this affection in themselves, even these
persons will be under great restraints from the same
affection in others. Thus a man who has himself
no sense of injustice, cruelty, oppression, will be
kept from running the utmost lengths of wickedness
by fear of that detestation and even resentment of
inhumanity, in many particular instances of it, which
compassion for the object towards which such inhumanity is exercised excites in the bulk of mankind. And this is frequently the chief danger and
the chief restraint which tyrants and the great op-
pressors of the world feel.

[17] In general, experience will show that, as
want of natural appetite to food supposes and proceeds from some bodily disease, so the apathy the
Stoics talk of, as much supposes, or is accompanied with, somewhat amiss in the moral character,
in that which is the health of the mind. Those who

formerly aimed at this upon the foot of philosophy appear to have had better success in eradicating the affections of tenderness and compassion than they had with the passions of envy, pride, and resentment: these latter, at best, were but concealed, and that imperfectly too. How far this observation may be extended to such as endeavour to suppress the natural impulses of their affections, in order to form themselves for business and the world, I shall not determine. But there does not appear any capacity or relation to be named, in which men ought to be entirely deaf to the calls of affection, unless the judicial one is to be excepted.

[18] And as to those who are commonly called the men of pleasure, it is manifest that the reason they set up for hardness of heart is, to avoid being interrupted in their course by the ruin and misery they are the authors of; neither are persons of this character always the most free from the impotencies of envy and resentment. What may not men at last bring themselves to, by suppressing their passions and affections of one kind, and leaving those of the other in their full strength? But surely it might be expected that persons who make pleasure their study and their business, if they understood what they profess, would reflect, how many of the entertainments of life, how many of those kind of amusements which seem peculiarly to belong to men of leisure and education, they become insensible to by this acquired hardness of heart.

[19] I shall close these reflections with barely mentioning the behaviour of that Divine Person, who was the example of all perfection in human nature, as represented in the Gospels mourning, and even, in a literal sense, weeping over the distresses of his creatures.

[20] The observation already made,—that, of the two affections mentioned in the text, the latter exerts itself much more than the former, that, from the original constitution of human nature, we much more generally and sensibly compassionate the distressed, than rejoice with the prosperous, requires to be particularly considered. This observation, therefore, with the reflections which arise out of it, and which it leads our thoughts to, shall be the subject of another discourse.

[21] For the conclusion of this, let me just take notice of the danger of over-great refinements, of going beside or beyond the plain, obvious, first appearances of things, upon the subject of morals and religion. The least observation will show how little the generality of men are capable of speculations. Therefore morality and religion must be somewhat plain and easy to be understood; they must appeal to what we call plain common sense, as distinguished from superior capacity and improvement, because they appeal to mankind. [22] Persons of superior capacity and improvement have often fallen into errors, which no one of mere common understanding could. Is it possible that one of this latter character could ever himself have thought, that there was absolutely no such thing in mankind as affection to the good of others; suppose of parents to their children? Or that what he felt upon seeing a friend in distress was only fear for himself? Or, upon supposition of the affections of kindness and compassion, that it was the business of wisdom and virtue to set him about extirpating them as fast as he could? And yet each of these manifest contradictions to nature has been laid down by men of speculation, as a discovery in moral philosophy, which they, it seems, have found out through all the specious appearances

to the contrary. [23] This reflection may be extended further. The extravagances of enthusiasm and superstition do not at all lie in the road of common sense, and therefore, so far as they are *original mistakes*, must be owing to going beside or beyond it. Now, since inquiry and examination can relate only to things so obscure and uncertain as to stand in need of it, and to persons who are capable of it; the proper advice to be given to plain honest men, to secure them from the extremes both of superstition and irreligion, is that of the Son of Sirach—*In every good work trust thy own soul; for this is the keeping of the commandment.*[1]

[1] Ecclus. xxxii. 23.

F

SERMON VI.

" Rejoice with them that do rejoice, and weep with
them that weep."—Rom. xii. 15.

THERE is a much more exact correspondence between the natural and
moral world than we are apt to take
notice of. The inward frame of man
does in a peculiar manner answer to
the external condition and circumstances of life, in
which he is placed. This is a particular instance of
that general observation of the son of Sirach : *All*
things are double one against another, and God hath
made nothing imperfect.[1] The several passions and
affections in the heart of man, compared with the
circumstances of life in which he is placed, afford,
to such as will attend to them, as certain instances
of final causes as any whatever which are more commonly alleged for such : since those affections lead
him to a certain determinate course of action suitable to those circumstances, as (for instance) compassion, to relieve the distressed. And as all observations of final causes, drawn from the principles of
action in the heart of man, compared with the condition he is placed in, serve all the good uses which
instances of final causes in the material world about
us do, and both these are equally proofs of wisdom
and design in the Author of Nature ; so the former

[1] Ecclus. xlii. 24.

serve to further good purposes, they show us what course of life we are made for, what is our duty, and in a peculiar manner enforce upon us the practice of it.

[25] Suppose we are capable of happiness and of misery in degrees equally intense and extreme, yet we are capable of the latter for a much longer time, beyond all comparison. We see men in the tortures of pain for hours, days, and, excepting the short suspensions of sleep, for months together, without intermission; to which no enjoyments of life do, in degree and continuance, bear any sort of proportion. And such is our make and that of the world about us, that anything may become the instrument of pain and sorrow to us. Thus almost any one man is capable of doing mischief to any other, though he may not be capable of doing him good; and if he be capable of doing him some good, he is capable of doing him more evil. And it is in numberless cases much more in our power to lessen the miseries of others than to promote their positive happiness, any otherwise than as the former often includes the latter, ease from misery occasioning for some time the greatest positive enjoyment. [26] This constitution of nature, namely, that it is so much more in our power to occasion and likewise to lessen misery than to promote positive happiness, plainly required a particular affection, to hinder us from abusing, and to incline us to make a right use of the former powers, *i. e.* the powers both to occasion and to lessen misery, over and above what was necessary to induce us to make a right use of the latter power, that of promoting positive happiness. The power we have over the misery of our fellow-creatures, to occasion or lessen it, being a more important trust than the power we have of promoting their positive

happiness, the former requires and has a further,
'an additional security and guard against its being
violated, beyond and over and above what the latter
has. The social nature of man and general good-
will to his species equally prevent him from doing
evil, incline him to relieve the distressed, and to
promote the positive happiness of his fellow-creatures: but compassion only restrains him from the
first, and carries him to the second, it hath nothing
to do with the third.

[27] The final causes, then, of compassion are to
prevent and to relieve misery.

As to the former—this affection may plainly be a
restraint upon resentment, envy, unreasonable self-
love, that is, upon all the principles from which men
do evil to one another. Let us instance only in resentment. It seldom happens, in regulated societies,
that men have an enemy so entirely in their power,
as to be able to satiate their resentment with safety.
But if we were to put this case, it is plainly supposable that a person might bring his enemy into
such a condition as, from being the object of anger
and rage, to become an object of compassion even
to himself, though the most malicious man in the
world; and in this case compassion would stop him,
if he could stop with safety, from pursuing his revenge any further. But since nature has placed
within us more powerful restraints to prevent mischief, and since the final cause of compassion is
much more to relieve misery, let us go on to the
consideration of it in this view.

[28] As this world was not intended to be a state
of any great satisfaction or high enjoyment, so neither was it intended to be a mere scene of unhappiness and sorrow. Mitigations and reliefs are provided by the merciful Author of Nature for most of

the afflictions in human life. There is kind provision
made even against our frailties,. as we are so constituted that *time* abundantly abates our sorrows and
begets in us that resignment of temper which ought
to have been produced by a better cause, a due
sense of the authority of God and our state of dependence. This holds in respect to far the greatest
part of the evils of life, I suppose, in some degree
as to pain and sickness. Now this part of the constitution or make of man, considered as some relief
to misery and not as provision for positive happiness,
is, if I may so speak, an instance of nature's compassion for us, and every natural remedy or relief to
misery may be considered in the same view.

[29] But since in many cases it is very much in our
power to alleviate the miseries of each other, and
benevolence, though natural in man to man, yet is in
a very low degree kept down by interest and competitions, and men for the most part are so engaged
in the business and pleasures of the world as to overlook and turn away from objects of misery, which
are plainly considered as interruptions to them in
their way, as intruders upon their business, their
gaiety and mirth—compassion is an advocate within
us in their behalf, to gain the unhappy admittance
and access, to make their case attended to. If it
sometimes serve a contrary purpose and make men
industriously turn away from the miserable, these
are only instances of abuse and perversion; for
the end for which the affection was given us most
certainly is not to make us avoid, but to make us
attend to, the objects of it. And if men would
only resolve to allow thus much to it—let it bring
before their view, the view of their mind, the miseries
of their fellow-creatures—let it gain for them that
their case be considered—I am persuaded it would

not fail of gaining more, and that very few real objects of charity would pass unrelieved. Pain and sorrow and misery have a right to our assistance; compassion puts us in mind of the debt, and that we owe it to ourselves as well as to the distressed. For to endeavour to get rid of the sorrow of compassion by turning from the wretched, when yet it is in our power to relieve them, is as unnatural as to endeavour to get rid of the pain of hunger, by keeping from the sight of food. That we can do one with greater success than we can the other, is no proof that one is less a violation of nature than the other. Compassion is a call, a demand of nature, to relieve the unhappy, as hunger is a natural call for food. This affection plainly gives the objects of it an additional claim to relief and mercy, over and above what our fellow-creatures in common have to our good-will. [30] Liberality and bounty are exceedingly commendable and a particular distinction in such a world as this, where men set themselves to contract their heart, and close it to all interest but their own. It is by no means to be opposed to mercy, but always accompanies it; the distinction between them is only, that the former leads our thoughts to a more promiscuous and undistinguished distribution of favours—to those who are not, as well as those who are necessitous—whereas the object of compassion is misery. But in the comparison and where there is not a possibility of both, mercy is to have the preference; the affection of compassion manifestly leads us to this preference. Thus, to relieve the indigent and distressed, to single out the unhappy from whom can be expected no returns either of present entertainment or future service, for the objects of our favours—to esteem a man's being friendless as a recommendation—dejection,

and incapacity of struggling through the world, as
a motive for assisting him—in a word, to consider
these circumstances of disadvantage which are
usually thought a sufficient reason for neglect and
overlooking a person, as a motive for helping him
forward: this is the course of benevolence which
compassion marks out and directs us to; this is
that humanity, which is so peculiarly becoming our
nature and circumstances in this world.

[31] To these considerations, drawn from the
nature of man, must be added the reason of the
thing itself we are recommending, which accords to
and shows the same. For since it is so much more
in our power to lessen the misery of our fellow-
creatures than to promote their positive happiness,
in cases where there is an inconsistency, we shall
be likely to do much more good by setting ourselves
to mitigate the former than by endeavouring to
promote the latter. Let the competition be between
the poor and the rich. It is easy, you will say, to
see which will have the preference. True: but the
question is, which ought to have the preference?
What proportion is there between the happiness
produced by doing a favour to the indigent, and that
produced by doing the same favour to one in easy
circumstances? It is manifest that the addition of
a very large estate to one who before had an affluence, will in many instances yield him less new
enjoyment or satisfaction, than an ordinary charity
would yield to a necessitous person. So that it is
not only true, that our nature, *i. e.* the voice of God
within us, carries us to the exercise of charity and
benevolence in the way of compassion or mercy,
preferably to any other way; but we also manifestly
discern much more good done by the former: or, if
you will allow me the expressions, more misery anni-

hilated, and happiness created. If charity and benevolence and endeavouring to do good to our fellow-
creatures be anything, this observation deserves to
be most seriously considered by all who have to
bestow. And it holds with great exactness when
applied to the several degrees of greater and less
indigency throughout the various ranks in human
life, the happiness or good produced not being in
proportion to what is bestowed, but in proportion to
this joined with the need there was of it.

[32] It may perhaps be expected that, upon this
subject, notice should be taken of occasions, circumstances, and characters, which seem at once to call
forth affections of different sorts. Thus vice may
be thought the subject both of pity and indignation ;
folly, of pity and of laughter. How far this is strictly
true, I shall not inquire ; but only observe upon the
appearance, how much more humane it is to yield
and give scope to affections which are most directly
in favour of, and friendly towards, our fellow-creatures ; and that there is plainly much less danger of
being led wrong by these, than by the other.

[33] But notwithstanding all that has been said
in recommendation of compassion, that it is most
amiable, most becoming human nature, and most
useful to the world ; yet it must be owned, that
every affection, as distinct from a principle of reason,
may rise too high and be beyond its just proportion.
And by means of this one carried too far, a man
throughout his life is subject to much more uneasiness
than belongs to his share, and, in particular instances,
it may be in such a degree as to incapacitate him
from assisting the very person who is the object of
it. But as there are some who upon principle set up
for suppressing this affection itself as a weakness,
there is also I know not what of fashion on this side,

and by some means or other the whole world almost
is run into the extremes of insensibility towards the
distresses of their fellow-creatures; so that general
rules and exhortations must always be on the other
side.

[34] And now to go on to the uses we should
make of the foregoing reflections, the further ones
they lead to, and the general temper they have a
tendency to beget in us. There being that distinct
affection implanted in the nature of man tending to
lessen the miseries of life, that particular provision
made for abating its sorrows more than for increasing
its positive happiness, as before explained; this may
suggest to us what should be our general aim respecting ourselves in our passage through this world,
namely, to endeavour chiefly to escape misery, keep
free from uneasiness, pain, and sorrow, or to get
relief and mitigation of them; to propose to ourselves peace and tranquillity of mind, rather than
pursue after high enjoyments. This is what the constitution of nature before explained marks out as the
course we should follow, and the end we should aim at.
To make pleasure and mirth and jollity our business,
and be constantly hurrying about after some gay
amusement, some new gratification of sense or appetite, to those who will consider the nature of man and
our condition in this world, will appear the most romantic scheme of life that ever entered into thought.
And yet how many are there who go on in this
course, without learning better from the daily, the
hourly disappointments, listlessness, and satiety,
which accompany this fashionable method of wast-
ing away their days!

[35] The subject we have been insisting upon
would lead us into the same kind of reflections, by a
different connection. The miseries of life brought

home to ourselves by compassion, viewed through this affection considered as the sense by which they are perceived, would beget in us that moderation, humility, and soberness of mind, which has been now recommended, and which particularly belongs to a season of recollection, the only purpose of which is to bring us to a just sense of things, to recover us out of that forgetfulness of ourselves and our true state, which it is manifest far the greatest part of men pass their whole life in. [36] Upon this account Solomon says, that *it is better to go to the house of mourning, than to go to the house of feasting; i. e.* it is more to a man's advantage to turn his eyes towards objects of distress, to recall sometimes to his remembrance the occasions of sorrow, than to pass all his days in thoughtless mirth and gaiety. And he represents the wise as choosing to frequent the former of these places, to be sure not for its own sake, but because *by the sadness of the countenance the heart is made better.* Every one observes how temperate and reasonable men are when humbled and brought low by afflictions, in comparison of what they are in high prosperity. By this voluntary resort to the house of mourning, which is here recommended, we might learn all those useful instructions which calamities teach, without undergoing them ourselves, and grow wiser and better at a more easy rate than men commonly do. The objects themselves, which in that place of sorrow lie before our view, naturally give us a seriousness and attention, check that wantonness which is the growth of prosperity and ease, and lead us to reflect upon the deficiencies of human life, itself —that *every man, at his best estate, is altogether vanity.* This would correct the florid and gaudy prospects and expectations which we are too apt to indulge, teach us to lower our notions of happiness and enjoyment, bring them down to the reality of things, to what is attainable, to what the frailty of our condition will admit of, which for any continuance, is only tranquillity, ease, and moderate satisfactions. Thus we might at once become proof against the temptations with which the whole world almost is carried away, since it is plain, that not only what is called a life of pleasure, but also vicious pursuits in general, aim at somewhat besides and beyond these moderate satisfactions.

[37] And as to that obstinacy and wilfulness which render men so insensible to the motives of religion, this right sense of ourselves and of the world about us would bend the stubborn mind, soften the heart, and make it more apt to receive impression; and this is the proper temper in which to call our ways to remembrance, to review and set home upon ourselves the miscarriages of our past life. In such a compliant state of mind, reason and conscience will have a fair hearing, which is the preparation for, or rather the beginning of, that repentance, the outward show of which we all put on at this season.

[38] Lastly, The various miseries of life which lie before us wherever we turn our eyes, the frailty of this mortal state we are passing through, may put us in mind that the present world is not our home, that we are merely strangers and travellers in it, as all our fathers were. It is therefore to be considered as a foreign country, in which our poverty and wants and the insufficient supplies of them, were designed to turn our views to that higher and better state we are heirs to, a state where will be no follies to be overlooked, no miseries to be pitied, no wants to be relieved, where the affection we have

been now treating of will happily be lost, as there
will be no objects to exercise it upon, for *God shall
wipe away all tears from their eyes, and there shall
be no more death, neither sorrow nor crying, neither
shall there be any more pain, for the former things
are passed away.*

SERMON VII.

*" Let me die the death of the righteous, and let my
last end be like his."*—NUMB. xxiii. 10.

THESE words taken alone and without
respect to him who spoke them, lead
our thoughts immediately to the different ends of good and bad men.
For though the comparison is not ex-
pressed, yet it is manifestly implied, as is also the
preference of one of these characters to the other
in that last circumstance, death. And, since dying
the death of the righteous or of the wicked necessarily implies men's being righteous or wicked, *i. e.*
having lived righteously or wickedly, a comparison
of them in their lives also might come into consideration, from such a single view of the words themselves. But my present design is to consider them
with a particular reference or respect to him who
spoke them; which reference, if you please to attend, you will see. And if what shall be offered to
your consideration at this time be thought a discourse
upon the whole history of this man, rather than upon
the particular words I have read, this is of no con-

sequence; it is sufficient, if it afford reflections of use and service to ourselves.

[2] But, in order to avoid cavils respecting this remarkable relation in Scripture, either that part of it which you have heard in the first lesson for the day, or any others; let me just observe, that as this is not a place for answering them, so they no way affect the following discourse, since the character there given is plainly a real one in life and such as there are parallels to.

[3] The occasion of Balaam's coming out of his own country into the land of Moab, where he pronounced this solemn prayer or wish, he himself relates in the first parable or prophetic speech, of which it is the conclusion. In which is a custom referred to, proper to be taken notice of: that of devoting enemies to destruction, before the entrance upon a war with them. This custom appears to have prevailed over a great part of the world, for we find it amongst the most distant nations. The Romans had public officers, to whom it belonged as a stated part of their office. But there was somewhat more particular in the case now before us, Balaam being looked upon as an extraordinary person whose blessing or curse was thought to be always effectual.

[4] In order to engage the reader's attention to this passage, the sacred historian has enumerated the preparatory circumstances, which are these. Balaam requires the king of Moab to build him seven altars, and to prepare him the same number of oxen and of rams. The sacrifice being over, he retires alone to a solitude sacred to these occasions, there to wait the divine inspiration or answer for which the foregoing rites were the preparation. *And*

God met Balaam, and put a word in his mouth,[1]
upon receiving which he returns back to the altars,
where was the king, who had all this while attended
the sacrifice, as appointed; he and all the princes
of Moab standing, big with expectation of the prophet's reply. [2]*And he took up his parable, and said,
Balak the king of Moab hath brought me from
Aram, out of the mountains of the east, saying, Come,
curse me Jacob, and come, defy Israel. How shall
I curse, whom God hath not cursed? Or how shall
I defy, whom the Lord hath not defied? For from
the top of the rocks I see him, and from the hills I
behold him: lo, the people shall dwell alone, and
shall not be reckoned among the nations. Who can
count the dust of Jacob, and the number of the fourth
part of Israel? Let me die the death of the righteous, and let my last end be like his.*

[5] It is necessary, as you will see in the progress of this discourse, particularly to observe what
he understood by *righteous.* And he himself is introduced in the book of Micah[3] explaining it; if by
righteous, is meant *good,* as to be sure it is. *O my
people, remember now what Balak king of Moab
consulted, and what Balaam the son of Beor answered
him from Shittim unto Gilgal.* From the mention
of Shittim, it is manifest, that it is this very story
which is here referred to, though another part of it,
the account of which is not now extant; as there
are many quotations in Scripture out of books which
are not come down to us. *Remember what Balaam
answered, that ye may know the righteousness of
the Lord;* i.e. the righteousness which God will
accept. Balak demands, *Wherewith shall I come
before the Lord, and bow myself before the high
God? Shall I come before him with burnt offer-*

[1] v. 4, 5. [2] v. 7-10. [3] Chap. vi.

*ings, with calves of a year old? Will the Lord be
pleased with thousands of rams, or with ten thousands of rivers of oil? Shall I give my first-born
for my transgression, the fruit of my body for the
sin of my soul?* Balaam answers him, *He hath
showed thee, O man, what is good: and what doth
the Lord require of thee, but to do justly, and to love
mercy, and to walk humbly with thy God?* Here
is a good man expressly characterized, as distinct
from a dishonest and a superstitious man. No words
can more strongly exclude dishonesty and falseness
of heart, than *doing justice*, and *loving mercy:* and
both these, as well as *walking humbly with God*, are
put in opposition to those ceremonial methods of
recommendation, which Balak hoped might have
served the turn. From hence appears what he
meant by the *righteous* whose *death* he desires to
die.

[6] Whether it was his own character shall now
be inquired: and in order to determine it, we must
take a view of his whole behaviour upon this occasion. When the elders of Moab came to him, though
he appears to have been much allured with the rewards offered, yet he had such regard to the authority of God, as to keep the messengers in suspense
until he had consulted his will. *And God said to
him, Thou shall not go with them; thou shalt not
curse the people: for they are blessed.*[1] Upon this
he dismisses the ambassadors, with an absolute refusal of accompanying them back to their king.
Thus far his regards to duty prevailed, neither does
there anything appear as yet amiss in his conduct.
[7] His answer being reported to the king of Moab,
a more honourable embassy is immediately dis-
patched, and greater rewards proposed. Then the

[1] Chap. xxii. 12.

iniquity of his heart began to disclose itself. A thorough honest man would without hesitation have repeated his former answer, that he could not be guilty of so infamous a prostitution of the sacred character with which he was invested, as in the name of a prophet to curse those whom he knew to be blessed. But instead of this, which was the only honest part in these circumstances that lay before him, he desires the princes of Moab to tarry that night with him also; and for the sake of the reward deliberates, whether by some means or other he might not be able to obtain leave to curse Israel; to do that which had been before revealed to him to be contrary to the will of God, which yet he resolves not to do without that permission. [8] Upon which as when this nation afterward rejected God from reigning over them, he gave them a king in his anger; in the same way, as appears from other parts of the narration, he gives Balaam the permission he desired; for this is the most natural sense of the words. [9] Arriving in the territories of Moab, and being received with particular distinction by the king, and he repeating in person the promise of the rewards he had before made to him by his ambassadors: he seeks, the text says, by *sacrifices* and *enchantments* (what these were is not to our purpose), to obtain leave of God to curse the people, keeping still his resolution not to do it without that permission; which not being able to obtain, he had such regard to the command of God, as to keep this resolution to the last. The supposition of his being under a supernatural restraint is a mere fiction of Philo: he is plainly represented to be under no other force or restraint, than the fear of God. However, he goes on persevering in that endeavour, after he had declared that *God had not beheld ini-*

G

quity in Jacob, neither had he seen perverseness in Israel,[1] *i. e.* they were a people of virtue and piety, so far as not to have drawn down, by their iniquity, that curse which he was soliciting leave to pronounce upon them. So that the state of Balaam's mind was this: he wanted to do what he knew to be very wicked, and contrary to the express command of God; he had inward checks and restraints, which he could not entirely get over; he therefore casts about for ways to reconcile this wickedness with his duty. How great a paradox soever this may appear, as it is indeed a contradiction in terms, it is the very account which the Scripture gives us of him.

[10] But there is a more surprising piece of iniquity yet behind. Not daring in his religious character, as a prophet, to assist the king of Moab, he considers whether there might not be found some other means of assisting him against that very people, whom he himself by the fear of God was restrained from cursing in words. One would not think it possible, that the weakness, even of religious self-deceit in its utmost excess, could have so poor a distinction, so fond an evasion, to serve itself of. But so it was: and he could think of no other method, than to betray the children of Israel to provoke His wrath, who was their only strength and defence. The temptation which he pitched upon, was that concerning which Solomon afterward observed, that it had *cast down many wounded; yea, many strong men had been slain by it:* and of which he himself was a sad example, when *his wives turned away his heart after other gods.* This succeeded: the people sin against God: and thus the prophet's counsel brought on that destruction, which he could by no

[1] v. 21.

means be prevailed upon to assist with the religious
ceremony of execration, which the king of Moab
thought would itself have effected it.   Their crime
and punishment are related in Deuteronomy,[1] and
Numbers.[2]   And from the relation repeated in
Numbers,[3] it appears, that Balaam was the contriver
of the whole matter.   It is also ascribed to him in
the Revelation,[4] where he is said to have *taught
Balak to cast a stumbling-block before the children
of Israel.*

[11] This was the man, this Balaam, I say, was
the man who desired to *die the death of the righteous,* and that his *last end might be like his :* and
this was the state of his mind, when he pronounced
these words.

So that the object we have now before us is the
most astonishing in the world : a very wicked man,
under a deep sense of God and religion, persisting
still in his wickedness and preferring the wages of
unrighteousness, even when he had before him a
lively view of death and that approaching period of
his days which should deprive him of all those advantages for which he was prostituting himself, and
likewise a prospect, whether certain or uncertain,
of a future state of retribution : all this joined with
an explicit ardent wish, that, when he was to leave
this world, he might be in the condition of a righteous man.   Good God, what inconsistency, what
perplexity is here !   With what different views of
things, with what contradictory principles of action,
must such a mind be torn and distracted !   It was
not unthinking carelessness, by which he ran on
headlong in vice and folly, without ever making a
stand to ask himself what he was doing.   No, he
acted upon the cool motives of interest and advan-

[1] Chap. iv.   [2] Chap. xxv.   [3] Chap. xxxi.   [4] Chap. ii.

tage. Neither was he totally hard and callous to impressions of religion, what we call abandoned; for he absolutely denied to curse Israel. When reason assumes her place, when convinced of his duty, when he owns and feels, and is actually under the influence of the divine authority; whilst he is carrying on his views to the grave, the end of all temporal greatness; under this sense of things, with the better character and more desirable state present— full before him—in his thoughts, in his wishes— voluntarily to choose the worse, what fatality is here! Or how otherwise can such a character be explained? And yet, strange as it may appear, it is not altogether an uncommon one: nay, with some small alterations, and put a little lower, it is applicable to a very considerable part of the world. For if the reasonable choice be seen and acknowledged, and yet men make the unreasonable one, is not this the same contradiction, that very inconsistency which appeared so unaccountable?

[12] To give some little opening to such characters and behaviour, it is to be observed, in general, that there is no account to be given in the way of reason, of men's so strong attachments to the present world: our hopes and fears and pursuits are in degrees beyond all proportion to the known value of the things they respect. This may be said without taking into consideration religion and a future state; and when these are considered, the disproportion is infinitely heightened. [13] Now when men go against their reason, and contradict a more important interest at a distance, for one nearer, though of less consideration; if this be the whole of the case, all that can be said is, that strong passions, some kind of brute force within, prevail over the principle of rationality. However, if this be with a clear, full,

and distinct view of the truth of things, then it is
doing the utmost violence to themselves, acting in
the most palpable contradiction to their very nature.
[14] But if there be any such thing in mankind as
putting half deceits upon themselves; which there
plainly is, either by avoiding reflection, or (if they
do reflect) by religious equivocation, subterfuges,
and palliating matters to themselves; by these
means conscience may be laid asleep, and they may
go on in a course of wickedness with less disturbance. All the various turns, doubles, and intrica-
cies in a dishonest heart, cannot be unfolded or laid
open; but that there is somewhat of that kind is
manifest, be it to be called self-deceit, or by any
other name. [15] Balaam had before his eyes the
authority of God, absolutely forbidding him what he,
for the sake of a reward, had the strongest inclination to: he was likewise in a state of mind sober
enough to consider death and his last end: by these,
considerations he was restrained, first from going to
the king of Moab, and, after he did go, from cursing
Israel. But notwithstanding this, there was great
wickedness in his heart. He could not forego
the rewards of unrighteousness: he therefore first
seeks for indulgences; and when these could not
be obtained, he sins against the whole meaning, end,
and design of the prohibition, which no consideration
in the world could prevail with him to go against
the letter of. And surely that impious counsel he
gave to Balak against the children of Israel was, considered in itself, a greater piece of wickedness than
if he had cursed them in words.

[16] If it be inquired what his situation, his hopes,
and fears were, in respect to this his wish; the
answer must be, that consciousness of the wickedness of his heart must necessarily have destroyed

all settled hopes of dying the death of the righteous:
he could have no calm satisfaction in this view of
his last end: yet, on the other hand, it is possible
that those partial regards to his duty, now mentioned, might keep him from perfect despair.

[17] Upon the whole, it is manifest that Balaam
had the most just and true notions of God and religion; as appears, partly from the original story itself, and more plainly from the passage in Micah,
where he explains religion to consist in real virtue
and real piety, expressly distinguished from superstition, and in terms which most strongly exclude
dishonesty and falseness of heart. Yet you see his
behaviour: he seeks indulgences for plain wickedness, which not being able to obtain, he glosses over
the same wickedness, dresses it up in a new form,
in order to make it pass off more easily with himself. That is, he deliberately contrives to deceive
and impose upon himself, in a matter which he
knew to be of the utmost importance.

[18] To bring these observations home to ourselves: it is too evident, that many persons allow
themselves in very unjustifiable courses, who yet
make great pretences to religion,—not to deceive the
world, none can be so weak as to think this will pass
in our age,—but from principles, hopes, and fears,
respecting God and a future state; and go on thus
with a sort of tranquillity and quiet of mind. This
cannot be upon a thorough consideration and full
resolution that the pleasures and advantages they
propose are to be pursued at all hazards, against
reason, against the law of God, and though everlasting destruction is to be the consequence. This
would be doing too great violence upon themselves.
No, they are for making a composition with the
Almighty. These of his commands they will obey:

but as to others—why they will make all the atonements in their power; the ambitious, the covetous,
the dissolute man, each in a way which shall not
contradict his respective pursuit. Indulgences before, which was Balaam's first attempt, though he
was not so successful in it as to deceive himself, or
atonements afterwards, are all the same. And here
perhaps come in faint hopes that they may, and half-
resolves that they will, one time or other, make a
change.

[19] Besides these, there are also persons who, from
a more just way of considering things, see the infinite
absurdity of this, of substituting sacrifice instead of
obedience; there are persons far enough from superstition, and not without some real sense of God and
religion upon their minds, who yet are guilty of most
unjustifiable practices, and go on with great coolness
and command over themselves. The same dishonesty and unsoundness of heart discover themselves in these another way. [20] In all common
ordinary cases we see intuitively at first view what
is our duty, what is the honest part. This is the
ground of the observation, that the first thought is
often the best. In these cases doubt and deliberation is itself dishonesty; as it was in Balaam upon
the second message. That which is called considering what is our duty in a particular case, is very
often nothing but endeavouring to explain it away.
Thus those courses, which, if men would fairly attend to the dictates of their own consciences, they
would see to be corruption, excess, oppression, un-
charitableness; there are refined upon—things were
so and so circumstanced—great difficulties are raised
about fixing bounds and degrees; and thus every
moral obligation whatever may be evaded. Here
is scope, I say, for an unfair mind to explain away

every moral obligation to itself. [21] Whether men
reflect again upon this internal management and
artifice, and how explicit they are with themselves,
is another question. There are many operations of
the mind, many things pass within, which we never
reflect upon again, which a bystander, from having
frequent opportunities of observing us and our conduct, may make shrewd guesses at.

[22] That great numbers are in this way of deceiving themselves is certain. There is scarce a man
in the world, who has entirely got over all regards,
hopes, and fears, concerning God and a future state;
and these apprehensions in the generality, bad as
we are, prevail in considerable degrees; yet men
will and can be wicked, with calmness and thought;
we see they are. There must therefore be some
method of making it sit a little easy upon their
minds; which, in the superstitious, is those indulgences and atonements before mentioned, and this
self-deceit of another kind in persons of another
character. [23] And both these proceed from a
certain unfairness of mind, a peculiar inward dishonesty, the direct contrary to that simplicity which
our Saviour recommends, under the notion of *becoming little children,* as a necessary qualification
for our entering into the kingdom of heaven.

[24] But to conclude.—How much soever men
differ in the course of life they prefer, and in their
ways of palliating and excusing their vices to themselves, yet all agree in the one thing, desiring to *die
the death of the righteous.* This is surely remarkable. The observation may be extended further and
put thus: Even without determining what that is
which we call guilt or innocence, there is no man
but would choose, after having had the pleasure or
advantage of a vicious action, to be free of the guilt

of it, to be in the state of an innocent man. [25]
This shows at least the disturbance and implicit dissatisfaction in vice. If we inquire into the ground
of it, we shall find it proceeds partly from an immediate sense of having done evil and partly from an
apprehension that this inward sense shall one time
or another be seconded by a higher judgment, upon
which our whole being depends. [26] Now to suspend and drown this sense and these apprehensions,
be it by the hurry of business or of pleasure, or by
superstition, or moral equivocations, this is in a
manner one and the same, and makes no alteration
at all in the nature of our case. Things and actions
are what they are, and the consequences of them
will be what they will be : why then should we desire to be deceived ? As we are reasonable creatures and have any regard to ourselves, we ought
to lay these things plainly and honestly before our
mind, and upon this, act as you please, as you think
most fit ; make that choice, and prefer that course
of life, which you can justify to yourselves and which
sits most easy upon your own mind. It will immediately appear, that vice cannot be the happiness,
but must upon the whole be the misery, of such a
creature as man, a moral, an accountable agent.
Superstitious observances, self-deceit, though of a
more refined sort, will not in reality at all mend
matters with us. And the result of the whole can
be nothing else, but that with simplicity and fairness we *keep innocency, and take heed unto the
thing that is right; for this alone shall bring a man
peace at the last.*

SERMON VIII.

UPON RESENTMENT.

" Ye have heard that it hath been said, Thou shalt love thy neighbour, and hate thine enemy: but I say unto you, Love your enemies, bless them that curse you, do good to them that hate you, and pray for them which despitefully use you and persecute you."—MATT. v. 43, 44.

SINCE perfect goodness in the Deity is the principle from whence the universe was brought into being and by which it is preserved, and since general benevolence is the great law of the whole moral creation, it is a question which immediately occurs, *Why had man implanted in him a principle, which appears the direct contrary to benevolence?* Now the foot upon which inquiries of this kind should be treated is this: to take human nature as it is, and the circumstances in which it is placed as they are; and then consider the correspondence between that nature and those circumstances, or what course of action and behaviour, respecting those circumstances, any particular affection or passion leads us to. [2] This I mention

to distinguish the matter now before us from dis-
quisitions of quite another kind ; namely, Why we
are not made more perfect creatures, or placed in
better circumstances ? these being questions which
we have not, that I know of, anything at all to do
with.   God Almighty undoubtedly foresaw the disorders, both natural and moral, which would happen
in this state of things.   If upon this we set ourselves
to search and examine why he did not prevent them ;
we shall, I am afraid, be in danger of running into
somewhat worse than impertinent curiosity.   But
upon this to examine how far the nature which he
hath given us hath a respect to those circumstances
such as they are—how far it leads us to act a proper
part in them—plainly belongs to us : and such inquiries are in many ways of excellent use.   Thus
the thing to be considered is, not, Why we were
not made of such a nature, and placed in such circumstances, as to have no need of so harsh and turbulent a passion as resentment : but, taking our nature
and condition as being what they are, Why, or for
what end such a passion was given us : and this
chiefly in order to show what are the abuses of it.

[3] The persons who laid down for a rule " Thou
shalt love thy neighbour, and hate thine enemy,"
made short work with this matter.   They did not, it
seems, perceive anything to be disapproved in hatred,
more than in good-will : and, according to their
system of morals, our enemy was the proper natural
object of one of these passions, as our neighbour
was of the other of them.

This was all they had to say, and all they thought
needful to be said, upon the subject.   But this cannot be satisfactory, because hatred, malice, and revenge, are directly contrary to the religion we profess, and to the nature and reason of the thing itself.

[4] Therefore, since no passion God hath endued us with can be in itself evil; and yet since men frequently indulge a passion in such ways and degrees that at length it becomes quite another thing from what it was originally in our nature; and those vices of malice and revenge in particular take their occasion from the natural passion of resentment: it will be needful to trace this up to its original, that we may see what it is in itself, as placed in our nature by its Author, from which it will plainly appear, for what ends it was placed there. And when we know what the passion is in itself, and the ends of it, we shall easily see, what are the abuses of it in which malice and revenge consist, and which are so strongly forbidden in the text, by the direct contrary being commanded.

[5] Resentment is of two kinds: hasty and sudden, or settled and deliberate. The former is called anger, and often *passion ;* which, though a general word, is frequently appropriated and confined to the particular feeling, sudden anger, as distinct from deliberate resentment, malice, and revenge. In all these words there is usually implied somewhat vicious, somewhat unreasonable as to the occasion of the passion, or immoderate as to the degree or duration of it. But that the natural passion itself is indifferent, St. Paul has asserted in that precept, *Be ye angry, and sin not ;*[1] which though it is by no means to be understood as an encouragement to indulge ourselves in anger, the sense being certainly this, *Though ye be angry, sin not ;* yet here is evidently a distinction made between anger and sin; between the natural passion, and sinful anger.

[6] *Sudden anger,* upon certain occasions, is mere instinct: as merely so, as the disposition to close our

[1] Ephes. iv. 26.

eyes upon the apprehension of somewhat falling into
them, and no more necessarily implies any degree
of reason.   I say *necessarily*, for to be sure *hasty*,
as well as *deliberate*, anger may be occasioned by
injury or contempt, in which cases reason suggests
to our thoughts that injury and contempt, which is
the occasion of the passion : but I am speaking of the
former only so far as it is to be distinguished from
the latter.   The only way in which our reason and
understanding can raise anger, is by representing
to our mind injustice or injury of some kind or other.
Now momentary anger is frequently raised, not only
without any real, but without any apparent reason ;
that is, without any appearance of injury, as distinct
from hurt or pain.   It cannot, I suppose, be thought,
that this passion in infants, in the lower species of
animals, and, which is often seen, in men towards
them—it cannot, I say, be imagined, that these instances of this passion are the effect of reason : no,
they are occasioned by mere sensation and feeling.
It is opposition, sudden hurt, violence, which naturally excites the passion; and the real demerit or
fault of him who offers that violence, or is the cause
of that opposition or hurt, does not, in many cases,
so much as come into thought.

[7] The reason and the end, for which man was
made thus liable to this passion, is, that he might
be better qualified to prevent, and likewise (or perhaps chiefly) to resist and defeat, sudden force, violence, and opposition, considered merely as such,
and without regard to the fault or demerit of him
who is the author of them.   Yet, since violence may
be considered in this other and further view, as
implying fault; and since injury, as distinct from
harm, may raise sudden anger ; sudden anger may
likewise accidentally serve to prevent, or remedy,

such fault or injury. But, considered as distinct
from settled anger, it stands in our nature for self-
defence, and not for the administration of justice.
There are plainly cases (and in the uncultivated
parts of the world, where regular governments are
not formed, they frequently happen), in which there
is no time for consideration, and yet to be passive
is certain destruction ; in which sudden resistance is
the only security.

[8] But from this, deliberate anger or resentment is essentially distinguished, as the latter is not
naturally excited by, or intended to prevent, mere
harm without appearance of wrong or injustice.
[9] Now, in order to see, as exactly as we can, what
is the natural object and occasion of such resentment, let us reflect upon the manner in which we
are touched with reading, suppose, a feigned story
of baseness and villany, properly worked up to move
our passions. This immediately raises indignation,
somewhat of a desire that it should be punished.
And though the designed injury be prevented, yet
that it was designed is sufficient to raise this inward feeling. Suppose the story true, this inward
feeling would be as natural and as just: and one
may venture to affirm, that there is scarce a man
in the world, but would have it upon some occasions. It seems *in us* plainly connected with a
sense of virtue and vice, of moral good and evil.
Suppose further, we knew both the persons who
did and who suffered the injury: neither would this
make any alteration, only that it would probably
affect us more. [10] The indignation raised by
cruelty and injustice, and the desire of having it
punished, which persons unconcerned would feel,
is by no means malice. No, it is resentment against
vice and wickedness : it is one of the common bonds,

by which society is held together, a fellow feeling,
which each individual has in behalf of the whole species, as well as of himself. And it does not appear that
this, generally speaking, is at all too high amongst
mankind. [11] Suppose now the injury I have been
speaking of to be done against ourselves, or those
whom we consider as ourselves. It is plain the way
in which we should be affected would be exactly
the same in kind, but it would certainly be in a
higher degree, and less transient, because a sense
of our own happiness and misery is most intimately
and always present to us; and from the very
constitution of our nature, we cannot but have a
greater sensibility to, and be more deeply interested
in, what concerns ourselves. And this seems to be
the whole of this passion which is, properly speaking,
natural to mankind, namely, a resentment against
injury and wickedness in general, and in a higher
degree when towards ourselves in proportion to the
greater regard which men naturally have for themselves than for others. [12] From hence it appears
that it is not natural, but moral evil, it is not suffering,
but injury, which raises that anger or resentment,
which is of any continuance. The natural object of
it is not one who appears to the suffering person to
have been only the innocent occasion of his pain or
loss, but one who has been in a moral sense injurious either to ourselves or others. [13] This is
abundantly confirmed by observing what it is which
heightens or lessens resentment, namely, the same
which aggravates or lessens the fault—friendship,
and former obligations, on one hand; or inadvertency, strong temptations, and mistake on the other.
[14] All this is so much understood by mankind,
how little soever it be reflected upon, that a person
would be reckoned quite distracted who should

coolly resent a harm which had not to himself the appearance of injury or wrong. [15] Men do indeed resent what is occasioned through carelessness: but then they expect observance as their due, and so that carelessness is considered as faulty. [16] It is likewise true that they resent more strongly an injury done, than one which, though designed, was prevented, in cases where the guilt is perhaps the same: the reason however is, not that bare pain or loss raises resentment, but that it gives a new and, as I may speak, additional sense of the injury or injustice. [17] According to the natural course of the passions, the degrees of resentment are in proportion, not only to the degree of design and deliberation in the injurious person, but in proportion to this, joined with the degree of the evil designed or premeditated; since this likewise comes in to make the injustice greater or less. And the evil or harm will appear greater when they feel it, than when they only reflect upon it: so therefore will the injury: and consequently the resentment will be greater.

[18] The natural object or occasion of settled resentment then being injury, as distinct from pain or loss; it is easy to see, that to prevent and to remedy such injury, and the miseries arising from it, is the end for which this passion was implanted in man. It is to be considered as a weapon, put into our hands by nature, against injury, injustice, and cruelty: how it may be innocently employed and made use of, shall presently be mentioned.

[19] The account which has been now given of this passion is, in brief, that sudden anger is raised by, and was chiefly intended to prevent or remedy, mere harm distinct from injury; but that it *may* be raised by injury, and *may* serve to prevent or to

remedy it, and then the occasions and effects of it are the same with the occasions and effects of deliberate anger. But they are essentially distinguished in this, that the latter is never occasioned by harm, distinct from injury; and its natural proper end is to remedy or prevent only that harm, which implies, or is supposed to imply, injury or moral wrong. Every one sees that these observations do not relate to those who have habitually suppressed the course of their passions and affections, out of regard either to interest or virtue, or who, from habits of vice and folly, have changed their nature. But I suppose there can be no doubt but this, now described, is the general course of resentment, considered as a natural passion, neither increased by indulgence, nor corrected by virtue, nor prevailed over by other passions, or particular habits of life.

[20] As to the abuses of anger, which it is to be observed may be in all different degrees, the first which occurs is what is commonly called *passion*, to which some men are liable, in the same way as others are to the *epilepsy*, or any sudden particular disorder. This distemper of the mind seizes them upon the least occasion in the world, and perpetually without any real reason at all: and by means of it they are plainly every day, every waking hour of their lives, liable and in danger of running into the most extravagant outrages. [21] Of a less boisterous, but not of a less innocent kind, is *peevishness*, which I mention with pity, with real pity to the unhappy creatures, who, from their inferior station, or other circumstances and relations, are obliged to be in the way of, and to serve for a supply to it. [22] Both these, for aught that I can see, are one and the same principle; but as it takes root in minds of different makes, it appears differently,

H

and so is come to be distinguished by different names. That which in a more feeble temper is peevishness and languidly discharges itself upon everything which comes in its way, the same principle in a temper of greater force and stronger passions, becomes rage and fury. In one, the humour discharges itself at once; in the other, it is continually discharging. This is the account of *passion* and *peevishness*, as distinct from each other, and appearing in different persons. It is no objection against the truth of it, that they are both to be seen sometimes in one and the same person.

[23] With respect to deliberate resentment, the chief instances of abuse are: when, from partiality to ourselves, we imagine an injury done us, when there is none: when this partiality represents it to us as greater than it really is: when we fall into that extravagant and monstrous kind of resentment towards one who has innocently been the occasion of evil to us, that is, resentment upon account of pain or inconvenience, without injury, which is the same absurdity as settled anger at a thing that is inanimate; when the indignation against injury and injustice rises too high and is beyond proportion to the particular ill action it is exercised upon: or, lastly, when pain or harm of any kind is inflicted merely in consequence of, and to gratify, that resentment, though naturally raised.

[24] It would be endless to descend into and explain all the peculiarities of perverseness and wayward humour which might be traced up to this passion. But there is one thing which so generally belongs to and accompanies all excess and abuse of it as to require being mentioned, a certain determination and resolute bent of mind not to be convinced or set right, though it be ever so plain that there is

no reason for the displeasure, that it was raised
merely by error or misunderstanding. In this there
is doubtless a great mixture of pride; but there
is somewhat more, which I cannot otherwise express, than that resentment has taken possession
of the temper and of the mind, and will not quit its
hold. It would be too minute to inquire whether
this be anything more than bare obstinacy : it is
sufficient to observe, that it, in a very particular
manner and degree, belongs to the abuses of this
passion.

[25] But, notwithstanding all these abuses, " Is
not just indignation against cruelty and wrong one
of the instruments of death, which the Author of our
nature hath provided ?   Are not cruelty, injustice,
and wrong, the natural objects of that indignation ?
Surely then it may one way or other be innocently
employed against them." True. Since, therefore,
it is necessary for the very subsistence of the world,
that injury, injustice, and cruelty, should be punished;
and since compassion, which is so natural to mankind, would render that execution of justice exceedingly difficult and uneasy ; indignation against vice
and wickedness is, and may be allowed to be, a
balance to that weakness of pity, and also to anything else which would prevent the necessary methods
of severity. Those who have never thought upon
these subjects may perhaps not see the weight of
this : but let us suppose a person guilty of murder,
or any other action of cruelty, and that mankind had
naturally no indignation against such wickedness
and the authors of it; but that everybody was affected
towards such a criminal in the same way as towards
an innocent man: compassion, amongst other things,
would render the execution of justice exceedingly
painful and difficult, and would often quite prevent

it. And notwithstanding that the principle of benevolence is denied by some and is really in so very
low a degree, that men are in great measure insensible to the happiness of their fellow-creatures; yet
they are not insensible to their misery, but are very
strongly moved with it, insomuch that there plainly
is occasion for that feeling which is raised by guilt
and demerit, as a balance to that of compassion.
Thus much may, I think, justly be allowed to resentment, in the strictest way of moral consideration.

[26] The good influence which this passion has
in fact upon the affairs of the world, is obvious to
every one's notice. Men are plainly restrained from
injuring their fellow-creatures by fear of their resentment, and it is very happy that they are so, when
they would not be restrained by a principle of virtue.
And after an injury is done and there is a necessity
that the offender should be brought to justice, the
cool consideration of reason, that the security and
peace of society require examples of justice should
be made, might indeed be sufficient to procure laws
to be enacted, and sentence passed: but is it that
cool reflection in the injured person which, for the
most part, brings the offender to justice? Or is it
not resentment and indignation against the injury
and the author of it? I am afraid there is no doubt
which is commonly the case. This however is to
be considered as a good effect, notwithstanding it
were much to be wished that men would act from
a better principle, reason and cool reflection.

[27] The account now given of the passion of
resentment, as distinct from all the abuses of it, may
suggest to our thoughts the following reflections.

[28] First. That vice is indeed of ill desert, and
must finally be punished. Why should men dis-

pute concerning the reality of virtue, and whether
it be founded in the nature of things, which yet
surely is not matter of question; but why should this,
I say, be disputed, when every man carries about
him this passion, which affords him demonstration
that the rules of justice and equity are to be the
guide of his actions ? For every man naturally feels
an indignation upon seeing instances of villany and
baseness, and therefore cannot commit the same
without being self-condemned.

[29] Secondly. That we should learn to be cautious lest we *charge God foolishly* by ascribing that
to him, or the nature he has given us, which is
owing wholly to our own abuse of it. Men may
speak of the degeneracy and corruption of the world,
according to the experience they have had of it;
but human nature, considered as the divine work-
manship, should methinks be treated as sacred, for
in the image of God made he man. That passion,
from whence men take occasion to run into the dreadful vices of malice and revenge, even that passion,
as implanted in our nature by God, is not only innocent, but a generous movement of mind. It is
in itself, and in its original, no more than indignation against injury and wickedness, that which is
the only deformity in the creation, and the only
reasonable object of abhorrence and dislike. How
manifold evidence have we of the divine wisdom and
goodness, when even pain in the natural world, and
the passion we have been now considering in the
moral, come out instances of it !

SERMON IX.

UPON FORGIVENESS OF INJURIES.

AS God Almighty foresaw the irregularities and disorders, both natural and moral, which would happen in this state of things, he hath graciously made some provision against them, by giving us several passions and affections, which arise from, or whose objects are, those disorders. Of this sort are fear, resentment, compassion, and others, of which there could be no occasion or use in a perfect state; but in the present we should be exposed to greater inconveniences without them, though there are very considerable ones which they themselves are the occasions of. They are encumbrances indeed, but such as we are obliged to carry about with us through this various journey of life, some of them as a guard against the violent assaults of others and in our own defence, some in behalf of others, and all of them to put us upon, and help to carry us through a course of behaviour suitable to our condition, in default of that perfection of wisdom and virtue which would be in all respects our better security.

[31] The passion of anger or resentment hath already been largely treated of. It hath been shown that mankind naturally feel some emotion of mind

against injury and injustice, whoever are the sufferers by it; and even though the injurious design be
prevented from taking effect. Let this be called
anger, indignation, resentment, or by whatever name
any one shall choose, the thing itself is understood,
and is plainly natural. It has likewise been observed that this natural indignation is generally
moderate and low enough in mankind, in each particular man, when the injury which excites it doth
not affect himself or one whom he considers as himself. [32] Therefore the precepts to *forgive*, and to
love our enemies, do not relate to that general indignation against injury and the authors of it, but to this
feeling, or resentment, when raised by private or personal injury. But no man could be thought in earnest
who should assert that, though indignation against
injury, when others are the sufferers, is innocent and
just, yet the same indignation against it, when we
ourselves are the sufferers, become faulty and blamable. These precepts therefore cannot be understood to forbid this in the latter case more than in
the former. Nay they cannot be understood to forbid this feeling in the latter case, though raised to
a higher degree than in the former; because, as
we have also observed further, from the very constitution of our nature we cannot but have a greater
sensibility to what concerns ourselves. Therefore
the precepts in the text, and others of the like im-
port with them, must be understood to forbid only
the excess and abuse of this natural feeling, in cases
of personal and private injury; the chief instances
of which excess and abuse have likewise been already
remarked, and all of them, excepting that of retaliation, do so plainly in the very terms express somewhat unreasonable, disproportionate, and absurd, as
to admit of no pretence or shadow of justification.

[33] But since custom and false honour are on the side of retaliation and revenge, when the resentment is natural and just; and reasons are sometimes offered in justification of revenge in these cases; and since love of our enemies is thought too hard a saying to be obeyed: I will show the absolute unlawfulness of the former; the obligations we are under to the latter; and then proceed to some reflections which may have a more direct and immediate tendency to beget in us a right temper of mind towards those who have offended us.

[34] In showing the unlawfulness of revenge, it is not my present design to examine what is alleged in favour of it, from the tyranny of custom and false honour, but only to consider the nature and reason of the thing itself, which ought to have prevented, and ought now to extirpate, everything of that kind.

[35] First. Let us begin with the supposition of that being innocent which is pleaded for, and which shall be shown to be altogether vicious, the supposition that we were allowed to *render evil for evil*, and see what would be the consequence. Malice or resentment towards any man hath plainly a tendency to beget the same passion in him who is the object of it; and this again increases it in the other. It is of the very nature of this vice to propagate itself, not only by way of example, which it does in common with other vices, but in a peculiar way of its own; for resentment itself, as well as what is done in consequence of it, is the object of resentment: hence it comes to pass, that the first offence, even when so slight as presently to be dropped and forgotten, becomes the occasion of entering into a long intercourse of ill offices: neither is it at all uncommon to see persons, in this progress of strife and variance, change parts; and him, who was at first the injured person, become more in-

jurious and blamable than the aggressor. Put the
case then that the law of retaliation was universally
received and allowed, as an innocent rule of life, by
all; and the observance of it thought by many (and
then it would soon come to be thought by all) a
point of honour: this supposes every man in private
cases to pass sentence in his own cause, and likewise that anger or resentment is to be the judge.
Thus, from the numberless partialities which we
all have for ourselves, every one would often think
himself injured when he was not: and in most cases
would represent an injury as much greater than it
really is; the imagined dignity of the person offended
would scarce ever fail to magnify the offence. And
if bare retaliation, or returning just the mischief
received, always begets resentment in the person
upon whom we retaliate, what would that excess
do? Add to this, that he likewise has his partialities—there is no going on to represent this scene of
rage and madness: it is manifest there would be no
bounds, nor any end. If "the beginning of strife
is as one that letteth out water," what would it come
to when allowed this free and unrestrained course?
"As coals are to burning coals, or wood to fire; so
would these contentious men be to kindle strife."
And, since the indulgence of revenge hath manifestly this tendency, and does actually produce these
effects in proportion as it is allowed, a passion of so
dangerous a nature ought not to be indulged, were
there no other reason against it.

[36] Secondly. It hath been shown that the
passion of resentment was placed in man, upon supposition of, and as a prevention or remedy to, irregularity and disorder. Now whether it be allowed
or not, that the passion itself and the gratification
of it joined together are painful to the malicious
person; it must however be so with respect to the

person towards whom it is exercised, and upon whom the revenge is taken. Now if we consider mankind, according to that fine allusion of St. Paul, as " one body, and every one members. one of another," it must be allowed that resentment is, with respect to society, a painful remedy. Thus then the very notion or idea of this passion, as a remedy or prevention of evil, and as in itself a painful means, plainly shows that it ought never to be made use of, but only in order to produce some greater good.

[37] It is to be observed, that this argument is not founded upon an allusion or simile, but that it is drawn from the very nature of the passion itself, and the end for which it was given us. We are obliged to make use of words taken from sensible things to explain what is the most remote from them ; and every one sees from whence the words prevention and remedy are taken. But, if you please, let these words be dropped: the thing itself, I suppose, may be expressed without them.

That mankind is a community, that we all stand in a relation to each other, that there is a public end and interest of society which each particular is obliged to promote, is the sum of morals. Consider then the passion of resentment, as given to this one body, as given to society. Nothing can be more manifest than that resentment is to be considered as a secondary passion placed in us upon supposition, upon account of, and with regard to, injury; not, to be sure, to promote and further it, but to render it, and the inconveniences and miseries arising from it, less and fewer than they would be without this passion. It is as manifest, that the indulgence of it is, with regard to society, a painful means of obtaining these ends. Considered in itself, it is very undesirable, and what society must very much wish

to be without.   It is in every instance absolutely an
evil in itself, because it implies producing misery:
and consequently must never be indulged or gratified for itself, by any one who considers mankind
as a community or family, and himself as a member
of it.

[38] Let us now take this in another view. Every
natural appetite, passion, and affection, may be gratified in particular instances, without being subservient to the particular chief end for which these
several principles were respectively implanted in our
nature. And, if neither this end nor any other moral
obligation be contradicted, such gratification is innocent.   Thus I suppose there are cases in which
each of these principles, this one of resentment excepted, may innocently be gratified, without being
subservient to what is the main end of it: that is,
though it does not conduce to, yet it may be gratified without contradicting, that end, or any other
obligation.   But the gratification of resentment, if
it be not conducive to the end for which it was
given us, must necessarily contradict, not only the
general obligation to benevolence, but likewise that
particular end itself.   The end, for which it was
given, is to prevent or remedy injury, *i.e.*, the misery
occasioned by injury, *i. e.*, misery itself; and the
gratification of it consists in producing misery, *i.e.*,
in contradicting the end for which it was implanted
in our nature.

[39] This whole reasoning is built upon the difference there is between this passion and all others.
No other principle or passion hath for its end the
misery of our fellow-creatures.   But malice and revenge meditates evil itself; and to do mischief, to
be the author of misery, is the very thing which
gratifies the passion: this is what it directly tends

towards as its proper design. Other vices even-
tually do mischief: this alone aims at it as an end.

[40] Nothing can with reason be urged in justification of revenge, from the good effects which
the indulgence of it were before mentioned[1] to have
upon the affairs of the world ; because, though it be
a remarkable instance of the wisdom of Providence
to bring good out of evil, yet vice is vice to him who
is guilty of it. " But suppose these good effects
are foreseen ;" that is, suppose reason in a particular case leads a man the same way as passion ? Why
then, to be sure, he should follow his reason, in this
as well as in all other cases. So that, turn the
matter whichever way you will, no more can be
allowed to this passion than what hath been already.[2]

[41] As to that love of our enemies, which is
commanded : this supposes the general obligation
to benevolence or good-will towards mankind ; and
this being supposed, that precept is no more than
to forgive injuries, that is, to keep clear of those
abuses before mentioned ; because that we have the
habitual temper of benevolence is taken for granted.

[42] Resentment is not inconsistent with good-
will, for we often see both together in very high
degrees, not only in parents towards their children,
but in cases of friendship and dependence where
there is no natural relation. These contrary passions, though they may lessen, do not necessarily
destroy each other. We may therefore love our
enemy, and yet have resentment against him for
his injurious behaviour towards us. But when this
resentment entirely destroys our natural benevolence
towards him, it is excessive, and becomes malice or
revenge. The command to prevent its having this
effect, *i. e.*, to forgive injuries, is the same as to love

[1] Sermon viii. p. 100.   ·   [2] Ibid. p. 99.

our enemies; because that love is always supposed, unless destroyed by resentment.

[43] "But though mankind is the natural object of benevolence, yet may it not be lessened upon vice, *i. e.*, injury?" Allowed: but if every degree of vice or injury must destroy that benevolence, then no man is the object of our love; for no man is without faults.

"But if lower instances of injury may lessen our benevolence, why may not higher, or the highest, destroy it?" The answer is obvious. It is not man's being a social creature, much less his being a moral agent, from whence *alone* our obligations to good-will towards him arise. There is an obligation to it prior to either of these, arising from his being a sensible creature, that is, capable of happiness or misery. Now this obligation cannot be superseded by his moral character. What justifies public executions is, not that the guilt or demerit of the criminal dispenses with the obligation of good-will, neither would this justify any severity; but, that his life is inconsistent with the quiet and happiness of the world: that is, a general and more enlarged obligation necessarily destroys a particular and more confined one of the same kind inconsistent with it. Guilt or injury, then, does not dispense with, or supersede the duty of, love and good-will.

[44] Neither does that peculiar regard to ourselves, which was before allowed to be natural[1] to mankind, dispense with it: because that can no way innocently heighten our resentment against those who have been injurious to ourselves in particular, any otherwise than as it heightens our sense of the injury or guilt; and guilt, though in the highest

[1] Sermon viii. p. 95.

If we could place ourselves at a due distance, *i. e.*, be really unprejudiced, we should frequently discern that to be in reality inadvertence and mistake in our enemy, which we now fancy we see to be malice or scorn. From this proper point of view we should likewise in all probability see something of these latter in ourselves, and most certainly a great deal of the former. Thus the indignity or injury would almost infinitely lessen, and perhaps at last come out to be nothing at all. Self-love is a medium of a peculiar kind; in these cases it magnifies everything which is amiss in others, at the same time that it lessens everything amiss in ourselves.

[51] Anger also or hatred may be considered as another false medium of viewing things, which always represents characters and actions much worse than they really are. Ill-will not only never speaks, but never thinks, well of the person towards whom it is exercised. Thus in cases of offence and enmity, the whole character and behaviour is considered with an eye to that peculiar part which has offended us, and the whole man appears monstrous, without anything right or human in him: whereas the resentment should surely at least be confined to that particular part of the behaviour which gave offence, since the other parts of a man's life and character stand just the same as they did before.

[52] In general, there are very few instances of enmity carried to any length, but inadvertency, misunderstanding, some real mistake of the case, on one side however, if not on both, has a great share in it.

[53] If these things were attended to, these ill-humours could not be carried to any length amongst good men, and they would be exceedingly abated amongst all. And one would hope they might be

attended to : for all that these cautions come to, is
really no more than desiring that things may be
considered and judged of as they are in themselves,
that we should have an eye to, and beware of, what
would otherwise lead us into mistakes. So that to
make allowances for inadvertence, misunderstanding, for the partialities of self-love, and the false
light which anger set things in—I say, to make
allowances for these—is not to be spoken of as an
instance of humbleness of mind, or meekness and
moderation of temper; but as what common sense
should suggest, to avoid judging wrong of a matter
before us, though virtue and morals were out of the
case. And therefore it as much belongs to ill men,
who will indulge the vice I have been arguing against,
as to good men, who endeavour to subdue it in themselves. In a word, all these cautions concerning
anger and self-love, are no more than desiring a
man, who was looking through a glass which either
magnified or lessened, to take notice that the objects are not in themselves what they appear through
that medium.

[54] To all these things one might add that, resentment being out of the case, there is not, properly speaking, any such thing as direct ill-will in
one man towards another : therefore the first indignity or injury, if it be not owing to inadvertence or
misunderstanding, may however be resolved into
other particular passions or self-love, principles
quite distinct from ill-will, and which we ought all
to be disposed to excuse in others, from experiencing
so much of them in ourselves. A great man of
antiquity is reported to have said that, as he never
was indulgent to any one fault in himself, he could
not excuse those of others. This sentence could
scarce with decency come out of the mouth of any

If we could place ourselves at a due distance, *i. e.*, be really unprejudiced, we should frequently discern that to be in reality inadvertence and mistake in our enemy, which we now fancy we see to be malice or scorn. From this proper point of view we should likewise in all probability see something of these latter in ourselves, and most certainly a great deal of the former. Thus the indignity or injury would almost infinitely lessen, and perhaps at last come out to be nothing at all. Self-love is a medium of a peculiar kind; in these cases it magnifies everything which is amiss in others, at the same time that it lessens everything amiss in ourselves.

[51] Anger also or hatred may be considered as another false medium of viewing things, which always represents characters and actions much worse than they really are. Ill-will not only never speaks, but never thinks, well of the person towards whom it is exercised. Thus in cases of offence and enmity, the whole character and behaviour is considered with an eye to that peculiar part which has offended us, and the whole man appears monstrous, without anything right or human in him: whereas the resentment should surely at least be confined to that particular part of the behaviour which gave offence, since the other parts of a man's life and character stand just the same as they did before.

[52] In general, there are very few instances of enmity carried to any length, but inadvertency, misunderstanding, some real mistake of the case, on one side however, if not on both, has a great share in it.

[53] If these things were attended to, these ill-humours could not be carried to any length amongst good men, and they would be exceedingly abated amongst all. And one would hope they might be

attended to: for all that these cautions come to, is really no more than desiring that things may be considered and judged of as they are in themselves, that we should have an eye to, and beware of what would otherwise mislead us into mistakes: — So that to make allowances for... the particular... light which anger sets things in... allowances for these — is... instance of... moderation of temper... should suggest... before we thought... case, and therefore... which will change the... as to good men who... better... anger and... that so we should be... magnitude of... there ought to be... that reason.

...

human creature.   But if we invert the former part,
and put it thus—that he was indulgent to many
faults in himself, as it is to be feared the best of us
are, and yet was implacable—how monstrous would
such an assertion appear?   And this is the case in
respect to every human creature, in proportion as
he is without the forgiving spirit I have been recommending.

[55] Further, though injury, injustice, oppression, the baseness of ingratitude, are the natural
objects of indignation, or if you please of resentment,
as before explained ; yet they are likewise the objects of compassion, as they are their own punishment, and without repentance will for ever be so.
No one ever did a designed injury to another, but
at the same time he did a much greater to himself.
If therefore we would consider things justly, such a
one is, according to the natural course of our affections, an object of compassion, as well as of displeasure : and to be affected really in this manner,
I say really, in opposition to show and pretence,
argues the true greatness of mind.   We have an
example of forgiveness in this way in its utmost
perfection, and which indeed includes in it all that
is good, in that prayer of our blessed Saviour on the
cross: " Father, forgive them ; for they know not
what they do."

[56] But lastly, the offences which we are all
guilty of against God, and the injuries which men
do to each other are often mentioned together, and
—making allowances for the infinite distance between the Majesty of heaven and a frail mortal, and
likewise for this, that he cannot possibly be affected
or moved as we are—offences committed by others
against ourselves, and the manner in which we are
apt to be affected with them, give a real occasion

for calling to mind our own sins against God. Now
there is an apprehension and presentiment natural
to mankind that we ourselves shall one time or
other be dealt with as we deal with others, and a
peculiar acquiescence in, and feeling of, the equity
and justice of this equal distribution. This natural
notion of equity the Son of Sirach has put in the
strongest way. " He that revengeth shall find
vengeance from the Lord, and he will surely keep
his sins in remembrance. Forgive thy neighbour
the hurt he hath done unto thee, so shall thy sins be
forgiven when thou prayest. One man beareth
hatred against another; and doth he seek pardon
from the Lord? He sheweth no mercy to a man
which is like himself; and doth he ask forgiveness
of his own sins ?"[1] Let any one read our Saviour's
parable of the king who took account of his servants,[2] and the equity and rightness of the sentence
which was passed upon him who was unmerciful to
his fellow-servant will be felt. There is somewhat
in human nature, which accords to and falls in with
that method of determination. Let us then place
before our eyes the time which is represented in
the parable, that of our own death, or the final
judgment. Suppose yourselves under the apprehensions of approaching death; that you are just
going to appear naked and without disguise before
the Judge of all the earth, to give an account of
your behaviour towards your fellow creatures:
could anything raise more dreadful apprehensions
of that judgment, than the reflection that you had
been implacable, and without mercy towards those
who had offended you—without that forgiving spirit
towards others, which, that it may now be exercised

---

[1] Ecclus. xxviii. 1—4.   [2] Matt. xviii.

towards yourselves, is your only hope ? [57] And these natural apprehensions are authorized by our Saviour's application of the parable : " So likewise shall my heavenly Father do also unto you, if ye from your hearts forgive not every one his brother their trespasses." On the other hand, suppose a good man in the same circumstance, in the last part and close of life ; conscious of many frailties, as the best are, but conscious too that he had been meek, forgiving, and merciful ; that he had in simplicity of heart been ready to pass over offences against himself: the having felt this good spirit will give him, not only a full view of the amiableness of it, but the surest hope that he shall meet with it in his Judge. This likewise is confirmed by his own declaration : " If ye forgive men their trespasses, your heavenly Father will likewise forgive you." And that we might have a constant sense of it upon our mind, the condition is expressed in our daily prayer. A forgiving spirit is therefore absolutely necessary, as ever we hope for pardon of our own sins, as ever we hope for peace of mind in our dying moments, or for the divine mercy at that day when we shall most stand in need of it.

SERMON X.

UPON SELF-DECEIT.

" And Nathan said to David, Thou art the man."—
2 SAM. xii. 7.

THESE words are the application of Nathan's parable to David, upon occasion of his adultery with Bathsheba and the murder of Uriah her husband. The parable, which is related in the most beautiful simplicity, is this : " There were two men in one city; the one rich, and the other poor. The rich man had exceeding many flocks and herds ; but the poor man had nothing, save one little ewe lamb, which he had bought and nourished up ; and it grew up together with him, and with his children; it did eat of his own meat, and drank of his own cup, and lay in his bosom, and was unto him as a daughter. And there came a traveller unto the rich man, and he spared to take of his own flock and of his own herd, to dress for the wayfaring man that was come unto him; but took the poor man's lamb, and dressed it for the man that was come to him. And David's anger was greatly kindled against the man ; and he said to Nathan, As the Lord liveth, the man that hath done this thing shall surely die : and he shall restore the lamb fourfold, because he did this thing, and because he had no pity."[1] [2] David passes sentence, not only that there should be a fourfold restitution made, but he proceeds to the rigour of justice, " the man that hath done this thing shall die :" and this judgment is pronounced with the utmost indignation against such an act of inhumanity: " As the Lord liveth, he shall surely die ; and his anger was greatly kindled against the man." And the prophet answered, " Thou art the man." He had been guilty of much greater inhumanity, with the utmost deliberation, thought, and contrivance. Near a year must have passed between the time of the commission of his crimes and the time of the prophet's coming to him ; and it does not appear from the story that he had in all this while the least remorse or contrition.

[3] There is not anything relating to men and characters more surprising and unaccountable than this partiality to themselves which is observable in many ; as there is nothing of more melancholy reflection, respecting morality, virtue, and religion. Hence it is that many men seem perfect strangers to their own characters. They think, and reason, and judge quite differently upon any matter relating to themselves, from what they do in cases of others where they are not interested. Hence it is one hears people exposing follies, which they themselves are eminent for ; and talking with great severity against particular vices, which, if all the world be not mistaken, they themselves are notoriously guilty of. This self-ignorance and self-partiality may be in all different degrees. It is a lower degree of it which David himself refers to in these words, " Who can tell how oft he offendeth ?

[1] 2 Sam. xii. 1—6.

O cleanse thou me from my secret faults." This is
the ground of that advice of Elihu to Job : " Surely
it is meet to be said unto God, That which I see not,
teach thou me ; if I have done iniquity, I will do no
more." And Solomon saw this thing in a very
strong light, when he said, " He that trusteth his
own heart is a fool." This likewise was the reason
why that precept, " Know thyself," was so frequently
inculcated by the philosophers of old. For if it were
not for that partial and fond regard to ourselves, it
would certainly be no great difficulty to know our
own character, what passes within the bent and bias
of our mind ; much less would there be any difficulty
in judging rightly of our own actions. But from
this partiality it frequently comes to pass, that the
observation of many men's being themselves last of
all acquainted with what falls out in their own
families, may be applied to a nearer home, to what
passes within their own breasts.

[4] There is plainly in the generality of mankind
an absence of doubt or distrust, in a very great
measure, as to their moral character and behaviour ;
and likewise a disposition to take for granted that all
is right and well with them in these respects. The
former is owing to their not reflecting, not exercising their judgment upon themselves ; the latter, to
self-love. I am not speaking of that extravagance
which is sometimes to be met with ; instances of
persons declaring in words at length, that they
never were in the wrong, nor had ever any diffidence of the justness of their conduct, in their
whole lives. No, these people are too far gone to
have anything said to them. The thing before us
is indeed of this kind, but in a lower degree, and
confined to the moral character ; somewhat of which
we almost all of us have, without reflecting upon it.

[5] Now consider how long and how grossly a person of the best understanding might be imposed upon by one of whom he had not any suspicion and in whom he placed an entire confidence, especially if there were friendship and real kindness in the case: surely this holds even stronger with respect to that self we are all so fond of. [6] Hence arises in men a disregard of reproof and instruction, rules of conduct and moral discipline, which occasionally come in their way: a disregard, I say, of these not in every respect, but in this single one, namely, as what may be of service to them in particular towards mending their own hearts and tempers, and making them better men. It never in earnest comes into their thoughts whether such admonitions may not relate and be of service to themselves; and this quite distinct from a positive persuasion to the contrary, a persuasion from reflection that they are innocent and blameless in those respects. Thus we may invert the observation which is somewhere made upon Brutus, that he never read but in order to make himself a better man. It scarce comes into the thoughts of the generality of mankind, that this use is to be made of moral reflections which they meet with; that this use, I say, is to be made of them by themselves, for everybody observes and wonders that it is not done by others.

[7] Further, there are instances of persons having so fixed and steady an eye upon their own interest, whatever they place it in, and the interest of those whom they consider as themselves, as in a manner to regard nothing else; their views are almost confined to this alone. Now we cannot be acquainted with, nor in any propriety of speech be said to know, anything, but what we attend to. If

therefore they attend only to one side, they really will not, cannot see or know what is to be alleged on the other. Though a man hath the best eyes in the world, he cannot see any way but that which he turns them. Thus these persons, without passing over the least, the most minute thing, which can possibly be urged in favour of themselves, shall overlook entirely the plainest and most obvious things on the other side. And whilst they are under the power of this temper, thought and consideration upon the matter before them has scarce any tendency to set them right; because they are engaged, and their deliberation concerning an action to be done, or reflection upon it afterwards, is not to see whether it be right, but to find out reasons to justify or palliate it; palliate it, not to others, but to themselves.

[8] In some there is to be observed a general ignorance of themselves, and wrong way of thinking and judging in everything relating to themselves—their fortune, reputation, everything in which self can come in: and this perhaps attended with the rightest judgment in all other matters. In others this partiality is not so general, has not taken hold of the whole man, but is confined to some particular favourite passion, interest, or pursuit; suppose ambition, covetousness, or any other. And these persons may probably judge and determine what is perfectly just and proper, even in things in which they themselves are concerned, if these things have no relation to their particular favourite passion or pursuit. [9] Hence arises that amazing incongruity, and seeming inconsistency of character, from whence slight observers take it for granted, that the whole is hypocritical and false, not being able otherwise to reconcile the several parts;

whereas in truth there is real honesty, so far as it goes. There is such a thing as men's being honest to such a degree, and in such respects, but no further. And this, as it is true, so it is absolutely necessary to be taken notice of, and allowed them; such general and undistinguishing censure of their whole character, as designing and false, being one main thing which confirms them in their self-deceit. They know that the whole censure is not true, and so take for granted that no part of it is.

[10] But to go on with the explanation of the thing itself.—Vice in general consists in having an unreasonable and too great a regard to ourselves, in comparison of others. Robbery and murder are never from the love of injustice or cruelty, but to gratify some other passion, to gain some supposed advantage : and it is false selfishness alone, whether cool or passionate, which makes a man resolutely pursue that end, be it ever so much to the injury of another. But whereas, in common and ordinary wickedness, this unreasonableness, this partiality and selfishness, relates only or chiefly to the temper and passions, in the characters we are now considering, it reaches to the understanding, and influences the very judgment.[1] And, besides that general want of

[1] That peculiar regard for ourselves which frequently produces this partiality of judgment in our own favour, may have a quite contrary effect, and occasion the utmost diffidence and distrust of ourselves; were it only, as it may set us upon a more frequent and strict survey and review of our own character and behaviour. This search or recollection itself implies somewhat of diffidence; and the discoveries we make, what is brought to our view, may possibly increase it. Good-will to another may either blind our judgment, so as to make us overlook his faults ; or it may put us upon exercising that judgment with greater strictness, to see whether he is so faultless and perfect as we wish him. (*a*) If that peculiar regard to ourselves lead us to examine our own character with this greater severity, in order

distrust and diffidence concerning our own character, there are, you see, two things, which may thus prejudice and darken the understanding itself: that over-fondness for ourselves, which we are all so liable to; and also being under the power of any particular passion or appetite, or engaged in any particular pursuit. And these, especially the last of the two, may be in so great a degree, as to influence our judgment, even of other persons and their behaviour. Thus a man, whose temper is formed to ambition or covetousness, shall even approve of them sometimes in others.

[11] This seems to be in a good measure the account of self-partiality and self-deceit, when traced up to its original. Whether it be or be not thought satisfactory, that there is such a thing is manifest; and that it is the occasion of great part of the unreasonable behaviour of men towards each other: that by means of it they palliate their vices and follies to themselves: and that it prevents their applying to themselves those reproofs and instructions, which they meet with either in scripture or in moral and religious discourses, though exactly suitable to the state of their own mind and the course of their behaviour. There is one thing further to be added here, that the temper we distinguish by hardness of heart with respect to others, joined with this self-partiality, will carry a man almost any lengths of

really to improve and grow better, it is the most commendable turn of mind possible, and can scarce be to excess. But if, as everything hath its counterfeit, we are so much employed about ourselves in order to disguise what is amiss, and to make a better appearance; or if our attention to ourselves has chiefly this effect; it is liable to run up into the greatest weakness and excess, and is, like all other excesses, its own disappointment: for scarce any show themselves to advantage, who are over solicitous of doing so.

wickedness, in the way of oppression, hard usage of
others, and even to plain injustice; without his having from what appears, any real sense at all of it.
This indeed was not the general character of David:
for he plainly gave scope to the affections of compassion and good-will, as well as to his passions of
another kind.

[12] But as some occasions and circumstances
lie more open to this self-deceit, and give it greater
scope and opportunities than others, these require
to be particularly mentioned.

[13] It is to be observed then that as there are
express determinate acts of wickedness, such as
murder, adultery, theft: so, on the other hand,
there are numberless cases in which the vice and
wickedness cannot be exactly defined; but consists
in a certain general temper and course of action, or
in the neglect of some duty, suppose charity or any
other, whose bounds and degrees are not fixed.
This is the very province of self-deceit and self-
partiality; here it governs without check or control. " For what commandment is there broken?
Is there a transgression where there is no law? a
vice which cannot be defined?"

[14] Whoever will consider the whole commerce
of human life, will see that a great part, perhaps
the greatest part, of the intercourse amongst mankind, cannot be reduced to fixed determinate rules.
Yet in these cases there is a right and a wrong: a
merciful, a liberal, a kind and compassionate behaviour, which surely is our duty; and an unmerciful
contracted spirit, a hard and oppressive course of
behaviour, which is most certainly immoral and vicious. But who can define precisely, wherein that
contracted spirit and hard usage of others consist,
as murder and theft may be defined! There is

not a word in our language which expresses more
detestable wickedness than *oppression ;* yet the nature of this vice cannot be so exactly stated, nor
the bounds of it so determinately marked, as that
we shall be able to say in all instances, where rigid
right and justice ends, and oppression begins.
[15] In these cases there is great latitude left for
every one to determine for, and consequently to
deceive himself. It is chiefly in these cases that
self-deceit comes in; as every one must see that
there is much larger scope for it here, than in express, single, determinate acts of wickedness. However it comes in with respect to the *circumstances*
attending the most gross and determinate acts of
wickedness. Of this the story of David, now before us, affords the most astonishing instance. It
is really prodigious to see a man, before so remarkable for virtue and piety, going on deliberately from
adultery to murder, with the same cool contrivance,
and, from what appears, with as little disturbance,
as a man would endeavour to prevent the ill consequences of a mistake he had made in any common
matter. That total insensibility of mind with respect to those horrid crimes, after the commission
of them, manifestly shows that he did some way or
other delude himself: and this could not be with
respect to the crimes themselves, they were so
manifestly of the grossest kind. What the particular circumstances were with which he extenuated
them, and quieted and deceived himself is not related.

[16] Having thus explained the nature of internal hypocrisy and self-deceit, and remarked the
occasions upon which it exerts itself, there are several things further to be observed concerning it:
that all of the sources, to which it was traced up,

are sometimes observable together in one and the
same person: but that one of them is more remarkable, and to a higher degree, in some, and others
of them are so in others: that in general it is a
complicated thing; and may be in all different degrees and kinds: that the temper itself is essentially in its own nature vicious and immoral. It is
unfairness: it is dishonesty: it is falseness of heart:
and is therefore so far from extenuating guilt, that
it is itself the greatest of all guilt in proportion to
the degree it prevails, for it is a corruption of the
whole moral character in its principle. Our understanding and sense of good and evil, is the light and
guide of life: " If therefore the light that is in thee
be darkness, how great is that darkness!" [1] For
this reason our Saviour puts an *evil eye* as the direct opposite to a *single eye;* the absence of that
simplicity, which these last words imply, being itself evil and vicious. And whilst men are under
the power of this temper, in proportion still to the
degree they are so, they are fortified on every side
against conviction: and when they hear the vice
and folly of what is in truth their own course of life,
exposed in the justest and strongest manner, they
will often assent to it, and even carry the matter
further; persuading themselves, one does not know
how, but some way or other persuading themselves,
that they are out of these, and that it hath no relation to them. [17] Yet notwithstanding this there
frequently appears a suspicion that all is not right,
or as it should be: and perhaps there *is always* at
bottom somewhat of this sort. There are, doubtless, many instances of the ambitious, the revengeful, the covetous, and those whom with too great
indulgence we only call the men of pleasure, who

[1] Matt. vi. 23.

will not allow themselves to think how guilty they are, who explain and argue away their guilt to themselves: and though they do really impose upon themselves in some measure, yet there are none of them but have, if not a proper knowledge, yet at least an implicit suspicion, where the weakness lies, and what part of their behaviour they have reason to wish unknown or forgotten for ever. Truth and real good sense and thorough integrity carry along with them a peculiar consciousness of their own genuineness: there is a feeling belonging to them, which does not accompany their counterfeits, error, folly, half-honesty, partial and slight regards to virtue and right, so far only as they are consistent with that course of gratification which men happen to be set upon. [18] And if this be the case, it is much the same as if we should suppose a man to have had a general view of some scene, enough to satisfy him that it was very disagreeable, and then to shut his eyes, that he might not have a particular or distinct view of its several deformities. It is as easy to close the eyes of the mind as those of the body: and the former is more frequently done with wilfulness, and yet not attended to, than the latter; the actions of the mind being more quick and transient, than those of the senses. This may be further illustrated by another thing observable in ordinary life. It is not uncommon for persons who run out their fortunes, entirely to neglect looking into the state of their affairs, and this from a general knowledge that the condition of them is bad. These extravagant people are perpetually ruined before they themselves expected it: and they tell you for an excuse, and tell you truly, that they did not think they were so much in debt, or that their expenses so far exceeded their income. And

yet no one will take this for an excuse, who is sensible that their ignorance of their particular circumstances was owing to their general knowledge of
them; that is, their general knowledge, that matters were not well with them, prevented their looking into particulars. , There is somewhat of the
like kind with this in respect to morals, virtue, and
religion.   Men find that the survey of themselves,
their own heart and temper, their own life and behaviour, doth not afford them satisfaction: things
are not as they should be: therefore they turn
away, will not go over particulars, or look deeper,
lest they should find more amiss.   For who would
choose to be put out of humour with himself?   No
one, surely, if it were not in order to mend, and to
be more thoroughly and better pleased with himself for the future.

[19] If this sincere self-enjoyment and home
satisfaction be thought desirable and worth some
pains and diligence, the following reflections will
I suppose deserve your attention, as what may
be of service and assistance to all who are in any
measure honestly disposed for avoiding that fatal
self-deceit and towards getting acquainted with
themselves.

[20] The *first* is that those who have never had
any suspicion of, who have never made allowances
for, this weakness in themselves, who have never
(if I may be allowed such a manner of speaking)
caught themselves in it, may almost take for granted
that they have been very much misled by it.   For
consider: nothing is more manifest, than that affection and passion of all kinds influence the judgment.   Now as we have naturally a greater regard
to ourselves than to others, as the private affection
is more prevalent than the public, the former will

have proportionally a greater influence upon the
judgment, upon our way of considering things.
People are not backward in owning this partiality
of judgment in cases of friendship and natural relation.   The reason is obvious why it is not so readily
acknowledged when the interest which misleads us
is more confined, confined to ourselves: but we all
take notice of it in each other in these cases.   There
is not any observation more common than that there
is no judging of a matter from hearing only one
side.   This is not founded upon supposition, at
least it is not always, of a formed design in the re-
later to deceive: for it holds in cases, where he ex-
pects that the whole will be told over again by the
other side.   But the supposition which this observation is founded upon, is the very thing now before
us, namely, that men are exceedingly prone to deceive themselves, and judge too favourably in every
respect where themselves and their own interest
are concerned.   Thus though we have not the least
reason to suspect that such an interested person
hath any intention to deceive us, yet we of course
make great allowances for his having deceived himself.   If this be general, almost universal, it is prodigious that every man can think himself an exception, and that he is free from this self-partiality.
The direct contrary is the truth.   Every man may
take for granted that he has a great deal of it till
from the strictest observation upon himself, he finds
particular reason to think otherwise.

[21] *Secondly.*   There is one easy and almost
sure way to avoid being misled by this self-partiality and to get acquainted with our real character:
to have regard to the suspicious part of it, and keep
a steady eye over ourselves in that respect.   Suppose then a man fully satisfied with himself and his

K

own behaviour; such a one, if you please, as the Pharisee in the Gospel, or a better man.—Well; but allowing this good opinion you have of yourself to be true, yet every one is liable to be misrepresented. Suppose then an enemy were to set about defaming you, what part of your character would he single out? What particular scandal, think you, would he be most likely to fix upon you? And what would the world be most ready to believe? There is scarce a man living but could, from the most transient superficial view of himself, answer this question. What is that ill thing, that faulty behaviour, which I am apprehensive an enemy, who was thoroughly acquainted with me, would be most likely to lay to my charge, and which the world would be most apt to believe? It is indeed possible that a man may not be guilty in that respect. All that I say is, let him in plainness and honesty fix upon that part of his character for a particular survey and reflection; and by this he will come to be acquainted, whether he be guilty or innocent in that respect, and how far he is one or the other.

[22] *Thirdly.* It would very much prevent our being misled by this self-partiality, to reduce that practical rule of our Saviour, "Whatsoever ye would that men should do to you, even so do unto them," to our judgment and way of thinking. This rule, you see, consists of two parts. One is, to substitute another for yourself, when you take a survey of any part of your behaviour, or consider what is proper and fit and reasonable for you to do upon any occasion: the other part is, that you substitute yourself in the room of another; consider yourself as the person affected by such a behaviour,

or towards whom such an action is done: and then
you would not only see, but likewise feel, the rea-
sonableness or unreasonableness of such an action
or behaviour. But, alas! the rule itself may be
dishonestly applied: there are persons who have
not impartiality enough with respect to themselves,
nor regard enough for others, to be able to make a
just application of it. This just application, if men
would honestly make it, is in effect all that I have
been recommending; it is the whole thing, the direct contrary to that inward dishonesty as respecting
our intercourse with our fellow-creatures. And
even the bearing this rule in their thoughts may be
of some service; the attempt thus to apply it, is an
attempt towards being fair and impartial, and may
chance unawares to show them to themselves, to
show them the truth of the case they are considering.

[23] Upon the whole it is manifest, that there is
such a thing as this self-partiality and self-deceit;
that in some persons it is to a degree which would
be thought incredible, were not the instances before
our eyes, of which the behaviour of David is perhaps the highest possible one in a single particular
case, for there is not the least appearance, that it
reached his general character: that we are almost
all of us influenced by it in some degree, and in
some respects: that therefore every one ought to
have an eye to and beware of it. And all that I have
further to add upon this subject is, that either there
is a difference between right and wrong, or there
is not: religion is true, or it is not. If it be not,
there is no reason for any concern about it: but if
it be true, it requires real fairness of mind and
honesty of heart. And, if people will be wicked,

they had better of the two be so from the common
vicious passions without such refinements, than
from this deep and calm source of delusion, which
undermines the whole principle of good, darkens
that light, "that candle of the Lord within," which
is to direct our steps, and corrupts conscience, which
is the guide of life.

SERMON XI.

PREACHED ON ADVENT SUNDAY.

" And if there be any other commandment, it is briefly comprehended in this saying, namely, Thou shalt love thy neighbour as thyself."— ROM. xiii. 9.

IT is commonly observed that there is a disposition in men to complain of the viciousness and corruption of the age in which they live as greater than that of former ones; which is usually followed with this further observation, that mankind has been in that respect much the same in all times. Now, not to determine whether this last be not contradicted by the accounts of history, thus much can scarce be doubted, that vice and folly take different turns, and some particular kinds of it are more open and avowed in some ages than in others: and I suppose it may be spoken of as very much the distinction of the present to profess a contracted spirit and greater regards to self-interest than appears to have been done formerly.

Upon this account it seems worth while to inquire whether private interest is likely to be promoted in proportion to the degree in which self-love engrosses us, and prevails over all other principles; or whether the contracted affection may not possibly be so prevalent as to disappoint itself, and even contradict its own end, private good.

[2] And since, further, there is generally thought to be some peculiar kind of contrariety between self-love and the love of our neighbour, between the pursuit of public and of private good; insomuch that when you are recommending one of these, you are supposed to be speaking against the other; and from hence arises a secret prejudice against, and frequently open scorn of, all talk of public spirit, and real good-will to our fellow-creatures; it will be necessary to inquire what respect benevolence hath to self-love, and the pursuit of private interest to the pursuit of public: or whether there be anything of that peculiar inconsistence and contrariety between them, over and above what there is between self-love and other passions and particular affections, and their respective pursuits.

These inquiries, it is hoped, may be favourably attended to, for there shall be all possible concessions made to the favourite passion, which hath so much allowed to it and whose cause is so universally pleaded; it shall be treated with the utmost tenderness and concern for its interests.

[3] In order to do this, as well to determine the forementioned questions, it will be necessary to consider the nature, the object, and end of that self-love, as distinguished from other principles or affections in the mind, and their respective objects.

[4] Every man hath a general desire of his own happiness; and likewise a variety of particular

affections, passions, and appetites to particular external objects. The former proceeds from, or is,
self-love, and seems inseparable from all sensible
creatures, who can reflect upon themselves and
their own interest or happiness, so as to have that
interest an object to their minds: what is to be said
of the latter is, that they proceed from, or together
make up that particular nature, according to which
man is made. The object the former pursues is
somewhat internal, our own happiness, enjoyment,
satisfaction, whether we have, or have not, a distinct
particular perception what it is, or wherein it consists: the objects of the latter are this or that
particular external thing, which the affections tend
towards, and of which it hath always a particular
idea or perception. The principle we call self-love
never seeks anything external for the sake of the
thing, but only as a means of happiness or good ;
particular affections rest in the external things
themselves. One belongs to man as a reasonable
creature reflecting upon his own interest or happiness. The other, though quite distinct from reason,
are as much a part of human nature.

[5] That all particular appetites and passions are
towards external things themselves, distinct from
the pleasure arising from them, is manifested from
hence, that there could not be this pleasure, were
it not for that prior suitableness between the object
and the passion: there could be no enjoyment or
delight from one thing more than another, from
eating food more than from swallowing a stone, if
there were not an affection or appetite to one thing
more than another.

[6] Every particular affection, even the love of
our neighbour, is as really our own affection, as
self-love ; and the pleasure arising from its gratifi-

cation is as much my own pleasure as the pleasure self-love would have from knowing I myself
should be happy some time hence, would be
my own pleasure. And if, because every particular
affection is a man's own, and the pleasure arising
from its gratification his own pleasure or pleasure
to himself, such particular affection must be called
self-love; according to this way of speaking, no
creature whatever can possibly act but merely from
self-love; and every action and every affection
whatever is to be resolved upon this one principle.
But then this is not the language of mankind; or,
if it were, we should want words to express the
difference between the principle of an action proceeding from cool consideration that it will be to
my own advantage, and an action, suppose of revenge or of friendship, by which a man runs upon
certain ruin, to do evil or good to another. It is
manifest the principles of these actions are totally
different, and so want different words to be distinguished by: all that they agree in is, that they
both proceed from, and are done to gratify, an inclination in a man's self. But the principle or inclination in one case is self-love: in the other, hatred
or love of another. There is then a distinction
between the cool principle of self-love, or general
desire of our own happiness, as one part of our
nature and one principle of action, and the particular affections towards particular external objects,
as another part of our nature and another principle
of action. How much soever therefore is to be
allowed to self-love, yet it cannot be allowed to be
the whole of our inward constitution; because, you
see, there are other parts or principles which come
into it.

[7] Further, private happiness or good is all

which self-love can make us desire, or be concerned
about : in having this consists its gratification ; it is
an affection to ourselves, a regard to our own interest, happiness, and private good ; and in the
proportion a man hath this, he is interested or a
lover of himself. Let this be kept in mind, because
there is commonly, as I shall presently have occasion to observe, another sense put upon these
words. On the other hand, particular affections
tend towards particular external things : these are
their objects, having these is their end, in this consists their gratification, no matter whether it be, or
be not, upon the whole, our interest or happiness.
An action done from the former of these principles
is called an interested action : an action proceeding
from any of the latter has its denomination of passionate, ambitious, friendly, revengeful, or any other,
from the particular appetite or affection from which
it proceeds. Thus self-love as one part of human
nature, and the several particular principles as the
other part, are, themselves, their objects and ends,
stated and shown.

[8] From hence it will be easy to see how far,
and in what ways, each of these can contribute and
be subservient to the private good of the individual.
Happiness does not consist in self-love. The desire of happiness is no more the thing itself, than
the desire of riches is the possession or enjoyment
of them. People may love themselves with the
most entire and unbounded affection, and yet be
extremely miserable. Neither can self-love any
way help them out, but by setting them on work to
get rid of the causes of their misery, to gain or make
use of those objects which are by nature adapted to
afford satisfaction. [9] Happiness or satisfaction
consists only in the enjoyment of those objects which

are by nature suited to our several particular appetites, passions, and affections. So that if self-love
wholly engrosses us, and leaves us no room for any
other principle, there can be absolutely no such
thing at all as happiness, or enjoyment of any kind
whatever: since happiness consists in the gratification of particular passions, which supposes the having of them. Self-love then does not constitute *this*
or *that* to be our interest or good; but our interest
or good being constituted by nature and supposed,
self-love only puts us upon obtaining and securing
it. [10] Therefore, if it be possible that self-love
may prevail and exert itself in a degree or manner
which is not subservient to this end, then it will not
follow, that our interests will be promoted in proportion to the degree in which that principle engrosses
us, and prevails over others. Nay, further, the
private and contracted affection, when it is not subservient to this end, private good, may, for anything
that appears, have a direct contrary tendency and
effect. And if we will consider the matter, we shall
see that it often really has. [11] Disengagement is
absolutely necessary to enjoyment: and a person
may have so steady and fixed an eye upon his own
interest, whatever he places it in, as may hinder him
from attending to many gratifications within his
reach, which others have their minds free and open
to.   Over-fondness for a child is not generally
thought to be for its advantage: and, if there be any
guess to be made from appearances, surely that character we call selfish is not the most promising for
happiness. Such a temper may plainly be, and exert
itself in a degree and manner which may give unnecessary and useless solicitude and anxiety, in a
degree and manner which may prevent obtaining
the means and materials of enjoyment, as well as

the making use of them. [12] Immoderate self-love does very ill consult its own interest: and how much soever a paradox it may appear, it is certainly true, that even from self-love we should endeavour to get over all inordinate regard to and consideration of ourselves. Every one of our passions and affections hath its natural stint and bound, which may easily be exceeded; whereas our enjoyments can possibly be but in a determinate measure and degree. Therefore such excess of the affection, since it cannot procure any enjoyment, must in all cases be useless, but is generally attended with inconveniences, and often is downright pain and misery. This holds as much with regard to self-love as to all other affections. The natural degree of it, so far as it sets us on work to gain and make use of the materials of satisfaction, may be to our real advantage; but beyond or besides this, it is in several respects an inconvenience and disadvantage. Thus it appears, that private interest is so far from being likely to be promoted in proportion to the degree in which self-love engrosses us, and prevails over all other principles, that the contracted affection may be so prevalent as to disappoint itself and even contradict its own end, private good.

[13] " But who, except the most sordidly covetous, ever thought there was any rivalship between the love of greatness, honour, power, or between sensual appetites, and self-love ? No, there is a perfect harmony between them. It is by means of these particular appetites and affections that self-love is gratified in enjoyment, happiness, and satisfaction. The competition and rivalship is between self-love and the love of our neighbour. That affection which leads us out of ourselves, makes us regardless of our own interests, and substitutes that of another in its stead."

Whether then there be any peculiar competition and contrariety in this case, shall now be considered.

[14] Self-love and interestedness was stated to consist in or be an affection to ourselves, a regard to our own private good : it is therefore distinct from benevolence, which is an affection to the good of our fellow-creatures. But that benevolence is distinct from, that is, not the same thing with self-love, is no reason for its being looked upon with any peculiar suspicion ; because every principle whatever, by means of which self-love is gratified, is distinct from it : and all things which are distinct from each other are equally so. [15] A man has an affection or aversion to another : that one of these tends to, and is gratified by doing good, that the other tends to, and is gratified by doing harm, does not in the least alter the respect which either one or the other of these inward feelings has to self-love. We use the word *property* so as to exclude any other persons' having an interest in that of which we say a particular man has the property. And we often use the word *selfish* so as to exclude in the same manner all regards to the good of others. But the cases are not parallel : for though that exclusion is really part of the idea of property, yet such positive exclusion, or bringing this peculiar disregard to the good of others into the idea of self-love, is in reality adding to the idea, or changing it from what it was before stated to consist in, namely, in an affection to ourselves.[1] This being the whole idea of self-love, it can no otherwise exclude good-will or love of others, than merely by not including it, no otherwise, than it excludes love of arts or of reputation, or of anything else. Neither on the other hand does benevolence, any more than love of arts or of

[1] Sermon xi. p. 137.

reputation, exclude self-love. Love of our neighbour then has just the same respect to, is no more
distant from self-love, than hatred of our neighbour,
or than love or hatred of anything else. [16] Thus
the principles from which men rush upon certain
ruin for the destruction of an enemy, and for the
preservation of a friend, have the same respect to
the private affection, and are equally interested or
equally disinterested : and it is of no avail, whether
they are said to be one or the other. Therefore to
those who are shocked to hear virtue spoken of as
disinterested, it may be allowed that it is indeed
absurd to speak thus of it, unless hatred, several
particular instances of vice, and all the common
affections and aversions in mankind, are acknowledged to be disinterested too. Is there any less
inconsistence between the love of inanimate things
or of creatures merely sensitive, and self-love, than
between self-love and the love of our neighbour ?
Is desire of and delight in the happiness of another
any more a diminution of self-love, than desire of
and delight in the esteem of another ? They are
both equally desire of and delight in somewhat external to ourselves : either both or neither are so.
The object of self-love is expressed in the term
self; and every appetite of sense and every particular
affection of the heart is equally interested or disinterested, because the objects of them all are equally
self or somewhat else. Whatever ridicule, therefore,
the mention of a disinterested principle or action
may be supposed to lie open to, must, upon the
matter being thus stated, relate to ambition, and
every appetite and particular affection, as much as
to benevolence. And indeed all the ridicule and all
the grave perplexity of which this subject hath had
its full share, is merely from words. The most in-

telligible way of speaking of it seems to be this:
that self-love, and the actions done in consequence
of it (for these will presently appear to be the same
as to this question), are interested; that particular
affections towards external objects, and the actions
done in consequence of those affections, are not so.
But every one is at liberty to use words as he pleases.
All that is here insisted upon is, that ambition,
revenge, benevolence, all particular passions whatever, and the actions they produce, are equally interested or disinterested.

[17] Thus it appears that there is no peculiar
contrariety between self-love and benevolence; no
greater competition between these, than between
any other particular affections and self-love. This
relates to the affections themselves. Let us now see
whether there be any peculiar contrariety between
the respective courses of life which these affections
lead to; whether there be any greater competition
between the pursuit of private and of public good,
than between any other particular pursuits and that
of private good.

[18] There seems no other reason to suspect
that there is any such peculiar contrariety, but only
that the course of action which benevolence leads to,
has a more direct tendency to promote the good of
others, than that course of action which love of reputation, suppose, or any other particular affection
leads to. But that any affection tends to the happiness of another, does not hinder its tending to
one's own happiness too. That others enjoy the
benefit of the air and the light of the sun, does not
hinder but that these are as much one's own private
advantage now, as they would be if we had the property of them exclusive of all others. So a pursuit
which tends to promote the good of another, yet

may have as great tendency to promote private interest, as a pursuit which does not tend to the good of another at all, or which is mischievous to him. All particular affections whatever—resentment, benevolence, love of arts—equally lead to a course of action for their own gratification, *i. e.* the gratification of ourselves; and the gratification of each gives delight: so far, then, it is manifest they have all the same respect to private interest. [19] Now take into consideration further, concerning these three pursuits, that the end of the first is the harm, of the second, the good of another, of the last, somewhat indifferent; and is there any necessity, that these additional considerations should alter the respect, which we before saw these three pursuits had to private interest; or render any one of them less conducive to it, than any other? Thus one man's affection is to honour as his end; in order to obtain which he thinks no pains too great. Suppose another, with such a singularity of mind, as to have the same affection to public good as his end, which he endeavours with the same labour to obtain. In case of success, surely the man of benevolence hath as great enjoyment as the man of ambition—they both equally having the end their affections, in the same degree, tended to: but in case of disappointment the benevolent man has clearly the advantage, since endeavouring to do good considered as a virtuous pursuit, is gratified by its own consciousness, *i. e.* is in a degree its own reward.

[20] And as to these two, or benevolence and any other particular passions whatever, considered in a further view as forming a general temper, which more or less disposes us for enjoyment of all the common blessings of life, distinct from their own gratification: is benevolence less the temper of

tranquillity and freedom than ambition or covetousness? Does the benevolent man appear
less easy with himself from his love to his neighbour? Does he less relish his being? Is there any
peculiar gloom seated on his face? Is his mind
less open to entertainment, to any particular gratification? Nothing is more manifest, than that being
in good humour, which is benevolence whilst it lasts,
is itself the temper of satisfaction and enjoyment.

[21] Suppose then a man sitting down to consider
how he might become most easy to himself, and
attain the greatest pleasure he could, all that which
is his real natural happiness. This can only consist
in the enjoyment of those objects which are by nature adapted to our several faculties. These particular enjoyments make up the sum total of our
happiness, and they are supposed to arise from
riches, honour, and the gratification of sensual appetites. Be it so: yet none profess themselves so
completely happy in these enjoyments, but that there
is room left in the mind for others, if they were
presented to them: nay these, as much as they
engage us, are not thought so high but that human
nature is capable even of greater. [22] Now there
have been persons in all ages, who have professed
that they found satisfaction in the exercise of
charity, in the love of their neighbour, in endeavouring to promote the happiness of all they had to
do with, and in the pursuit of what is just, and
right, and good, as the general bent of their mind
and end of their life; and that doing an action of
baseness or cruelty, would be as great violence to
their self, as much breaking in upon their nature,
as any external force. Persons of this character
would add, if they might be heard, that they consider themselves as acting in the view of an infinite

Being, who is in a much higher sense the object of reverence and of love than all the world besides; and therefore they could have no more enjoyment from a wicked action done under his eye, than the persons to whom they are making their apology could, if all mankind were the spectators of it; and that the satisfaction of approving themselves to his unerring judgment, to whom they thus refer all their actions, is a more continued settled satisfaction than any this world can afford; as also that they have, no less than others, a mind free and open to all the common innocent gratifications of it, such as they are. [23] And if we go no further, does there appear any absurdity in this? Will any one take upon him to say, that a man cannot find his account in this general course of life, as much as in the most unbounded ambition and the excesses of pleasure? Or that such a person has not consulted so well for himself, for the satisfaction and peace of his own mind, as the ambitious or dissolute man? And though the consideration, that God himself will in the end justify their taste and support their cause, is not formally to be insisted upon here; yet thus much comes in, that all enjoyments whatever are much more clear and unmixed from the assurance that they will end well. Is it certain, then, that there is nothing in these pretensions to happiness? especially when there are not wanting persons, who have supported themselves with satisfactions of this kind in sickness, poverty, disgrace, and in the very pangs of death; whereas it is manifest all other enjoyments fail in these circumstances. This surely looks suspicious of having somewhat in it. Self-love, methinks, should be alarmed. May she not possibly pass over greater pleasures, than those she is so wholly taken up with.

L

[24] The short of the matter is no more than this. Happiness consists in the gratification of certain affections, appetites, passions, with objects which are by nature adapted to them. Self-love may indeed set us on work to gratify these; but happiness or enjoyment has no immediate connection with self-love, but arises from such gratification alone. Love of our neighbour is one of those affections. This, considered as *a virtuous principle*, is gratified by a consciousness of endeavouring to promote the good of others; but considered as *a natural affection*, its gratification consists in the actual accomplishment of this endeavour. Now indulgence or gratification of this affection, whether in that consciousness, or this accomplishment, has the same respect to interest, as indulgence of any other affection; they equally proceed from or do not proceed from self-love, they equally include or equally exclude this principle. Thus it appears, that benevolence and the pursuit of public good hath at least as great a respect to self-love and the pursuit of private good, as any other particular passions, and their respective pursuits.

[25] Neither is covetousness, whether as a temper or pursuit, any exception to this. For if by covetousness is meant the desire and pursuit of riches for their own sake, without any regard to or consideration of the uses of them, this hath as little to do with self-love as benevolence hath. But by this word is usually meant, not such madness and total distraction of mind, but immoderate affection to and pursuit of riches as possessions in order to some further end, namely, satisfaction, interest, or good. This therefore is not a particular affection, or particular pursuit, but it is the general principle

of self-love, and the general pursuit of our own
interest; for which reason, the word selfish is by
every one appropriated to this temper and pursuit.
Now as it is ridiculous to assert that self-love and
the love of our neighbour are the same, so neither
is it asserted, that following these different affections
hath the same tendency and respect to our own interest. The comparison is not between self-love
and the love of our neighbour, between pursuit of
our own interest, and the interest of others; but .
between the several particular affections in human
nature towards external objects, as one part of the
comparison, and the one particular affection to the
good of our neighbour, as the other part of it ; and it
has been shown that all these have the same respect
to self-love and private interest.

[26] There is indeed frequently an inconsistence
or interfering between self-love or private interest,
and the several particular appetites, passions, affections, or the pursuits they lead to. But this competition or interfering is merely accidental, and
happens much oftener between pride, revenge,
sensual gratifications, and private interest, than between private interest and benevolence. For nothing
is more common than to see men give themselves up
to a passion or an affection to their known prejudice
and ruin, and in direct contradiction to manifest and
real interest and the loudest calls of self-love:
whereas the seeming competitions and interfering
between benevolence and private interest, relate
much more to the materials or means of enjoyment,
than to enjoyment itself. There is often an interfering in the former when there is none in the
latter. Thus as to riches—so much money as a
man gives away, so much less will remain in his
possession. Here is a real interfering. But though

a man cannot possibly give without lessening his fortune, yet there are multitudes might give without lessening their own enjoyment, because they may have more than they can turn to any real use or advantage to themselves. Thus, the more thought and time any one employs about the interests and good of others, he must necessarily have less to attend to his own; but he may have so ready and large a supply of his own wants, that such thought might be really useless to himself, though of great service and assistance to others.

[27] The general mistake that there is some greater inconsistence between endeavouring to promote the good of another and self-interest, than between self-interest and pursuing anything else, seems, as hath already been hinted, to arise from our notions of property; and to be carried on by this property's being supposed to be itself our happiness or good. People are so very much taken up with this one subject that they seem from it to have formed a general way of thinking which they apply to other things that they have nothing to do with. Hence, in a confused and slight way, it might well be taken for granted, that another's having no interest in an affection (*i. e.* his good not being the object of it) renders, as one may speak, the proprietor's interest in it greater; and that if another had an interest in it, this would render his less, or occasion that such affection could not be so friendly to self-love, or conducive to private good, as an affection or pursuit which has not a regard to the good of another. This, I say, might be taken for granted whilst it was not attended to that the object of every particular affection is equally somewhat external to ourselves; and whether it be the good of another person, or whether it be any other external

thing, makes no alteration with regard to its being one's own affection, and the gratification of one's own private enjoyment. And so far as it is taken for granted that barely having the means and materials of enjoyment is what constitutes interest and happiness ; that our interest or good consists in possessions themselves, in having the property of riches, houses, lands, gardens, not in the enjoyment of them; so far it will even more strongly be taken for granted, in the way already explained, that an affection's conducing to the good of another must even necessarily occasion it to conduce less to private good, if not to be positively detrimental to it. For if property and happiness are one and the same thing, as by increasing the property of another you lessen your own property, so by promoting the happiness of another you must lessen your own happiness. But whatever occasioned the mistake, I hope it has been fully proved to be one, as it has been proved, that there is no peculiar rivalship or competition between self-love and benevolence ; that as there may be a competition between these two, so there may be also between any particular affection whatever and self-love; that every particular affection, benevolence among the rest, is subservient to self-love, by being the instrument of private enjoyment ; and that in one respect benevolence contributes more to private interest, *i. e.*, enjoyment or satisfaction, than any other of the particular common affections, as it is in a degree its own gratification.

[28] And to all these things may be added, that religion, from whence arises our strongest obligation to benevolence, is so far from disowning the principle of self-love, that it often addresses itself to that very principle, and always to the mind in that

state when reason presides: and there can no access be had to the understanding, but by convincing
men, that the course of life we would persuade them
to is not contrary to their interest. It may be
allowed; without any prejudice to the cause of
virtue and religion, that our ideas of happiness and
misery are of all our ideas the nearest and most
important to us; that they will, nay, if you please,
that they ought to prevail over those of order, and
beauty, and harmony, and proportion, if there should
ever be, as it is impossible there ever should be any
inconsistence between them: though these last,
too, as expressing the fitness of actions, are real as
truth itself. Let it be allowed, though virtue or
moral rectitude does indeed consist in affection to
and pursuit of, what is right and good, as such;
yet that when we sit down in a cool hour, we can
neither justify to ourselves this or any other pursuit, till we are convinced that it will be for our
happiness, or at least not contrary to it.

[29] Common reason and humanity will have
some influence upon mankind, whatever becomes
of speculations; but, so far as the interests of virtue
depend upon the theory of it being secured from
open scorn, so far its very being in the world depends upon its appearing to have no contrariety to
private interest and self-love. The foregoing observations, therefore, it is hoped, may have gained
a little ground in favour of the precept before us;
the particular explanation of which shall be the
subject of the next discourse.

[30] I will conclude at present with observing
the peculiar obligation which we are under to
virtue and religion, as enforced in the verses following the text, in the Epistle for the day, from our
Saviour's coming into the world, "The night is

far spent, the day is at hand; let us therefore cast off the works of darkness, and let us put on the armour of light," &c. The meaning and force of which exhortation is, that Christianity lays us under new obligations to a good life, as by it the will of God is more clearly revealed, and as it affords additional motives to the practice of it, over and above those which arise out of the nature of virtue and vice; I might add, as our Saviour has set us a perfect example of goodness in our own nature. Now love and charity is plainly the thing in which he hath placed his religion; in which, therefore, as we have any pretence to the name of Christians, we must place ours. He hath at once enjoined it upon us by way of command with peculiar force, and by his example, as having undertaken the work of our salvation out of pure love and goodwill to mankind. The endeavour to set home this example upon our minds is a very proper employment of this season, which is bringing on the festival of his birth: which as it may teach us many excellent lessons of humility, resignation, and obedience to the will of God, so there is none it recommends with greater authority, force, and advantage, than this of love and charity; since it was "for us men, and for our salvation, that he came down from heaven, and was incarnate, and was made man;" that he might teach us our duty, and more especially that he might enforce the practice of it, reform mankind, and finally bring us to that "eternal salvation," of which "he is the Author to all those that obey him."

SERMON XII.

UPON THE LOVE OF OUR NEIGHBOUR

*" And if there be any other commandment, it is
briefly comprehended in this saying, namely,
Thou shalt love thy neighbour as thyself."*—
ROM. xiii. 9.

HAVING already removed the prejudices
against public spirit, or the love of our
neighbour, on the side of private interest and self-love, I proceed to the
particular explanation of the precept
before us, by showing, Who is our neighbour—In
what sense we are required to love him as ourselves—The influence such love would have upon
our behaviour in life—and, lastly, How this commandment comprehends in it all others.

I. [32] The objects and due extent of this affection will be understood by attending to the nature
of it, and to the nature and circumstances of mankind in this world. The love of our neighbour is
the same with charity, benevolence, or good-will:
it is an affection to the good and happiness of our
fellow-creatures. This implies in it a disposition to
produce happiness: and this is the simple notion of
goodness, which appears so amiable wherever we

meet with it. From hence it is easy to see, that
the perfection of goodness consists in love to the
whole universe. This is the perfection of Almighty
God.

[33] But as man is so much limited in his capacity, as so small a part of the creation comes under
his notice and influence, and as we are not used to
consider things in so general a way ; it is not to be
thought of, that the universe should be the object
of benevolence to such creatures as we are. Thus
in that precept of our Saviour, " Be ye perfect, even
as your Father which is in heaven is perfect "[1] the
perfection of the divine goodness is proposed to
our imitation as it is promiscuous and extends to the
evil as well as the good, not as it is absolutely universal, imitation of it in this respect being plainly
beyond us. The object is too vast. For this reason
moral writers also have substituted a less general
object for our benevolence—mankind.   But this
likewise is an object too general, and very much
out of our view. Therefore persons more practical
have, instead of mankind, put our country; and
this is what we call a public spirit, which in men of
public stations is the character of a patriot. But this
is speaking to the upper part of the world. Kingdoms and governments are large, and the sphere of
action of far the greatest part of mankind is much
narrower than the government they live under ; or,
however, common men do not consider their actions
as affecting the whole community of which they are
members. There plainly is wanting a less general
and nearer object of benevolence for the bulk of
men, than that of their country. Therefore the
Scripture, not being a book of theory and speculation, but a plain rule of life for mankind, has with

[1] Matt. v. 48.

the utmost possible propriety put the principle of virtue upon the love of our *neighbour ;* which is that part of the universe, that part of mankind, that part of our country, which comes under our immediate notice, acquaintance, and influence, and with which we have to do.

This is plainly the true account or reason, why our Saviour places the principle of virtue in the love of our neighbour; and the account itself shows who are comprehended under that relation.

II. [34] Let us now consider in what sense we are commanded to love our neighbour as ourselves.

This precept, in its first delivery by our Saviour, is thus introduced : " Thou shalt love the Lord thy God with all thy heart, with all thy soul, and with all thy strength; and thy neighbour as thyself." These very different manners of expression do not lead our thoughts to the same measure or degree of love, common to both objects; but to one peculiar to each.   Supposing then, which is to be supposed, a distinct meaning and propriety in the words, " as thyself," the precepts we are considering will admit of any of these senses: that we bear the *same kind* of affection to our neighbour, as we do to ourselves; or, that the love we bear to our neighbour should have *some certain proportion or other* to self-love; or, lastly, that it should bear the particular proportion of *equality*, that it be in *the same degree.*

35] First.   The precept may be understood as requiring only, that we have the *same kind* of affection to our fellow-creatures as to ourselves: that, as every man has the principle of self-love, which disposes him to avoid misery and consult his own happiness, so we should cultivate the affection of

good-will to our neighbour, and that it should influence us to have the same kind of regard to him.
This at least must be commanded, and this will not
only prevent our being injurious to him, but will
also put us upon promoting his good. There are
blessings in life, which we share in common with
others; peace, plenty, freedom, healthful seasons.
But real benevolence to our fellow-creatures would
give us the notion of a common interest in a stricter sense, for in the degree we love another, his interests, his joys, and sorrows, are our own. It is
from self-love that we form the notion of private
good, and consider it as our own; love of our neighbour would teach us thus to appropriate to ourselves
his good and welfare, to consider ourselves as having a real share in his happiness. Thus the prin- ·
ciple of benevolence would be an advocate within
our own breasts, to take care of the interests of our
fellow-creatures in all the interfering and competitions which cannot but be, from the imperfection
of our nature, and the state we are in. It would
likewise, in some measure, lessen that interfering,
and hinder men from forming so strong a notion of
private good, exclusive of the good of others, as we
commonly do. Thus, as the private affection
makes us in a particular manner sensible of humanity, justice, or injustice, when exercised towards
ourselves; love of our neighbour would give us the
same kind of sensibility in his behalf. This would
be the greatest security of our uniform obedience to
that most equitable rule: "Whatsoever ye would
that men should do unto you, do ye even so unto
them."

All this indeed is no more than that we should
have a real love to our neighbour: but then, which
is to be observed, the words, *as thyself*, express

this in the most distinct manner, and determine the precept to relate to the affection itself. The advantage which this principle of benevolence has over other remote considerations, is, that it is itself the temper of virtue : and likewise that it is the chief, nay the only effectual security of our performing the several offices of kindness we owe to our fellow-creatures. When from distant considerations men resolve upon anything to which they have no liking, or perhaps an averseness, they are perpetually finding out evasions and excuses, which need never be wanting, if people look for them ; and they equivocate with themselves in the plainest cases in the world. This may be in respect to single determinate acts of virtue, but it comes in much more, where the obligation is to a general course of behaviour, and most of all, if it be such as cannot be reduced to fixed determinate rules. This observation may account for the diversity of expression, in that known passage of the prophet Micah : " to do justly, and to love mercy." A man's heart must be formed to humanity and benevolence, he must " love mercy," otherwise he will not act mercifully in any settled course of behaviour. As consideration of the future sanctions of religion is our only security of persevering in our duty, in cases of great temptations : so to get our heart and temper formed to a love and liking of what is good is absolutely necessary in order to our behaving rightly in the familiar and daily intercourses amongst mankind.

[36] Secondly. The precept before us may be understood to require, that we love our neighbour in some certain *proportion* or other, according as we love ourselves. And indeed a man's character cannot be determined by the love he bears to his neighbour, considered absolutely : but the propor-

tion which this bears to self-love, whether it be attended to or not, is the chief thing which forms the character, and influences the actions. For as the form of the body is a composition of various parts, so likewise our inward structure is not simple or uniform, but a composition of various passions, appetites, affections, together with rationality; including in this last both the discernment of what is right, and a disposition to regulate ourselves by it. There is greater variety of parts in what we call a character, than there are features in a face: and the morality of that is no more determined by one part, than the beauty or deformity of this is by one single feature; each is to be judged of by all the parts or features, not taken singly but together. In the inward frame the various passions, appetites, affections, stand in different respects to each other. The principles in our mind may be contradictory, or checks and allays only, or incentives and assistants to each other. And principles which in their nature have no kind of contrariety or affinity, may yet accidentally be each other's allays or incentives.

[37] From hence it comes to pass, that though we were able to look into the inward contexture of the heart, and see with the greatest exactness in what degree any one principle is in a particular man; we could not from thence determine, how far that principle would go towards forming the character, or what influence it would have upon the actions, unless we could likewise discern what other principles prevailed in him, and see the proportion which that one bears to the others. Thus, though two men should have the affection of compassion in the same degree exactly: yet one may have the principle of resentment, or of ambition so strong in him, as to prevail over that of compassion,

and prevent its having any influence upon his actions; so that he may deserve the character of an hard or cruel man: whereas the other having compassion in just the same degree only, yet having resentment or ambition in a lower degree, his compassion may prevail over them, so as to influence his actions, and to denominate his temper compassionate. So that, how strange soever it may appear to people who do not attend to the thing, yet it is quite manifest, that, when we say one man is more resenting or compassionate than another, this does not necessarily imply that one has the principle of resentment or of compassion stronger than the other. For if the proportion, which resentment or compassion bears to other inward principles, is greater in one than in the other, this is itself sufficient to denominate one more resenting or compassionate than the other.

[38] Further, the whole system, as I may speak, of affections (including rationality), which constitute the heart, as this word is used in Scripture and on moral subjects, are each and all of them stronger in some than in others. Now the proportion which the two general affections, benevolence and self-love, bear to each other, according to this interpretation of the text, denominates men's character as to virtue. Suppose then one man to have the principle of benevolence in a higher degree than another: it will not follow from hence, that his general temper, or character, or actions, will be more benevolent than the other's. For he may have self-love in such a degree as quite to prevail over benevolence, so that it may have no influence at all upon his actions: whereas benevolence in the other person, though in a lower degree, may yet be the strongest principle in his heart, and strong enough

to be the guide of his actions, so as to denominate him a good and virtuous man. The case is here as in scales: it is not one weight, considered in itself, which determines whether the scale shall ascend or descend; but this depends upon the proportion which that one weight hath to the other.

[39] It being thus manifest that the influence which benevolence has upon our actions, and how far it goes towards forming our character, is not determined by the degree itself of this principle in our mind, but by the proportion it has to self-love and other principles: a comparison also being made in the text between self-love and the love of our neighbour: these joint considerations afforded sufficient occasion for treating here of that proportion: it plainly is implied in the precept, though it should be questioned whether it be the exact meaning of the words, *as thyself*.

[40] Love of our neighbour, then, must bear some proportion to self-love, and virtue to be sure consists in the due proportion. What this due proportion is, whether as a principle in the mind, or as exerted in actions, can be judged of only from our nature and condition in this world. Of the degree in which affections and the principles of actions, considered in themselves, prevail, we have no measure: let us then proceed to the course of behaviour, the actions they produce.

[41] Both our nature and condition require, that each particular man should make particular provision for himself: and the inquiry, what proportion benevolence should have to self-love, when brought down to practice, will be, what is a competent care and provision for ourselves. And how certain soever it be, that each man must determine this for himself: and how ridiculous soever it would be, for

any to attempt to determine it for another; yet it
is to be observed, that the proportion is real, and
that a competent provision has a bound, and that it
cannot be all which we can possibly get and keep
within our grasp without legal injustice. Mankind
almost universally bring in vanity, supplies for what
is called a life of pleasure, covetousness, or ima-
ginary notions of superiority over others, to determine this question: but every one who desires to
act a proper part in society, would do well to consider, how far any of them come in to determine it,
in the way of moral consideration. All that can be
said is, supposing, what, as the world goes, is so
much to be supposed that it is scarce to be mentioned, that persons do not neglect what they really
owe to themselves; the more of their care and
thought, and of their fortune, they employ in doing
good to their fellow-creatures, the nearer they
come up to the law of perfection, " Thou shalt love
thy neighbour as thyself."

[42] Thirdly, if the words, *as thyself,* were to be
understood of an equality of affection, it would not
be attended with those consequences which perhaps
may be thought to follow from it. Suppose a person to have the same settled regard to others, as to
himself; that in every deliberate scheme or pursuit
he took their interest into the account in the same
degree as his own, so far as an equality of affection
would produce this; yet it would in fact, and ought
to be, much more taken up and employed about
himself and his own concerns, than about others
and their interests. For besides the one common
affection towards himself and his neighbour, he
would have several other particular affections, passions, appetites, which he could not possibly feel in
common both for himself and others: now these

sensations themselves very much employ us, and
have perhaps as great influence as self-love. So
far indeed as self-love, and cool reflection upon
what is for our interest, would set us on work to
gain a supply of our own several wants, so far the
love of our neighbour would make us do the same
for him: but the degree in which we are put upon
seeking and making use of the means of gratification, by the feeling of those affections, appetites,
and passions, must necessarily be peculiar to ourselves.

That there are particular passions (suppose
shame, resentment) which men seem to have, and
feel in common, both for themselves and others,
makes no alteration in respect to those passions
and appetites which cannot possibly be thus felt in
common.   From hence (and perhaps more things
of the like kind might be mentioned) it follows,
that though there were an equality of affection to
both, yet regard to ourselves would be more prevalent than attention to the concerns of others.

[43] And from moral considerations it ought to
be so, supposing still the equality of affection commanded, because we are in a peculiar manner, as I
may speak, intrusted with ourselves; and therefore
care of our own interests, as well as of our conduct, particularly belongs to us.

[44] To these things must be added, that moral
obligations can extend no further than to natural
possibilities. Now we have a perception of our own
interests, like consciousness of our own existence,
which we always carry about with us, and which, in
its continuation, kind, and degree, seems impossible to be felt in respect to the interests of
others.

[45] From all these things it fully appears, that

M

though we were to love our neighbour in the same degree as we love ourselves, so far as this is possible, yet the care of ourselves, of the individual, would not be neglected; the apprehended danger of which seems to be the only objection against understanding the precept in this strict sense.

III. [46] The general temper of mind which the due love of our neighbour would form us to, and the influence it would have upon our behaviour in life, is now to be considered.

[47] The temper and behaviour of charity is explained at large, in that known passage of St. Paul:[1] "Charity suffereth long, and is kind; charity envieth not; doth not behave itself unseemly, seeketh not her own, thinketh no evil, beareth all things, believeth all things, hopeth all things." As to the meaning of the expressions, "seeketh not her own, thinketh no evil, believeth all things"—however those expressions may be explained away, this meekness, and in some degree easiness of temper, readiness to forego our right for the sake of peace as well as in the way of compassion, freedom from mistrust, and disposition to believe well of our neighbour, this general temper, I say, accompanies, and is plainly the effect of love and good-will. And, though such is the world in which we live that experience and knowledge of it not only may, but must beget in us greater regard to ourselves, and doubtfulness of the characters of others, than is natural to mankind; yet these ought not to be carried further than the nature and course of things make necessary. It is still true, even in the present state of things, bad as it is, that a real good man had rather be deceived than be suspicious; had rather forego his known right, than run

[1] 1 Cor. xiii.

the venture of doing even a hard thing. This is
the general temper of that charity, of which the
Apostle asserts, that if he had it not, giving his
" body to be burned would avail him nothing;" and
which he says " shall never fail."

[48] The happy influence of this temper extends
to every different relation and circumstance in human life. It plainly renders a man better, more to
be desired, as to all the respects and relations we
can stand in to each other. The benevolent man
is disposed to make use of all external advantages
in such a manner as shall contribute to the good of
others, as well as to his own satisfaction. His own
satisfaction consists in this. He will be easy and
kind to his dependents, compassionate to the poor
and distressed, friendly to all with whom he has to
do. This includes the good neighbour, parent,
master, magistrate: and such a behaviour would
plainly make dependence, inferiority, and even ser-
vitude, easy. So that a good or charitable man of
superior rank in wisdom, fortune, authority, is a
common blessing to the place he lives in: happiness grows under his influence. This good principle in inferiors would discover itself in paying
respect, gratitude, obedience, as due. It were
therefore, methinks, one just way of trying one's
own character, to ask ourselves, am I in reality a
better master or servant, a better friend, a better
neighbour, than such and such persons; whom perhaps I may think not to deserve the character of
virtue and religion so much as myself?

[49] And as to the spirit of party, which unhappily prevails amongst mankind, whatever are the
distinctions which serve for a supply to it, some or
other of which have obtained in all ages and countries—one who is thus friendly to his kind will im-

mediately make due allowances for it, as what cannot
but be amongst such creatures as men, in such a
world as this.   And as wrath and fury and over-
bearing upon these occasions proceed, as I may
speak, from men's feeling only on their own side :
so a common feeling for others as well as for ourselves would render us sensible to this truth, which
it is strange can have so little influence ; that we
ourselves differ from others, just as much as they
do from us.   I put the matter in this way, because
it can scarce be expected that the generality of
men should see that those things which are made
the occasions of dissension and fomenting the party-
spirit are really nothing at all : but it may be expected from all people, how much soever they are in
earnest about their respective peculiarities, that humanity and common good-will to their fellow-creatures should moderate and restrain that wretched
spirit.

[50] This good temper of charity likewise would
prevent strife and enmity arising from other occasions : it would prevent our giving just cause of offence, and our taking it without cause.   And in
cases of real injury, a good man will make all the
allowances which are to be made, and, without any
attempts of retaliation, he will only consult his own
and other men's security for the future against injustice and wrong.

IV. [51] I proceed to consider lastly, what is
affirmed of the precept now explained, that it comprehends in it all others ; *i. e.,* that to love our
neighbour as ourselves includes in it all virtues.

Now the way in which every maxim of conduct,
or general speculative assertion, when it is to be
explained at large, should be treated, is, to show
what are the particular truths which were designed

to be comprehended under such a general observation, how far it is strictly true; and then the limitations, restrictions, and exceptions, if there be exceptions, with which it is to be understood. But
it is only the former of these, namely, how far the
assertion in the text holds, and the ground of the
pre-eminence assignéd to the precept of it, which
in strictness comes into our present consideration.

[52] However, in almost everything that is said,
there is somewhat to be understood beyond what
is explicitly laid down, and which we of course
supply; somewhat, I mean, which would not be
commonly called a restriction, or limitation. Thus,
when benevolence is said to be the sum of virtue,
it is not spoken of as a blind propension, but as a
principle in reasonable creatures, and so to be directed by their reason: for reason and reflection
come into our notion of a moral agent. And that
will lead us to consider distant consequences, as
well as the immediate tendency of an action: it
will teach us, that the care of some persons, suppose children and families, is particularly committed
to our charge by Nature and Providence; as also
that there are other circumstances, suppose friendship or former obligations, which require that we
do good to some preferably to others. Reason considered merely as subservient to benevolence, as
assisting to produce the greatest good, will teach
us to have particular regard to these relations and
circumstances; because it is plainly for the good
of the world that they should be regarded. And as
there are numberless cases in which, notwithstanding appearances, we are not competent judges
whether a particular action will upon the whole do
good or harm; reason, in the same way, will teach

us to be cautious how we act in these cases of uncertainty. It will suggest to our consideration
which is the safer side; how liable we are to be
led wrong by passion and private interest; and what
regard is due to laws, and the judgment of mankind. All these things must come into consideration, were it only in order to determine which way of
acting is likely to produce the greatest good. Thus
upon supposition that it were in the strictest sense
true, without limitation, that benevolence includes
in it all virtues; yet reason must come in as its
guide and director, in order to attain its own end,
the end of benevolence, the greatest public good.
Reason then being thus included, let us now consider the truth of the assertion itself.·

[53] First. It is manifest that nothing can be
of consequence to mankind or any creature, but
happiness. This then is all which any person can,
in strictness of speaking, be said to have a right
to. We can therefore "owe no man anything,"
but only to further and promote his happiness, according to our abilities. And therefore a disposition and endeavour to do good to all with whom
we have to do, in the degree and manner which
the different relations we stand in to them require,
is a discharge of all the obligations we are under to
them.

[54] As human nature is not one simple uniform
thing, but a composition of various parts, body,
spirit, appetites, particular passions, and affections,
for each of which reasonable self-love would lead
men to have due regard, and make suitable provision: so society consists of various parts, to which
we stand in different respects and relations, and
just benevolence would as surely lead us to have

due regard to each of these, and behave as the respective relations require. Reasonable good-will and right behaviour towards our fellow-creatures are in a manner the same: only that the former expresseth the principle as it is in the mind; the latter, the principle as it were become external, *i. e.,* exerted in actions.

[55] And so far as temperance, sobriety, and moderation in sensual pleasures, and the contrary vices, have any respect to our fellow-creatures, any influence upon their quiet, welfare, and happiness; as they always have a real, and often a near influence upon it; so far it is manifest those virtues may be produced by the love of our neighbour, and that the contrary vices would be prevented by it. Indeed, if men's regard to themselves will not restrain them from excess, it may be thought little probable, that their love to others will be sufficient; but the reason is, that their love to others is not, any more than their regard to themselves, just, and in its due degree. There are, however, manifest instances of persons kept sober and temperate from regard to their affairs, and the welfare of those who depend upon them. And it is obvious to everyone, that habitual excess, a dissolute course of life, implies a general neglect of the duties we owe towards our friends, our families, and our country.

[56] From hence it is manifest that the common virtues, and the common vices of mankind, may be traced up to benevolence, or the want of it. And this entitles the precept, " Thou shalt love thy neighbour as thyself," to the pre-eminence given to it, and is a justification of the Apostle's assertion, that all other commandments are compre-

hended in it; whatever cautions and restrictions[1]
there are, which might require to be considered,
if we were to state particularly and at length, what
is virtue and right behaviour in mankind. But,
  [57] Secondly. It might be added, that in a

[1] For instance: as we are not competent judges, what is
upon the whole for the good of the world, there may be other
immediate ends appointed us to pursue, besides that one of
doing good, or producing happiness. Though the good of the
creation be the only end of the Author of it, yet he may have
laid us under particular obligations, which we may discern
and feel ourselves under, quite distinct from a perception, that
the observance or violation of them is for the happiness or
misery of our fellow-creatures. (*b.*) And this is in fact the case.
For there are certain dispositions of mind, and certain actions,
which are in themselves approved or disapproved by mankind,
abstracted from the consideration of their tendency to the happiness or misery of the world; approved or disapproved by
reflection, by that principle within, which is the guide of life,
the judge of right and wrong. Numberless instances of this
kind might be mentioned. There are pieces of treachery,
which in themselves appear base and detestable to every one.
There are actions, which perhaps can scarce have any other
general name given them, than indecencies, which yet are
odious and shocking to human nature. There is such a thing
as meanness, a little mind; which as it is quite distinct from
incapacity, so it raises a dislike and disapprobation quite different from that of contempt, which men are too apt to have,
of mere folly. On the other hand, what we call greatness of
mind is the object of another sort of approbation, than superior
understanding. Fidelity, honour, strict justice, are themselves
approved in the highest degree, abstracted from the consideration of their tendency. Now, whether it be thought that
each of these is connected with benevolence in our nature
and so may be considered as the same thing with it; or whether some of them be thought an inferior kind of virtues and
vices, somewhat like natural beauties and deformities; or
lastly, plain exceptions to the general rule; thus much, however, is certain, that the things now instanced in, and numberless others, are approved or disapproved by mankind in
general, in quite another view than as conducive to the happiness or misery of the world.

higher and more general way of consideration, leaving out the particular nature of creatures, and the particular circumstances in which they are placed, benevolence seems in the strictest sense to include in it all that is good and worthy; all that is good, which we have any distinct particular notion of. We have no clear conception of any positive moral attribute in the Supreme Being, but what may be resolved up into goodness. And, if we consider a reasonable creature or moral agent, without regard to the particular relations and circumstances in which he is placed, we cannot conceive anything else to come in towards determining whether he is to be ranked in a higher or lower class of virtuous beings, but the higher or lower degree in which that principle, and what is manifestly connected with it, prevail in him.

[58] That which we more strictly call piety, or the love of God, and which is an essential part of a right temper, some may perhaps imagine no way connected with benevolence: yet surely they must be connected, if there be indeed in being an object infinitely good. Human nature is so constituted, that every good affection implies the love of itself; *i. e.*, becomes the object of a new affection in the same person. Thus, to be righteous, implies in it the love of righteousness; to be benevolent, the love of benevolence; to be good, the love of goodness; whether this righteousness, benevolence, or goodness, be viewed as in our own mind, or in another's; and the love of God as a being perfectly good, is the love of perfect goodness contemplated in a being or person. Thus morality and religion, virtue and piety, will at last necessarily coincide, run up into one and the same point, and love will be in all senses the end of the commandment.

O ALMIGHTY GOD, inspire us with this divine principle; kill in us all the seeds of
envy and ill-will; and help us, by cultivating within ourselves the love of our neighbour, to improve
in the love of thee. Thou hast placed us in various kindreds, friendships, and relations, as the
school of discipline for our affections: help us, by
the due exercise of them, to improve to perfection,
till all partial affection be lost in that entire universal
one, and thou, O God, shalt be all in all.

SERMON XIII.

UPON THE LOVE OF GOD.

" Thou shalt love the Lord thy God with all thy heart, and with all thy soul, and with all thy mind."—MATT. xxii. 37.

EVERYBODY knows, you therefore need only just be put in mind, that there is such a thing, as having so great horror of one extreme, as to run insensibly and of course into the contrary; and that a doctrine's having been a shelter for enthusiasm, or made to serve the purposes of superstition, is no proof of the falsity of it—truth or right being somewhat real in itself, and so not to be judged of by its liableness to abuse, or by its supposed distance from, or nearness to, error. It may be sufficient to have mentioned this in general, without taking notice of the particular extravagances, which have been vented under the pretence or endeavour of explaining the love of God; or how manifestly we are got into the contrary extreme, under the notion of a reasonable religion, so very reasonable as to have nothing to do with the heart and affections, if these words signify anything but the faculty by which we discern speculative truth.

[2] By the love of God, I would understand all those regards, all those affections of mind, which are due immediately to him from such a creature as man, and which rest in him as their end. As this does not include servile fear; so neither will any other regards, how reasonable soever, which respect anything out of or besides the perfection of divine nature, come into consideration here. But all fear is not excluded, because his displeasure is itself the natural proper object of fear. Reverence, ambition of his love and approbation, delight in the hope or consciousness of it, come likewise into this definition of the love of God; because he is the natural object of all those affections or movements of mind, as really as he is the object of the affection, which is in the strictest sense called love; and all of them equally rest in him, as their end. And they may all be understood to be implied in these words of our Saviour, without putting any force upon them, for he is speaking of the love of God and our neighbour, as containing the whole of piety and virtue.

[3] It is plain that the nature of man is so constituted as to feel certain affections, upon the sight or contemplation of certain objects. Now the very notion of affection implies resting in its object as an end. And the particular affection to good characters, reverence and moral love of them, is natural to all those who have any degree of real goodness in themselves. This will be illustrated by the description of a perfect character in a creature, and by considering the manner in which a good man, in his presence, would be affected towards such a

character. He would of course feel the affections of love, reverence, desire of his approbation, delight in the hope or consciousness of it. And surely all this is applicable, and may be brought up to that Being, who is infinitely more than an adequate object of all those affections, whom we are commanded to " love with all our *heart*, with all our *soul*, and with all our *mind.*" And of these regards towards Almighty God, some are more particularly suitable to and becoming so imperfect a creature as man, in this mortal state we are passing through; and some of them, and perhaps other exercises of the mind, will be the employment and happiness of good men in a state of perfection.

[4] This is a general view of what the following discourse will contain. And it is manifest the subject is a real one; there is nothing in it enthusiastical or unreasonable. And if it be indeed at all a subject, it is one of the utmost importance.

[5] As mankind have a faculty by which they discern speculative truth, so we have various affections towards external objects. Understanding and temper, reason and affection, are as distinct ideas, as reason and hunger; and one would think could no more be confounded. It is by reason that we get the ideas of the several objects of our affections: but, in these cases, reason and affection are no more the same, than sight of a particular object and the pleasure or uneasiness consequent thereupon, are the same. Now as reason tends to and rests in the discernment of truth, the object of it; so the very nature of affection consists in tending towards, and resting in, its objects as an end. We do, indeed, often in common language say, that things are loved, desired, esteemed, not for them-

selves, but for somewhat further, somewhat out of
and beyond them: yet, in these cases, whoever
will attend will see, that these things are not in
reality the objects of the affections, *i. e.*, are not
loved, desired, esteemed, but the somewhat further
and beyond them. If we have no affections which
rest in what are called their objects, then what is
called affection, love, desire, hope, in human nature, is only an uneasiness in being at rest; an un-
quiet disposition to action, progress, pursuit, without end or meaning. But if there be any such
thing as delight in the company of one person
rather than of another, whether in the way of friendship, or mirth and entertainment, it is all one, if it
be without respect to fortune, honour, or increasing
our stores of knowledge, or anything beyond the
present time, here is an instance of an affection absolutely resting in its object as its end, and being
gratified in the same way as the appetite of hunger
is satisfied with food. Yet nothing is more common than to hear it asked, what advantage a man
hath in such a course, suppose of study, particular
friendships, or in any other: nothing, I say, is
more common than to hear such a question put in
a way which supposes no gain, advantage, or interest, but as a means to somewhat further: and if
so, then there is no such thing at all as real interest, gain, or advantage. This is the same absurdity with respect to life, as an infinite series of
effects without a cause is, in speculation. The gain,
advantage, or interest, consists in the delight itself,
arising from such a faculty's having its object:
neither is there any such thing as happiness or enjoyment, but what arises from hence. The pleasures of hope and of reflection are not exceptions;
the former being only this happiness anticipated,

the latter the same happiness enjoyed over again after its time. And even the general expectation of future happiness can afford satisfaction, only as it is a present object to the principle of self-love.

[6] It was doubtless intended, that life should be very much a pursuit to the gross of mankind. But this is carried so much further than is reasonable, that what gives immediate satisfaction, *i. e.*, our present interest, is scarce considered as our interest at all. It is inventions, which have only a remote tendency towards enjoyment, perhaps but a remote tendency towards gaining the means only of enjoyment, which are chiefly spoken of as useful to the world. And though this way of thinking were just with respect to the imperfect state we are now in, where we know so little of satisfaction without satiety; yet it must be guarded against, when we are considering the happiness of a state of perfection, which happiness being enjoyment and not hope, must necessarily consist in this, that our affections have their objects, and rest in those objects as an end, *i. e.*, be satisfied with them. This will further appear in the sequel of this discourse.

[7] Of the several affections or inward sensations which particular objects excite in man, there are some the having of which implies the love of them, when they are reflected upon.[1] This cannot be said of all our affections, principles, and motives of action. It were ridiculous to assert, that a man upon reflection hath the same kind of approbation

---

[1] St. Augustin observes, " Amor ipse ordinatè amandus est, quo bene amatur quod amandum est, ut sit in nobis virtus quâ vivitur bene," *i. e.*, " The affection which we rightly have for what is lovely, must (ordinatè) justly, in due manner and proportion, become the object of a new affection, or be itself beloved, in order to our being endued with that virtue which is the principle of a good life."—*Civ. Dei,* l. xv. c. 22.

of the appetite of hunger, or the passion of fear, as he hath of good-will to his fellow-creatures. To be a just, a good, a righteous man, plainly carries with it a peculiar affection to, or love of, justice, goodness, righteousness, when these principles are the object of contemplation. Now if a man approves of, or hath an affection to, any principle in and for itself, incidental things allowed for, it will be the same whether he views it in his own mind, or in another; in himself, or in his neighbour. This is the account of our approbation of, our moral love and affection to, good characters, which cannot but be in those who have any degrees of real goodness in themselves, and who discern and take notice of the same principle in others.

[8] From observation of what passes within ourselves, our own actions, and the behaviour of others, the mind may carry on its reflections as far as it pleases, much beyond what we experience in ourselves, or discern in our fellow-creatures. It may go on, and consider goodness as become a uniform continued principle of action, as conducted by reason, and forming a temper and character absolutely good and perfect, which is in a higher sense excellent, and proportionably the object of love and approbation.

[9] Let us then suppose a creature perfect according to his created nature; let his form be human, and his capacities no more than equal to those of the chief of men: goodness shall be his proper character, with wisdom to direct it, and power within some certain determined sphere of action to exert it; but goodness must be the simple actuating principle within him, this being the moral quality which is amiable, or the immediate object of love, as distinct from other affections of appro-

bation. Here then is a finite object for our mind
to tend towards, to exercise itself upon : a creature,
perfect according to his capacity, fixed, steady,
equally unmoved by weak pity or more weak fury
and resentment ; forming the justest scheme of conduct : going on undisturbed in the execution of it,
through the several methods of severity and reward,
towards his end, namely, the general happiness of
all with whom he hath to do, as in itself right and
valuable. This character, though uniform in itself,
in its principle, yet exerting itself in different ways,
or considered in different views, may by its appearing variety move different affections. Thus, the
severity of justice would not affect us in the same
way as an act of mercy: the adventitious qualities
of wisdom and power may be considered in themselves : and even the strength of mind, which this
immovable goodness supposes, may likewise be
viewed as an object of contemplation, distinct from
the goodness itself. Superior excellence of any
kind, as well as superior wisdom and power, is the
object of awe and reverence to all creatures, whatever their moral character be : but so far as creatures of the lowest rank were good, so far the view
of this character, as simply good, must appear amiable to them, be the object of, or beget love. Further, suppose we were conscious, that this superior
person so far approved of us, that we had nothing
servilely to fear from him ; that he was really our
friend, and kind and good to us in particular, as he
had occasionally intercourse with us : we must be .
other creatures than we are, or we could not but
feel the same *kind* of satisfaction and enjoyment
(whatever would be the *degree* of it) from this
higher acquaintance and friendship, as we feel from
common ones ; the intercourse being real, and the

persons equally present in both cases. We should
have a more ardent desire to be approved by his
better judgment, and a satisfaction in that approbation of the same sort with what would be felt in
respect to common persons, or be wrought in us by
their présence.

[10] Let us now raise the character, and suppose this creature, for we are still going on with
the supposition of a creature, our proper guardian
and governor; that we were in a progress of being
towards somewhat further; and that his scheme of
government was too vast for our capacities to comprehend: remembering still that he is perfectly
good, and our friend as well as our governor. Wisdom, power, goodness, accidentally viewed anywhere, would inspire reverence, awe, love: and as
these affections would be raised in higher or lower
degrees, in proportion as we had occasionally more
or less intercourse with the creature endued with
those qualities; so this further consideration and
knowledge, that he was our proper guardian and
governor, would much more bring these objects
and qualities home to ourselves, teach us they had
a greater respect to us in particular, that we had a
higher interest in that wisdom, and power, and
goodness. We should, with joy, gratitude, reverence, love, trust, and dependence, appropriate the
character, as what we had a right in; and make
our boast in such our relation to it. And the conclusion of the whole would be, that we should refer
ourselves implicitly to him, and cast ourselves entirely upon him. As the whole attention of life
should be to obey his commands, so the highest
enjoyment of it must arise from the contemplation
of this character and our relation to it, from a consciousness of his favour and approbation, and from

the exercise of those affections towards him which
could not but be raised from his presence. A being who hath these attributes, who stands in this
relation, and is thus sensibly present to the mind,
must necessarily be the object of these affections:
there is as real a correspondence between them,
as between the lowest appetite of sense and its
object.

[11] That this being is not a creature, but the
Almighty God, that he is of infinite power, and
wisdom, and goodness, does not render him less
the object of reverence and love, than he would be
if he had those attributes only in a limited degree.
The Being who made us, and upon whom we entirely depend, is the object of some regards. He
hath given us certain affections of mind, which correspond to wisdom, power, goodness, *i. e.*, which
are raised upon view of those qualities. If then he
be really wise, powerful, good, he is the natural
object of those affections, which he has endued us
with and which correspond to those attributes.
That he is infinite in power, perfect in wisdom and
goodness, makes no alteration, but only that he is
the object of those affections raised to the highest
pitch. He is not indeed to be discerned by any of
our senses. " I go forward, but he is not there;
and backward, but I cannot perceive him: on the
left hand, where he doth work, but I cannot behold
him: he hideth himself on the right hand, that I
cannot see him. O that I knew where I might
find him! that I might come even to his seat!" [1]
But is he then afar off? does he not fill heaven and
earth with his presence? The presence of our
fellow-creatures affects our senses, and our senses
give us the knowledge of their presence, which hath

[1] Job xxiii.

different kinds of influence upon us, love, joy, sorrow, restraint, encouragement, reverence. However this influence is not immediately from our senses, but from that knowledge. Thus suppose a person neither to see nor hear another, not to know by any of his senses, but yet certainly to know, that another was with him; this knowledge might, and in many cases would, have one or more of the effects before mentioned. It is therefore not only reasonable, but also natural, to be affected with a presence, though it be not the object of our senses: whether it be, or be not, is merely an accidental circumstance, which needs not come into consideration: it is the certainty that he is with us, and we with him, which hath the influence. We consider persons then as present, not only when they are within reach of our senses, but also when we are assured by any other means that they are within such a nearness; nay, if they are not, we can recall them to our mind, and be moved towards them as present: and must he, who is so much more intimately with us, that "in him we live and move and have our being," be thought too distant to be the object of our affections? We own and feel the force of amiable and worthy qualities in our fellow-creatures: and can we be insensible to the contemplation of perfect goodness? Do we reverence the shadows of greatness here below, are we solicitous about honour and esteem, and the opinion of the world: and shall we not feel the same with respect to him, whose are wisdom and power in their original, who "is the God of judgment, by whom actions are weighed?" Thus love, reverence, desire of esteem, every faculty, every affection, tends towards, and is employed about its respective object in common cases: and must the exercise of them be sus-

pended with regard to him alone, who is an object,
an infinitely more than adequate object, to our most
exalted faculties—him, " of whom, and through
whom, and to whom are all things ?"

[12] As we cannot remove from this earth, or
change our general business on it, so neither can
we alter our real nature. Therefore no exercise of
the mind can be recommended, but only the exercise of those faculties you are conscious of. Religion does not demand new affections, but only claims
the direction of those you already have, those affections you daily feel—though unhappily confined to
objects, not altogether unsuitable, but altogether
unequal to them. We only represent to you the
higher, the adequate objects of those very faculties
and affections. Let the man of ambition go on
still to consider disgrace as the greatest evil; honour as his chief good. But disgrace, in whose
estimation ? Honour, in whose judgment ? This
is the only question. If shame, and delight in esteem, be spoken of as real, as any settled ground
of pain or pleasure ; both these must be in proportion to the supposed wisdom and worth of him, by
whom we are contemned or esteemed. Must it,
then, be thought enthusiastical to speak of a sensibility of this sort, which shall have respect to an
unerring judgment, to infinite wisdom ; when we
are assured this unerring judgment, this infinite
wisdom, does observe upon our actions.

It is the same with respect to the love of God in
the strictest and most confined sense. We only
offer and represent the highest object of an affection, supposed already in your mind. Some degree
of goodness must be previously supposed : this always implies the love of itself, an affection to goodness : the highest, the adequate object of this

affection, is perfect goodness; which, therefore, we
are to "love with all our heart, with all our soul,
and with all our strength."

[13] "Must we then, forgetting our own interest, as it were go out of ourselves, and love God
for his own sake?" No more forget your own interest, no more go out of yourselves, than when
you prefer one place, one prospect, the conversation of one man to that of another. Does not every
affection necessarily imply, that the object of it be
itself loved? If it be not, it is not the object of the
affection. You may and ought if you can, but it is
a great mistake to think you can, love, or fear, or
hate anything, from consideration that such love,
or fear, or hatred may be a means of obtaining
good or avoiding evil. But the question, whether
we *ought* to love God for his sake or for our own,
being a mere mistake in language; the real question, which this is mistaken for, will, I suppose, be
answered by observing, that the goodness of God
already exercised towards us, our present dependence upon him, and our expectation of future benefits, ought, and have a natural tendency, to *beget
in us* the affection of gratitude, and greater love
towards him, than the same goodness exercised towards others: were it only for this reason, that
every affection is moved in proportion to the sense
we have of the object of it; and we cannot but
have a more lively sense of goodness, when exercised towards ourselves, than when exercised towards others. I added expectation of future benefits, because the ground of that expectation is
present goodness.

[14] Thus Almighty God is the natural object of
the several affections, love, reverence, fear, desire
of approbation. For though he is simply one, yet

we cannot but consider him in partial and different
views. He is in himself one uniform being, and for
ever the same without " variableness or shadow of
turning :" but his infinite greatness, his goodness,
his wisdom, are different objects to our mind. To
which is to be added, that from the change in our
characters, together with his unchangeableness, we
cannot but consider ourselves as more or less the
objects of his approbation, and really be so. For
if he approves what is good, he cannot, merely from
the unchangeableness of his nature, approve what is
evil. Hence must arise more various movements
of mind, more different kind of affections. And
this greater variety also is just and reasonable
in such creatures as we are, though it respects a
Being simply one, good, and perfect. As some of
these affections are most particularly suitable to so
imperfect a creature as man, in this mortal state we
are passing through; so there may be other exercises of mind, or some of these in higher degrees,
our enjoyment and happiness in a state of perfection.

SERMON XIV.

ONSIDER then our ignorance, the imperfection of our nature, our virtue, and our condition in this world, with respect to an infinitely good and just Being, our Creator, and Governor; and you will see what religious affections of mind are most particularly suitable to this mortal state we are passing through.

[16] Though we are not affected with anything so strongly, as what we discern with our senses; and though our nature and condition require that we be much taken up about sensible things; yet our reason convinces us that God is present with us, and we see and feel the effects of his goodness: he is therefore the object of some regards. The imperfection of our virtue, joined with the consideration of his absolute rectitude or holiness, will scarce permit that perfection of love which entirely casts out all fear: yet goodness is the object of love to all creatures who have any degree of it themselves; and consciousness of a real endeavour to approve ourselves to him, joined with the consideration of his goodness, as it quite excludes servile dread and horror, so it is plainly a reasonable ground for hope of his favour. Neither fear, nor hope, nor

love, then is excluded: and one or another of these
will prevail, according to the different views we
have of God, and ought to prevail according to the
changes we find in our own character. There is a
temper of mind made up of, or which follows from
all three, fear, hope, love—namely, resignation to
the divine will, which is the general temper belonging to this state, which ought to be the habitual frame
of our mind and heart, and to be exercised at proper
seasons more distinctly in acts of devotion.

[17] Resignation to the will of God is the whole
of piety, it includes in it all that is good, and is a
source of the most settled quiet and composure of
mind. There is the general principle of submission
in our nature. Man is not so constituted as to desire things, and be uneasy in the want of them, in
proportion to their known value: many other considerations come in to determine the degrees of
desire, particularly whether the advantage we take
a view of be within the sphere of our rank. Who
ever felt uneasiness, upon observing any of the advantages brute creatures have over us? And yet
it is plain they have several. It is the same with
respect to advantages belonging to creatures of a
superior order. Thus though we see a thing to be
highly valuable, yet that it does not belong to our
condition of being, is sufficient to suspend our desires after it, to make us rest satisfied without such
advantage. Now there is just the same reason for
quiet resignation in the want of everything equally
unattainable and out of our reach in particular,
though others of our species be possessed of it.
All this may be applied to the whole of life; to positive inconveniences as well as wants; not indeed
to the sensations of pain and sorrow, but to all the
uneasinesses of reflection, murmuring, and discon-

tent. Thus is human nature formed to compliance, yielding, submission of temper. We find the principles of it within us, and every one exercises it towards some objects or other, *i. e.*, feels it with regard to some persons, and some circumstances. Now this is an excellent foundation of a reasonable and religious resignation. Nature teaches and inclines us to take up with our lot: the consideration, that the course of things is unalterable, hath a tendency to quiet the mind under it, to beget a submission of temper to it. But when we can add, that this unalterable course is appointed and continued by infinite wisdom and goodness, how absolute should be our submission, how entire our trust and dependence!

[18] This would reconcile us to our condition; prevent all the supernumerary troubles arising from imagination, distant fears, impatience; all uneasiness, except that which necessarily arises from the calamities themselves we may be under. How many of our cares should we by this means be disburdened of—cares not properly our own, how apt soever they may be to intrude upon us and we to admit them, the anxieties of expectation, solicitude about success and disappointment, which in truth are none of our concern! How open to every gratification would that mind be, which was clear of these incumbrances!

[19] Our resignation to the will of God may be said to be perfect, when our will is lost and resolved up into his; when we rest in his will as our end, as being itself most just, and right, and good. And where is the impossibility of such an affection to what is just, and right, and good, such a loyalty of heart to the Governor of the universe, as shall prevail over all sinister indirect desires of our own!

Neither is this at bottom anything more than faith, and honesty, and fairness of mind—in a more enlarged sense indeed, than those words are commonly used. And as in common cases, fear and hope and other passions are raised in us by their respective objects : so this submission of heart and soul and mind, this religious resignation, would be as naturally produced by our having just conceptions of Almighty God, and a real sense of his presence with us. In how low a degree soever this temper usually prevails amongst men, yet it is a temper right in itself : it is what we owe to our Creator : it is particularly suitable to our mortal condition, and what we should endeavour after for our own sakes in our passage through such a world as this, where there is nothing upon which we can rest or depend, nothing but what we are liable to be deceived and disappointed in. Thus we might " acquaint ourselves with God, and be at peace." This is piety and religion in the strictest sense, considered as an habit of mind—an habitual sense of God's presence with us—being affected towards him, as present, in the manner his superior nature requires from such a creature as man: this is to " walk with God."

[20] Little more need be said of devotion or religious worship, than that it is this temper exerted into act. The nature of it consists in the actual exercise of those affections towards God, which are supposed habitual in good men. He is always equally present with us: but we are so much taken up with sensible things, that " Lo, he goeth by us, and we see him not: he passeth on also, but we perceive him not."[1] Devotion is retirement, from the world he has made, to him alone : it is to withdraw from the avocations of sense, to employ our attention

[1] Job ix. 11.

wholly upon him as upon an object actually present, to yield ourselves up to the influence of the divine presence, and to give full scope to the affections of gratitude, love, reverence, trust and dependence; of which infinite power, wisdom, and goodness, are the natural and only adequate objects. We may apply to the whole of devotion those words of the Son of Sirach, " When you glorify the Lord, exalt him as much as you can, for even yet will he far exceed; and when you exalt him, put forth all your strength and be not weary, for you can never go far enough."[1] Our most raised affections of every kind cannot but fall short and be disproportionate when an infinite Being is the object of them. This is the highest exercise and employment of mind that a creature is capable of. As this divine service and worship is itself absolutely due to God, so also is it necessary, in order to a further end, to keep alive upon our minds a sense of his authority, a sense that in our ordinary behaviour amongst men we act under him as our governor and judge.

Thus you see the temper of mind respecting God, which is particularly suitable to a state of imperfection—to creatures in a progress of being towards somewhat further.

[21] Suppose now this something further attained; that we were arrived at it: what a perception will it be, to see and know and feel that our trust was not vain, our dependence not groundless —that the issue, event, and consummation came out such as fully to justify and answer that resignation? If the obscure view of the divine perfection, which we have in this world, ought in just consequence to beget an entire resignation; what will this resignation be exalted into, when "we shall see

[1] Ecclus. xliii. 30.

face to face, and know as we are known?" If we
cannot form any distinct notion of that perfection of
the love of God, which "casts out all fear"—of that
enjoyment of him, which will be the happiness of
good men hereafter—the consideration of our wants
and capacities of happiness, and that he will be an
adequate supply to them, must serve us instead of
such distinct conception of the particular happiness
itself.

[22] Let us then suppose a man entirely disen-
gaged from business and pleasure, sitting down alone at
leisure, to reflect upon himself and his own condition
of being.   He would immediately feel that he was
by no means complete of himself, but totally insufficient for his own happiness.   One may venture to
affirm, that every man hath felt this, whether he
hath again reflected upon it or not.   It is feeling
this deficiency, that they are unsatisfied with themselves, which makes men look out for assistance
from abroad ; and which has given rise to various
kinds of amusements, altogether needless any otherwise than as they serve to fill up the blank spaces
of time, and so hinder their feeling this deficiency
and being uneasy with themselves.   [23] Now if
these external things we take up with were really
an adequate supply to this deficiency of human
nature, if by their means our capacities and desires were all satisfied and filled up—then it might be
truly said, that we had found out the proper happiness of man ; and so might sit down satisfied, and
be at rest in the enjoyment of it.   But if it appears,
that the amusements, which men usually pass their
time in, are so far from coming up to or answering
our notions and desire of happiness or good, that
they are really no more than what they are commonly
called, somewhat to pass away the time, *i.e.*, that some-

what which serves to turn us aside from, and prevent
our attending to, this our internal poverty and want
—if they serve only, or chiefly, to suspend, instead
of satisfying our conceptions and desires of happiness
—if the want remains, and we have found out little
more than barely the means of making it less
sensible; then are we still to seek for somewhat to
be an adequate supply to it.   It is plain that there
is a capacity in the nature of man, which neither
riches, nor honours, nor sensual gratifications, nor
anything in this world can perfectly fill up, or satisfy:
there is a deeper and more essential want, than any
of these things can be the supply of.   [24] Yet
surely there is a possibility of somewhat, which may
fill up all our capacities of happiness—somewhat in
which our souls may find rest—somewhat, which
may be to us that satisfactory good we are inquiring after.   But it cannot be anything which is
valuable only as it tends to some further end. Those
therefore who have got this world so much into their
hearts, as not to be able to consider happiness as
consisting in anything but property and possessions,
which are only valuable as the means to somewhat
else, cannot have the least glimpse of the subject
before us, which is the end, not the means—the
thing itself, not somewhat in order to it.   [25] But
if you can lay aside that general, confused, undeterminate notion of happiness, as consisting in such
possessions; and fix in your thoughts, that it really
can consist in nothing but in a faculty's having its
proper object; you will clearly see that in the coolest
way of consideration, without either the heat of fanciful
enthusiasm, or the warmth of real devotion, nothing
is more certain than that an infinite Being may himself be, if he please, the supply to all the capacities
of our nature.   All the common enjoyments of life

are from the faculties he hath endued us with, and
the objects he hath made suitable to them.   He
may himself be to us infinitely more than all these :
he may be to us all that we want.   As our understanding can contemplate itself, and our affections be
exercised upon themselves by reflection, so may
each be employed in the same manner upon any
other mind : and since the Supreme Mind, the
Author and Cause of all things, is the highest possible object to himself, he may be an adequate
supply to all the faculties of our souls—a subject to
our understanding, and an object to our affections.

[26] Consider then: when we shall have put off
this mortal body, when we shall be divested of sensual appetites, and those possessions which are now
the means of gratification shall be of no avail—when
this restless scene of business and vain pleasures,
which now diverts us from ourselves, shall be all
over; we, our proper self, shall still remain : we
shall still continue the same creatures we are, with
wants to be supplied, and capacities of happiness.
We must have faculties of perception, though not
sensitive ones ; and pleasures or uneasiness from our
perceptions, as now we have.

[27] There are certain ideas which we express
by the words, order, harmony, proportion, beauty,
the furthest removed from anything sensual.   Now
what is there in those intellectual images, forms, or
ideas, which begets that approbation, love, delight,
and even rapture, which is seen in some persons'
faces upon having those objects present to their
minds?—"Mere enthusiasm !"—Be it what it will:
there are objects, works of nature and of art, which
all mankind have delight from, quite distinct from
their affording gratification to sensual appetites, and
from quite another view of them, than as being for

their interest and further advantage. The faculties from which we are capable of these pleasures, and the pleasures themselves, are as natural, and as much to be accounted for, as any sensual appetite whatever, and the pleasure from its gratification. Words, to be sure, are wanting upon this subject: to say, that everything of grace and beauty throughout the whole of nature, everything excellent and amiable shared in differently lower degrees by the whole creation, meet in the Author and Cause of all things —this is an inadequate, and perhaps improper way of speaking of the divine nature: but it is manifest that absolute rectitude, the perfection of being, must be in all senses, and in every respect, the highest object to the mind.

[28] In this world it is only the *effects* of wisdom, and power, and greatness, which we discern; it is not impossible, that hereafter the *qualities themselves* in the Supreme Being may be the immediate object of contemplation. What amazing wonders are opened to view by late improvements! What an object is the Universe to a creature, if there be a creature who can comprehend its system! But it must be an infinitely higher exercise of the understanding, to view the scheme of it in that mind, which projected it, before its foundations were laid. And surely we have meaning to the words, when we speak of going further and viewing, not only this system in his mind, but the wisdom and intelligence itself from whence it proceeded. The same may be said of power. But since wisdom and power are not God (he is a wise, a powerful *Being*), the divine Nature may therefore be a further object to the understanding. It is nothing to observe that our senses give us but an imperfect knowledge of things: effects themselves, if we knew them thoroughly, would give

us but imperfect notions of wisdom and power;
much less of his Being, in whom they reside. I
am not speaking of any fanciful notion of seeing all
things in God; but only representing to you, how
much an higher object to the understanding an infinite Being himself is, than the things which he has
made: and this is no more than saying that the
Creator is superior to the works of his hands.

[29] This may be illustrated by a low example.
Suppose a machine, the sight of which would raise,
and discoveries in its contrivance gratify, our curiosity: the real delight, in this case, would arise from
its being the effect of skill and contrivance. This
skill in the mind of the artificer would be an higher
object, if we had any senses or ways to discern it.
For, observe, the contemplation of that principle,
faculty, or power which produced any effect, must
be an higher exercise of the understanding, than the
contemplation of the effect itself.   The cause must
be an higher object to the mind than the effect.

[30] But whoever considers distinctly what the
delight of knowledge is, will see reason to be satisfied that it cannot be the chief good of man: all
this, as it is applicable, so it was mentioned with
regard to the attribute of goodness. I say, goodness.
Our being and all our enjoyments are the effects of it:
just men bear its resemblance: but how little do we
know of the original, of what it is in itself? Recall
what was before observed concerning the affection
to moral characters; which, in how low a degree
soever, yet is plainly natural to man, and the most
excellent part of his nature: suppose this improved,
as it may be improved, to any degree whatever, in
the "spirits of just men made perfect," and then
suppose that they had a real view of that "righteousness, which is an everlasting righteousness"—of the

conformity of the divine will to the law of truth, in which the moral attributes of God consist—of that goodness in the sovereign Mind, which gave birth to the universe: add, what will be true of all good men hereafter, a consciousness of having an interest in what they are contemplating; suppose them able to say, "This God is our God for ever and ever"— would they be any longer to seek for what was their chief happiness, their final good? Could the utmost stretch of their capacities look further? Would not infinite perfect goodness be their very end, the last end and object of their affections; beyond which they could neither have nor desire; beyond which they could not form a wish or thought?

[31] Consider wherein that presence of a friend consists, which has often so strong an effect as wholly to possess the mind and entirely suspend all other affections and regards, and which itself affords the highest satisfaction and enjoyment. He is within reach of the senses. Now, as our capacities of perception improve, we shall have, perhaps by some faculty entirely new, a perception of God's presence with us in a nearer and stricter way; since it is certain he is more intimately present with us than anything else can be. Proof of the existence and presence of any being is quite different from the immediate perception, the consciousness of it. What then will be the joy of heart, which his presence, and "the light of his countenance," who is the life of the universe, will inspire good men with, when they shall have a sensation, that he is the sustainer of their being, that they exist in him; when they shall feel his influence to cheer and enliven and support their frame, in a manner of which we have now no conception? He will be in a literal sense "their strength and their portion for ever."

[32] When we speak of things so much above our comprehension as the employment and happiness of a future state, doubtless it behoves us to speak with all modesty and distrust of ourselves. But the Scripture represents the happiness of that state under the notions of "seeing God, seeing him as he is, knowing as we are known, and seeing face to face." These words are not general nor undetermined, but express a particular determinate happiness. And I will be bold to say, that nothing can account for, or come up to these expressions, but only this, that God *himself* will be an object to our faculties, that he *himself* will be our happiness; as distinguished from the enjoyments of the present state, which seem to arise, not immediately from him, but from the objects he has adapted to give us delight.

[33] To conclude: Let us suppose a person tired with care and sorrow and the repetition of vain delights which fill up the round of life; sensible that everything here below in its best estate is altogether vanity. Suppose him to feel that deficiency of human nature, before taken notice of; and to be convinced that God alone was the adequate supply to it. What could be more applicable to a good man in this state of mind, or better express his present wants and distant hopes, his passage through this world as a progress towards a state of perfection, than the following passages in the devotions of the royal prophet? They are plainly in a higher and more proper sense applicable to this, than they could be to anything else. " I have seen an end of all perfection. Whom have I in heaven but thee? And there is none upon earth that I desire in comparison of thee. My flesh and my heart faileth: but God is the strength of my heart, and my portion

for ever.   Like as the hart desireth the water-brooks, so longeth my soul after thee, O God.   My soul is athirst for God, yea, even for the living God: when shall I come to appear before him?   How excellent is thy loving-kindness, O God! and the children of men shall put their trust under the shadow of thy wings.   They shall be satisfied with the plenteousness of thy house: and thou shalt give them drink of thy pleasures, as out of the river. For with thee is the well of life; and in thy light shall we see light.   Blessed is the man whom thou choosest, and receivest unto thee: he shall dwell in thy court, and shall be satisfied with the pleasures of thy house, even of thy holy temple.   Blessed is the people, O Lord, that can rejoice in thee: they shall walk in the light of thy countenance.   Their delight shall be daily in thy name, and in thy right-eousness shall they make their boast.   For thou art the glory of their strength: and in thy loving-kindness they shall be exalted.   As for me, I will behold thy presence in righteousness, and when I awake up after thy likeness, I shall be satisfied with it.   Thou shalt shew me the path of life; in thy presence is the fulness of joy, and at thy right hand there is pleasure for evermore."

SERMON XV.

"*When I applied mine heart to know wisdom, and to
see the business that is done upon the earth: then
I beheld all the work of God, that a man cannot
find out the work that is done under the sun :
because though a man labour to seek it out, yet
he shall not find it ; yea farther, though a wise
man think to know it, yet shall he not be able to
find it.*"—ECCLES. viii. 16, 17.

THE writings of Solomon are very much
taken up with reflections upon human
nature and human life, to which he
hath added, in this book, reflections
upon the constitution of things. And
it is not improbable that the little satisfaction and the
great difficulties he met with in his researches into
the general constitution of nature, might be the
occasion of his confining himself, so much as he
hath done, to life and conduct. However, upon
that joint review he expresses great ignorance of
the works of God, and the method of his providence
in the government of the world ; great labour and
weariness in the search and observation he had employed himself about ; and great disappointment,

pain, and even vexation of mind, upon that which
he had remarked of the appearances of things, and
of what was going forward upon this earth.   This
whole review and inspection, and the result of it,
sorrow, perplexity, a sense of his necessary ignorance, suggest various reflections to his mind.   But,
notwithstanding all this ignorance and dissatisfaction,
there is somewhat upon which he assuredly rests
and depends : somewhat which is the conclusion of
the whole matter, and the only concern of man.
Following this his method and train of reflection,
let us consider—

I. [2] The assertion of the text, the ignorance of
man ; that the wisest and most knowing cannot
comprehend the ways and works of God : and
then—

II. [3] What are the just consequences of this observation and knowledge of our own ignorance, and
the reflections which it leads us to.

I. [4] The wisest and most knowing cannot comprehend the works of God, the methods and designs
of his providence in the creation and government of
the world.

Creation is absolutely and entirely out of our
depth, and beyond the extent of our utmost reach.
And yet it is as certain that God made the world, as
it is certain that effects must have a cause.   It is
indeed in general no more than *effects,* that the
most knowing are acquainted with ; for as to *causes,*
they are as entirely in the dark as the most ignorant.
What are the laws by which matter acts upon matter,
but certain effects, which some, having observed to
be frequently repeated, have reduced to general
rules ?   The real nature and essence of beings likewise is what we are altogether ignorant of.   All
these things are so entirely out of our reach, that we

have not the least glimpse of them. And we know little more of ourselves, than we do of the world about us—how we were made, how our being is continued and preserved, what the faculties of our minds are, and upon what the power of exercising them depends. " I am fearfully and wonderfully made: marvellous are thy works, and that my soul knoweth right well." Our own nature, and the objects we are surrounded with, serve to raise our curiosity; but we are quite out of a condition of satisfying it. Every secret which is disclosed, every discovery which is made, every new effect which is brought to view, serves to convince us of numberless more which remain concealed, and which we had before no suspicion of. And what if we were acquainted with the whole creation, in the same way and as thoroughly as we are with any single object in it? What would all this natural knowledge amount to? It must be a low curiosity indeed which such superficial knowledge could satisfy. On the contrary, would it not serve to convince us of our ignorance still; and to raise our desire of knowing the nature of things themselves, the author, the cause, and the end of them?

[5] As to the government of the world: though from consideration of the final causes which come within our knowledge; of characters, personal merit and demerit; of the favour and disapprobation, which respectively are due and belong to the righteous and the wicked, and which therefore must necessarily be in a mind which sees things as they really are;—though, I say, from hence we may know somewhat concerning the designs of Providence in the government of the world, enough to enforce upon us religion and the practice of virtue: yet, since the monarchy of the universe is a dominion unlimited in extent and

everlasting in duration, the general system of it must necessarily be quite beyond our comprehension: and since there appears such a subordination and reference of the several parts to each other, as to constitute it properly one administration or government, we cannot have a thorough knowledge of any part, without knowing the whole. This surely should convince us that we are much less competent judges of the very small part which comes under our notice in this world than we are apt to imagine. " No heart can think upon these things worthily, and who is able to conceive his way ? It is a tempest which no man can see, for the most part of his works are hid. Who can declare the works of his justice ? for his covenant is afar off, and the trial of all things is in the end :" *i. e.*, The dealings of God with the children of men are not yet completed, and cannot be judged of by that part which is before us. " So that a man cannot say, This is worse than that : for in time they shall be well approved. Thy faithfulness, O Lord, reacheth unto the clouds : thy righteousness standeth like the strong mountains : thy judgments are like the great deep. He hath made everything beautiful in his time : also he hath set the world in their heart ; so that no man can find out the work that God maketh from the beginning to the end." And thus St. Paul concludes a long argument upon the various dispensations of Providence : " O the depth of the riches, both of the wisdom and knowledge of God ! How unsearchable are his judgments, and his ways past finding out ! For who hath known the mind of the Lord ?"

[6] Thus the scheme of Providence, the ways and works of God, are too vast, of too large extent for our capacities. There is, as I may speak, such an expanse of power, and wisdom, and goodness, in

the formation and government of the world, as is too much for us to take in or comprehend.   Power, and wisdom, and goodness, are manifest to us in all those works of God, which come within our view; but there are likewise infinite stores of each poured forth throughout the immensity of the creation, no part of which can be thoroughly understood, without taking in its reference and respect to the whole, and this is what we have not faculties for.

[7] And as the works of God, and his scheme of government, are above our capacities thoroughly to comprehend, so there possibly may be reasons which originally made it fit that many things should be concealed from us, which we have perhaps natural capacities of understanding—many things concerning the designs, methods, and ends of Divine Providence in the government of the world.   There is no manner of absurdity in supposing a veil on purpose drawn over some scenes of infinite power, wisdom, and goodness, the sight of which might some way or other strike us too strongly; or that better ends are designed and served by their being concealed, than could be by their being exposed to our knowledge.   The Almighty may cast clouds and darkness round about him, for reasons and purposes of which we have not the least glimpse or conception.

[8] However, it is surely reasonable, and what might have been expected, that creatures, in some stage of their being, suppose in the infancy of it, should be placed in a state of discipline and improvement, where their patience and submission are to be tried by afflictions, where temptations are to be resisted, and difficulties gone through in the discharge of their duty.   Now if the greatest pleasures and pains of the present life be overcome and suspended,

as they manifestly may, by hope and fear, and other passions and affections; then the evidence of religion, and the sense of the consequences of virtue and vice, might have been such as entirely in all cases to prevail over those afflictions, difficulties and temptations —prevail over them so, as to render them absolutely none at all.   But the very notion itself now mentioned, of a state of discipline and improvement, necessarily excludes such sensible evidence and conviction of religion, and of the consequences of virtue and vice.   Religion consists in submission and resignation to the Divine will.   Our condition in this world is a school of exercise for this temper: and our ignorance, the shallowness of our reason, the temptations, difficulties, afflictions, which we are exposed to, all equally contribute to make it so.   The general observation may be carried on ; and whoever will attend to the thing will plainly see, that less sensible evidence, with less difficulty in practice, is the same, as more sensible evidence, with greater difficulty in · practice.   Therefore difficulties in speculation as much come into the notion of a state of discipline, as difficulties in practice : and so the same reason or account is to be given of both.   Thus, though it is indeed absurd to talk of the greater merit of assent, upon *little or no* evidence, than upon demonstration ; yet the strict discharge of our duty, with *less sensible* evidence, does imply in it a better character, than the same diligence in the discharge of it upon more sensible evidence.   This fully accounts for and explains that assertion of our Saviour, " Blessed are they that have not seen, and yet have believed,"[1] have become Christians and obeyed the Gospel upon less sensible evidence than that which Thomas, to whom he is speaking, insisted upon.

[1] John xx. 29.   ·

[9] But, after all, the same account is to be given why we were placed in these circumstances of ignorance, as why nature has not furnished us with wings; namely, that we were designed to be inhabitants of this earth. I am afraid we think too highly of ourselves; of our rank in the creation, and of what is due to us. What sphere of action, what business, is assigned to man, that he has not capacities and knowledge fully equal to ? It is manifest he has reason, and knowledge, and faculties superior to the business of the present world—faculties which appear superfluous, if we do not take in the respect which they have to somewhat further and beyond it. If to acquire knowledge were our proper end, we should indeed be but poorly provided : but if somewhat else be our business and duty, we may, notwithstanding our ignorance, be well enough furnished for it; and the observation of our ignorance may be of assistance to us in the discharge of it.

II. [10] Let us then consider, what are the consequences of this knowledge and observation of our own ignorance, and the reflection it leads us to.

[11] *First.* We may learn from it, with what temper of mind a man ought to inquire into the subject of religion—namely, with expectation of finding difficulties, and with a disposition to take up and rest satisfied with any evidence whatever, *which is real.*

He should beforehand expect things mysterious, and such as he will not be able thoroughly to comprehend, or go to the bottom of. To expect a distinct comprehensive view of the whole subject, clear of difficulties and objections, is to forget our nature and condition, neither of which admits of such knowledge with respect to any science whatever. And to inquire with this expectation is not to inquire as a man, but as one of another order of creatures.

[12] Due sense of the general ignorance of man would also beget in us a disposition to take up and rest satisfied with any evidence whatever which is real. I mention this as the contrary to a disposition, of which there are not wanting instances, to find fault with and reject evidence, because it is not such as was desired. If a man were to walk by twilight, must he not follow his eyes as much as if it were broad day and clear sunshine? Or if he were obliged to take a journey by night, would he not "give heed to any light shining in the darkness, till the day should break and the day-star arise?" It would not be altogether unnatural for him to reflect how much better it were to have daylight; he might perhaps have great curiosity to see the country round about him; he might lament that the darkness concealed many extended prospects from his eyes, and wish for the sun to draw away the veil: but how ridiculous would it be to reject with scorn and disdain the guidance and direction which that lesser light might afford him, because it was not the sun itself! If the make and constitution of man, the circumstances he is placed in, or the reason of things, affords the least hint or intimation, that virtue is the law he is born under—scepticism itself should lead him to the most strict and inviolable practice of it; that he may not make the dreadful experiment of leaving the course of life marked out for him by nature, whatever that nature be, and entering paths of his own, of which he can know neither the dangers nor the end. For though no danger be seen, yet darkness, ignorance, and blindness are no manner of security.

[13] *Secondly.* Our ignorance is the proper answer to many things, which are called objections against religion, particularly to those which arise from the appearances of evil and irregularity in the constitu-

tion of nature and the government of the world. In all other cases it is thought necessary to be thoroughly acquainted with the whole of a scheme, even one of so narrow a compass as those which are formed by men, in order to judge of the goodness or badness of it : and the most slight and superficial view of any human contrivance comes abundantly nearer to a thorough knowledge of it, than that part which we know of the government of the world, does to the general scheme and system of it—to the whole set of laws by which it is governed. From our ignorance of the constitution of things and the scheme of Providence in the government of the world, from the reference the several parts have to each other and to the whole, and from our not being able to see the end and the whole, it follows, that however perfect things are, they must even necessarily appear to us otherwise less perfect than they are.[1]

---

[1] Suppose some very *complicated piece of work*, some *system* or *constitution*, formed for some *general end*, to which each of the *parts* had a *reference*. The perfection or justness of this work or constitution would consist in the reference and respect which the several parts have to the general design. This reference of parts to the general design may be infinitely various, both in degree and kind. Thus one part may only contribute and be subservient to another, this to a third, and so on through a long series, the last part of which alone may contribute immediately and directly to the general design : or a part may have this distant reference to the general design, and may also contribute immediately to it. For instance, if the general design or end, for which the complicated frame of nature was brought into being, is happiness, whatever affords present satisfaction, and likewise tends to carry on the course of things, hath this double respect to the general design. (*b*) Now suppose a spectator of that work or constitution was in a great measure ignorant of such various reference to the general end, whatever that end be ; and, that upon a very slight and partial view which he had of the work, several things appeared to his eye disproportionate

[14] *Thirdly.* Since the constitution of nature, and the methods and designs of Providence in the government of the world, are above our comprehension, we should acquiesce in, and rest satisfied with, our ignorance, turn our thoughts from that which is above and beyond us, and apply ourselves to that which is level to our capacities, and which is our real business and concern. Knowledge is not our proper happiness. Whoever will in the least attend to the thing will see that it is the gaining, not the having of it, which is the entertainment of the mind. Indeed, if the proper happiness of man consisted in knowledge considered as a possession or treasure, men who are possessed of the largest share would have a very ill time of it; as they would be infinitely more sensible than others of their poverty in this respect. Thus "he who increaseth knowledge would" eminently "increase sorrow." Men of deep research and curious inquiry should just be put in mind not to mistake what they are doing. If their discoveries serve the cause of virtue and religion, in

and wrong, others, just and beautiful: what would he gather from these appearances? He would immediately conclude there was a probability, if he could see the whole reference of the parts appearing wrong in the general design, that this would destroy the appearance of wrongness and disproportion: but there is no probability that the reference would destroy the particular right appearances, though that reference might show the things already appearing just, to be so likewise in a higher degree or another manner. There is a probability that the right appearances were intended: there is no probability that the wrong appearances were. We cannot suspect irregularity and disorder to be designed. The pillars of a building appear beautiful; but their being likewise its support does not destroy that beauty: there still remains a reason to believe that the architect intended the beautiful appearance, after we have found out the reference, support. It would be reasonable for a man of himself to think thus, upon the first piece of architecture he ever saw.

the way of proof, motive to practice, or assistance
in it; or if they tend to render life less unhappy,
and promote its satisfactions—then they are most .
usefully employed: but bringing things to light,
alone and of itself, is of no manner of use, any
otherwise than as entertainment or diversion. Neither
is this at all amiss, if it does not take up the time
which should be employed in better work. [15]
But it is evident that there is another mark set up for
us to aim at—another end appointed us to direct our
lives to—another end, which the most knowing may
fail of, and the most ignorant arrive at. "The secret
things belong unto the Lord our God; but those
things which are revealed belong unto us and to our
children for ever, that we may do all the words of
this law." Which reflection of Moses, put in general
terms, is, that the only knowledge which is of any
avail to us, is that which teaches us our duty or assists
us in the discharge of it. The economy of the
universe, the course of nature, almighty power
exerted in the creation and government of the world,
are out of our reach. What would be the consequence, if we could really get an insight into these
things, is very uncertain; whether it would assist us
in, or divert us from, what we have to do in this present state. If then there be a sphere of knowledge,
of contemplation, and employment, level to our
capacities, and of the utmost importance to us, we
ought surely to apply ourselves with all diligence to
this our proper business, and esteem everything else
nothing, nothing as to us, in comparison of it. Thus
Job, discoursing of natural knowledge, how much it
is above us, and of wisdom in general, says, "God
understandeth the way thereof, and he knoweth the
place thereof. And unto man he said, Behold the
fear of the Lord, that is wisdom, and to depart from

evil is understanding." Other orders of creatures may perhaps be let into the secret councils of Heaven, and have the designs and methods of Providence, in the creation and government of the world, communicated to them: but this does not belong to our rank or condition. "The fear of the Lord, and to depart from evil," is the only wisdom which man should aspire after, as his work and business. The same is said, and with the same connection and context, in the conclusion of the Book of Ecclesiastes. Our ignorance, and the little we can know of other things, afford a reason why we should not perplex ourselves about them; but no way invalidate that which is the "conclusion of the whole matter, Fear God, and keep his commandments; for this is the whole concern of man." So that Socrates was not the first who endeavoured to draw men off from labouring after and laying stress upon other knowledge, in comparison of that which related to morals. Our province is virtue and religion, life and manners—the science of improving the temper and making the heart better. This is the field assigned us to cultivate: how much it has lain neglected is indeed astonishing. Virtue is demonstrably the happiness of man: it consists in good actions, proceeding from a good principle, temper, or heart. Overt acts are entirely in our power. What remains is, that we learn to "keep our heart;" to govern and regulate our passions, mind, affections: that so we may be free from the impotencies of fear, envy, malice, covetousness, ambition; that we may be clear of these, considered as vices seated in the heart, considered as constituting a general wrong temper; from which general wrong frame of mind all the mistaken pursuits and far the greatest part of the unhappiness of life, proceed. He, who should find

out one rule to assist us in this work, would deserve
infinitely better of mankind, than all the improvers
of other knowledge put together.

[16] *Lastly.* Let us adore that infinite wisdom
and power and goodness, which is above our comprehension. "To whom hath the root of wisdom
been revealed? Or who hath known her wise coun-
sels? There is one wise and greatly to be feared;
the Lord sitting upon his throne. He created her,
and saw her, and numbered her, and poured her out
upon all his works." If it be thought a considerable
thing to be acquainted with a few, a very few, of the
effects of infinite power and wisdom, the situation,
bigness, and revolution of some of the heavenly
bodies—what sentiments should our minds be filled
with concerning Him, who appointed to each its
place and measure, and sphere of motion, all which
are kept with the most uniform constancy! "Who
stretched out the heavens, and telleth the number
of the stars, and calleth them all by their names.
Who laid the foundations of the earth, who compre-
hendeth the dust of it in a measure, and weighed
the mountains in scales, and the hills in a balance."
And, when we have recounted all the appearances
which come within our view, we must add, " Lo,
these are part of his ways: but how little a portion
is heard of him! Canst thou by searching find out
God? Canst thou find out the Almighty unto perfection? It is as high as heaven; what canst thou
do? deeper than hell; what canst thou know?"

[17] The conclusion is, that in all lowliness of
mind we set lightly by ourselves: that we form our
temper to an implicit submission to the Divine Majesty; beget within ourselves an absolute resignation
to all the methods of his Providence, in his dealings
with the children of men: that, in the deepest hu-

P

mility of our souls, we prostrate ourselves before him, and join in that celestial song : " Great and marvellous are thy works, Lord God Almighty! just and true are thy ways, thou King of saints ! Who shall not fear thee, O Lord, and glorify thy name ? "

END OF SERMONS AT THE ROLLS.

SIX SERMONS

PREACHED UPON

PUBLIC OCCASIONS.

SERMON I.

PREACHED BEFORE THE INCORPORATED SOCIETY FOR
THE PROPAGATION OF THE GOSPEL IN FOREIGN
PARTS, AT THEIR ANNIVERSARY MEETING IN THE
PARISH CHURCH OF ST. MARY-LE-BOW, ON FRIDAY,
FEBRUARY 16, 1738-9.

*" And this gospel of the kingdom shall be preached
in all the world, for a witness unto all nations."*
—MATT. xxiv. 14.

THE general doctrine of religion, that
all things are under the direction of
one righteous Governor, having been
established by repeated revelations in
the first ages of the world, was left
with the bulk of mankind, to be honestly preserved
pure and entire, or carelessly forgotten, or wilfully corrupted. And though reason, almost intuitively, bare witness to the truth of this moral system of nature, yet it soon appeared, that *they did
not like to retain God in their knowledge,*[1] as to
any purposes of real piety. Natural religion became gradually more and more darkened with superstition, little understood, less regarded in practice ; and the face of it scarce discernible at all, in

[1] Rom. i. 28.

the religious establishments of the most learned,
polite nations. And how much soever could have
been done towards the revival of it by the light of
reason, yet this light could not have discovered,
what so nearly concerned us, that important part in
the scheme of this world, which regards a Mediator; nor how far the settled constitution of its government admitted repentance to be accepted for
remission of sins; after the obscure intimations of
these things, from tradition, were corrupted or forgotten. One people indeed had clearer notices of
them, together with the genuine scheme of natural
religion, preserved in the primitive and subsequent
revelations committed to their trust; and were designed to be a witness of God and a Providence to
the nations around them: but this people also had
corrupted themselves and their religion to the
highest degree, that was consistent with keeping up
the form of it.

In this state of things, when infinite Wisdom saw
proper, the general doctrine of religion was autho-
ritatively republished in its purity; and the particular dispensation of Providence, which this world
is under, manifested to all men, even *the dispensation of the grace of God*[2] towards us, as sinful, lost
creatures, to be recovered by repentance through a
Mediator; who was *to make reconciliation for iniquity, and to bring in everlasting righteousness,*[3]
and at length establish that new state of things foretold by the prophet Daniel, under the character of *a
kingdom, which the God of heaven would set up,
and which should never be destroyed.*[4] This, including a more distinct account of the instituted
means, whereby Christ the Mediator would *gather*

[2] Eph. iii. 2.   [3] Dan. ix. 24.   [4] Dan. ii. 44.

*together in one the children of God, that were scat-
tered abroad,*[5] and conduct them to *the place he
is gone to prepare for them ;*[6] is *the gospel of the
kingdom,*[7] which he here foretells, and elsewhere
commands, should *be preached in all the world, for
a witness unto all nations.* And it *first began to be
spoken by the Lord, and was confirmed unto us by
them that heard him ; God also bearing them witness, both with signs and wonders, and with divers
miracles, and gifts of the Holy Ghost, according to
his own will :*[8] by which means it was spread very
widely among the nations of the world, and became
a witness unto them.*

When thus much was accomplished, as there is
a wonderful uniformity in the conduct of Providence,
Christianity was left with Christians, to be transmitted down pure and genuine, or to be corrupted
and sunk ; in like manner as the religion of nature
had been before left with mankind in general.
There was however this difference, that by an institution of external religion fitted for all men (consisting in a common form of Christian worship,
together with a standing ministry of instruction and
discipline), it pleased God to unite Christians in
communities or visible churches, and all along to
preserve them, over a great part of the world ; and
thus perpetuate a general publication of the gospel.
For these communities, which together make up
the catholic visible church, are, first, the repositories of the written oracles of God ; and, in every
age, have preserved and published them, in every
country, where the profession of Christianity has
obtained. Hence it has come to pass, and it is a

[5] John xi. 52. [6] John xiv. 2, 3.
[7] Matt. iv. 23. [8] Heb. ii. 3, 4.

thing very much to be observed in the appointment
of Providence, that even such of these communities,
as, in a long succession of years, have corrupted
Christianity the most, have yet continually carried,
together with their corruptions, the confutation of
them : for they have everywhere preserved the pure
original standard of it, the Scripture, to which recourse might have been had, both by the deceivers
and the deceived, in every successive age. Secondly,
any particular church, in whatever place established,
is like *a city that is set on a hill, which cannot be
hid,*[9] inviting all who pass by, to enter into it. All
persons, to whom any notices of it come, have, in
scripture language, *the kingdom of God come nigh
unto them.* They are reminded of that religion,
which natural conscience attests the truth of: and
they may, if they will, be instructed in it more distinctly, and likewise in the gracious means, whereby
sinful creatures may obtain eternal life ; that chief
and final good, which all men, in proportion to their
understanding and integrity, even in all ages and
countries of the heathen world, were ever in pursuit
of. And, lastly, out of these churches have all along
gone forth persons, who have preached the gospel
in remote places, with greater or less good effect :
for the establishment of any profession of Christianity, however corrupt, I call a good effect, whilst
accompanied with a continued publication of the
Scripture, notwithstanding it may for some time lie
quite neglected.

From these things, it may be worth observing by
the way, appears the weakness of all pleas for neglecting the public service of the church. For though
a man prays with as much devotion and less inter-

ruption at home, and reads better sermons there, yet that will by no means excuse the neglect of his appointed part in keeping up the profession of Christianity amongst mankind. And this neglect, were it universal, must be the dissolution of the whole visible church, *i. e.* of all Christian communities; and so must prevent those good purposes, which were intended to be answered by them, and which they have, all along, answered over the world. For we see that by their means the event foretold in the text, which began in the preaching of Christ and the apostles, has been carried on, more or less, ever since, and is still carrying on; these being the providential means of its progress. And it is, I suppose, the completion of this event, which St. John had a representation of, under the figure of *an angel flying in the midst of heaven, having the everlasting gospel to preach unto them that dwell on the earth, and to every nation, and kindred, and tongue, and people.*[10]

Our Lord adds in the text, that this should be *for a witness unto them;* for an evidence of their duty, and an admonition to perform it. But what would be the effect, or success of the general preaching of the gospel, is not here mentioned. And therefore the prophecy of the text is not parallel to those others in scripture, which seem to foretell the glorious establishment of Christianity in the last days: nor does it appear that they are coincident; otherwise than as the former of these events must be supposed preparatory to the latter. Nay, it is not said here that *God willeth all men should be saved, and come unto the knowledge of the truth :*[11] though this is the language of scripture elsewhere. The

[10] Rev. xiv. 6.   [11] 1 Tim. ii. 4.

text declares no more, than that it was the appointment of God, in his righteous government over the world, that *the gospel of the kingdom should be preached for a witness unto it.*

The visible constitution and course of nature, the moral law written in our hearts, the positive institutions of religion, and even any memorial of it, are all spoken of in Scripture under this or the like denomination: so are the prophets, apostles, and our Lord himself. They are all *witnesses,* for the most part unregarded witnesses, in behalf of God, to mankind. They inform us of his being and providence, and of the particular dispensation of religion which we are under; and continually remind us of them. And they are equally witnesses of these things, whether we regard them or not. Thus after a declaration, that Ezekiel should be sent with a divine message to the children of Israel, it is added, *and they, whether they will hear, or whether they will forbear (for they are a rebellious house), yet shall know that there hath been a prophet among them.*[12] And our Lord directs the seventy disciples, upon their departure from any city, which refused to receive them, to declare, *Notwithstanding, be ye sure of this, that the kingdom of God is come nigh unto you.*[13] The thing intended in both these passages is that which is expressed in the text by the word *witness.* And all of them together evidently suggest thus much, that the purposes of Providence are carried on, by the preaching of the gospel to those who reject it, as well as to those who embrace it. It is indeed true, *God willeth that all men should be saved:* yet, from the unalterable constitution of his government, the salvation of every man cannot but

[12] Ezek. ii. 5. 7.   [13] Luke x. 11.

depend upon his behaviour, and therefore cannot
but depend upon himself; and is necessarily his
own concern, in a sense, in which it cannot be another's.   All this the scripture declares, in a manner
the most forcible and alarming: *Can a man be pro-*
fitable unto God, as he that is wise may be profitable
unto himself? Is it any pleasure to the Almighty,
that thou art righteous? or is it gain to Him, that
thou makest thy way perfect?[14] *If thou be wise, thou*
shalt be wise for thyself: but if thou scornest, thou
alone shalt bear it.[15] *He that beareth, let him bear;*
and he that forbeareth, let him forbear.[16] And again,
He that hath ears to hear, let him hear: but if any
man be ignorant, i. e. wilfully, *let him be ignorant.*[17]
To the same purpose are those awful words of the
angel, in the person of Him, to whom *all judgment*
is committed:[18] *He that is unjust, let him be unjust*
still: and he which is filthy, let him be filthy still:
and he that is righteous, let him be righteous still:
and he that is holy, let him be holy still.   And be-
hold, I come quickly; and my reward is with me,
to give every man according as his work shall be.[19]
The righteous government of the world must be
carried on; and, of necessity, men shall remain the
subjects of it, by being examples of its mercy or of
its justice. *Life and death are set before them, and*
whether they like shall be given unto them.[20]   They
are to make their choice, and abide by it: but which
soever their choice be, the gospel is equally a *wit-*
ness to them; and the purposes of Providence are
answered by this *witness* of the gospel.

From the foregoing view of things we should be
reminded, that the same reasons which make it our

[14] Job xxii. 2, 3.   [15] Prov. ix. 12.   [16] Ezek. iii. 27.
[17] 1 Cor. xiv. 38.   [18] John v. 22.   [19] Rev. xxii. 11, 12.
[20] Ecclus. xv. 17.

duty to instruct the ignorant in the relation, which
the light of nature shows they stand in to God their
maker, and in the obligations of obedience, resignation, and love to him, which arise out of that relation; make it our duty likewise to instruct them
in all those other relations, which revelation informs
us of, and in the obligations of duty, which arise out
of them.   And the reasons for instructing men in
both these are of the very same kind, as for com-
municating any useful knowledge 'whatever.   God,
if he had so pleased, could indeed miraculously have
revealed every religious truth which concerns mankind, to every individual man; and so he could
have every common truth; and thus have superseded all use of human teaching in either.   Yet he
has not done this: but has appointed, that men
should be instructed by the assistance of their fellow-creatures in both.   Further: though all knowledge from reason is as really from God as revelation is; yet this last is a distinguished favour to us,
and naturally strikes us with the greatest awe, and
carries in it an assurance, that those things which
we are informed of by it are of the utmost importance to us to be informed of.   Revelation therefore,
as it demands to be received with a regard and
reverence peculiar to itself; so it lays us under obligations, of a like peculiar sort, to communicate the
light of it.   Further still: it being an indispensable
law of the gospel, that Christians should unite in
religious communities, and these being intended for
repositories[21] of the written *oracles of God*, for standing memorials of religion to unthinking men, and
for the propagation of it in the world; Christianity
is very particularly to be considered as a trust, de-

[21] Pp. 213, 214.

posited with us in behalf of others, in behalf of mankind, as well as for our own instruction. No one
has a right to be called a Christian, who doth not
do somewhat in his station towards the discharge
of this trust; who doth not, for instance, assist in
keeping up the profession of Christianity where he
lives. And it is an obligation but little more remote, to assist in doing it in our factories abroad;
and in the colonies to which we are related, by
their being peopled from our own mother-country,
and subjects, indeed very necessary ones, to the
same government with ourselves : and nearer yet is
the obligation upon such persons in particular, as
have the intercourse of an advantageous commerce
with them.

Of these our colonies, the slaves ought to be
considered as inferior members, and therefore to be
treated as members of them; and not merely as
cattle or goods, the property of their masters. Nor
can the highest property, possible to be acquired in
these servants, cancel the obligation to take care of
their religious instruction. Despicable as they may
appear in our eyes, they are the creatures of God,
and of the race of mankind, for whom Christ died :
and it is inexcusable to keep them in ignorance of
the end for which they were made, and the means
whereby they may become partakers of the general
redemption. On the contrary, if the necessity of
the case requires, that they may be treated with the
very utmost rigour that humanity will at all permit,
as they certainly are; and, for our advantage, made
as miserable as they well can be in the present
world; this surely heightens our obligation to put
them into as advantageous a situation as we are
able, with regard to another.

The like charity we owe to the natives; owe to

them in a much stricter sense than we are apt to
consider, were it only from neighbourhood, and our
having gotten possessions in their country.   For incidental circumstances of this kind appropriate all
the general obligations of charity to particular persons; and make such and such instances of it the
duty of one man rather than another.   We are most
strictly bound to consider these poor uninformed
creatures, as being in all respects, of one family
with ourselves, the family of mankind; and instruct
them in our *common salvation*:[22] that they may not
pass through this stage of their being like brute
beasts; but be put into a capacity of moral improvements, how low soever they must remain as to
others, and so into a capacity of qualifying themselves for an higher state of life hereafter.

All our affairs should be carried on in the fear of
God, in subserviency to his honour, and the good
of mankind.   And thus navigation and commerce
should be consecrated to the service of religion, by
being made the means of propagating it in every
country with which we have any intercourse.   And
the more widely we endeavour to spread its
light and influence, as the forementioned circumstances, and others of a like kind, open and direct
our way, the more faithful shall we be judged in the
discharge of that trust,[23] which is committed to us
as Christians, when our Lord shall require an account of it.

And it may be some encouragement to cheerful
perseverance in these endeavours to observe, not
only that they are our duty, but also that they seem
the means of carrying on a great scheme of Providence, which shall certainly be accomplished.   For

[22] Jude 3.   [23] P. 219.

the everlasting gospel shall be preached to every nation:[24] *and the kingdoms of this world shall become the kingdoms of our Lord, and of his Christ.*[25]

However, we ought not to be discouraged in this good work, though its future success were less clearly foretold; and though its effect now in reforming mankind appeared to be as little as our adversaries pretend. They indeed, and perhaps some others, seem to require more than either experience or scripture give ground to hope for, in the present course of the world. But the bare establishment of Christianity in any place, even the external form and profession of it, is a very important and valuable effect. It is a serious call upon men to attend to the natural and the revealed doctrine of religion. It is a standing publication of the gospel, and renders it a *witness* to them: and by this means the purposes of Providence are carrying on, with regard to remote ages, as well as to the present. *Cast thy bread upon the waters: for thou shalt find it after many days. In the morning sow thy seed, and in the evening withhold not thine hand: for thou knowest not whether shall prosper, either this or that, or whether they both shall be alike good.*[26] We can look but a very little way into the connections and consequences of things: our duty is to spread the *incorruptible seed* as widely as we can, and leave it to *God to give the increase.*[27] Yet thus much we may be almost assured of, that the gospel, wherever it is planted, will have its genuine effect upon some few; upon more perhaps than are taken notice of in the hurry of the world. There are, at least, a few persons in every country and successive age, scattered

[24] Rev. xiv. 6.   [25] Rev. xi. 15.
[26] Eccles xi. 1, 6.   [27] 1 Cor. iii. 6.

up and down, and mixed among the rest of mankind ; who, not being corrupted past amendment,
but having within them the principles of recovery,
will be brought to a moral and religious sense of
things, by the establishment of Christianity where
they live ; and then will be influenced by the peculiar doctrines of it, in proportion to the integrity
of their minds, and to the clearness, purity, and
evidence, with which it is offered them.   Of these
our Lord speaks in the parable of the sower, as *understanding the word, and bearing fruit, and bringing forth, some an hundredfold, some sixty, some
thirty*.[28]   One might add, that these persons, in
proportion to their influence, do at present better the
state of things : better it even in the civil sense, by
giving some check to that avowed profligateness,
which is a contradiction to all order and government ;
and, if not checked, must be the subversion of it.

These important purposes, which are certainly to
be expected from the good work before us, may
serve to show, how little weight there is in that objection against it, from the want of those miraculous
assistances, with which the first preachers of Christianity proved its truth.   The plain state of the case
is, that the gospel, though it be not in the same degree a *witness* to all, who have it made known to
them ; yet in some degree is so to all.   Miracles to
the spectators of them are intuitive proofs of its
truth : but the bare preaching of it is a serious admonition to all who hear it, to attend to the notices
which God has given of himself by the light of
nature ;   and, if Christianity be preached with its
proper evidence, to submit to its peculiar discipline
and laws; if not, to inquire honestly after its evidence,

[28] Mat. xiii. 23.

in proportion to their capacities. And there are
persons of small capacities for inquiry and examination, who yet are wrought upon by it, to *deny un-
godliness and worldly lusts, and live soberly, righteously, and godly in this present world,*[29] in expectation of a future judgment by Jesus Christ. Nor
can any Christian, who understands his religion,
object, that these persons are Christians without
evidence: for he cannot be ignorant who has declared, that *if any man will do his will, he shall know
of the doctrine, whether it be of God.*[30] And, since
the whole end of Christianity is to influence the
heart and actions, were an unbeliever to object in
that manner, he should be asked, whether he would
think it to the purpose to object against persons of
like capacities, that they are prudent without evidence, when, as is often the case, they are observed
to manage their worldly affairs with discretion.

The design before us being therefore in general
unexceptionably good, it were much to be wished,
that serious men of all denominations would join in
it. And let me add, that the foregoing view of
things affords distinct reasons why they should.
For, first, by so doing, they assist in a work of the
most useful importance, that of spreading over the
world the scripture itself, as a divine revelation: and
it cannot be spread under this character, for a continuance, in any country, unless Christian churches
be supported there ; but will always more or less, so
long as such churches subsist; and therefore their
subsistence ought to be provided for. In the next
place, they should remember, that if Christianity is
to be propagated at all, which they acknowledge it
should, it must be in some particular form of pro-

[29] Titus ii. 12, 13.   [30] John vii. 17.

Q

fession. And though they think ours liable to objections, yet it is possible they themselves may be mistaken: and whether they are or no, the very nature of society requires some compliance with others. And whilst, together with our particular form of Christianity, the confessed standard of Christian religion, the Scripture, is spread; and especially whilst every one is freely allowed to study it, and worship God according to his conscience; the evident tendency is, that genuine Christianity will be understood and prevail. Upon the whole, therefore, these persons would do well to consider, how far they can with reason satisfy themselves in neglecting what is certainly right, on account of what is doubtful, whether it be wrong; and when the right is of so much greater consequence one way, than the supposed wrong can be the other.

To conclude: Atheistical immorality and profaneness, surely, is not better in itself, nor less contrary to the design of revelation, than superstition. Nor is superstition the distinguishing vice of the present age, either at home or abroad. But if our colonies abroad are left without a public religion, and the means of instruction, what can be expected, but that, from living in a continued forgetfulness of God, they will at length cease to believe in him; and so sink into stupid atheism? And there is too apparent danger of the like horrible depravity at home, without the like excuse for it. Indeed amongst creatures naturally formed for religion, yet so much under the powers of imagination, so apt to deceive themselves, and so liable to be deceived by others, as men are; superstition is an evil, which can never be out of sight. But even against this, true religion is a great security; and the only one. True religion takes up that place in the mind, which superstition would usurp, and so leaves little room for it; and likewise lays us under the strongest obligations to oppose it. On the contrary, the danger of superstition cannot but be increased by the prevalence of irreligion: and by its general prevalence, the evil will be unavoidable. For the common people, wanting a religion, will of course take up with almost any superstition, which is thrown in their way: and, in process of time, amidst the infinite vicissitudes of the political world, the leaders of parties will certainly be able to serve themselves of that superstition, whatever it be, which is getting ground; and will not fail to carry it on to the utmost length their occasions require. The general nature of the thing shows this; and history and fact confirm it. But what brings the observation home to ourselves is, that the great superstition of which this nation, in particular, has reason to be afraid, is imminent; and the ways in which we may, very supposably, be overwhelmed by it, obvious. It is therefore wonderful, those people who seem to think there is but one evil in life, that of superstition, should not see, that atheism and profaneness must be the introduction of it. So that in every view of things, and upon all accounts, irreligion is at present our chief danger. Now the several religious associations among us, in which many good men have of late united, appear to be providentially adapted to this present state of the world. And as all good men are equally concerned in promoting the end of them; to do it more effectually, they ought to unite in promoting it: which yet is scarce practicable upon any new models, and quite impossible upon such as every one would think unexceptionable. They ought therefore to come into those already formed to their hands; and even take advantage of any occasion of union, to add

mutual force to each other's endeavours in further-
ing their common end; however they may differ as
to the best means, or anything else subordinate to
it.   Indeed there are well-disposed persons, who
much want to be admonished, how dangerous a
thing it is, to discountenance what is good, because
it is not better; and hinder what they approve, by
raising prejudices against some under-part of it.
Nor can they assist in rectifying what they think
capable of amendment, in the manner of carrying
on these designs, unless they will join in the designs
themselves; which they must acknowledge to be
good and necessary ones.   For what can be called
good and necessary by Christians, if it be not so, to
support Christianity where it must otherwise sink,
and propagate it where it must otherwise be unknown; to restrain abandoned, barefaced vice, by
making useful examples, at least of shame, perhaps
of repentance; and to take care of the education of
such children, as otherwise must be, even educated
in wickedness, and trained up to destruction?   Yet
good men separately can do nothing, proportionable
to what is wanting, in any of these ways; but their
common, united endeavours may do a great deal in
all of them.

And besides the particular purposes, which these
several religious associations serve, the more general ones, which they all serve, ought not to be passed
over.   Everything of this kind is, in some degree, a
safeguard to religion; an obstacle, more or less, in
the way of those who want to have it extirpated out
of the world.   Such societies also contribute more
especially towards keeping up the face of Christianity among ourselves; and by their obtaining here,
the gospel is rendered more and more a *witness* to
us.

And if it were duly attended to, and had its genuine influence upon our minds, there would be no need of persuasions to impart the blessing : nor would the means of doing it be wanting.   Indeed the present income of this Society, which depends upon voluntary contributions, with the most frugal management of it, can in no wise sufficiently answer the bare purposes of our charter : but the nation, or even this opulent city itself, has it in its power to do so very much more, that I fear the mention of it may be thought too severe a reproof, since so little is done.   But if the gospel had its proper influence upon the Christian world in general, as it is the centre of trade and seat of learning, a very few ages, in all probability, would settle Christianity in every country, without miraculous assistances.   For scarce anything else, I am persuaded, would be wanting to effect this, but laying it before men in its divine simplicity, together with an exemplification of it in the lives of Christian nations.   *The unlearned and un-believers, falling down on their faces, would worship God, and report that God is in us of a truth.*[31]

[31] 1 Cor. xiv. 24, 25.

SERMON II.

PREACHED BEFORE THE RIGHT HON. THE LORD
MAYOR, THE COURT OF ALDERMEN, THE SHERIFFS,
AND THE GOVERNORS OF THE SEVERAL HOSPI-
TALS OF THE CITY OF LONDON, AT THE PARISH
CHURCH OF ST. BRIDGET, ON MONDAY IN EASTER
WEEK, 1740.

*" The rich and poor meet together: the Lord is the
maker of them all."*—Prov. xxii. 2.

THE constitution of things being such,
that the labour of one man, or the
united labour of several, is sufficient
to procure more *necessaries* than he
or they stand in need of, which it may
be supposed was, in some degree, the case, even in
the first ages; this immediately gave room for riches
to arise in the world, and for men's acquiring them
by honest means; by diligence, frugality, and prudent management. Thus some would very soon
acquire greater plenty of *necessaries* than they had
occasion for; and others by contrary means, or by
cross accidents, would be in want of them: and he
who should supply their wants would have the property in a proportionable labour of their hands;
which he would scarce fail to make use of, instead
of his own, or perhaps together with them, to pro-

vide future *necessaries* in greater plenty. Riches
then were first bestowed upon the world, as they
are still continued in it, by the blessing of God upon
the industry of men, in the use of their understanding and strength. Riches themselves have always
this source; though the possession of them is con-
veyed to particular persons by different channels.
Yet still, *the hand of the diligent maketh rich,*[1] and,
other circumstances being equal, in proportion to its
diligence.

But to return to the first rich man; whom we
left in possession of dependents, and plenty of *necessaries* for himself and them. A family would not
be long in this state, before *conveniences,* somewhat
ornamental, and for *entertainment,* would be wanted,
looked for, and found out. And, by degrees, these
secondary wants, and inventions for the supply of
them, the fruits of leisure and ease, came to employ much of men's time and labour. Hence *a new
species of riches* came into the world, consisting of
things which it might have done well enough without, yet thought desirable, as affording pleasure to
the imagination or the senses. And these went on
increasing, till, at length, the *superfluities* of life
took in a vastly larger compass of things than the
necessaries of it. Thus luxury made its inroad, and
all the numerous train of evils its attendants; of
which poverty, as bad an one as we may account
it, is far from being the worst. Indeed the hands
of the generality must be employed: and a very
few of them would now be sufficient to provide the
world with necessaries; and therefore the rest of
them must be employed about what may be called
superfluities, which could not be, if these superflui-

[1] Prov. x. 4.

ties were not made use of. Yet the desire of such
things, insensibly, becomes immoderate, and the use
of them, almost of course, degenerates into luxury;
which, in every age, has been the dissipation of
riches, and, in every sense, the ruin of those who
were possessed of them: and therefore cannot be
too much guarded against by all opulent cities.
And as men sink into luxury as much from fashion
as direct inclination, the richer sort together may
easily restrain this vice, in almost what degree they
please: and a few of the chief of them may contribute a great deal towards the restraining it.

It is to be observed further concerning the progress of riches, that had they continued to consist only
in the possession of *the things themselves* which were
necessary, and of *the things themselves* which were,
upon their own account, otherwise desirable; this,
in several respects, must have greatly embarrassed
trade and commerce; and have set bounds to the
increase of riches in all hands, as well as have confined them in the hands of a few.   But, in process
of time, it was agreed to substitute somewhat more
lasting and portable, which should pass everywhere,
in commerce, for real natural riches; as sounds had
before, in language, been substituted for thoughts.
And this general agreement, (by what means soever
it became general) that *money* should answer all
things, together with some other improvements,
gave full scope for riches to increase in the hands of
particular persons, and likewise to circulate into
more hands.   Now this, though it was not the first
origin of covetousness, yet it gives greater scope,
encouragement, and temptation to covetousness than
it had before.   And there is moreover the appearance, that this artificial kind of riches, money, has
begot an artificial kind of passion for them: both

which follies well-disposed persons must, by all
means, endeavour to keep clear of. For indeed *the
love of riches is the root of all evil* :[2] though riches
themselves may be made instrumental in promoting
everything that is good.

The improvement of trade and commerce has
made another change, just hinted at, and I think a
very happy one, in the state of the world, as it has
enlarged the middle rank of people : many of which
are, in good measure, free from the vices of the
highest and the lowest part of mankind. Now these
persons must remember, that whether, in common
language, they do or do not pass under the denomination of rich, yet they really are so, with regard to the indigent and necessitous ; and that considering the great numbers which make up this
middle rank among us, and how much they mix
with the poor, they are able to contribute very
largely to their relief, and have in all respects a very
great influence over them.

You have heard now the origin and progress of what this great city so much abounds
with, riches; as far as I had occasion to speak
of these things. For this brief account of them
has been laid before you for the sake of the
good admonitions it afforded. Nor will the admonitions be thought foreign to the charities, which we
are endeavouring to promote. For these must necessarily be less, and the occasions for them greater,
in proportion as industry should abate, or luxury increase. And the temper of covetousness is, we all
know, directly contrary to that of charity, and eats
out the very heart of it. Then, lastly, there are
good sort of people who really want to be told, that
they are included in the admonitions to be given to

[2] 1 Tim. vi. 10.

the rich, though they do see others richer than themselves.

The ranks of rich and poor being thus formed, they *meet together;* they continue to make up one society.   The mutual want, which they still have of each other, still unites them inseparably.   But they *meet* upon a foot of great inequality.   For, as Solomon expresses it in brief, and with much force, *the rich ruleth over the poor.*[3]   And this their general intercourse, with the superiority on one hand, and dependance on the other, are in no sort accidental, but arise necessarily from a settled providential disposition of things, for their common good. Here then is a real, standing relation between the rich and the poor.   And the former must take care to perform the duties belonging to their part of it, for these chiefly the present occasion leads me to speak to, from regard to Him, who placed them in that relation to the poor, from whence those duties arise, and who *is the Maker of them all.*

What these duties are, will easily be seen, and the obligations to them strongly enforced, by a little further reflection upon both these ranks, and the natural situation which they are in with respect to each other.

The lower rank of mankind go on, for the most part, in some tract of living, into which they got by direction or example ; and to this their understanding and discourse, as well as labour, are greatly confined.   Their opinions of persons and things they take upon trust.   Their behaviour has very little in it original or of home-growth ; very little which may not be traced up to the influence of others, and less which is not capable of being changed by such

[3] Prov. xxii. 7.

influence. Then as God has made plentiful provision for all his creatures, the wants of all, even of
the poorest, might be supplied, so far as it is fit they
should, by a proper distribution of it. This being
the condition of the lower part of mankind, consider
now what influence, as well as power, their superiors
must, from the nature of the case, have over them.
For they can instil instruction, and recommend it in
a peculiar manner by their example, and enforce it
still further with favour and discouragement of
various kinds. And experience shows, that they do
direct and change the course of the world as they
please. Not only the civil welfare, but the morals
and religion of their fellow-creatures, greatly depend
upon them : much more indeed than they would, if
the common people were not greatly wanting to
their duty. All this is evidently true of superiors in
general ; superiors in riches, authority, and understanding, taken together. And need I say how much
of this whole superiority goes along with riches ?
It is no small part of it, which arises out of riches
themselves. In all governments, particularly in our
own, a good share of civil authority accompanies
them. Superior natural understanding may, or may
not : but when it does not, yet riches afford great
opportunities for improvement, and may command
information ; which things together are equivalent
to natural superiority of understanding.

But I am sure you will not think I have been re-
minding you of these advantages of riches in order
to beget in you that complacency and trust in them,
which you find the Scripture everywhere warning
you against. No : the importance of riches, this
their power and influence, affords the most serious
admonition in the world to those who are possessed
of them. For it shows, how very blamable even

their carelessness in the use of that power and influence must be: since it must be blamable in a degree proportionate to the importance of what they
are thus careless about.

But it is not only true, that the rich have the
power of doing a great deal of good, and must be
highly blamable for neglecting to do it: but it is
moreover true, that this power is given them by way
of trust, in order to their keeping down that vice
and misery, with which the lower people would
otherwise be quite overrun. For without instruction, and good influence they, of course, grow rude
and vicious, and reduce themselves to the utmost
distresses; often to very terrible ones without deserving much blame. And to these must be added
their unavoidable distresses, which yet admit of
relief. This their case plainly requires, that some
natural provision should be made for it: as the case
of children does, who, if left to their own ways, would
almost infallibly ruin themselves. Accordingly Providence has made provision for this case of the poor:
not only by forming their minds peculiarly apt to be
influenced by their superiors, and giving those superiors abilities to direct and relieve them; but also
by putting the latter under the care and protection
of the former: for this is plainly done, by means of
that intercourse of various kinds between them, which,
in the natural course of things, is unavoidably necessary. In the primitive ages of the world, the
manner in which *the rich and the poor met together*,
was in families. Rich men had the poor for their
servants: not only a few for the offices about their
persons, and for the care of what we now call domestic affairs; but great numbers also for the keeping
of their cattle, the tillage of their fields, for working
up their wool into furniture and vestments of neces-

sary use as well as ornament, and for preparing them
those many things at home, which now pass through
a multitude of unknown poor hands successively, and
are by them prepared, at a distance, for the use of
the rich. The instruction of these large families,
and the oversight of their morals and religion,
plainly belonged to the heads of them. And that
obvious humanity, which every one feels, must have
induced them to be kind to all whom they found
under their roof, in sickness and old age. In this
state of the world, the relation between the rich and
the poor could not but be universally seen and acknowledged. Now indeed it is less in sight, by
means of artificial methods of carrying on business,
which yet are not blamable. But the relation still
subsists, and the obligations arising out of it; and
cannot but remain the same, whilst the rich have the
same want of the poor, and make the same use of
them, though not so immediately under their eye;
and whilst the instruction and manners, and good or
bad state of the poor, really depend in so great a
degree upon the rich, as all these things evidently
do; partly in their capacity of magistrates, but very
much also in their private capacity. In short, he
who has distributed men into these different ranks,
and at the same time united them into one society,
in such sort as men are united, has, by this constitution of things, formally put the poor under the
superintendency and patronage of the rich. The
rich then are charged, by natural providence, as
much as by revealed appointment, with the care of
the poor: not to maintain them idle; which, were
it possible they could be so maintained, would produce greater mischiefs than those which charity is to
prevent; but to take care, that they maintain themselves by their labour, or in case they cannot, then to

relieve them ; to restrain their vices, and form their
minds to virtue and religion. This is a trust, yet it
is not a burden, but a privilege, annexed to riches.
And if every one discharged his share of the trust
faithfully, whatever be his share of it, the world would
be quite another place from what it is. But that
cannot be, till covetousness, debauchery, and every
vice, be unknown among the rich. Then, and not
before, will the manners of the poor be, in all respects, what they ought to be, and their distresses
find the full relief which they ought to find. And,
as far as things of this sort can be calculated, in proportion to the right behaviour of persons whom God
has placed in the former of these ranks, will be the
right behaviour and good condition of those who are
cast into the latter. Every one of ability then is to
be persuaded to do somewhat towards this, keeping
up a sense of virtue and religion among the poor,
and relieving their wants ; each as much as he can
be persuaded to. Since the generality will not part
with their vices, it were greatly to be wished, they
would bethink themselves, and do what good they
are able, so far only as is consistent with them. A
vicious rich man cannot pass through life without
doing an incredible deal of mischief, were it only by
his example and influence ; besides neglecting the
most important obligations, which arise from his
superior fortune. Yet still, the fewer of them he
neglects, and the less mischief he does, the less
share of the vices and miseries of his inferiors will
lie at his door : the less will be his guilt and punishment. But conscientious persons of this rank must
revolve again and again in their minds, how great
the trust is, which God has annexed to it. They
must each of them consider impartially, what is his
own particular share of that trust; which is de-

termined by his situation, character, and fortune together: and then set himself to be as useful as he can in those particular ways, which he finds thus marked out for him. This is exactly the precept of St. Peter; *As every man hath received the gift, even so minister the same one to another, as good stewards of the manifold grace of God.*[4] And as rich men, by a right direction of their greater capacity, may entitle themselves to a greater reward; so by a wrong direction of it, or even by great negligence, they may become *partakers of other men's sins,*[5] and chargeable with other men's miseries. For if there be at all any measures of proportion, any sort of regularity and order in the administration of things, it is self-evident, that *unto whomsoever much is given, of him shall much be required; and to whom much is committed, of him shall more be demanded.*[6]

But still it is to be remembered, that every man's behaviour is his own concern, for every one must give account of his own works; and that the lower people are very greatly to blame in yielding to any ill influence, particularly following the ill example of their superiors; though these are more to blame in setting them such an example. For, as our Lord declares, in the words immediately preceding those just mentioned, *that servant which knew his lord's will, and prepared not himself, neither did according to his will, shall be beaten with many stripes. But he that knew not, and did commit things worthy of stripes, shall be beaten with few stripes.*[7] Vice is itself of ill-desert, and therefore shall be punished in all: though its ill-desert is greater or less, and so shall be its punishment, in proportion to men's

---

[4] 1 Pet. iv. 10.   [5] 1 Tim. v. 22.
Luke xii. 48.   [7] Luke xii. 47, 48.

knowledge of God and religion : but it is in the most literal sense true, that *be who knew not his lord's will, and committed things worthy of stripes, shall be beaten,* though *with few stripes.* For it being the discernment, that such and such actions are evil, which renders them vicious in him who does them, ignorance of other things, though it may lessen, yet it cannot remit the punishment of such actions in a just administration, because it cannot destroy the guilt of them : much less can corrupt deference and regard to the example of superiors in matters of plain duty and sin have this effect. Indeed the lowest people know very well, that such ill example affords no reason why they should do ill ; but they hope it will be an excuse for them, and thus deceive themselves to their ruin : which is a forcible reason why their superiors should not lay this snare in their way.

All this approves itself to our natural understanding ; though it is by means of Christianity chiefly, that it is thus enforced upon our consciences. And Christianity, as it is more than a dispensation of goodness, in the general notion of goodness, even a dispensation of forgiveness, of mercy and favour, on God's part, does in a peculiar manner heighten our obligations to charity among ourselves. *In this was manifested the love of God towards us,*—that *be sent his Son to be the propitiation for our sins. Beloved, if God so loved us, we ought also to love one another.*[8] With what unanswerable force is that question of our Lord to be applied to every branch of this duty, *Shouldest not thou also have had compassion on thy fellow-servant, even as I had pity on thee ?*[9] And can there be a stronger inducement to endeavour

---

[8] 1 John iv. 9, 10, 11.   [9] Matt. xviii. 33.

the reformation of the world, and bringing it to a
sense of virtue and religion, than the assurance given
us, *that be which converteth a sinner from the error
of his way*, and, in like manner, he also who pre-
venteth a person's being corrupted, by taking care
of his education, *shall save a soul from death, and
hide a multitude of sins ?*[10]

These things lead us to the following observations
on the several charities which are the occasion of
these annual solemnities:

1. What we have to bestow in charity being a
trust, we cannot discharge it faithfully, without taking some care to satisfy ourselves in some degree,
that we bestow it upon the proper objects of charity.
One hears persons complaining, that it is difficult to
distinguish who are such; yet often seeming to forget, that this is a reason for using their best endeavours to do it.   And others make a custom of
giving to idle vagabonds: a kind of charity, very improperly so called, which one really wonders people
can allow themselves in; merely to be relieved from
importunity, or at best, to gratify a false good-
nature.   For they cannot but know, that it is, at
least, very doubtful, whether what they thus give
will not immediately be spent in riot and debauchery.
Or suppose it be not, yet still they know, they do a
great deal of certain mischief, by encouraging this
shameful trade of begging in the streets, and all the
disorders which accompany it.   But the charities
towards which I now ask your assistance, as they are
always open, so every one may contribute to them
with full assurance, that he bestows upon proper
objects, and in general that he does vastly more
good, than by equal sums given separately to particular persons.   For that these charities really have

[10] James v. 20.

R

these advantages, has been fully made out, by some
who have gone before me in the duty I am discharging, and by the reports annually published at this
time.

[*Here the Report annexed was read.*] [11]

Let us thank God for these charities, in behalf of
the poor ; and also on our own behalf, as they give
us such clear opportunities of doing good.   Indeed
without them, vice and misery, of which there is
still so much, would abound so much more in this
populous city, as to render it scarce an habitable
place.

2. Amongst the peculiar advantages of public
charities above private ones, is also to be mentioned,
that they are examples of great influence.   They
serve for perpetual memorials of what I have been
observing, of the relation which subsists between the
rich and the poor, and the duties which arise out of
it.   They are standing admonitions to all within
sight or hearing of them, to *go and do likewise.*[12]
Educating poor children in virtue and religion, relieving the sick, and correcting offenders in order to
their amendment, are, in themselves, some of the
very best of good works.   These charities would
indeed be the glory of your city, though their influence were confined to it.   But important as they
are in themselves, their importance still increases,
by their being examples to the rest of the nation ;
which, in process of time, of course copies after the

[11] [The report consisted of a statement of the number of
children and grown persons educated, assisted, and maintained by the horpitals under the care of the Lord Mayor and
Corporation ; these were Christ's Hospital, St. Bartholomew's,
St. Thomas's, Bridewell, Bethlem, and the London Work-
house.]

[12] Luke x. 37.

metropolis. It has indeed already imitated every one of these charities; for of late, the most difficult and expensive of them, hospitals for the sick and wounded, have been established; some within your sight, others in remote parts of the kingdom. You will give me leave to mention particularly that[13] in its second trading city: which is conducted with such disinterested fidelity and prudence, as I dare venture to compare with yours. Again, there are particular persons very blamably unactive and careless, yet not without good dispositions, who, by these charities, are reminded of their duty, and *provoked to love and to good works*.[14] And let me add, though one is sorry any should want so slight a reason for contributing to the most excellent designs, yet if any are supposed to do so merely of course, because they see others do it, still they help to support these monuments of charity, which are a continued admonition to the rich, and relief to the poor: and herein all good men *rejoice*, as St. Paul speaks of himself in a like case, *yea, and will rejoice*.[15]

3. As all human schemes admit of improvement,

[13] As it is of very particular benefit to those who ought always to be looked upon with particular favour by us, I mean our seamen; so likewise it is of very extensive benefit to the large tracts of country west and north of it. Then the medicinal waters near the city render it a still more proper situation for an infirmary. And so likewise doth its neighbourhood to the Bath hospital. For it may well be supposed, that some poor objects will be sent thither in hopes of relief from the Bath waters, whose case may afterwards be found to require the assistance of physic or surgery: and on the other hand, that some may be sent to our infirmary for help from those arts, whose case may be found to require the Bath waters. So that if I am not greatly partial, the Bristol infirmary as much deserves encouragement as any charitable foundation in the kingdom.

[14] Heb. x. 24.   [15] Phil. i. 18.

all public charities, methinks, should be considered
as standing open to proposals for it; that the whole
plan of them, in all its parts, may be brought to as
great perfection as is possible. Now it should seem,
that employing some share of the children's time in
easy labour, suitable to their age, which is done in
some of our charity-schools, might be done in most
others of them, with very good effect; as it is in
all those of a neighbouring kingdom. Then as the
only purposes of punishments less than capital are
to reform the offenders themselves, and warn the
innocent by their example, every thing which should
contribute to make this kind of punishments
answer these purposes better than it does, would be
a great improvement. And whether it be not a
thing practicable, and what would contribute somewhat towards it, to exclude utterly all sorts of revel-
mirth from places where offenders are confined, to
separate the young from the old, and force them
both, in solitude, with labour and low diet, to make
the experiment, how far their natural strength of
mind can support them under guilt and shame and
poverty; this may deserve consideration. Then
again, some religious instruction particularly adapted to their condition would as properly accompany
those punishments which are intended to reform, as
it does capital ones. God forbid that I should be
understood to discourage the provision which is
made for it in this latter case: I heartily wish it
were better than it is; especially since it may well
be supposed, as the state of religion is at present
among us, that some condemned malefactors may
have never had the doctrine of the gospel enforced
upon their consciences. But since it must be acknowledged of greater consequence, in a religious
as well as civil respect, how persons live, than how

they die; it cannot but be even more incumbent on us to endeavour, in all ways, to reclaim those offenders who are to return again into the world, than those who are to be removed out of it: and the only effectual means of reclaiming them, is to instil into them a principle of religion. If persons of authority and influence would take things of this and a like kind under their consideration, they might perhaps still improve those charities; which are already, I truly believe, under a better management than any other of so large a compass in the world. But,

4. With regard to the two particular branches of them last mentioned, I would observe, that our laws and whole constitution, civil and ecclesiastical, go more upon supposition of an equality amongst mankind, than the constitution and laws of other countries. Now this plainly requires that more particular regard should be had to the education of the lower people here, than in places where they are born slaves of power, and to be made slaves of superstition. It is, I suppose, acknowledged, that they have greater liberty here, than they have any where else in the world. But unless care be taken for giving them some inward principle, to prevent their abusing this greater liberty which is their birthright, can we expect it will prove a blessing to them? or will they not in all probability become more dissolute, or more wild and extravagant, whatever wrong turn they happen to take, than people of the same rank in other countries?

5. Let me again remind you of the additional reason, which persons of fortune have to take particular care of their whole behaviour, that it be in all respects good and exemplary, upon account of the influence which it will have upon the manners of their inferiors. And pray observe how strictly

this is connected with the occasion of our present
meeting; how much your good behaviour in private
life will contribute to promote the good design of all
these charities; and how much the contrary would
tend to defeat it, and even to produce the evils
which they are intended to prevent or to remedy.
Whatever care be taken in the education of these
poor children at school, there is always danger of
their being corrupted, when they come from it. And
this danger is greater, in proportion to the greater
wickedness of the age they are to pass through.
But if, upon their coming abroad into the world,
they find the principles of virtue and religion recommended by the example of their superiors, and vice
and irreligion really discountenanced, this will confirm them in the good principles in which they have
been brought up, and give the best ground to hope
they will never depart from them. And the like is
to be said of offenders, who may have had a sense of
virtue and religion wrought in them, under the discipline of labour and confinement. Again: dissolute
and debauched persons of fortune greatly increase
the general corruption of manners; and this is what
increases want and misery of all kinds. So that they
may contribute largely to any or all of these charities, and yet undo but a very small part of the mischief which they do, by their example, as well as in
other ways. But still the mischief which they do,
suppose by their example, is an additional reason
why they should contribute to them; even in justice
to particular persons, in whose ruin they may have
an unknown share of guilt; or however in justice to
society in general; for which they will deserve commendation, how blamable soever they are for the
other. And indeed amidst the dark prospect before
us, from that profligateness of manners, and scorn of

religion, which so generally abound, this good spirit of charity to the poor discovering itself in so great a degree, upon these occasions, and likewise in the late necessitous time, even amongst persons far from being blameless in other respects; this cannot but afford hopes, that we are not given over by Providence, and also that they themselves will at length consider, and not go on contributing, by the example of their vices, to the introduction of that distress, which they so commendably relieve by their liberality.

To conclude : let our charity towards men be exalted into piety towards God, from the serious consideration, that we are all his creatures ; consideration which enforces that duty upon our consciences, as we have any regard to him. This kind of abjuration, and a most solemn one it is, one often hears profaned by a very unworthy sort of people, when they ask relief *for God's sake*. But surely the principle itself, which contains in it every thing great and just and good, is grievously forgotten among us. To relieve the poor *for God's sake*, is to do it in conformity to the order of nature, and to his will, and his example, who is the Author and Governor of it ; and in thankful remembrance, that all we have is from his bounty. It is to do it in his behalf, and as to him. *For he that hath pity upon the poor lendeth unto the Lord* ;[16] and our Saviour has declared, that he will take as given to himself, what is given in a well-chosen charity.[16] Lastly, it is to do it under a sense of the account which will be required of what is committed to our trust, when *the rich and poor*, who *meet* here upon terms of so great inequality, shall *meet* hereafter upon a level, before Him who *is the Maker of them all*.

[16] Prov. xix. 17.   [17] Matt. xxv. 40.

SERMON III.

PREACHED BEFORE THE HOUSE OF LORDS, IN THE
ABBEY-CHURCH OF WESTMINSTER, ON FRIDAY,
JANUARY 30, 1740-41, BEING THE DAY APPOINTED
TO BE OBSERVED AS THE DAY OF THE MARTYRDOM
OF KING CHARLES I.

*And not using your liberty for a cloak of malicious-
ness, but as the servants of God.*—1 Peter ii. 16.

AN history so full of important and interesting events as that which this
day recalls annually to our thoughts,
cannot but afford them very different
subjects for their most serious and
useful employment. But there seems none which
it more naturally leads us to consider than that of
hypocrisy, as it sets before us so many examples of
it ; or which will yield us more practical instruction,
as these examples so forcibly admonish us, not only
to be upon our guard against the pernicious effects of
this vice in others, but also to watch over our own
hearts, against everything of the like kind in ourselves : for hypocrisy, in the moral and religious
consideration of things, is of much larger extent
than every one may imagine.

In common language, which is formed upon the

common intercourses amongst men, hypocrisy signifies little more than their pretending what they
really do not mean, in order to delude one another.
But in scripture, which treats chiefly of our behaviour towards God and our own consciences, it
signifies, not only the endeavour to delude our
fellow-creatures, but likewise insincerity towards
him, and towards ourselves. And therefore, according to the whole analogy of scripture language,
to use liberty as a cloak of maliciousness,[1] must be

[1] The hypocrisy laid to the charge of the Pharisees and Sad-
ducees, in Matt. xvi. at the beginning, and in Luke xii. 54, is
determinately this, that their vicious passions blinded them so
as to prevent their discerning the evidence of our Saviour's mission; though no more understanding was necessary to discern
it, than what they had, and made use of in common matters.
Here they are called hypocrites merely upon account of their
insincerity towards God and their own consciences, and not at
all on account of any insincerity towards men. This last indeed is included in that general hypocrisy, which, throughout
the gospels, is represented as their distinguished character; but
the former is as much included. For they were not men, who,
without any belief at all of religion, put on the appearance of
it only in order to deceive the world: on the contrary, they
believed their religion, and were zealous in it. But their religion, which they believed, and were zealous in, was in its nature hypocritical: for it was the form, not the reality; it
allowed them immoral practices; and indeed was itself in some
respects immoral, as they indulged their pride and uncharitable-
ness under the notion of zeal for it. See Jer. ix. 6. Psalm
lxxviii. 36. Job iii. 19. and Matt. xv. 7—14. and xxiii. 13, 16,
19, 24, 26. where *hypocrite* and *blind* are used promiscuously.
Again, the Scripture speaks of the *deceitfulness of sin,* and its
deceiving those who are guilty of it; Heb. iii. 13. Eph. iv.
22. Rom. vii. 11: of men's acting as if they could *deceive and
mock God;* Isa. xxix. 15. Acts v. 3. Gal. vi. 7: of their *blind-
ing their own eyes;* Matt. xiii. 15. Acts xxviii. 27: and *deceiving themselves;* which is quite a different thing from being
deceived; 1 Cor. iii. 18. 1 John i. 8. Galatians vi. 3. James
i. 22, 26. Many more coincident passages might be mentioned: but I will add only one. In 2 Thess. ii. it is foretold,

understood to mean, not only endeavouring to impose upon others, by indulging wayward passions, or carrying on indirect designs, under pretences of it; but also excusing and palliating such things to ourselves; serving ourselves of such pretences to quiet our own minds in anything which is wrong.

Liberty in the writings of the New Testament, for the most part, signifies, being delivered from the bondage of the ceremonial law; or of sin and the devil, which St. Paul calls *the glorious liberty of the children of God.*[2] This last is a progressive state: and the perfection of it, whether attainable in this world or not, consists in that *perfect love,*[3] which St. John speaks of; and which, as it implies an entire

that by means of some *force,* some *energy of delusion,* men should believe *the lie* which is there treated of: this *force of delusion* is not anything without them, but somewhat within them, which it is expressly said they should bring upon themselves, by *not receiving the love of the truth, but having pleasure in unrighteousness.* Answering to all this is that very remarkable passage of our Lord, Matt. vi. 22, 23. Luke xi. 34, 35, and that admonition repeated fourteen times in the New Testament, *He that hath ears to hear, let him hear.* And the ground of this whole manner of considering things; for it is not to be spoken of as only a peculiar kind of phraseology, but is a most accurate and strictly just manner of considering characters and moral conduct; the ground of it, I say, is, that when persons will not be influenced by such evidence in religion as they act upon in the daily course of life, or when their notions of religion (and I might add of virtue) are in any sort reconcilable with what is vicious, it is some faulty negligence or prejudice which thus deludes them; in very different ways, perhaps, and very different degrees. But when any one is thus deluded through his own fault, in whatever way or degree it is, he deludes himself. And this is as properly hypocrisy towards himself, as deluding the world is hypocrisy towards the world: and he who is guilty of it acts as if he could deceive and mock God; and therefore is an hypocrite towards Him, in as strict and literal a sense as the nature of the subject will admit.

[2] Rom. viii. 21.   [3] 1 John iv. 18.

coincidence of our wills with the will of God, must be a state of the most absolute freedom, in the most literal and proper sense. But whatever St. Peter distinctly meant by this word, *liberty,* the text gives occasion to consider any kind of it, which is liable to the abuse he here warns us against. However, it appears that he meant to comprehend that liberty, were it more or less, which they to whom he was writing enjoyed under civil government: for of civil government he is speaking just before and afterwards: *Submit yourselves to every ordinance of man for the Lord's sake: whether it be to the king, as supreme ; or unto governors, as unto them that are sent by him.* For so it is the will of God, that *with well-doing,* of which dutiful behaviour towards authority is a very material instance, *ye may put to silence the ignorance of foolish men :* as free, perhaps in distinction from the servile state, of which he speaks afterwards, *and not using your liberty for a cloak of maliciousness,* of anything wrong, for so the word signifies; and therefore comprehends petulance, affectation of popularity, with any other like frivolous turn of mind, as well as the more hateful and dangerous passions such as malice, or ambition; for all of which *liberty* may equally be *used as a cloak.* The apostle adds, *but as the servants of God: as free—but as his servants,* who requires dutiful submission to *every ordinance of man,* to his magistracy; and to whom we are accountable for our manner of using the liberty we enjoy under it; as well as for all other parts of our behaviour. *Not using your liberty as a cloak of maliciousness, but as the servants of God.*

Here are three things offered to our consideration:

1 Pet. ii. 13—15.   5 Ver. 16.

First, A general supposition, that what is wrong cannot be avowed in its proper colours, but stands in need of some *cloak* to be thrown over it: secondly, A particular one, that there is danger, some singular danger, of liberty's being made use of for this purpose: lastly, An admonition not to make this ill use of our liberty, *but* to use it *as the servants of God.*

I. Here is a general supposition, that what is wrong cannot be avowed in its proper colours, but stands in need of some *cloak* to be thrown over it. God has constituted our nature, and the nature of society, after such a manner, that, generally speaking, men cannot encourage or support themselves in wickedness upon the foot of there being no difference between right and wrong, or by a direct avowal of wrong; but by disguising it, and endeavouring to spread over it some colours of right. And they do this in every capacity and every respect, in which there is a right or a wrong. They do it, not only as social creatures under civil government, but also as moral agents under the government of God; in one case to make a proper figure in the world, and delude their fellow-creatures; in the other to keep peace within themselves, and delude their own consciences. And the delusion in both cases being voluntary, is, in scripture, called by one name, and spoken against in the same manner: though doubtless they are much more explicit with themselves, and more distinctly conscious of what they are about, in one case than in the other.

The fundamental laws of all governments are virtuous ones, prohibiting treachery, injustice, cruelty: and the law of reputation enforces those civil laws, by rendering these vices every where infamous, and the contrary virtues honourable and of good report.

Thus far the constitution of society is visibly moral: and hence it is, that men cannot live in it without taking care to cover those vices when they have them, and make some profession of the opposite virtues, fidelity, justice, kind regard to others, when they have them not: but especially is this necessary in order to disguise and colour over indirect purposes, which require the concurrence of several persons.

Now all false pretences of this kind are to be called hypocritical, as being contrary to simplicity; though not always designed, properly speaking, to beget a false belief. For it is to be observed, that they are often made without any formal intention to have them believed, or to have it thought that there is any reality under these pretences. Many examples occur of verbal professions of fidelity, justice, public regards, in cases where there could be no imagination of their being believed. And what other account can be given of these merely verbal professions, but that they were thought the proper language for the public ear; and made in business for the very same kind of reasons as civility is kept up in conversation?

These false professions of virtue, which men have, in all ages, found it necessary to make their appearance with abroad, must have been originally taken up in order to deceive in the proper sense: then they became habitual, and often intended merely by way of form: yet often still, to serve their original purpose of deceiving.

There is doubtless amongst mankind a great deal of this hypocrisy towards each other: but not so much as may sometimes be supposed. For part which has, at first sight, this appearance, is in reality that other hypocrisy before mentioned; that

self-deceit, of which the scripture so remarkably
takes notice. There are indeed persons who live
without God in the world.[6] and some appear so
hardened as to keep no measures with themselves.
But as very ill men may have a real and strong
sense of virtue and religion, in proportion as this is
the case with any, they cannot be easy within themselves but by deluding their consciences. And
though they should, in great measure, get over
their religion, yet this will not do. For as long as
they carry about with them any such sense of things,
as makes them condemn what is wrong in others,
they could not but condemn the same in themselves,
and dislike and be disgusted with their own character
and conduct, if they would consider them distinctly,
and in a full light. But this sometimes they carelessly neglect to do, and sometimes carefully avoid
doing. And as *the integrity of the upright guides
him,*[7] guides even a man's judgment; so wickedness may distort it to such a degree, as that he may
*call evil good, and good evil; put darkness for
light, and light for darkness ;*[8] and *think wickedly,
that God is such an one as himself.*[9] Even the
better sort of men are, in some degree, liable to
disguise and palliate their failings to themselves :
but perhaps there are few men who go on calmly
in a course of very bad things, without somewhat
of the kind now described in a very high degree.
They try appearances upon themselves as well as
upon the world, and with at least as much success;
and choose to manage so as to make their own
minds easy with their faults, which can scarce be
without management, rather than to mend them.
But whether from men's deluding themselves, or

[6] Eph. ii. 12.   [7] Prov. xi. 3.
[8] Isa. v. 20.   [9] Psalm l. 21.

from their intending to delude the world, it is evident scarce anything wrong in public has ever been
accomplished, or even attempted, but under false
colours : either by pretending one thing, which was
right, to be designed, when it was really another
thing, which was wrong ; or if that which was wrong
was avowed, by endeavouring to give it some appearance of right. For tyranny, and faction so
friendly to it, and which is indeed tyranny out of
power, and unjust wars, and persecution, by which
the earth has been laid waste ; all this has all along
been carried on with pretences of truth, right, general good. So it is, men cannot find in their heart
to join in such things, without such honest words
to be the bond of the union, though they know
among themselves, that they are only words, and
often though they know, that every body else knows
it too.

These observations might be exemplified by numerous instances in the history which led to them:
and without them it is impossible to understand in
any sort the general character of the chief actors in
it, who were engaged in the black design of sub-
verting the constitution of their country. This they
completed with the most enormous act of mere
power, in defiance of all laws of God and man, and
in express contradiction to the real design and public votes of that assembly, whose commission, they
professed, was their only warrant for anything they
did throughout the whole rebellion. Yet with un-
heard-of hypocrisy towards men, towards God and
their own consciences—for without such a complication of it their conduct is inexplicable—even this
action, which so little admitted of any cloak, was,
we know, contrived and carried into execution, under pretences of authority, religion, liberty, and by

profaning the forms of justice in an arraignment and trial, like to what is used in regular legal procedures.   No age indeed can shew an example of hypocrisy parallel to this.   But the history of all ages and all countries will shew, what has been really going forward over the face of the earth, to be very different from what has been always pretended; and that virtue has. been everywhere professed much more than it has been anywhere practised: nor could society, from the very nature of its constitution, subsist without some general public profession of it.   Thus the face and appearance which the world has in all times put on, for the ease and ornament of life, and in pursuit of further ends, is the justest satire upon what has in all times been carrying on under it: and ill men are destined, by the condition of their being as social creatures, always to bear about with them, and, in different degrees, to profess, that law of virtue, by which they shall finally be judged and condemned.

II. As fair pretences, of one sort or other, have thus always been made use of by mankind to colour over indirect and wrong designs from the world, and to palliate and excuse them to their own minds; liberty, in common with all other good things, is liable to be made this use of, and is also liable to it in a way more peculiar to itself: which was the second thing to be considered.

In the history which this day refers us to, we find our constitution, in Church and State, destroyed under pretences, not only of religion, but of securing liberty, and carrying it to a greater height. The destruction of the former was with zeal of such a kind, as would not have been warrantable, though it had been employed in the destruction of heathenism.   And the confusions, the persecuting spirit, and incredible fanaticism, which grew up upon its ruins, cannot but teach sober-minded men to reverence so mild and reasonable an establishment, now it is restored; for the preservation of Christianity, and keeping up a sense of it amongst us, and for the instruction and guide of the ignorant; nay were it only for guarding religion from such extravagances: especially as these important purposes are served by it without bearing hard in the least upon any.

And the concurrent course of things, which brought on the ruin of our civil constitution, and what followed upon it, are no less instructive. The opposition, by legal and parliamentary methods, to prerogatives unknown to the constitution, was doubtless formed upon the justest fears in behalf of it. But new distrusts arose: new causes were given for them: these were most unreasonably aggravated. The better part gradually gave way to the more violent: and the better part themselves seem to have insisted upon impracticable securities against that one danger to liberty, of which they had too great cause to be apprehensive; and wonderfully overlooked all other dangers to it, which yet were, and ever will be, many and great. Thus they joined in the current measures, till they were utterly unable to stop the mischiefs, to which, with too much distrust on one side, and too little on the other, they had contributed. Never was a more remarkable example of the Wise Man's observation, that *the beginning of strife is as when one letteth out water.*[10] For this opposition, thus begun, surely without intent of proceeding to violence; yet, as it went on, like an overflowing stream in its progress, it collected all sort of impurities, and grew more

[10] Prov. xvii. 14.

s

outrageous as it grew more corrupted; till at length it bore down everything good before it. This naturally brought on arbitrary power in one shape, which was odious to every body, and which could not be accommodated to the forms of our constitution; and put us in the utmost danger of having it entailed upon us under another, which might. For at the king's return, such was the just indignation of the public at what it had seen, and fear of feeling again what it had felt, from the popular side; such the depression and compliance, not only of the more guilty, but also of those, who with better meaning had gone on with them; and a great deal too far many of this character had gone; and such the undistinguishing distrust the people had of them all, that the chief security of our liberties seems to have been, their not being attempted at that time.

But though persons contributed to all this mischief and danger with different degrees of guilt, none could contribute to them with innocence, who at all knew what they were about. Indeed the destruction of a free constitution of government, though men see or fancy many defects in it, and whatever they design or pretend, ought not to be thought of without horror. For the design is in itself unjust, since it is romantic to suppose it legal: it cannot be prosecuted without the most wicked means; nor accomplished but with the present ruin of liberty, religious as well as civil; for it must be the ruin of its present security. Whereas the restoration of it must depend upon a thousand future contingencies, the integrity, understanding, power of the persons, into whose hands anarchy and confusion should throw things; and who they will be, the history before us may surely serve to shew, no

human foresight can determine ; even though such
a terrible crisis were to happen in an age, not distinguished for the want of principle and public spirit,
and when nothing particular were to be apprehended from abroad.   It would be partiality to say,
that no constitution of government can possibly be
imagined more perfect than our own.   And ingenuous youth may be warmed with the idea of
one, against which nothing can be objected.   But
it is the strongest objection against attempting to
put in practice the most perfect theory, that it is
impracticable, or too dangerous to be attempted.
And whoever will thoroughly consider, in what degree mankind are really influenced by reason, and
in what degree by custom, may, I think, be convinced, that the state of human affairs does not even
admit of an equivalent for the mischief of setting
things afloat ; and the danger of parting with those
securities of liberty, which arise from regulations of
long prescription and ancient usage : especially at
a time when the directors are so very numerous,
and the obedient so few.   Reasonable men therefore will look upon the general plan of our constitution, transmitted down to us by our ancestors, as
sacred ; and content themselves with calmly doing
what their station requires, towards rectifying the
particular things which they think amiss, and sup-
plying the particular things which they think deficient in it, so far as is practicable without endanger-
ing the whole.

But liberty is in many other dangers from itself,
besides those which arise from formed designs of
destroying it, under hypocritical pretences, or
romantic schemes of restoring it upon a more
perfect plan.   It is particularly liable to become
excessive, and to degenerate insensibly into licen-

tiousness; in the same manner as liberality, for example, is apt to degenerate into extravagance. And as men cloak their extravagance to themselves under the notion of liberality, and to the world under the name of it, so licentiousness passes under the name and notion of liberty. Now it is to be observed, that there is, in some respects or other, a very peculiar contrariety between those vices which consist in excess, and the virtues of which they are said to be the excess, and the resemblance, and whose names they affect to bear; the excess of anything being always to its hurt, and tending to its destruction. In this manner licentiousness is, in its very nature, a present infringement upon liberty, and dangerous to it for the future. Yet it is treated by many persons with peculiar indulgence under this very notion, as being an excess of liberty. And an excess of liberty it is to the licentious themselves: but what is it to those who suffer by them, and who do not think, that amends is at all made them by having it left in their power to retaliate safely? When by popular insurrections, or defamatory libels, or in any like way, the needy and the turbulent securely injure quiet people in their fortune or good name, so far quiet people are no more free than if a single tyrant used them thus. A particular man may be licentious without being less free: but a community cannot; since the licentiousness of one will unavoidably break in upon the liberty of another. Civil liberty, the liberty of a community, is a severe and a restrained thing; implies in the notion of it, authority, settled subordinations, subjection, and obedience; and is altogether as much hurt by too little of this kind, as by too much of it. And the love of liberty, when it is indeed the love of liberty, which carries us to withstand tyranny,

will as much carry us to reverence authority, and
support it; for this most obvious reason, that one
is as necessary to the very being of liberty, as the
other is destructive of it. And therefore the love
of liberty, which does not produce this effect; the
love of liberty, which is not a real principle of dutiful behaviour towards authority; is as hypocritical,
as the religion which is not productive of a good
life. Licentiousness is, in truth, such an excess of
liberty as is of the same nature with tyranny. For
what is the difference between them, but that one
is lawless power exercised under pretence of authority, or by persons invested with it; the other lawless power exercised under pretence of liberty,
or without any pretence at all? A people then must
always be less free in proportion as they are more
licentious; licentiousness being not only different
from liberty, but directly contrary to it; a direct
breach upon it.

It is moreover of a growing nature; and of
speedy growth too; and, with the culture which it
has amongst us, needs no great length of time to
get to such an height as no legal government will
be able to restrain, or subsist under: which is the
condition the historian describes in saying, they
could neither bear their vices nor the remedies of
them.[11] I said legal government: for, in the present state of the world, there is no danger of our
becoming savages. Had licentiousness finished its
work, and destroyed our constitution, power would
not be wanting, from one quarter or another, sufficient to subdue us, and keep us in subjection. But
government, as distinguished from mere power,
free government, necessarily implies reverence in
the subjects of it, for authority, or power regulated

[11] Nec vitia nostra, nec remedia pati possumus, Liv. lib. i. c. 1.

by laws; and an habit of submission to the subordinations in civil life, throughout its several ranks:
nor is a people capable of liberty without somewhat
of this kind.   But it must be observed, and less
surely cannot be observed, this reverence and submission will at best be very precarious, if it be not
founded upon a sense of authority being God's
ordinance, and the subordinations in life a providen-
tal appointment of things.   Now let it be considered—for surely it is not duly considered—what
is really the short amount of those representations
which persons of superior rank give, and encourage
to be given of each other, and which are spread
over the nation?   Is it not somewhat, in itself, and
in its circumstances, beyond anything in any other
age or country of the world?   And what effect must
the continuance of this extravagant licentiousness
in them, not to mention other kinds of it, have upon
the people in those respects just mentioned?   Must
it not necessarily tend to wear out of their minds
all reverence for authority, and respect for superiors
of every sort; and, joined with the irreligious principles we find so industriously propagated, to introduce a total profligateness amongst them; since,
let them be as bad as they will, it is scarce possible
they can be so bad as they are instructed they may
be, or worse than they are told their superiors are?
And is there no danger that all this—to mention
only one supposable course of it—may raise somewhat like that levelling spirit, upon atheistical
principles, which in the last age, prevailed upon en-
thusiastic ones? not to speak of the possibility, that
different sorts of people may unite in it upon these
contrary principles.   And may not this spirit, together with a concurrence of ill humours, and of
persons who hope to find their account in confusion,

soon prevail to such a degree, as will require more of the good old principles of loyalty and of religion to withstand it, than appear to be left amongst us?

What legal remedies can be provided against these mischiefs, or whether any at all, are considerations the farthest from my thoughts. No government can be free, which is not administered by general stated laws: and these cannot comprehend every case, which wants to be provided against: nor can new ones be made for every particular case, as it arises: and more particular laws, as well as more general ones, admit of infinite evasions: and legal government forbids any but legal methods of redress; which cannot but be liable to the same sort of imperfections: besides the additional one of delay; and whilst redress is delayed, however unavoidably, wrong subsists. Then there are very bad things, which human authority can scarce provide against at all, but by methods dangerous to liberty; nor fully, but by such as would be fatal to it. These things shew, that liberty, in the very nature of it, absolutely requires, and even supposes, that people be able to govern themselves in those respects in which they are free; otherwise their wickedness will be in proportion to their liberty, and this greatest of blessings will become a curse.

III. These things shew likewise, that there is but one adequate remedy to the forementioned evils, even that which the apostle prescribes in the last words of the text, to consider ourselves *as the servants of God*, who enjoins dutiful submission to civil authority, as his ordinance; and to whom we are accountable for the use we make of the lib. rty which we enjoy under it. Since men cannot live out of society, nor in it without government, government is plainly a divine appointment; and consequently submission to it, a most evident duty of the law of nature. And we all know in how forcible a manner it is put upon our consciences in scripture. Nor can this obligation be denied formally upon any principles, but such as subvert all other obligations. Yet many amongst us seem not to consider it as any obligation at all. This doubtless is, in a great measure, owing to dissoluteness and corruption of manners: but I think it is partly owing to their having reduced it to nothing in theory. Whereas this obligation ought to be put upon the same foot with all other general ones, which are not absolute and without exception: and our submission is due in all cases but those, which we really discern to be exceptions to the general rule. And they who are perpetually displaying the exceptions, though they do not indeed contradict the meaning of any particular texts of scripture, which surely intended to make no alteration in men's civil rights; yet they go against the general tenor of scripture. For the scripture, throughout the whole of it, commands submission; supposing men apt enough of themselves to make the exceptions, and not to need being continually reminded of them. Now if we are really under any obligations of duty at all to magistrates, honour and respect, in our behaviour towards them, must doubtless be their due. And they who refuse to pay them this small and easy regard, who *despise dominion, and speak evil of dignities*,[12] should seriously ask themselves, what restrains them from any other instance whatever of undutifulness? And if it be principle, why not from

[12] Jude ver. 8.

this? Indeed free government supposes, that the conduct of affairs may be inquired into, and spoken of with freedom. Yet surely this should be done with decency, for the sake of liberty itself; for its honour and its security. But be it done as it will, it is a very different thing from libelling, and endeavouring to vilify the persons of such as are in authority. It will be hard to find an instance, in which a serious man could calmly satisfy himself in doing this. It is in no case necessary, and in every case of very pernicious tendency. But the immorality of it increases in proportion to the integrity and superior rank of the persons thus treated. It is therefore in the highest degree immoral, when it extends to the supreme authority in the person of a prince, from whom our liberties are in no imaginable danger, whatever they may be from ourselves; and whose mild and strictly legal government could not but make any virtuous people happy.

A free government, which the good providence of God has preserved to us through innumerable dangers, is an invaluable blessing. And our ingratitude to him in abusing of it must be great in proportion to the greatness of the blessing, and the providential deliverances by which it has been preserved to us. Yet the crime of abusing this blessing receives further aggravation from hence, that such abuse always is to the reproach, and tends to ruin of it. The abuse of liberty has directly overturned many free governments, as well as our own, on the popular side; and has, in various ways, contributed to the ruin of many, which have been overturned on the side of authority. Heavy therefore must be their guilt, who shall be found to have given such advantages against it, as well as theirs who have taken them.

Lastly, The consideration, that we are the servants of God, reminds us, that we are accountable to him for our behaviour in those respects, in which it is out of the reach of all human authority; and is the strongest enforcement of sincerity, as *all things are naked and open unto the eyes of him with whom we have to do.*[13] Artificial behaviour might perhaps avail much towards quieting our consciences, and making our part good in the short competitions of this world: but what will it avail us considered as under the government of God? Under his government, *there is no darkness, nor shadow of death, where the workers of iniquity may hide themselves.*[14] He has indeed instituted civil government over the face of the earth, *for the punishment of evildoers, and for the praise,* the apostle does not say the rewarding, but, *for the praise of them that do well.*[15] Yet as the worst answer these ends in some measure, the best can do it very imperfectly. Civil government can by no means take cognizance of *every work,* which is good or evil: many *things* are done in *secret;* the authors unknown to it, and often the things themselves: then it cannot so much consider actions, under the view of their being morally *good* or *evil,* as under the view of their being mischievous or beneficial to society: nor can it in any wise execute *judgment* in rewarding what is *good,* as it can and ought and does, in punishing what is *evil.* But *God shall bring every work into judgment, with every secret thing, whether it be good, or whether it be evil.*[16]

[13] Heb. iv. 13.   [14] Job xxxiv. 22.
[15] 1 Pet. ii. 14.   [16] Eccles. xii. 14.

SERMON IV.

PREACHED IN THE PARISH CHURCH OF CHRIST-
CHURCH, LONDON, ON THURSDAY, MAY 9, 1745,
BEING THE TIME OF THE YEARLY MEETING OF THE
CHILDREN EDUCATED IN THE CHARITY-SCHOOLS IN
AND ABOUT THE CITIES OF LONDON AND WEST-
MINSTER.

*" Train up a child in the way he should go: and
when he is old, he will not depart from it."*—
PROV. xxii. 6.

HUMAN creatures, from the constitution
of their nature and the circumstances
in which they are placed, cannot but
acquire habits during their childhood,
by the impressions which are given
them, and their own customary actions. And long
before they arrive at mature age, these habits form
a general settled character. And the observation of
the text, that the most early habits are usually the
most lasting, is likewise every one's observation.
Now whenever children are left to themselves, and
to the guides and companions which they choose,
or by hazard light upon, we find by experience,·
that the first impressions they take, and course of
action they get into, are very bad; and so con-

sequently must be their habits and character and
future behaviour. Thus if they are not trained up in
the way they *should go*, they will certainly be trained
up in the way they *should not go;* and in all probability will persevere in it, and become miserable
themselves, and mischievous to society; which, in
event, is worse, upon account of both, than if they
had been exposed to perish in their infancy.   On
the other hand, the ingenuous docility of children
before they have been deceived, their distrust of
themselves, and natural deference to grown people,
whom they find here settled in a world where they
themselves are strangers; and to whom they have
recourse for advice, as readily as for protection;
which deference is still greater towards those who
are placed over them: these things give the justest
grounds to expect that they may receive such impressions, and be influenced to such a course of
behaviour, as will produce lasting good habits; and,
together with the dangers before mentioned, are as
truly a natural demand upon us to *train them up in
the way they should go*, as their bodily wants are a
demand to provide them bodily nourishment. Brute
creatures are appointed to do no more than this last
for their offspring, nature forming them by instincts
to the particular manner of life appointed them;
from which they never deviate. But this is so far
from being the case of men, that, on the contrary,
considering communities collectively, every successive generation is left, in the ordinary course of
Providence, to be formed by the preceding one;
and becomes good or bad, though not without its
own merit or demerit, as this trust is discharged or
violated, chiefly in the management of youth. '

We ought, doubtless, to instruct and admonish
grown persons; to restrain them from what is evil,

and encourage them in what is good, as we are able :
but this care of youth, abstracted from all consideration of the parental affection, I say, this care of
youth, which is the general notion of *education*, becomes a distinct subject, and a distinct duty, from
the particular danger of their ruin, if left to themselves, and the particular reason we have to expect
they will do well, if due care be taken of them.
And from hence it follows, that children have as much
right to some proper education, as to have their
lives preserved ; and that when this is not given
them by their parents, the care of it devolves upon all
persons, it becomes the duty of all, who are capable
of contributing to it, and whose help is wanted.

These trite, but most important things, implied
indeed in the text, being thus premised as briefly
as I could express them, I proceed to consider distinctly the general manner in which the duty of
education is there laid before us : which will further
shew its extent, and further obviate the idle objections which have been made against it. And all
this together will naturally lead us to consider the
occasion and necessity of schools for the education
of poor children, and in what light the objections
against them are to be regarded.

Solomon might probably intend the text for a
particular admonition to educate children in a manner suitable to their respective ranks and future
employments : but certainly he intended it for a
general admonition to educate them in virtue and
religion, and good conduct of themselves in their
temporal concerns. And all this together, in which
they are to be educated, he calls *the way they should
go, i. e.* he mentions it not as a matter of speculation, but of practice. And conformably to this description of the things in which children are to be

educated, he describes education itself: for he calls
it *training them up;* which is a very different thing
from merely teaching them some truths, necessary
to be known or believed. It is endeavouring to form
such truths into practical principles in the mind, so
as to render them of habitual good influence upon the
temper and actions, in all the various occurrences
of life. And this is not done by bare instruction;
but by that, together with admonishing them frequently as occasion offers; restraining them from
what is evil, and exercising them in what is good.
Thus the precept of the apostle concerning this
matter is, to *bring up children in the nurture
and admonition of the Lord;* [1] as it were by way of
distinction from acquainting them merely with the
principles of Christianity, as you would with any
common theory. Though education were nothing
more than informing children of some truths of importance to them, relating to religion and common
life, yet there would be great reason for it, notwithstanding the frivolous objections concerning the
danger of giving them prejudices. But when we
consider that such information itself is really the
least part of it; and that it consists in endeavouring
to put them into right dispositions of mind, and
right habits of living, in every relation and every
capacity; this consideration shews such objections
to be quite absurd: since it shews them to be objections against doing a thing of the utmost importance at the natural opportunity of our doing it,
childhood and youth; and which is indeed, properly
speaking, our only one. For when they are grown
up to maturity, they are out of our hands, and must
be left to themselves. The natural authority on one

[1] Eph. vi. 4.

side ceases, and the deference on the other. God
forbid, that it should be impossible for men to recollect themselves, and reform at an advanced age:
but it is in no sort in the power of others to gain
upon them; to turn them away from what is wrong,
and enforce upon them what is right, at that season
of their lives, in the manner we might have done in
their childhood.

Doubtless religion requires instruction, for it is
founded in knowledge and belief of some truths.
And so is common prudence in the management of
our temporal affairs. Yet neither of them consists
in the knowledge or belief even of these fundamental truths; but in our being brought by such knowledge or belief to a correspondent temper and behaviour. Religion, as it stood under the Old Testament, is perpetually styled *the fear of God:* under
the New, *faith in Christ.* But as that fear of God
does not signify literally being afraid of him, but
having a good heart, and leading a good life, in
consequence of such fear; so this faith in Christ
does not signify literally *believing* in him in the
sense that word is used in common language, but
becoming his real disciples in consequence of such
belief.

Our religion being then thus practical, consisting
in a frame of mind and course of behaviour, suitable
to the dispensation we are under, and which will
bring us to our final good; children ought, by
education, to be habituated to this course of behaviour, and formed into this frame of mind. And
it must ever be remembered, that if no care be
taken to do it, they will grow up in a direct contrary behaviour, and be hardened in direct contrary
habits. They will more and more corrupt themselves, and spoil their proper nature. They will

alienate themselves further from God; and not only neglect, but *trample under foot*, the means which he in his infinite mercy has appointed for our recovery. And upon the whole, the same reasons, which shew, that they ought to be instructed and exercised in what will render them useful to society, secure them from the present evils they are in danger of incurring, and procure them that satisfaction which lies within the reach of human prudence; shew likewise, that they ought to be instructed and exercised in what is suitable to the highest relations in which we stand, and the most important capacity in which we can be considered; in that temper of mind and course of behaviour, which will secure them from their chief evil, and bring them to their chief good. Besides that religion is the principal security of men's acting a right part in society, and even in respect to their own temporal happiness, all things duly considered.

It is true indeed, children may be taught superstition, under the notion of religion; and it is true also, that, under the notion of prudence, they may be educated in great mistakes as to the nature of real interest and good, respecting the present world. But this is no more a reason for not educating them according to the best of our judgment, than our knowing how very liable we all are to err in other cases, is a reason why we should not, in those other cases, act according to the best of our judgment.

It being then of the greatest importance, that children should be thus educated, the providing schools to give this education to such of them as would not otherwise have it, has the appearance, at least at first sight, of deserving a place amongst the very best of good works. One would be backward, methinks, in entertaining prejudices against it; and very forward, if one had any, to lay them aside, upon being shewn that they were groundless. Let us consider the whole state of the case. For though this will lead us some little compass, yet I choose to do it ; and the rather, because there are people who speak of charity-schools as a new-invented scheme, and therefore to be looked upon with I know not what suspicion. Whereas it will appear, that the scheme of charity-schools, even the part of it which is most looked upon in this light, teaching the children letters and accounts, is no otherwise new, than as the occasion for it is so.

Formerly not only the education of poor children, but also their maintenance, with that of the other poor, were left to voluntary charities. But great changes of different sorts happening over the nation, and charity becoming more cold, or the poor more numerous, it was found necessary to make some legal provision for them. This might, much more properly than charity-schools, be called a new scheme. For, without question, the education of poor children was all along taken care of by voluntary charities, more or less: but obliging us by law to maintain the poor, was new in the reign of queen Elizabeth. Yet, because a change of circumstances made it necessary, its novelty was no reason against it. Now in that legal provision for the maintenance of the poor, poor children must doubtless have had a part in common with grown people. But this could never be sufficient for children, because their case always requires more than mere maintenance ; it requires that they be educated in some proper manner. Wherever there are poor who want to be maintained by charity, there must be poor children who, besides this, want to be educated by charity. And whenever there began

T

to be need of *legal* provision for the *maintenance* of the poor, there must immediately have been need also of some *particular* legal provision in behalf of poor children for their *education ;* this not being included in what we call their maintenance.   And many whose parents are able to maintain them, and do so, may yet be utterly neglected as to their education.   But possibly it might not at first be attended to, that the case of poor children was thus a case by itself, which required its own particular provision.   Certainly it would not appear, to the generality, so urgent an one as the want of food and raiment.   And it might be necessary, that a burden so entirely new as that of a poor-tax was at the time I am speaking of, should be as light as possible.   Thus the legal provision for the poor was first settled; without any particular consideration of that additional want in the case of children ; as it still remains, with scarce any alteration in this respect.   In the mean time, as the poor still increased, or charity still lessened, many poor children were left exposed, not to perish for want of food, but to grow up in society, and learn everything that is evil and nothing that is good in it ; and when they were grown up, greatly at a loss in what honest way to provide for themselves, if they could be supposed inclined to it. And larger numbers, whose case was not so bad as this, yet were very far from having due care taken of their education.   And the evil went on increasing, till it was grown to such a degree, as to be quite out of the compass of separate charities to remedy. At length some excellent persons, who were united in a Society[2] for carrying on almost every good work, took into consideration the neglected case I

[2] Society for promoting Christian Knowledge.

\ve been representing; and first of all, as I un-
:rstand, it, set up charity-schools; or however
omoted them, as far as their abilities and influence
uld extend.   Their design was not in any sort to
move poor children out of the rank in which they
:re born, but, keeping them in it, to give them
e assistance which their circumstances plainly
lled for; by educating them in the principles of
ligion, as well as civil life; and likewise making
me sort of provision for their maintenance: under
hich last I include clothing them, giving them
ich learning, if it is to be called by that name, as
ay qualify them for some common employment,
id placing them out to it, as they grow up.   These
vo general designs coincide in many respects, and
innot be separated.   For teaching the children to
ad, though I have ranked it under the latter,
jually belongs to both: and without some advan-
ges of the latter sort, poor people would not send
eir children to our charity-schools: nor could the
iorest of all be admitted into any schools, without
me charitable provision of clothing.   And care is
ken, that it be such as cannot but be a restraint
ion the children.   And if this, or any part of their
lucation, gives them any little vanity, as has been
iorly objected, whilst they are children, it is scarce
issible but that it will have even a quite contrary
fect when they are grown up, and ever after re-
ind them of their rank.   Yet still we find it is
iprehended, that what they here learn may set
em above it.

'But why should people be so extremely apprehensive of the danger, that poor persons will make
a perverse use of every the least advantage, even
the being able to read, whilst they do not appear at
all apprehensive of the like danger for themselves

or their own children, in respect of riches or power,
how much soever; though the danger of perverting
these advantages is surely as great, and the perversion itself of much greater and worse consequence!
And by what odd reverse of things has it happened,
that such as pretend to be distinguished for the love
of liberty should be the only persons who plead for
keeping down the poor, as one may speak; for
keeping them more inferior in this respect, and,
which must be the consequence, in other respects,
than they were in times past? For till within a
century or two all ranks were nearly upon a level
as to the learning in question. The art of printing
appears to have been providentially reserved till these
latter ages, and then providentially brought into
use, as what was to be instrumental for the future
in carrying on the appointed course of things. The
alterations which this art has even already made in the
face of the world are not inconsiderable. By means
of it, whether immediately or remotely, the methods
of carrying on business are, in several respects, improved, *knowledge has been increased*,[3] and some
sort of literature is become general. And if this be
a blessing, we ought to let the poor, in their degree,
share it with us. The present state of things and
course of providence plainly leads us to do so. And
if we do not, it is certain, how little soever it be
attended to, that they will be upon a greater disadvantage, on many accounts, especially in populous
places, than they were in the dark ages: for they
will be more ignorant, comparatively with the people about them, than they were then; and the
ordinary affairs of the world are now put in a way
which requires that they should have some know-

[3] Dan. xii. 4.

ledge of letters, which was not the case then. And
therefore, to bring up the poor in their former ignorance, now this knowledge is so much more common and wanted, would be, not to keep them in the
same, but to put them into a lower condition of life
than what they were in formerly. Nor let people
of rank flatter themselves, that ignorance will keep
their inferiors more dutiful and in greater subjection
to them: for surely there must be danger that it
will have a contrary effect under a free government
such as ours, and in a dissolute age. Indeed the
principles and manners of the poor, as to virtue and
religion, will always be greatly influenced, as they
always have been, by the *example* of their superiors,
if that would mend the matter. And this influence
will, I suppose, be greater, if they are kept more
inferior than formerly in all knowledge and improvement. But unless their superiors of the present age, superiors, I mean, of the middle, as well
as higher ranks in society, are greater examples of
public spirit, of dutiful submission to authority, human and divine, of moderation in diversions, and
proper care of their families and domestic affairs;
unless, I say, superiors of the present age are greater
examples of decency, virtue, and religion, than those
of former times; for what reason in the world is it
desirable that their example should have this greater
influence over the poor? On the contrary, why
should not the poor, by being taught to read, be
put into a capacity of making some improvement in
moral and religious knowledge, and confirming
themselves in those good principles, which will be
a great security for their following the example of
their superiors if it be good, and some sort of pre-
servative against their following it if it be bad?
And serious persons will further observe very sin-

gular reasons for this amongst us; from the dis-
continuance of that religious intercourse between
pastors and people in private, which remains in pro-
testant churches abroad, as well as in the church of
Rome; and from our small public care and provision for keeping up a sense of religion in the
lower rank, except by distributing religious books.
For in this way they have been assisted; and any
well-disposed person may do much good amongst
them, and at a very trifling expense, since the worthy Society before mentioned has so greatly lessened the price of such books. But this pious
charity is an additional reason why the poor should
be taught to read, that they may be in a capacity
of receiving the benefit of it. Vain indeed would
be the hope, that anything in this world can be
fully secured from abuse. For as it is the general
scheme of Divine Providence to bring good out of
evil; so the wickedness of men will, if it be possible, bring evil out of good. But upon the whole,
incapacity and ignorance must be favourable to error
and vice; and knowledge and improvement contribute, in due time, to the destruction of impiety as
well as superstition, and to the general prevalence
of true religion. But some of these observations
may perhaps be thought too remote from the present occasion. It is more obviously to the purpose
of it to observe, that reading, writing, and accounts,
are useful, and, whatever cause it is owing to, would
really now be wanted in the very lowest stations:
and that the trustees of our charity-schools are fully
convinced of the great fitness of joining to instruction easy labour, of some sort or other, as fast as it
is practicable; which they have already been able
to do in some of them.

Then as to placing out the poor children, as soon

as they are arrived at a fit age for it; this must be
approved by every one, as it is putting them in a
way of industry under domestic government, at a
time of life, in some respects, more dangerous than
even childhood. And it is a known thing, that care
is taken to do it in a manner which does not set
them above their rank: though it is not possible
'always to do it exactly as one would wish. Yet, I
hope it may be observed without offence, if any of
them happen to be of a very weakly constitution, or
of a very distinguished capacity, there can be no
impropriety in placing these in employments adapted
to their particular cases; though such as would be
very improper for the generality.

But the principal design of this charity is to
educate poor children in such a manner, as has a
tendency to make them good and useful and con-
tented, whatever their particular station be. The
care of this is greatly neglected by the poor: nor
truly is it more regarded by the rich, considering what might be expected from them. And if it
were as practicable to provide charity-schools, which
should supply this shameful neglect in the rich, as
it is to supply the like, though more excusable,
neglect in the poor, I should think certainly, that
both ought to be done for the same reasons. And
most people, I hope, will think so too, if they attend
to the thing I am speaking of; which is the moral
and religious part of education; what is equally
necessary for all ranks, and grievously wanting in
all. Yet in this respect the poor must be greatly
upon a disadvantage, from the nature of the case;
as will appear to any one who will consider it.

For if poor children are not sent to school, several
years of their childhood of course pass away in
idleness and loitering. This has a tendency to give

them perhaps a feeble listlessness, perhaps an headstrong profligateness of mind; certainly an indisposition to proper application as they grow up, and an aversion afterwards, not only to the restraints of religion, but to those which any particular calling, and even the nature of society, require. Whereas children kept to stated orders, and who many hours of the day are in employment, are by this means habituated both to submit to those who are placed over them, and to govern themselves; and they are also by. this means prepared for industry, in any way of life in which they may be placed. And all this holds abstracted from the consideration of their being taught to read; without which, however, it will be impracticable to employ their time: not to repeat the unanswerable reasons for it before mentioned. Now several poor people cannot, others will not be at the expense of sending their children to school. And let me add, that such as can and are willing, yet if it be very inconvenient to them, ought to be eased of it, and the burden of children made as light as may be to their poor parents.

Consider next the manner in which the children of the poor, who have vicious parents, are brought up, in comparison with other children whose parents are of the same character. The children of dissolute men of fortune may have the happiness of not seeing much of their parents. And this, even though they are educated at home, is often the case, by means of a customary distance between them, which cannot be kept amongst the poor. Nor is it impossible, that a rich man of this character, desiring to have his children better than himself, may provide them such an education as may make them so, without his having any restraint or trouble in the matter. And the education which children of better

rank must have, for their improvement in the common accomplishments belonging to it, is of course,
as yet, for the most part, attended with some sort
of religious education.   But the poor, as they cannot provide persons to educate their children; so,
from the way in which they live together in poor
families, a child must be an eye and ear witness of
the worst part of his parents' talk and behaviour.
And it cannot but be expected, that his own will be
formed upon it.   For as example in general has
very great influence upon all persons, especially
children, the example of their parents is of authority
with them, when there is nothing to balance it on
the other side.   Now take in the supposition, that
these parents are dissolute, profligate people; then,
over and above giving their children no sort of good
instruction, and a very bad example, there are more
crimes than one in which, it may be feared, they will
directly instruct and encourage them; besides letting them ramble abroad wherever they will, by
which, of course, they learn the very same principles and manners they do at home.   And from all
these things together, such poor children will have
their characters formed to vice, by those whose
business it is to restrain them from it.   They will
be disciplined and trained up in it.   This surely is
a case which ought to have some public provision
made for it.   If it cannot have an adequate one, yet
such an one as it can: unless it be thought so rare
as not to deserve our attention.   But in reality,
though there should be no more parents of this
character amongst the poor, in proportion, than
amongst the rich, the case which I have been putting will be far from being uncommon.   Now notwithstanding the danger to which the children of
such wretched parents cannot but be exposed, from

what they see at home; yet by instilling into them
the principles of virtue and religion at school, and
placing them soon out in sober families, there is
ground to hope they may avoid those ill courses,
and escape that ruin, into which, without this care,
they would almost certainly run. I need not add
how much greater ground there is to expect, that
those of the children who have religious parents
will do well. For such parents, besides setting their
children a good example, will likewise repeat and
enforce upon them at home the good instructions
they receive at school.

After all, we find the world continues very corrupt.
And it would be miraculous indeed, if charity-schools
alone should make it otherwise; or if they should
make even all who are brought up in them proof
against its corruptions. The truth is, every method
that can be made use of to prevent or reform the
bad manners of the age, will appear to be of less
effect, in proportion to the greater occasion there is
for it: as cultivation, though the most proper that
can be, will produce less fruit, or of a worse sort, in
a bad climate than in a good one. And thus the
character of the common people, with whom these
children are to live, in the ordinary intercourse of
business and company when they come out into the
world, may more or less defeat the good effects of
their education. And so likewise may the character of men of rank, under whose influence they
are to live. But whatever danger may be apprehended from either or both of these, it can be no
reason why we should not endeavour, by the like-
liest methods we can, to better the world, or keep
it from growing worse. The good tendency of the
method before us is unquestionable. And I think
myself obliged to add, that upon a comparison of

parishes where charity-schools have been for a considerable time established, with neighbouring ones, in like situations, which have had none, the good effects of them, as I am very credibly informed, are most manifest. Notwithstanding I freely own, that it is extremely difficult to make the necessary comparisons in this case, and form a judgment upon them. And a multitude of circumstances must come in to determine, from appearances only, concerning the positive good which is produced by this charity, and the evil which is prevented by it; which last is full as material as the former, and can scarce be estimated at all. But surely there can be no doubt whether it be useful or not, to educate children in order, virtue, and religion.

However, suppose, which is yet far from being the case, but suppose it should seem, that this undertaking did not answer the expense and trouble of it, in the civil or political way of considering things. What is this to persons who profess to be engaged in it, not only upon mere civil views, but upon moral and Christian ones? We are to do our endeavours to promote virtue and religion amongst men, and leave the success to God: the designs of his providence are answered by these endeavours, *whether they will hear, or whether they will forbear; i.e.* whatever be the success of them: and the least success in such endeavours is a great and valuable effect.[4]

From these foregoing observations, duly considered, it will appear, that the objections, which have been made against charity-schools, are to be regarded in the same light with those which are made against any other necessary things; for instance,

[4] See the Sermon before the Society for the Propagation of the Gospel.

against providing for the sick and the aged poor. Objections in this latter case could be considered no otherwise than merely as warnings of some inconvenience which might accompany such charity, and might, more or less, be guarded against, the charity itself being still kept up ; or as proposals for placing it upon some better foot. For though, amidst the disorder and imperfection in all human things, these objections were not obviated, they could not however possibly be understood as reasons for discontinuing such charity ; because, thus understood, they would be reasons for leaving necessitous people to perish. Well-disposed persons therefore will take care, that they be not deluded with objections against this before us, any more than against other necessary charities ; as though such objections were reasons for suppressing them, or not contributing to their support, unless we can procure an alteration of that to which we object. There can be no possible reasons for leaving poor children in that imminent danger of ruin, in which many of these must be left, were it not for this charity. Therefore objections against it cannot, from the nature of the case, amount to more than reasons for endeavouring, whether with or without success, to put it upon a right and unexceptionable foot, in the particular respects objected against. And if this be the intention of the objectors, the managers of it have shewn themselves remarkably ready to second them : for they have shewn even a docility in receiving admonitions of anything thought amiss in it, and proposals for rendering it more complete : and, under the influence of this good spirit, the management of it is really improving; particularly in greater endeavours to introduce manufactures into these schools; and in more particular care to place the

children out to employments in which they are most
wanted, and may be most serviceable, and which
are most suitable to their ranks.   But if there be
anything in the management of them, which some
particular persons think should be altered, and others
are of a contrary opinion, these things must be referred to the judgment of the public, and the determination of the public complied with.   Such compliance is an essential principle of all charitable
associations; for without it they could not subsist
at all: and by charitable associations, multitudes are
put in mind to do good, who otherwise would not
have thought of it; and infinitely more good may
be done, than possibly can by the separate endeavours of the same number of charitable persons.
Now he who refuses to help forward the good work
before us, because it is not conducted exactly in his
own way, breaks in upon that general principle of
union, which those who are friends to the indigent
and distressed part of our fellow-creatures will be
very cautious how they do in any case: but more
especially will they beware, how they break in upon
that necessary principle in a case of so great importance as is the present.   For the public is as
much interested in the education of poor children,
as in the preservation of their lives.

This last, I observed, is legally provided for.
The former is left amongst other works of charity,
neglected by many who care for none of these things,
and to be carried on by such only as think it their
concern to be doing good.   Some of you are able,
and in a situation, to assist in it in an eminent degree, by being trustees, and overlooking the management of these schools; or in different ways
countenancing and recommending them; as well as
by contributing to their maintenance: others can

assist only in this latter way. In what manner and degree then it belongs to you, and to me, and to any particular person, to help it forward, let us all consider seriously, not for one another, but each of us for himself.

> And may the blessing of Almighty God accompany this work of charity, which he has put into the hearts of his servants, in behalf of these poor children; that being now *trained up in the way they should go, when they are old they may not depart from it.* May he, of his mercy, keep them safe amidst the innumerable dangers of this bad world, through which they are to pass, and preserve them unto his heavenly kingdom.

SERMON V.

PREACHED BEFORE THE HOUSE OF LORDS, IN THE ABBEY-CHURCH OF WESTMINSTER, ON THURSDAY, JUNE 11, 1747, BEING THE ANNIVERSARY OF HIS MAJESTY'S HAPPY ACCESSION TO THE THRONE.

" *I exhort, that, first of all, supplications, prayers, intercessions, and giving of thanks, be made for all men ; for kings, and for all that are in authority ; that we may lead a quiet and peaceable life, in all godliness and honesty.*"—1 TIM. ii. 1, 2.

IT is impossible to describe the general end which Providence has appointed us to aim at in our passage through the present world, in more expressive words than these very plain ones of the apostle, *to lead a quiet and peaceable life, in all godliness and honesty: a quiet and peaceable life,* by way of distinction, surely, from eager, tumultuary pursuits in our private capacity, as well as in opposition both to our making insurrections in the state, and to our suffering oppression from it. *To lead a quiet and peaceable life in all godliness and honesty,* is the whole that we have any reason to be concerned for. To this the constitution of our na-

ture carries us; and our external condition is adapted
to it.

Now in aid to this general appointment of Providence, civil government has been instituted over the
world, both by the light of nature and by revelation,
to instruct men in the duties of fidelity, justice, and
regard to common good, and enforce the practice of
these virtues, without which there could have been
no peace or quiet amongst mankind; and to preserve, in different ways, a sense of religion as well
as virtue, and of God's authority over us.   For if
we could suppose men to have lived out of government, they must have run wild, and all knowledge
of divine things must have been lost from among
them.   But by means of their uniting under it, they
have been preserved in some tolerable security from
the fraud and violence of each other; order, a sense
of virtue, and the practice of it, has been in some
measure kept up; and religion, more or less pure,
has been all along spread and propagated.   So that
I make no scruple to affirm, that civil government
has been, in all ages, a standing publication of the
law of nature, and an enforcement of it; though
never in its perfection, for the most part greatly
corrupted, and I suppose always so in some degree.

And considering that civil government is that part
of God's government over the world, which he exercises by the instrumentality of men, wherein that
which is oppression, injustice, cruelty, as coming
from them, is, under his direction, necessary discipline, and just punishment; considering that *all
power is of God*,[1] all authority is properly of divine
appointment; men's very living under magistracy
might naturally have led them to the contemplation

[1] Rom. xiii. 1.

of authority in its source and origin; the one, supreme, absolute authority of Almighty God; by
which he *doeth according to his will in the army of
heaven, and among the inhabitants of the earth:*[2]
which he now exerts, visibly and invisibly, by different instruments, in different forms of administration, different methods of discipline and punishment;
and which he will continue to exert hereafter, not
only over mankind when this mortal life shall be
ended, but throughout his universal kingdom; till,
by having rendered to all according to their works,
he shall have completely executed that just scheme
of government, which he has already begun to execute in this world, by their hands, whom he has appointed, for the present *punishment of evil doers,
and for the praise of them that do well.*[3]

And though that perfection of justice cannot in
any sort take place in this world, even under the
very best governments; yet under the worst, men
have been enabled to lead much more quiet and
peaceable lives, as well as attend to and keep up a
sense of religion much more, than they could possibly have done without any government at all. But
a free Christian government is adapted to answer
these purposes in a higher degree, in proportion to
its just liberty, and the purity of its religious establishment. And as we enjoy these advantages, civil
and religious, in a very eminent degree, under a
good prince, and those he has placed in authority
over us, we are eminently obliged to offer up supplications and thanksgivings in their behalf; to pay
them all that duty which these prayers imply; and
to lead, as those advantages enable and have a tendency to dispose us to do, *quiet and peaceable lives
in all godliness and honesty.*

[2] Dan. iv. 35.   [3] 1 Pet. ii. 14.

U

290 A Sermon preached before [*Ser.* 5.

Of the former of these advantages, our free constitution of civil government, we seem to have a very
high value. And if we would keep clear from abuses
of it, it could not be overvalued; otherwise than
as everything may, when considered as respecting
this world only.   We seem, I say, sufficiently sensible of the value of our civil liberty.   It is our daily
boast, and we are in the highest degree jealous of
it.   Would to God we were somewhat more judi-
cious in our jealousy of it, so as to guard against its
chief enemy, one might say, the only enemy of it,
we have at present to fear; I mean licentiousness;
which has undermined so many free governments,
and without whose treacherous help no free government, perhaps, ever was undermined.   This licentiousness indeed is not only dangerous to liberty,
but it is actually a present infringement of it in
many instances.—But I must not turn this good
day into a day of reproach.   Dropping then the
encroachments which are made upon our liberty,
peace, and quiet by licentiousness, we are certainly
a freer nation than any other we have an account
of; and as free, it seems, as the very nature of government will permit.   Every man is equally under
the protection of the laws; may have equal justice
against the most rich and powerful; and securely enjoy
all the common blessings of life, with which the industry of his ancestors, or his own, has furnished
him.   In some other countries the upper part of the
world is free, but in Great Britain the whole body of
the people is free.   For we have at length, to the
distinguished honour of those who began, and have
more particularly laboured in it, emancipated our
northern provinces from most of their *legal* remains of
slavery: for *voluntary* slavery cannot be abolished, at
least not directly, by law. I take leave to speak of this

long-desired work as done; since it wants only his concurrence, who, as we have found by many years' experience, considers the good of his people as his own. And I cannot but look upon these acts of the legislature in a further view, as instances of regard to posterity; and declarations of its readiness to put every subject upon an equal foot of security and freedom, if any of them are not so, in any other respects, which come into its view; and as a precedent and example for doing it.

Liberty, which is the very genius of our civil constitution, and runs through every branch of it, extends its influence to the ecclesiastical part of it. A religious establishment without a toleration of such as think they cannot in conscience conform to it, is itself a general tyranny; because it claims absolute authority over conscience; and would soon beget particular kinds of tyranny of the worst sort, tyranny over the mind, and various superstitions; after the way should be paved for them, as it soon must, by ignorance. On the other hand, a constitution of civil government without any religious establishment is a chimerical project, of which there is no example: and which, leaving the generality without guide and instruction, must leave religion to be sunk and forgotten amongst them; and at the same time give full scope to superstition, and the gloom of enthusiasm; which last, especially, ought surely to be diverted and checked, as far as it can be done without force. Now a reasonable establishment provides instruction for the ignorant, withdraws them, not in the way of force, but of guidance, from running after those kinds of conceits. It doubtless has a tendency likewise to keep up a sense of real religion and real Christianity in a nation: and is moreover necessary for the encouragement of learn-

ing; some parts of which the scripture-revelation
absolutely requires should be cultivated.

It is to be remarked further, that the value of any
particular religious establishment is not to be estimated merely by what it is in itself, but also by
what it is in comparison with those of other nations;
a comparison which will sufficiently teach us not to
expect perfection in human things. And what is
still more material, the value of our own ought to be
very much heightened in our esteem, by considering
what it is a security from; I mean that great corruption of Christianity, popery, which is ever hard
at work to bring us again under its yoke. Whoever
will consider the popish claims, to the disposal of
the whole earth, as of divine right, to dispense with
the most sacred engagements, the claims to supreme
absolute authority in religion; in short, the general
claims which the canonists express by the words
plenitude of power—whoever, I say, will consider
popery as it is professed at Rome, may see, that it
is manifest, open usurpation of all human and divine
authority. But even in those Roman catholic countries where these monstrous claims are not admitted,
and the civil power does, in many respects, restrain
the papal; yet persecution is professed, as it is absolutely enjoined by what is acknowledged to be
their highest authority, a general council, so called,
with the pope at the head of it; and is practised in
all of them, I think without exception, where it can
be done safely. Thus they go on to substitute force
instead of argument; and external profession made
by force instead of reasonable conviction. And thus
corruptions of the grossest sort have been in vogue,
for many generations, in many parts of Christen-
dom; and are so still, even where popery obtains
in its least absurd form: and their antiquity and

wide extent are insisted upon as proofs of their
truth ; a kind of proof, which at best can be only
presumptive, but which loses all its little weight, in
proportion as the long and large prevalence of such
corruptions have been obtained by force.

Indeed it is said in the book of Job, that the worship of *the sun and moon was an iniquity to be
punished by the judge.*[4] And this, though it is not
so much as a precept, much less a general one, is,
I think, the only passage of scripture which can
with any colour be alleged in favour of persecution
of any sort: for what the Jews did, and what they
were commanded to do, under their theocracy, are
both quite out of the case. But whenever that book
was written, the scene of it is laid at a time when
idolatry was in its infancy, an acknowledged novelty,
essentially destructive of true religion, arising perhaps from mere wantonness of imagination. In these
circumstances, this greatest of evils, which afterwards laid waste true religion over the face of the
earth, might have been suppressed at once, without
danger of mistake or abuse. And one might go on to
add, that if those to whom the care of this belonged,
instead of serving themselves of prevailing superstitions, had in all ages and countries opposed them in
their rise ; and adhered faithfully to that primitive
religion, which was received *of old, since man was
placed upon earth ;*[5] there could not possibly have
been any such difference of opinion concerning the
Almighty Governor of the world, as could have given
any pretence for tolerating the idolatries which over-
spread it. On the contrary, his universal monarchy
must have been universally recognized, and the general laws of it more ascertained and known, than

[4] Job xxxi. 26, 27, 28.　　　[5] Job xx. 4.

the municipal ones of any particular country can be.   In such a state of religion, as it could not but have been acknowledged by all mankind, that immorality of every sort was disloyalty to him, *the high and lofty One that inhabiteth eternity, whose name is Holy ;* [6] so it could not but have been manifest, that idolatry, in those determinate instances of it, was plain rebellion against him ; and therefore might have been punished as an offence, of the highest kind, against the Supreme Authority in nature.   But this is in no sort applicable to the present state of religion in the world.   For if the principle of punishing idolatry were now admitted amongst the several different parties in religion, the weakest in every place would run a great risk of being convicted of it; or however heresy and schism would soon be found crimes of the same nature, and equally deserving punishment.   Thus the spirit of persecution would range without any stop or control, but what should arise from its want of power.   But our religious establishment disclaims all principles of this kind, and desires not to keep persons in its communion, or gain proselytes to it, by any other methods than the Christian ones of argument and conviction.

These hints may serve to remind us of the value we ought to set upon our constitution in Church and State, the advantages of which are the proper subjects of our commemoration on this day, as his majesty has shewn himself, not in words, but in the whole course of his reign, the guardian and protector of both.   And the blessings of his reign are not only rendered more sensible, but are really heightened, by its securing us from that pretender

[6] Isaiah lvii. 15.

to his crown, whom we had almost forgot, till our
late danger renewed our apprehensions; who, we
know, is a professed enemy to our church; and
grown old in resentments and maxims of government directly contrary to our civil constitution; nay
his very claim is founded in principles destructive
of it. Our deliverance and our security from this
danger, with all the other blessings of the king's
government, are so many reasons, *for supplications,
prayers, intercessions, and giving of thanks,* to
which we are exhorted; as well as for all other
dutiful behaviour towards it; and should also remind us to take care and make due improvement
of those blessings, by *leading,* in the enjoyment of
them, *quiet and peaceable lives, in all godliness and
honesty.*

The Jewish church offered sacrifices even for
heathen princes to whom they were in subjection:
and the primitive Christian church, the Christian
sacrifices of supplications and prayers for the prosperity of the emperor and the state; though they
were falsely accused of being enemies to both, because they would not join in their idolatries. In
conformity to these examples of the church of God
in all ages, prayers for the king and those in authority under him are part of the daily service of our
own. And for the day of his inauguration a particular service is appointed, which we are here assembled in the house of God to celebrate. This is
the first duty we owe to kings, and those who are
in authority under them, that we may make prayers
and thanksgivings for them. And in it is comprehended, what yet may be considered as another,
paying them honour and reverence. Praying for
them is itself an instance and expression of this, as
it gives them a part in our highest solemnities. It

also reminds us of that further honour and reverence which we are to pay them, as occasions offer, throughout the whole course of our behaviour. *Fear God, honour the king,*[7] are apostolic precepts; and *despising government, and speaking evil of dignities,*[8] apostolic descriptions of such as *are reserved until the day of judgment to be punished.*[9] And if these *evil speeches* are so highly criminal, it cannot be a thing very innocent to make a custom of entertaining ourselves with them.

Further, if we are to pray, *that we may*, that it may be permitted us, to *lead a quiet and peaceable life*, we ought surely to live so, when, by means of a mild, equal government, it is permitted us; and be very thankful, first to God, and then to those whom he makes the instruments of so great good to us, and pay them all obedience and duty; though everything be not conducted according to our judgment, nor every person in employment whom we may think deserving of it. Indeed opposition, in a legal, regular way, to measures which a person thinks wrong, cannot but be allowed in a free government. It is in itself just, and also keeps up the spirit of liberty. But opposition, from indirect motives, to measures which he sees to be necessary, is itself immoral: it keeps up the spirit of licentiousness; is the greatest reproach of liberty, and in many ways most dangerous to it; and has been a principal means of overturning free governments. It is well too if the *legal subjection* to the government we live under, which may accompany such behaviour, be not the reverse of *Christian subjection; subjection for wrath only*, and *not for*

[7] 1 Pet. ii. 17.   [8] 2 Pet. ii. 10.
[9] 2 Pet. ii. 9.

conscience sake.[10] And one who wishes well to his
country will beware how he inflames the common
people against measures, whether right or wrong,
which they are not judges of. For no one can foresee how far such disaffection will extend; but every
one sees, that it diminishes the reverence which is
certainly owing to authority. Our due regards to these
things are indeed instances of our loyalty, but they
are in reality as much instances of our patriotism
too. Happy the people who live under a prince,
the justice of whose government renders them
coincident.

Lastly, As by the good providence of God we
were born under a free government, and are members of a pure reformed church, both of which he
has wonderfully preserved through infinite dangers;
if we do not take heed to live like Christians, nor to
govern ourselves with decency in those respects in
which we are free, we shall be a dishonour to both.
Both are most justly to be valued: but they may
be valued in the wrong place. It is no more a recommendation of civil, than it is of natural liberty,[11]
that it must put us into a capacity of behaving ill.
Let us then value our civil constitution, not because
it leaves us the power of acting as mere humour
and passion carry us, in those respects, in which
governments less free lay men under restraints;
but for its equal laws, by which the great are disabled from oppressing those below them. Let us
transfer, each of us, the equity of this our civil constitution to our whole personal character; and be sure
to be as much afraid of subjection to mere arbitrary
will and pleasure in ourselves, as to the arbitrary

[10] Rom. xiii. 5.
[11] Natural liberty as opposed to necessity, or fate.

will of others.   For the tyranny of our own lawless
passions is the nearest and most dangerous of all
tyrannies.

Then as to the other part of our constitution ; let
us value it, not because it leaves us at liberty to
have as little religion as we please, without being
accountable to human judicatories; but because it
affords us the means and assistances to worship God
according to his word; because it exhibits to our
view, and enforces upon our conscience, genuine
Christianity, free from the superstitions with which
it is defiled in other countries.   These superstitions
naturally tend to *abate* its force: our profession of
it in its purity is a particular call upon us to yield
ourselves up to its *full* influence ; *to be pure in
heart ;*[12] *to be holy in all manner of conversation.*[13]
Much of *the form of godliness* is laid aside amongst
us : this itself should admonish us to attend more to
the power thereof.[14]   We have discarded many bur-
densome ceremonies : let us be the more careful to
cultivate inward religion.   We have thrown off a
multitude of superstitious practices, which were
called good works: let us the more abound in all
moral virtues, these being unquestionably such.
Thus our lives will justify and recommend the reformation ; and we shall *adorn the doctrine of God
our Saviour in all things.*[15]

[12] Matt. v. 8.   [13] 1 Pet. i. 15.
[14] 2 Tim. iii. 5.   [15] Titus ii. 10.

SERMON VI.

PREACHED BEFORE HIS GRACE CHARLES DUKE OF
RICHMOND, PRESIDENT, AND THE GOVERNORS OF
THE LONDON INFIRMARY, FOR THE RELIEF OF SICK
AND DISEASED PERSONS, ESPECIALLY MANUFAC-
TURERS, AND SEAMEN IN MERCHANT-SERVICE, &c.
AT THE PARISH CHURCH OF ST. LAWRENCE-JEWRY,
ON THURSDAY, MARCH 31, 1748.

*" And above all things have fervent charity among
yourselves: for charity shall cover the multitude
of sins."*—1 PET. iv. 8.

AS we owe our being, and all our faculties, and the very opportunities of
exerting them, to Almighty God,
and are plainly his and not our own,
we are admonished, even though we
should *have done all those things which are commanded us*, to say, *We are unprofitable servants.*[1]
And with much deeper humility must we make this
acknowledgment, when we consider in how *many
things we have all offended.*[2] But still the behaviour
of such creatures as men, highly criminal in some

[1] Luke xvii. 10.   [2] James iii. 2.

respects, may yet in others be such as to render them the proper objects of mercy, and, our Saviour does not decline saying, *thought worthy of it.*[3] And, conformably to our natural sense of things, the scripture is very express, that mercy, forgiveness, and, in general, charity to our fellow-creatures, has this efficacy in a very high degree.

Several copious and remote reasons have been alleged, why such pre-eminence is given to this grace or virtue; some of great importance, and none of them perhaps without its weight. But the proper one seems to be very short and obvious, that by fervent charity, with a course of beneficence proceeding from it, a person may make amends for the good he has blamably omitted, and the injuries he has done, so far, as that society would have no demand upon him for such his misbehaviour; nor consequently would justice have any in behalf of society, whatever it might have upon other accounts. Thus by fervent charity he may even merit forgiveness of men: and this seems to afford a very singular reason why it may be graciously granted him by God; a very singular reason, the Christian covenant of pardon always supposed, why divine justice should permit, and divine mercy appoint, that such his charity should be allowed to *cover the multitude of sins.*

And this reason leads me to observe, what scripture and the whole nature of the thing shews, that the charity here meant must be such hearty love to our fellow-creatures, as produceth a settled endeavour to promote, according to the best of our judgment, their real lasting good, both present and future; and not that easiness of temper, which with

[3] Luke xx. 35.

peculiar propriety is expressed by the word *good-humour*, and is a sort of benevolent instinct left to itself, without the direction of our judgment. For this kind of good-humour is so far from making the amends before mentioned, that, though it be agreeable in conversation, it is often most mischievous in every other intercourse of life; and always puts men out of a capacity of doing the good they might, if they could withstand importunity, and the sight of distress, when the case requires they should be withstood; many instances of which case daily occur, both in public and private. Nor is it to be supposed, that we can any more promote the lasting good of our fellow-creatures, by acting from mere kind inclinations, without considering what are the proper means of promoting it, than that we can attain our own personal good, by a *thoughtless* pursuit of everything which pleases us. For the love of our neighbour, as much as self-love, the social affections, as much as the private ones, from their very nature, require to be under the direction of our judgment. Yet it is to be remembered, that it does in no sort become such a creature as man to harden himself against the distresses of his neighbour, except where it is really necessary; and that even well-disposed persons may run into great perplexities, and great mistakes too, by being over-solicitous in distinguishing what are the most proper occasions for their charity, or who the greatest objects of it. And therefore, as on the one side we are obliged to take some care not to squander that which, one may say, belongs to the poor, as we shall do, unless we competently satisfy ourselves beforehand, that what we put to our account of charity will answer some good purpose; so on the other side, when we are competently satisfied of this, in any particular instance before us, we ought by no means to neglect such present opportunity of doing good, under the notion of making further inquiries : for of these delays there will be no end.

Having thus briefly laid before you the ground of that singular efficacy, which the text ascribes to charity in general; obviated the objection against its having this efficacy; and distinguished the virtue itself from its counterfeits; let us now proceed to observe the genuineness and excellency of the particular charity, which we are here met together to promote.

Medicine and every other relief, *under the calamity of bodily diseases and casualties,* no less than the daily necessaries of life, are natural provisions, which God has made for our present indigent state; and which he has granted in common to the children of men, whether they be poor or rich : to the rich by inheritance, or acquisition; and by their hands to the disabled poor.

Nor can there be any doubt, but that public infirmaries are the most effectual means of administering such relief; besides that they are attended with incidental advantages of great importance : both which things have been fully shewn; and excellently enforced, in the annual sermons upon this and the like occasions.

But indeed public infirmaries are not only the best, they are the only possible means by which the poor, especially in this city, can be provided, in any competent measure, with the several kinds of assistance, which *bodily diseases and casualties* require. Not to mention poor foreigners; it is obvious no other provision can be made for poor strangers out of the country, when they are overtaken by these calamities, as they often must be, whilst they are occasionally attending their affairs in this centre of business. But even the poor who are settled here are in a manner strangers to the people amongst whom they live ; and, were it not for this provision, must unavoidably be neglected, in the hurry and concourse around them, and be left unobserved to languish in sickness, and suffer extremely, much more than they could in less populous places; where every one is known to every one ; and any great distress presently becomes the common talk ; and where also poor families are often under the particular protection of some or other of their rich neighbours, in a very different way from what is commonly the case here. Observations of this kind shew, that there is a peculiar occasion, and even a necessity, in such a city as this, for public infirmaries, to which easy admittance may be had ; and here in ours no security is required, nor any sort of gratification allowed ; and that they ought to be multiplied or enlarged proportionably to the increase of our inhabitants : for to this the increase of the poor will always bear proportion ; though less in ages of sobriety and diligence, and greater in ages of profusion and debauchery.

Now though nothing, to be called an objection in the way of argument, can be alleged against thus providing for poor sick people, in the properest, indeed the only way in which they can be provided for ; yet persons of too severe tempers can, even upon this occasion, talk in a manner, which, contrary surely to their intention, has a very malignant influence upon the spirit of charity—talk of the ill-deserts of the poor, the good uses they might make of being let to suffer more than they do, under distresses which they bring upon themselves, or however might, by diligence and frugality, provide

against; and the idle uses they may make of knowing beforehand that they shall be relieved in case of
those distresses.   Indeed there is such a thing as a
prejudice against them, arising from their very state
of poverty, which ought greatly to be guarded
against; a kind of prejudice, to which perhaps most
of us, upon some occasions, and in some degree,
may inattentively be liable, but which pride and
interest may easily work up to a settled hatred of
them; the utter reverse of that amiable part of the
character of Job, that *be was a father to the poor.*⁴
But it is undoubtedly fit, that such of them as are
good and industrious should have the satisfaction of
knowing beforehand, that they shall be relieved
under *diseases and casualties:* and those, it is most
obvious, ought to be relieved preferably to others.
But these others, who are not of that good character, might possibly have the apprehension of
those calamities in so great a degree, as would be
very mischievous, and of no service, if they thought
they must be left to perish under them.   And
though their idleness and extravagance are very
inexcusable, and ought by all reasonable methods
to be restrained; and they are highly to be blamed
for not making some provision against age and supposable disasters, when it is in their power; yet it
is not to be desired, that the anxieties of avarice
should be added to the natural inconveniences of
poverty.
It is said, that our common fault towards the poor
is not harshness, but too great lenity and indulgence.   And if allowing them in debauchery, idleness, and open beggary; in drunkenness, profane
cursing and swearing in our streets, nay in our

⁴ Job xxix. 16.

houses of correction; if this be lenity, there is
doubtless a great deal too much of it. And such
lenity towards the poor is very consistent with the
most cruel neglects of them, in the extreme misery
to which those vices reduce them. Now though
this last certainly is not our general fault; yet it
cannot be said every one is free from it. For this
reason, and that nothing, which has so much as the
shadow of an objection against our public charities,
may be entirely passed over, you will give me leave
to consider a little the supposed case above mentioned, though possibly some may think it unnecessary, that of persons reduced to poverty and distress by their own faults.

Instances of this there certainly are. But it ought
to be very distinctly observed, that in judging which
are such, we are liable to be mistaken: and more
liable to it, in judging to what degree those are
faulty, who really are so in some degree. However, we should always look with mildness upon the
behaviour of the poor; and be sure not to expect
more from them than can be expected, in a moderate
way of considering things. We should be forward
not only to admit and encourage the good deserts
of such as do well, but likewise as to those of them
who do not, be ever ready to make due allowances
for their bad education, or, which is the same, their
having had none; for what may be owing to the ill
example of their superiors, as well as companions,
and for temptations of all kinds. And remember
always, that be men's vices what they will, they
have not forfeited their claim to relief under necessities, till they have forfeited their lives to justice.

*Our heavenly Father is kind to the unthankful
and to the evil ; and sendeth his rain on the just*

x

and on the unjust. And, in imitation of him, our
Saviour expressly requires, that our beneficence be
promiscuous. But we have moreover the divine
example for relieving those distresses which are
brought upon persons by their own faults; and this
is exactly the case we are considering. Indeed the
general dispensation of Christianity is an example of
this; for its general design is to save us from our
sins, and the punishments which would have been
the just consequence of them. But the divine example in the daily course of nature is a more obvious and sensible one. And though the natural
miseries which are foreseen to be annexed to a
vicious course of life are providentially intended to
prevent it, in the same manner as civil penalties are
intended to prevent civil crimes; yet those miseries,
those natural penalties admit of and receive natural
reliefs, no less than any other miseries, which could
not have been foreseen or prevented. Charitable
providence then, thus manifested in the course of
nature, which is the example of our heavenly Father, most evidently leads us to relieve, not only
such distresses as were unavoidable, but also such
as people by their own faults have brought upon
themselves. The case is, that we cannot judge in
what degree it was intended they should suffer, by
considering what, in the natural course of things,
would be the whole bad consequences of their faults,
if those consequences were not prevented, when
nature has provided means to prevent great part of
them. We cannot, for instance, estimate what degree of present sufferings God has annexed to
drunkenness, by considering the diseases which follow from this vice, as they would be if they admit-

* Matt. v.45. Luke vi. 35.

ted of no reliefs or remedies; but by considering
the remaining misery of those diseases, after the
application of such remedies as nature has provided. For as it is certain on the one side, that
those diseases are providential corrections of intemperance, it is as certain on the other, that the remedies are providential mitigations of those corrections;
and altogether as much providential, when administered by the good hand of charity in the case of
our neighbour, as when administered by self-love
in our own. Thus the pain and danger, and other
distresses of sickness and poverty remaining, after
all the charitable relief which can be procured; and
the many uneasy circumstances which cannot but
accompany that relief, though distributed with all
supposable humanity; these are the natural corrections of idleness and debauchery, supposing these
vices brought on those miseries. And very severe
corrections they are: and they ought not to be increased by withholding that relief, or by harshness
in the distribution of it. Corrections of all kinds,
even the most necessary ones, may easily exceed
their proper bound: and when they do so, they become mischievous; and mischievous in the measure
they exceed it. And the natural corrections which
we have been speaking of would be excessive, if the
natural mitigations provided for them were not administered.

Then persons who are so scrupulously apprehensive of everything which can possibly, in the
most indirect manner, encourage idleness and vice,
(which, by the way, anything may accidentally do,)
ought to turn their thoughts to the moral and religious tendency of infirmaries. The religious manner in which they are carried on has itself a direct
tendency to bring the subject of religion into the

consideration of those whom they relieve; and, in some degree, to recommend it to their love and practice, as it is productive of so much good to them, as restored ease and health, and a capacity of resuming their several employments. It is to virtue and religion, they may mildly be admonished, that they are indebted for their relief. And this, amongst other admonitions of their spiritual guide, and the quiet and order of their house, out of the way of bad examples, together with a regular course of devotion, which it were greatly to be wished might be daily; these means, it is to be hoped, with the common grace of God, may enforce deeply upon their consciences those serious considerations, to which a state of affliction naturally renders the mind attentive, and that they will return, as from a religious retreat, to their several employments in the world, with lasting impressions of piety in their hearts. By such united advantages, which these poor creatures can in no sort have any other way, very remarkable reformations have been wrought. Persons of the strictest characters therefore would give a more satisfactory proof, not to the world, but to their own consciences, of their desire to suppress vice and idleness, by setting themselves to cultivate the religious part of the institution of infirmaries, which, I think, would admit of great improvements;[6] than by allowing themselves to talk in a manner which tends to discountenance the institution itself, or any particular branch of it.

Admitting then the usefulness and necessity of these kinds of charity, which indeed cannot be denied; *yet everything has its bounds*. And, in the spirit of severity before mentioned, it is imagined,

[6] See Mr. Tucker's Sermon before the Governors of the Bristol Infirmary, 1746.

that *people are enough disposed*, such, it seems, is the present turn, *to contribute largely to them.* And some, whether from dislike of the charities themselves, or from mere profligateness, think *these formal recommendations of them at church every year might very well be spared.*

But surely it is desirable, that a customary way should be kept open for removing prejudices as they may arise against these institutions; for rectifying any misrepresentations which may, at any time, be made of them; and informing the public of any new emergencies; as well as for repeatedly enforcing the known obligations of charity, and the excellency of this particular kind of it. Then sermons, you know, amongst protestants, always of course accompany these more solemn appearances in the house of God: nor will these latter be kept up without the other. Now public devotions should ever attend and consecrate public charities. And it would be a sad presage of the decay of these charities, if ever they should cease to be professedly carried on in the fear of God, and upon the principles of religion. It may be added, that real charitable persons will approve of these frequent exhortations to charity, even though they should be conscious that they do not themselves stand in need of them, upon account of such as do. And such can possibly have no right to complain of being too often admonished of their duty, till they are pleased to practise it. It is true indeed, we have the satisfaction of seeing a spirit of beneficence prevail, in a very commendable degree, amongst all ranks of people, and in a very distinguished manner in some persons amongst the highest; yet it is evident, too many of all ranks are very deficient in it, who are of great ability, and of whom much might be expected. Though every-

thing therefore were done in behalf of the poor
which is wanted, yet these persons ought repeatedly
to be told, how highly blamable they are for letting
it be done without them; and done by persons, of
whom great numbers must have much less ability
than they.

But whoever can really think, that the necessities
of the disabled poor are sufficiently provided for
already, must be strangely prejudiced. If one were to
send you to them themselves to be better informed,
you would readily answer, that their demands would
be very extravagant; that persons are not to be
their own judges in claims of justice, much less in
those of charity. You then, I am speaking to the
hard people above mentioned, you are to judge,
what provision is to be made for the necessitous, so
far as it depends upon your contributions. But
ought you not to remember that you are interested,
that you are parties in the affair as well as they.
For is not the giver as really so as the receiver?
And as there is danger that the receiver will err
one way, is there not danger that the giver may err
the other? since it is not matter of arbitrary choice,
which has no rule, but matter of real equity, to be
considered as in the presence of God, what provision shall be made for the poor? And therefore,
though you are yourselves the only judges, what
you will do in their behalf, for the case admits no
other; yet let me tell you, you will not be impartial, you will not be equitable judges, until you have
guarded against the influence which interest is apt
to have upon your judgment, and cultivated within
you the spirit of charity to balance it. Then you
will see the various remaining necessities which call
for relief. But that there are many such must be
.evident at first sight to the most careless observer,

were it only from hence, that both this and the
other hospitals are often obliged to reject poor objects which offer, even for want of room, or wards
to contain them.

Notwithstanding many persons have need of these
admonitions, yet there is a good spirit of beneficence, as I observed, pretty generally prevailing.
And I must congratulate you upon the great success it has given to the particular good work before
us ; great, I think, beyond all example for the time
it has subsisted.   Nor would it be unsuitable to the
present occasion to recount the particulars of this
success.   For the necessary accommodations which
have been provided, and the numbers who have
been relieved, in so short a time, cannot but give
high reputation to the London Infirmary. And the
reputation of any particular charity, like credit in
trade, is so much real advantage, without the inconveniences to which that is sometimes liable.   It
will bring in contributions for its support ; and men
of character, as they shall be wanted, to assist in the
management of it ; men of skill in the professions,
men of conduct in business, to perpetuate, improve,
and bring it to perfection.   So that you, the con-
tributors to this charity, and more especially those
of you by whose immediate care and economy it is
in so high repute, are encouraged to go on with *your
labour of love*,[7] not only by the present good, which
you see is here done, but likewise by the prospect
of what will probably be done, by your means, in
future times, when this infirmary shall become, as I
hope it will, no less renowned than the city in which
it is established.

But to see how far it is from being yet complete,

[7] Heb. vi. 10.

for want of contributions, one need only look upon
the settled rules of the house for *admission of pa-
tients.* See there the limitations which necessity
prescribes, as to the persons to be admitted. Read
but that one order, though others might be mentioned, that *none who are judged to be in an asth-
matic, consumptive, or dying condition be admitted
on any account whatsoever.* Harsh as these words
sound, they proceed out of the mouth of Charity
herself. Charity pronounces it to be better, that poor
creatures, who might receive much ease and relief,
should be denied it, if their case does not admit of
recovery, rather than that others, whose case does
admit of it, be left to perish. But it shocks humanity to hear such an alternative mentioned; and
to think, that there should be a necessity, as there
is at present, for such restrictions, in one of the
most beneficent and best managed schemes in the
world. May more numerous or larger contributions, at length, open a door to such as these; that
what renders their case in the highest degree com-
passionable, their languishing under incurable diseases, may no longer exclude them from the house
of mercy!

But besides the persons to whom I have been
now more particularly speaking, there are others,
who do not cast about for excuses for not contributing to the relief of the necessitous; perhaps are
rather disposed to relieve them; who yet are not so
careful as they ought to be, to put themselves into a
capacity of doing it. For we are as really accountable for not doing the good which we might have in
our power to do, if we would manage our affairs with
prudence, as we are for not doing the good which is
in our power now at present. And hence arise the
obligations of economy upon people in the highest,

as well as in the lower stations of life, in order to enable themselves to do that good, which, without economy, both of them must be incapable of; even though without it they could answer the strict demands of justice; which yet we find neither of them can. *A good man sheweth favour, and lendeth; and,* to enable him to do so, *he will guide his affairs with discretion.*[8] For want of this, many a one has reduced his family to the necessity of asking relief from those public charities, to which he might have left them in a condition of largely contributing.

As economy is the duty of all persons, without exception, frugality and diligence are duties which particularly belong to the middle as well as lower ranks of men; and more particularly still to persons in trade and commerce, whatever their fortunes be. For trade and commerce cannot otherwise be carried on, but is plainly inconsistent with idleness and profusion: though indeed were it only from regard to propriety, and to avoid being absurd, every one should conform his behaviour to what his situation in life requires, without which the order of society must be broken in upon. And considering how inherited riches and a life of leisure are often employed, the generality of mankind have cause to be thankful that their station exempts them from so great temptations; that it engages them in a sober care of their expenses, and in a course of application to business: especially as these virtues, moreover, tend to give them, what is an excellent groundwork for all others, a stayed equality of temper and command of their passions. But when a man is diligent and frugal, in order to have it in his

---

[8] Psalm cxii. 5.

power to do good; when he is more industrious, or more sparing perhaps than his circumstances necessarily require, that he may *have to give to him that needeth ;*[9] when he *labours in order to support the weak ;*[10] such care of his affairs is itself charity, and the actual beneficence which it enables him to practise is additional charity.

You will easily see why I insist tnus upon these things, because I would particularly recommend the good work before us to all ranks of people in this great city. And I think I have reason to do so, from the consideration, that it very particularly belongs to them to promote it. The gospel indeed teaches us to look upon every one in distress as our neighbour, yet neighbourhood in the literal sense, and likewise several other circumstances, are providential recommendations of such and such charities, and excitements to them; without which the necessitous would suffer much more than they do at present. For our general disposition to beneficence would not be sufficiently directed, and in other respects would be very ineffectual, if it were not called forth into action by some or other of those providential circumstances, which form particular relations between the rich and the poor, and are of course regarded by every one in some degree. But though many persons among you, both in the way of contributions, and in other ways no less useful, have done even more than was to be expected, yet I must be allowed to say, that I do not think the relation the inhabitants of this city bear to the persons for whom our infirmary was principally designed, is sufficiently attended to by the generality: which may be owing to its late

---

[9] Eph. iv. 28.   [10] Acts xx. 35.

establishment. It is, you know, designed principally
for *diseased manufacturers, seamen in merchant-*
service, and their wives and children: and *poor*
manufacturers comprehend all who are employed
in any labour whatever belonging to trade and commerce. The description of these objects shews their
relation, and a very near one it is, to you, my
neighbours, the inhabitants of this city. If any of
your domestic servants were disabled by sickness,
there is none of you but would think yourself bound
to do somewhat for their relief. Now these seamen
and manufacturers are employed in your immediate
business. They are servants of merchants, and
other principal traders; as much your servants as if
they lived under your roof: though by their not
doing so, the relation is less in sight. And supposing they do not all depend upon traders of lower
rank in exactly the same manner, yet many of them
do; and they have all connections with you, which
give them a claim to your charity preferably to
strangers. They are indeed servants of the public;
and so are all industrious poor people as well as
they. But that does not hinder the latter from
being more immediately yours. And as their being
servants to the public is a general recommendation
of this charity to all other persons, so their being
more immediately yours is, surely, a particular recommendation of it to you. Notwithstanding all
this, I will not take upon me to say, that every one
of you is blamable who does not contribute to your
infirmary, for yours it is in a peculiar sense; but I will
say, that those of you who do are highly commendable. I will say more, that you promote a very
excellent work, which your particular station is a
providential call upon you to promote. And there
can be no stronger reason than this for doing any-

thing, except the one reason, that it would be criminal to omit it.

These considerations, methinks, might induce every trader of higher rank in this city to become a subscriber to the infirmary which is named from it; and others of you to contribute somewhat yearly to it, in the way in which smaller contributions are given. This would be a most proper offering out of your increase to Him, whose *blessing maketh rich.*[11] Let it be more or less, *every man according as he purposeth in his heart ; not grudgingly, or of necessity: for God loveth a cheerful giver.*[12]

The large benefactions of some persons of ability may be necessary in the first establishment of a public charity, and are greatly useful afterwards in maintaining it : but the expenses of this before us, in the extent and degree of perfection to which one would hope it might be brought, cannot be effectually supported, any more than the expenses of civil government, without the contribution of great numbers. You have already the assistance of persons of highest rank and fortune, of which the list of our governors, and the present appearance, are illustrious examples. And their assistance would be far from lessening by a general contribution to it amongst yourselves. On the contrary, the general contribution to it amongst yourselves, which I have been proposing, would give it still higher repute, and more invite such persons to continue their assistance, and accept the honour of being in its direction. For the greatest persons receive honour from taking the direction of a good work, as they likewise give honour to it. And by these concurrent endeavours, our infirmary might at length be brought

[11] Prov. x. 22.   [12] 2 Cor. ix. 7.

to answer, in some competent measure, to the occasions of our city.

Blessed are they who employ their riches in promoting so excellent a design. The temporal advantages of them are far from coming up, in enjoyment, to what they promise at a distance. But the distinguished privilege, the prerogative of riches, is, that they increase our power of doing good. This is their proper use. In proportion as men make this use of them, they imitate Almighty God; and co-operate together with him in promoting the happiness of the world; and may expect the most favourable judgment, which their case will admit of, at the last day, upon the general, repeated maxim of the gospel, that we shall then be treated ourselves as we now treat others. They have moreover the prayers of all good men, those of them particularly whom they have befriended; and, by such exercise of charity, they improve within themselves the temper of it, which is the very temper of heaven. Consider next the peculiar force with which this branch of charity, almsgiving, is recommended to us in these words; *He that hath pity upon the poor lendeth unto the Lord;*[13] and in these of our Saviour, *Verily I say unto you, Inasmuch as ye have done it,* relieved the sick and needy, *unto one of the least of these my brethren, ye have done it unto me.*[14] Beware you do not explain away these passages of scripture, under the notion, that they have been made to serve superstitious purposes: but ponder them fairly in your heart; and you will feel them to be of irresistible weight. Lastly, let us remember, in how many instances we have all left undone those things which we ought to have done, and

[13] Prov. xix. 17.   [14] Matt. xxv. 40.

done those things which we ought not to have done. Now whoever has a serious sense of this will most earnestly desire to supply the good, which he was obliged to have done, but has not, and undo the evil which he has done, or neglected to prevent; . and when that is impracticable, to make amends, in some other way for his offences——I *can* mean only to our fellow-creatures. To make amends, in some way or other, to a particular person, against whom we have offended, either by positive injury or by neglect; is an express condition of our obtaining forgiveness of God, when it is in our power to make it. And when it is not, surely the next best thing is to make amends to society by fervent charity, in a course of doing good: which riches, as I observed, put very much within our power.

How unhappy a choice then do those rich men make, who sacrifice all these high prerogatives of their state, to the wretched purposes of dissoluteness and vanity, or to the sordid itch of heaping up, to no purpose at all; whilst in the meantime they stand charged with the important trust, in which they are thus unfaithful, and of which a strict account remains to be given!

END OF THE SERMONS.

A CHARGE DELIVERED TO THE CLERGY AT THE PRIMARY VISITATION OF THE DIOCESE OF DURHAM IN THE YEAR 1751

I T is impossible for me, my brethren, upon our first meeting of this kind, to forbear lamenting with you the general decay of religion in this nation; which is now observed by every one, and has been for some time the complaint of all serious persons. The influence of it is more and more wearing out of the minds of men, even of those who do not pretend to enter into speculations upon the subject: but the number of those who do, and who profess themselves unbelievers, increases, and with their numbers their zeal. Zeal, it is natural to ask—for what? Why truly *for* nothing, but *against* everything that is good and sacred amongst us.

Indeed, whatever efforts are made against our religion, no Christian can possibly despair of it. For he, who has *all power in heaven and earth*, has promised, that *he will be with us to the end of the world.* Nor can the present decline of it be any stumbling-block to such as are considerate;

since he himself has so strongly expressed what is
as remarkably predicted in other passages of scripture, the great defection from his religion which
should be in the latter days, by that prophetic question, *When the Son of man cometh, shall he find
faith upon the earth?* How near this time is, God
only knows; but this kind of scripture signs of it is
too apparent. For as different ages have been distinguished by different sorts of particular errors and
vices, the deplorable distinction of ours is an avowed
scorn of religion in some, and a growing disregard
to it in the generality.

As to the professed enemies of religion, I know
not how often they may come in your way; but
often enough, I fear, in the way of some at least
amongst you, to require consideration, what is the
proper behaviour towards them. One would, to be
sure, avoid great familiarities with these persons;
especially if they affect to be licentious and profane
in their common talk. Yet if you fall into their
company, treat them with the regards which belong
to their rank; for so we must people who are vicious in any other respect. We should study what
St. James, with wonderful elegance and expressive-
ness, calls *meekness of wisdom*, in our behaviour
towards all men; but more especially towards these
men; not so much as being what we owe to them,
but to ourselves and our religion; that we may
adorn the doctrine of God our Saviour, in our car-
riage towards those who labour to vilify it.

For discourse with them; the caution commonly
given, not to attempt answering objections which
we have not considered, is certainly just. Nor need
any one in a particular case be ashamed frankly to
acknowledge his ignorance, provided it be not general. And though it were, to talk of what he is not

acquainted with, is a dangerous method of endeavouring to conceal it. But a considerate person,
however qualified he be to defend his religion, and
answer the objections he hears made against it, may
sometimes see cause to decline that office. Sceptical and profane men are extremely apt to bring up
this subject at meetings of entertainment, and such
as are of the freer sort: innocent ones I mean,
otherwise I should not suppose you would be present at them. Now religion is by far too serious a
matter to be the hackney subject upon these occasions. And by preventing its being made so, you
will better secure the reverence which is due to it,
than by entering into its defence. Every one observes, that men's having examples of vice often
before their eyes, familiarizes it to the mind, and
has a tendency to take off that just abhorrence of it
which the innocent at first felt, even though it
should not alter their *judgment* of vice, or make
them really *believe* it to be less evil or dangerous.
In like manner, the. hearing religion often disputed
about in light familiar conversation has a tendency
to lessen that sacred regard to it, which a good
man would endeavour always to keep up, both in
himself and others. But this is not all: people are
too apt inconsiderately to take for granted, that
things are really questionable, because they hear
them often disputed. This indeed is so far from
being a consequence, that we know demonstrated
truths have been disputed, and even matters of fact,
the objects of our senses. But were it a consequence, were the evidence of religion no more than
doubtful, then it ought not to be concluded false
any more than true, nor denied any more than affirmed ; for suspense would be the reasonable state
of mind with regard to it. And then it ought in all

Y

reason, considering its infinite importance, to have
nearly the same influence upon practice, as if it
were thoroughly believed. For would it not be madness for a man to forsake a safe road, and prefer to
it one in which he acknowledges there is an even
chance he should lose his life, though there were an
even chance likewise of his getting safe through it!
Yet there are people absurd enough, to take the
supposed doubtfulness of religion for the same thing
as a proof of its falsehood, after they have concluded it doubtful from hearing it often called in
question. This shews how infinitely unreasonable
sceptical men are, with regard to religion, and that
they really lay aside their reason upon this subject
as much as the most extravagant enthusiasts. But
further, cavilling and objecting upon any subject is
much easier than clearing up difficulties : and this
last part will always be put upon the defenders of
religion. Now a man may be fully convinced of the
truth of a matter, and upon the strongest reasons,
and yet not be able to answer all the difficulties
which may be raised upon it.

Then again, the general evidence of religion is
complex and various. It consists of a long series of
things, one preparatory to and confirming another,
from the very beginning of the world to the present
time. And it is easy to see how impossible it must
be, in a cursory conversation, to unite all this into
one argument, and represent it as it ought ; and,
could it be done, how utterly indisposed people
would be to attend to it—I say in a cursory conversation : whereas unconnected objections are
thrown out in a few words, and are easily apprehended, without more attention than is usual in
common talk. So that, notwithstanding we have
the best cause in the world, and though a man were

very capable of defending it, yet I know not why he should be forward to undertake it upon so great a disadvantage, and to so little good effect, as it must be done amidst the gaiety and carelessness of common conversation.

But then it will be necessary to be very particularly upon your guard, that you may not *seem*, by way of compliance, to join in with any levity of discourse respecting religion. Nor would one let any pretended argument against it pass entirely without notice ; nor any gross ribaldry upon it, without expressing our thorough disapprobation. This last may sometimes be done by silence : for silence sometimes is very expressive ; as was that of our blessed Saviour before the Sanhedrim and before Pilate. Or it may be done by observing mildly, that religion deserves another sort of treatment, or a more thorough consideration, than such a time, or such circumstances admit. However, as it is absolutely necessary, that we take care, by diligent reading and study, to be always prepared, to be *ready always to give to every man that asketh a reason of the hope that is in us ;* so there may be occasions when it will highly become us to do it. And then we must take care to do it in the spirit which the apostle requires, *with meekness and fear :* [1] *meekness* towards those who give occasions for entering into the defence of our religion ; and with *fear*, not of them, but of God ; with that reverential fear, which the nature of religion requires, and which is so far from being inconsistent with, that it will inspire proper courage towards men. Now this reverential fear will lead us to insist strongly upon the infinite greatness of God's scheme of go-

[1] 1 Pet. iii. 15.

vernment, both in extent and duration, together
with the wise connection of its parts, and the impossibility of accounting fully for the several parts,
without seeing the whole plan of Providence to
which they relate; which is beyond the utmost
stretch of our understanding. And to all this must
be added the necessary deficiency of human language, when things divine are the subject of it.
These observations are a proper full answer to many
objections, and very material with regard to all.

But your standing business, and which requires
constant attention, is with the body of the people;
to revive in them the spirit of religion, which is so
much declining. And it may seem, that whatever
reason there be for caution as to entering into an
argumentative defence of religion *in common conversation,* yet that it is necessary to do this, *from
the pulpit,* in order to guard the people against being
corrupted, however in some places. But then surely
it should be done in a manner as little controversial
as possible. For though such as are capable of
seeing the force of objections are capable also of
seeing the force of the answers which are given to
them; yet the truth is, the people will not competently attend to either. But it is easy to see
which they will attend to most. And to hear religion treated of as what many deny, and which has
much said against it as well as for it; this cannot
but have a tendency to give them ill impressions at
any time; and seems particularly improper for all
persons at a time of devotion; even for such as are
arrived at the most settled state of piety: I say at a
time of devotion, when we are assembled to yield
ourselves up to the full influence of the Divine Presence, and to call forth into actual exercise every
pious affection of heart. For it is to be repeated,

that the heart and course of affections may be dis-
turbed when there is no alteration of judgment.
Now the evidence of religion may be laid before
men without any air of controversy. The proof of
the being of God, from final causes, or the design
and wisdom which appears in every part of nature;
together with the law of virtue written upon our
hearts: the proof of Christianity from miracles, and
the accomplishment of prophecies; and the confirmation which the natural and civil history of the
world give to the scripture account of things: these
evidences of religion might properly be insisted on,
in a way to affect and influence the heart, though
there were no professed unbelievers in the world;
and therefore may be insisted on, without taking
much notice that there are such. And even their
particular objections may be obviated without a formal mention of them. Besides, as to religion in
general, it is a practical thing, and no otherwise a
matter of speculation, than common prudence in
the management of our worldly affairs is so. And
if one were endeavouring to bring a plain man to be
more careful with regard to this last, it would be
thought a strange method of doing it, to perplex
him with stating formally the several objections
which men of gaiety or speculation have made
against prudence, and the advantages which they
pleasantly tell us folly has over it; though one
could answer those objections ever so fully.

Nor does the want of religion in the generality of
the common people appear owing to a speculative
disbelief or denial of it, but chiefly to thoughtless-
ness and the common temptations of life. Your
chief business therefore is to endeavour to beget a
practical sense of it upon their hearts, as what they
acknowledge their belief of, and profess they ought

to conform themselves to. And this is to be done
by keeping up, as we are able, the form and face
of religion with decency and reverence, and in such
a degree as to bring the thoughts of religion often
to their minds; and then endeavouring to make this
form more and more subservient to promote the
reality and power of it. The form of religion may
indeed be where there is little of the thing itself;
but the thing itself cannot be preserved amongst
mankind without the form. And this form frequently
occurring in some instance or other of it will be a
frequent admonition to bad men to repent, and to
good men to grow better; and also be the means of
their doing so.

That which men have accounted religion in the
several countries of the world, generally speaking,
has had a great and conspicuous part in all public
appearances, and the face of it been kept up with great
reverence throughout all ranks, from the highest
to the lowest; not only upon occasional solemnities,
but also in the daily course of behaviour. In the
heathen world, their superstition was the chief subject of statuary, sculpture, painting, and poetry. It
mixed itself with business, civil forms, diversions,
domestic entertainments, and every part of common
life. The Mahometans are obliged to short devotions
five times between morning and evening. In Roman
catholic countries, people cannot pass a day without
having religion recalled to their thoughts, by some
or other memorial of it; by some ceremony or public religious form occurring in their way: besides
their frequent holydays, the short prayers they are
daily called to, and the occasional devotions enjoined
by confessors. By these means their superstition
sinks deep into the minds of the people, and their
religion also into the minds of such among them as

are serious and well-disposed. Our reformers, considering that some of these observances were in
themselves wrong and superstitious, and others of
them made subservient to the purposes of superstition, abolished them, reduced the form of religion
to great simplicity, and enjoined no more particular
rules, nor left anything more of what was external
in religion, than was in a manner necessary to preserve a sense of religion itself upon the minds of
the people. But a great part of this is neglected
by the generality amongst us; for instance, the
service of the church, not only upon common days,
but also upon saints' days; and several other things
might be mentioned. Thus they have no customary admonition, no public call to recollect the
thoughts of God and religion from one Sunday to
another.

It was far otherwise under the law. *These words,*
says Moses to the children of Israel, *which I command thee, shall be in thine heart: and thou shalt
teach them diligently unto thy children, and shalt
talk of them when thou sittest in thine house, and
when thou walkest by the way, and when thou liest
down, and when thou risest up.*[2] And as they were
commanded this, so it is obvious how much the
constitution of that law was adapted to effect it, and
keep religion ever in view. And without somewhat
of this nature, piety will grow languid even among
the better sort of men; and the worst will go on
quietly in an abandoned course, with fewer interruptions from within than they would have, were religious reflections forced oftener upon their minds,
and consequently with less probability of their
amendment. Indeed in most ages of the church,
the care of reasonable men has been, as there has

[2] Deut. vi. 6, 7.

been for the most part occasion, to draw the people
off from laying too great weight upon external
things; upon formal acts of piety. But the state of
matters is quite changed now with us. These
things are neglected to a degree, which is, and
cannot but be attended with a decay of all that is
good. It is highly seasonable now to instruct the
people in the importance of external religion.

And doubtless under this head must come into
consideration a proper regard to the structures which
are consecrated to the service of God. In the present turn of the age, one may observe a wonderful
frugality in everything which has respect to religion, and extravagance in everything else. But
amidst the appearances of opulence and improvement in all common things, which are now seen
in most places, it would be hard to find a reason
why these monuments of ancient piety should not
be preserved in their original beauty and mag-
nificence. But in the least opulent places they
must be preserved in becoming repair; and everything relating to the divine service be, however,
decent and clean; otherwise we shall vilify the face
of religion whilst we keep it up. All this is indeed
principally the duty of others. Yours is to press
strongly upon them what is their duty in this respect, and admonish them of it often, if they are
negligent.

But then you must be sure to take care and not
neglect that part of the sacred fabric which belongs
to you to maintain in repair and decency. Such
neglect would be great impiety in you, and of most
pernicious example to others. Nor could you, with
any success, or any propriety, urge upon them their
duty in a regard in which you yourselves should be
openly neglectful of it.

Bishop Fleetwood has observed,[a] that *unless the good public spirit of building, repairing, and adorning* churches *prevails a great deal more among us, and be more encouraged, an hundred years will bring to the ground an huge number of our churches.* This excellent prelate made this observation forty years ago: and no one, I believe, will imagine that the good spirit he has recommended prevails more at present than it did then.

But if these appendages of the divine service are to be regarded, doubtless the divine service itself is more to be regarded; and the conscientious attendance upon it ought often to be inculcated upon the people, as a plain precept of the gospel, as the means of grace, and what has peculiar promises annexed to it. But external acts of piety and devotion, and the frequent returns of them, are, moreover, necessary to keep up a sense of religion, which the affairs of the world will otherwise wear out of men's hearts. And the frequent returns, whether of public devotions, or of anything else, to introduce religion into men's serious thoughts, will have an influence upon them, in proportion as they are susceptible of religion, and not given over to a reprobate mind. For this reason, besides others, the service of the church ought to be celebrated as often as you can have a congregation to attend it.

But since the body of the people, especially in country places, cannot be brought to attend it oftener than one day in a week; and since this is in no sort enough to keep up in them a due sense of religion; it were greatly to be wished they could be persuaded to anything which might, in some measure, supply the want of more frequent public

[a] Charge to the Clergy of St. Asaph, 1710

devotions, or serve the like purposes. Family prayers, regularly kept up in every house, would have a great and good effect.

Secret prayer, as expressly as it is commanded by our Saviour, and as evidently as it is implied in the notion of piety, will yet, I fear, be grievously forgotten by the generality, till they can be brought to fix for themselves certain times of the day for it; since this is not done to their hands, as it was in the Jewish church by custom or authority. Indeed custom, as well as the manifest propriety of the thing, and examples of good men in scripture, justify us in insisting, that none omit their prayers morning or evening, who have not thrown off all regards to piety. But secret prayer comprehends not only devotions before men begin and after they have ended the business of the day, but such also as may be performed while they are employed in it, or even in company. And truly, if, besides our more set devotions, morning and evening, all of us would fix upon certain times of the day, so that the return of the hour should remind us, to say short prayers, or exercise our thoughts in a way equivalent to this; perhaps there are few persons in so high and habitual a state of piety, as not to find the benefit of it. If it took up no more than a minute or two, or even less time than that, it would serve the end I am proposing; it would be a recollection, that we are in the Divine presence, and contribute to our *being in the fear of the Lord all the day long.*

A duty of the like kind, and serving to the same purpose, is the particular acknowledgment of God when we are partaking of his bounty at our meals. The neglect of this is said to have been scandalous to a proverb in the heathen world;[4] but it is without shame laid aside at the tables of the highest and the lowest rank among us.

And as parents should be admonished, and it should be pressed upon their consciences, to teach their children their prayers and catechism, it being what they are obliged to upon all accounts; so it is proper to be mentioned here, as a means by which they will bring the principles of Christianity often to their own minds, instead of laying aside all thoughts of it from week's-end to week's-end.

General exhortations to piety, abstracted from the particular circumstances of it, are of great use to such as are already got into a religious course of life; but, such as are not, though they be touched with them, yet when they go away from church, they scarce know where to begin, or how to set about what they are exhorted to. And it is with respect to religion, as in the common affairs of life, in which many things of great consequence intended, are yet never done at all, because they may be done at any time, and in any manner; which would not be, were some determinate time and manner voluntarily fixed upon for the doing of them. Particular rules and directions then concerning the times and circumstances of performing acknowledged duties, bring religion nearer to practice; and such as are really proper, and cannot well be mistaken, and are easily observed.—Such particular rules in religion, prudently recommended, would have an influence upon the people.

All this indeed may be called form; as everything external in religion may be merely so. And

[4] Cudworth on the Lord's Supper, p. 8. Casaub. in Athenæum, l. i. c. xi. p. 22. Duport. Præl. in Theophrastum, ed. Needham, c. ix. p. 335, &c.

therefore whilst we endeavour, in these and other like instances, to keep up the *form of godliness*[s] amongst those who are our care, and over whom we have any influence, we must endeavour also that this form be made more and more subservient to promote the *power* of it.[s] Admonish them to take heed that they mean what they say in their prayers, that their thoughts and intentions go along with their words, that they really in their hearts exert and exercise before God the affections they express with their mouth. Teach them, not that external religion is nothing, for this is not true in any sense; it being scarce possible, but that it will lay some sort of restraint upon a man's morals; and it is moreover of good effect with respect to the world about him. But teach them that regard to one duty will in no sort atone for the neglect of any other. Endeavour to raise in their hearts such a sense of God as shall be an habitual, ready principle of reverence, love, gratitude, hope, trust, resignation, and obedience. Exhort them to make use of every circumstance, which brings the subject of religion at all before them; to turn their hearts habitually to him; to recollect seriously the thoughts of his presence *in whom they live and move and have their being,* and by a short act of their mind devote themselves to his service.—If, for instance, persons would accustom themselves to be thus admonished by the very sight of a church, could it be called superstition? Enforce upon them the necessity of making religion their principal concern, as what is the express condition of the gospel covenant, and what the very nature of the thing requires. Explain to them the terms of that covenant of

---

[s] 2 Tim. iii. 5.

mercy, founded in the incarnation, sacrifice, and intercession of Christ, together with the promised assistance of the Holy Ghost, not to supersede our own endeavours, but to render them effectual. The greater festivals of the church, being instituted for commemorating the several parts of the gospel history, of course lead you to explain these its several doctrines, and shew the Christian practice which arises out of them. And the more occasional solemnities of religion, as well as these festivals, will often afford you the fairest opportunities of enforcing all these things in familiar conversation. Indeed all *affectation* of talking piously is quite nauseous: and though there be nothing of this, yet men will easily be disgusted at the too great frequency or length of these occasional admonitions. But a word of God and religion dropped sometimes in conversation, gently, and without anything severe or forbidding in the manner of it, this is not unacceptable. It leaves an impression, is repeated again by the hearers, and often remembered by plain well-disposed persons longer than one would think. Particular circumstances too, which render men more apt to receive instruction, should be laid hold of to talk seriously to their consciences. For instance, after a man's recovery from a dangerous sickness, how proper is it to advise him to recollect and ever bear in mind, what were his hopes or fears, his wishes and resolutions, when under the apprehension of death; in order to bring him to repentance, or confirm him in a course of piety, according as his life and character has been. So likewise the terrible accidents which often happen from riot and debauchery, and indeed almost every vice, are occasions providentially thrown in your way, to discourse against these vices in common

conversation, as well as from the pulpit, upon any
such accidents happening in your parish, or in a
neighbouring one. Occasions and circumstances of
a like kind to some or other of these occur often,
and ought, if I may so speak, to be catched at, as
opportunities of conveying instruction, both public
and private, with great force and advantage.

Public instruction is absolutely necessary, and can
in no sort be dispensed with. But as it is common
to all who are present, many persons strangely
neglect to appropriate what they hear to themselves,
to their own heart and life. Now the only remedy
for this in our power is a particular personal application. And a personal application makes a very
different impression from a common, general one.
It were therefore greatly to be wished, that every
man should have the principles of Christianity, and
his own particular duty enforced upon his conscience, in a manner suited to his capacity, in private. And besides the occasional opportunities of
doing this, some of which have been intimated,
there are stated opportunities of doing it. Such,
for instance, is confirmation: and the usual age for
confirmation is that time of life, from which youth
must become more and more their own masters,
when they are often leaving their father's house,
going out into the wide world and all its numerous
temptations; against which they particularly want
to be fortified, by having strong and lively impressions of religion made upon their minds. Now the
61st canon expressly requires, that every minister
that hath care of souls shall use his best endeavour
to prepare and make able as many as he can to be
confirmed; which cannot be done as it ought without such personal application to each candidate in
particular as I am recommending. Another oppor-

tunity for doing this is, when any one of your parishioners signifies his name, as intending for the
first time to be partaker of the communion. The
rubric requires, that all persons, whenever they intend to receive, shall signify their names beforehand
to the minister; which, if it be not insisted upon in
all cases, ought absolutely to be insisted upon for
the first time. Now this even lays it in your way
to discourse with them in private upon the nature
and benefits of this sacrament, and enforce upon
them the importance and necessity of religion.
However I do not mean to put this upon the same
foot with catechizing youth, and preparing them for
confirmation; these being indispensable obligations,
and expressly commanded by our canons. This
private intercourse with your parishioners preparatory to their first communion, let it, if you please,
be considered as a voluntary service to religion on
your part, and a voluntary instance of docility on
theirs. I will only add as to this practice, that it is
regularly kept up by some persons, and particularly
by one, whose exemplary behaviour in every part
of the pastoral office is enforced upon you by his
station of authority and influence in (this part[6]
especially of) the diocese.

I am very sensible, my brethren, that some of
these things in places where they are greatly wanted
are impracticable, from the largeness of parishes,
suppose. And where there is no impediment of
this sort, yet the performance of them will depend
upon others, as well as upon you. People cannot
be admonished or instructed in private, unless they
will permit it. And little will you be able to do in
forming the minds of children to a sense of religion,

---

[6] The archdeaconry of Northumberland.

if their parents will not assist you in it; and yet much less, if they will frustrate your endeavours, by their bad example, and giving encouragement to their children to be dissolute. The like is to be said also of your influence in reforming the common people in general, in proportion as their superiors act in like manner to such parents; and whilst they, the lower people I mean, must have such numerous temptations to drunkenness and riot everywhere placed in their way. And it is cruel usage we often meet with, in being censured for not doing what we cannot do, without, what we cannot have, the concurrence of our censurers. Doubtless very much reproach which now lights upon the clergy would be found to fall elsewhere, if due allowances were made for things of this kind. But then we, my brethren, must take care and not make more than due allowances for them. If others deal uncharitably with us, we must deal impartially with ourselves, as in a matter of conscience, in determining what good is in our power to do: and not let indolence keep us from setting about what really is in our power; nor any heat of temper create obstacles in the prosecution of it, or render insuperable such as we find, when perhaps gentleness and patience would prevent or overcome them.

Indeed all this diligence to which I have been exhorting you and myself, for God forbid I should not consider myself as included in all the general admonitions you receive from me; all this diligence in these things does indeed suppose, that we *give ourselves wholly to them*. It supposes, not only that we have a real sense of religion upon our own minds, but also, that to promote the practice of it in others is habitually uppermost in our thought and intention, as the business of our lives. And this, my brethren,

is the business of our lives, in every sense, and upon
every account.   It is the general business of all
Christians as they have opportunity : it is our particular business.   It is so, as we have devoted ourselves to it by the most solemn engagements ; as,
according to our *Lord's appointment*, we *live of the
gospel ;* [7] and as the preservation and advancement
of religion, in such and such districts, are, in some
respects, our appropriated trust.

By being faithful in the discharge of this our
trust, by thus *taking heed to the ministry we have
received in the Lord that we fulfil it,* [8] we shall do
our part towards reviving a practical sense of religion amongst the people committed to our care.
And this will be the securest barrier against the
efforts of infidelity ; a great source of which plainly
is, the endeavour to get rid of religious restraints.
But whatever be our success with regard to others,
we shall have the approbation of our consciences,
and may rest assured, that, as to ourselves at least,
our labour is not in vain in the Lord. [9]

[7] 1 Cor. ix. 14.   [8] Col. iv. 17.   [9] 1 Cor. xv. 58.

z

FRAGMENTS.

I.

VISITATION OF THE SICK.

Extract from Bishop Butler's fourth Charge at Bristol, 1749, (taken from a MS. in Archbishop Secker's handwriting, and now printed from a Copy belonging to the Rev. Henry J. Rose.)

EXTREMES beget each other. Papists lay too much stress on the dying state of mind; but extravagantly too much on the forms used then: others quiet themselves in hopes of what they shall do for themselves, or their minister for them, at death. Hence bad men ridicule, and better men neglect the office of visiting the sick. But things are not useless because they have not all the extravagant uses which are ascribed to them. Ministers having knowledge of sickness [are] required to visit (Canon 67) and promise it in ordination. We should take it for granted we are desired, unless we see cause to the contrary. Our assistance would be kindly taken when not asked through lowness of spirits, negligence of attendants, or fear of being troublesome.

God means to remind us by sickness of our dependence on Him. Desiring the minister to pray

with or for them owns that dependence ; not desiring
it is a mark of the increase of irreligion. Many
avoid as much as possible the thought of death, even
when it happens to one in their own family. But
leaving men to die, like the beasts that perish, without religious admonition, or any exercise of piety performed by them, with them, or for them, helps to separate the ideas of Death and Religion and future
Judgment ; and thus the view of death will harden
persons in impenitence, whereas the occasion is a
very advantageous one for serious impressions to all
by-standers as well as the persons concerned.

Indeed without a good life no preparation for
death can be depended on ; men are so exceedingly
liable to mistake mere terrors of conscience for
repentance. But if God gives men the particular
warning of sickness, they should take it though they
have made a general preparation ; and if they have
led bad lives, it is not indifferent how they [may]
die, and we know not how important it may be.

Men are often easily brought in sickness to give and
ask forgiveness, which in health they neglect, though
a strict duty ; and also to settle their affairs. Now
these the minister is directed to remind them of. Also
to wean their hearts from the world, repent, exercise
faith, trust, resignation, thankfulness for which may
produce the peaceable fruits of righteousness. And
when sickness is the plain consequence of vice, we
should humbly acquiesce in it as a correction for
them, and *accept the punishment of our iniquities*,
Lev. xxvi. 41. 43. Thus we should look on death.
We say it is natural, the Scripture more properly
saith, it is appointed unto man to die. We should
receive it as the penalty of sin. But when we consider it as introductory to a future judgment, we
are apt to despond in a dangerous sickness, and our

mind needs as much assistance as our bodies, and
common humanity as much requires giving it.   The
sins and imperfections of the best as viewed by
them then, require to have His mercies, who is able
to save to the uttermost all that come to the Father
by Him set before them.   But the difficulty is
speaking to bad persons, who seem penitent, and to
their friends concerning them.   Anything that can
be called repentance is better than impenitence, and
doth good in proportion. to its kind and degree.
We know not how far ignorance, temptation, want
of admonition, may alleviate; nor can set bounds to
the mercy of the gospel, which is a dispensation of
mercy beyond the ordinary course of nature.   But
neither we, nor deathbed penitents can say whether
their penitence be true, so many having returned to
bad courses according to that most just, because
most loathsome description—*the Dog is turned to
his own vomit again, &c.*   The efficacy of Christ's
atonement is infinite, but the question is whether
they are qualified to partake of it, consistently with
the ends of Divine Government; and this, in this
case, God only knows.   They must be brought to
resign themselves to Him, submitting to die, in fear
that should they live they might return to their sins,
yet resolving and hoping the contrary, and so quietly
leave themselves in God's good hands.   Such distrust, not God, but themselves, as the case requires.
It is easier to compose such a dying penitent thus,
than to satisfy his friends. For real contrition renders
men humble and reasonable, and ready to acquiesce
in a doubtful hope of what they feel themselves unworthy of. But the love, and sorrow, and partiality
of friends makes them violent, and we must be infinitely cautious not to encourage them in wrong
presumptions, by what we say to the sick.

Visitation of the sick is as necessary with a view to their recovery as to their death, that they may use their restored health and threatened life better. They easily resolve well then, and if reminded afterwards of their fears, wishes and resolutions, it may be hoped these will settle into a principle of faith, or Christian piety, which faith always means, when it is made the condition of acceptance in the gospel, as fear of God always doth in the Old Testament. Thus their sickness will be, not unto death, but for the glory of God.

Ministers should not only be ready to visit the sick, but in preaching and conversation show them their need of this assistance. And should remember the time will soon come when we shall be in the circumstance in which we are now called upon to assist others. Happy if we can then apply to ourselves the transporting words of St. Paul " I have fought a good fight," &c., 2 *Tim.* iv.

II.

From the autographs of Bp. Butler now in the library at the British Museum. [Add. MS. 9815.]

GOD cannot approve of anything but what is in itself Right, Fit, Just. We should worship and endeavour to obey Him with this Consciousness and Recollection. To endeavour to please a man merely, is a different thing from endeavouring to please him as a wise and good man, *i. e.* endeavouring to please him in the particular way, of behaving towards him as we think the relations we stand in to him, and the intercourse we have with him, require.

Almighty God is to be sure infinitely removed from all those human weaknesses which we express by the words, captious, apt to take offence, &c. But an unthinking world does not consider what may be absolutely due to Him from all Creatures capable of considering themselves as His Creatures. Recollect the idea, inadequate as it is, which we have of God, and the idea of ourselves, and carelessness with regard to Him, whether we are to worship Him at all, whether we worship Him in a right manner, or conceited confidence that we do so, will seem to imply unspeakable Presumption. Neither do we know what necessary, unalterable connection there may be, between moral right and happiness, moral wrong and misery.

Sincerity is doubtless the thing, and not whether we hit the right manner, &c. But a sense of the imperfection of our worship, apprehension that it may be, and a degree of fear that it is, in some respects erroneous, may perhaps be a temper of mind not unbecoming such poor creatures as we are, in our addresses to God. In proportion as we are assured that we are honest and sincere, we may rest satisfied that God cannot be offended with us, but indifference whether what we do be materially, or in the nature of the thing abstracted from our way of considering it, Good and Right,—such indifference is utterly inconsistent with Sincerity.

No person who has just notions of God can be afraid of His displeasure any further than as he is afraid of his own Character, whether it be what it ought: but so far as a man has reason to fear his own character, so far there must be reason to fear God's displeasure or disapprobation ; not from any doubt of His Perfection and Goodness, but merely from the belief of it.

Is it possible that people can be Scepticks in *Opinion*, and yet without any doubtfulness, or solicitude about their *Actions* and *Behaviour?*

WHAT a wonderful incongruity it is for a man to see the doubtfulness in which things are involved, and yet be impatient out of action, or vehement in it! Say a man is a Sceptick, and add what was said of Brutus, *quicquid vult valde vult*, and you say, there is the greatest Contrariety between his Understanding and his Temper that can be expressed in words.

IN general a man ought not to do other people's duty for them; for their duty was appointed them for their exercise; and besides, who will do it in case of his death? Nor has a man any right to raise in others such a dependance upon him as that they must be miserable in case of his death, though whilst he lives he answers that dependance.

HOBBS' definition of Benevolence, that 'tis the love of power, is base and false, but there is more of truth in it than appears at first sight; the real Benevolence of men being, I think, for the most part, not indeed the single love of power, but the love of power to be exercised in the way of doing good; that is a different thing from the love of the good or happiness of others by whomsoever effected, which last I call single or simple Benevolence. How little there is of this in the world may appear by observing, how many persons can bear with great tranquillity that a friend or a child should live in misery, who yet cannot bear the thought of their death.

GOOD men surely are not treated in this world as

they deserve, yet 'tis seldom, very seldom their
goodness which makes them disliked, even in cases
where it may seem to be so: but 'tis some behaviour
or other, which however excusable, perhaps infinitely
overbalanced by their virtues, yet is offensive, possibly wrong; however such, it may be, as would pass
off very well in a man of the world.

SHALL I not be faithful to God? If he puts a part
upon me to do, shall I neglect or refuse it? A
part to suffer, and shall I say I would not if I could
help it? Can words more ill-sorted, more shocking
be put together? And is not the thing expressed
by them more so, though not expressed in words?
What then shall I prefer to the sovereign Good,
supreme Excellence, absolute Perfection? To
whom shall I apply for direction in opposition to
Infinite Wisdom? To whom for protection against
Almighty Power?
                    Sunday Evening, June 13, 1742.

HUNGER and thirst after Righteousness till filled
with it by being made partaker of the Divine nature.

AD te levo oculos meos, qui habitas in coelis. Sicut
oculi servorum *intenti sunt* ad manum dominorum
suorum, sicut oculi ancillae ad manum dominae
suae; ita oculi nostri ad Deum nostrum, donec
misereatur nostri.
   As all my passions and affections to my Reason
such as it is, so in consideration of the fallibility
and infinite deficiencies of this my Reason, I would
subject it to God, that He may guide and succour it.
   Our wants as Creatures: our Demerits as Sinners.
   That I may have a due sense of the hand of God
in everything, and then put myself into His hand

to lead me through whatever ways He shall think fit; either to add to my burden, or lighten it, or wholly discharge me of it.

Be more afraid of myself than of the world.

To discern the hand of God in everything and have a due sense of it.

Instead of deluding oneself in imagining one should behave well in times and circumstances other than those in which one is placed, to take care and be faithful and behave well in those one is placed in.

That God would please to make my way plain before my face, and deliver me from offendiculum of scrupulousness, or if not, O assist me to act the right part under it!

CORRESPONDENCE WITH

DR. CLARKE.

I.

REVEREND SIR,

I SUPPOSE you will wonder at the present trouble from one who is a perfect stranger to you, though you are not so to him; but I hope the occasion will excuse my boldness. I have made it, sir, my business, ever since I thought myself capable of such sort of reasoning, to prove to myself the being and attributes of God. And being sensible that it is a matter of the last consequence, I endeavoured after a demonstrative proof; not only more fully to satisfy my own mind, but also in order to defend the great truths of natural religion, and those of the Christian revelation which follow from them, against all opposers: but must own with concern, that hitherto I have been unsuccessful; and though I have got very probable arguments, yet I can go but a very little way with demonstration in the proof of those things. When first your book on those subjects (which by all, whom I have discoursed with, is so justly esteemed) was recommended to me, I was in great hopes of having all my inquiries answered. But since in some places, either through my not understanding your meaning, or what else I know not, even that has failed me, I almost despair of ever arriving to such a satisfaction as I aim at, unless by the method I now use. You cannot but know, sir, that of two different expressions of the same thing, though equally clear to some persons, yet to others one of them is sometimes very obscure, though the other be perfectly intelligible. Perhaps this may be my case here; and could I see those of your arguments, of which I doubt, differently proposed, possibly I might yield a ready assent to them. This, sir, I cannot but think a sufficient excuse for the present trouble; it being such an one as I hope may prevail for an answer, with one who seems to aim at nothing more than that good work of instructing others.

In your Demonstration of the Being and Attributes of God, Prop. VI.[1] [edit. 2d. p. 69, 70.] you propose to prove the infinity or omnipresence of the self-existent Being. The former part of the proof seems highly probable; but the latter part, which seems to aim at demonstration, is not to me convincing. The latter part of the paragraph is, if I mistake not, an entire argument of itself, which runs thus: "To suppose a finite being to be self-existent, is to say that it is a contradiction for that being not to exist, the absence of which may yet be conceived without a contradiction; which is the greatest absurdity in the world." The sense of these words ["the absence of which"] seems plainly

[1] P. 45. edit. 4; p. 41. edit. 6; p. 43. edit. 7; p. 44. edit. 8.

to be determined by the following sentence, to
mean its absence from any particular place. Which
sentence is to prove it to be an absurdity; and is
this: " For if a being can, without a contradiction,
be absent from one place, it may, without a contradiction, be absent from another place, and from all
places."   Now supposing this to be a consequence,
all that it proves is, that if a being can, without a
contradiction, be absent from one place at one time,
it may, without a contradiction, be absent from
another place, and so from all places, at different
times; (for I cannot see, that if a being can be absent from one place at one time, therefore it may,
without a contradiction, be absent from all places
at the same time, i.e. may cease to exist.) Now,
if it proves no more than this, I cannot see that it
reduces the supposition to an absurdity. Suppose
I could demonstrate, that any particular man should
live a thousand years; this man might, without a
contradiction, be absent from one and all places at
different times; but it would not from thence follow, that he might be absent from all places at the
same time, i.e. that he might cease to exist. No;
this would be a contradiction, because I am supposed
to have demonstrated that he should live a thousand
years.   It would be exactly the same, if, instead of
a thousand years, I should say, for ever; and the
proof seems the same, whether it be applied to a
self-existent or a dependent being.

What else I have to offer is in relation to your
proof, that the self-existent being must of necessity
be but one. Which proof is as follows, in Prop.
VII.[2] [edit. 2d. p. 74.] " To suppose two or more

---

[2] P. 48. edit. 4; p. 44. edit. 6; p. 46. edit. 7; p. 47. edit. 8.

different natures existing of themselves, necessarily,
and independent from each other, implies this plain
contradiction; that, each of them being independent
from the other, they may either of them be supposed to exist alone; so that it will be no contradiction to imagine the other not to exist, and consequently neither of them will be necessarily existing." The supposition indeed implies, that since
each of these beings is independent from the other,
they may either of them exist alone, *i.e.* without
any relation to, or dependence on, the other: but
where is the third idea, to connect this proposition
and the following one, viz. " so that it will be no
contradiction to imagine the other not to exist?"
Were this a consequence of the former proposition,
I allow it would be demonstration, by the first co-
rollary of Prop. III.[3] [2d edit. p. 26.] but since these
two propositions, ["they may either of them be
supposed to exist alone,"] and, [" so that it will be
no contradiction to imagine the other not to exist,"]
are very widely different; since likewise it is no
immediate consequence, that because either may
be supposed to exist independent from the other,
therefore the other may be supposed not to exist
at all; how is what was proposed, proved? That
the propositions are different, I think is plain; and
whether there be an immediate connection, everybody that reads your book must judge for themselves. I must say, for my own part, the absurdity
does not appear at first sight, any more than the
absurdity of saying that the angles below the base
in an isosceles triangle are unequal; which though
it is absolutely false, yet I suppose no one will lay

[3] P. 16, 17. edit. 4, 6, 7, and 8.

down the contrary for an axiom; because, though it is true, yet there is need of a proof to make it appear so.

Perhaps it may be answered, that I have not rightly explained the words, " to exist alone ;" and that they do not mean only, to exist independent from the other; but that " existing alone" means that nothing exists with it. Whether this or the other was meant, I cannot determine: but which ever it was, what I have said will hold. For if this last be the sense of those words, ["they either of them may be supposed to exist alone ;"] it indeed implies that it will be no contradiction to suppose the other not to exist: but then I ask, how come these two propositions to be connected; that, to suppose two different natures existing of themselves necessarily and independent from each other, implies that each of them may be supposed to exist alone in this sense? Which is exactly the same as I said before, only applied to different sentences. So that if " existing alone" be understood as I first took it, I allow it is implied in the supposition; but cannot see that the consequence is, that it will be no contradiction to suppose the other not to exist. But if the words, " existing alone," are meant in the latter sense, I grant, that if either of them may be supposed thus to exist alone, it will be no contradiction to suppose the other not to exist: but then I cannot see, that to suppose two different natures existing, of themselves, necessarily and independent from each other, implies that either of them may be supposed to exist alone in this sense of the words; but only, that either of them may be supposed to exist without having any relation to the other, and that there will be no need of the existence of the one in order to the existence of the other. But though upon this account, were there no other principle of its existence, it might cease to exist; yet on the account of the necessity of its own nature, which is quite distinct from the other, it is an absolute absurdity to suppose it not to exist.

Thus, sir, I have proposed my doubts, with the reasons of them. In which if I have wrested your words to another sense than you designed them, or in any respect argued unfairly, I assure you it was without design. So I hope you will impute it to mistake. And, if it will not be too great a trouble, let me once more beg the favour of a line from you, by which you will lay me under a particular obligation to be, what, with the rest of the world, I now am,

Reverend Sir,

Your most obliged servant, &c.

Nov. 4, 1713.

THE ANSWER.

Sir,

DID men who publish controversial papers accustom themselves to write with that candour and ingenuity, with which you propose your difficulties, I am persuaded almost all disputes might be very amicably terminated, either by men's coming at last to agree in opinion, or at least finding reason to suffer each other friendly to differ.

Your two objections are very ingenious, and urged with great strength and acuteness. Yet I am not without hopes of being able to give you satisfaction in both of them.   To your first, therefore, I answer : Whatever may, without a contradiction, be absent from any one place, at any one time, may also, without a contradiction, be absent from all places at all times.   For, whatever is absolutely necessary at all, is absolutely necessary in every part of space, and in every point of duration.   Whatever can at any time be conceived possible to be absent from any one part of space, may for the same reason, [viz. the implying no contradiction in the nature of things] be conceived possible to be absent from every other part of space at the same time ; either by ceasing to be, or by supposing it never to have begun to be.   Your instance about demonstrating a man to live a thousand years, is what, I think, led you into the mistake ; and is a good instance to lead you out of it again.   You may suppose a man shall live a thousand years, or God may reveal and promise he shall live a thousand years ; and upon that supposition, it shall not be possible for the man to be absent from all places in any part of that time. Very true : but why shall it not be possible ? only because it is contrary to the supposition, or to the promise of God ; but not contrary to the absolute nature of things ; which would be the case, if the man existed necessarily, as every part of space does. In supposing you could demonstrate, a man should live a thousand years, or one year ; you make an impossible and contradictory supposition. For though you may know certainly (by revelation suppose) that he will live so long ; yet this is only the certainty of a thing true in fact, not in itself necessary : and demonstration is applicable to nothing but what is necessary in itself, necessary in all places and at all times equally.

To your second difficulty, I answer: What exists
necessarily, not only must so exist alone, as to be
independent of anything else; but (being self-suf-
ficient) may also so exist alone, as that everything
else may possibly (or without any contradiction in
the nature of things) be supposed not to exist at
all: and consequently, (since that which may possibly be supposed not to exist at all, is not necessarily existent,) no other thing can be necessarily
existent. Whatever is necessarily existing, there is
need of its existence in order to the supposal of the
existence of any other thing; so that nothing can
possibly be supposed to exist, without presupposing
and including antecedently the existence of that
which is necessary. For instance; the supposal
of the existence of anything whatever includes necessarily a presupposition of the existence of space
and time; and if anything could exist without space
or time, it would follow that space and time were
not necessarily existing. Therefore, the supposing
anything possibly to exist alone, so as not necessarily
to include the presupposal of some other thing,
proves demonstrably that that other thing is not
necessarily existing; because, whatever has necessity of existence cannot possibly, in any conception
whatsoever be supposed away. There cannot possibly be any notion of the existence of anything,
there cannot possibly be any notion of existence at
all, but what shall necessarily preinclude the notion
of that which has necessary existence. And consequently the two propositions, which you judged independent, are really necessarily connected. These
sorts of things are indeed very difficult to express,
and not easy to be conceived but by very attentive
minds: but to such as can and will attend, nothing,
I think, is more demonstrably convictive.

If anything still sticks with you in this or any
other part of my books, I shall be very willing to be
informed of it; who am,

Sir,

Your assured friend and servant,

S. C.

Nov. 10, 1713.

P. S. Many readers, I observe, have misunderstood my second general proposition; as if the
words ["some one unchangeable and independent
being"] meant [one only—being;] whereas the
true meaning, and all that the argument there requires, is, [some one at least.] That there can be
but one, is the thing proved afterwards in the se-
venth proposition.

II.

Reverend Sir,

I HAVE often thought that the chief occasions
of men's differing so much in their opinions,
were, either their not understanding each other;
or else, that, instead of ingenuously searching after
truth, they have made it their business to find out
arguments for the proof of what they have once
asserted. However, it is certain there may be other
reasons for persons not agreeing in their opinions:
and where it is so, I cannot but think with you,
that they will find reason to suffer each other to
differ friendly; every man having a way of thinking,
in some respects, peculiarly his own.

I am sorry I must tell you, your answers to my
objections are not satisfactory. The reasons why
I think them not so are as follow:—

You say, "Whatever is absolutely necessary at
all is absolutely necessary in every part of space,
and in every point of duration." Were this evident,
it would certainly prove what you bring it for; viz.
that "whatever may, without a contradiction, be
absent from one place, at one time, may also be
absent from all place at all times." But I do not
conceive, that the idea of ubiquity is contained in
the idea of self-existence, or directly follows from
it; any otherwise than as, whatever exists must
exist somewhere. You add, "Whatever can at any
time be conceived possible to be absent from any
one part of space, may for the same reason [viz. the
implying no contradiction in the nature of things]
be conceived possible to be absent from every other
part of space at the same time." Now I cannot
see, that I can make these two suppositions for the
same reason, or upon the same account. The reason why I conceive this being may be absent from
one place, is because it doth not contradict the
former proof, [drawn from the nature of things,] in
which I proved only that it must necessarily exist.
But the other supposition, viz. that I can conceive
it possible to be absent from every part of space
at one and the same time, directly contradicts the
proof that it must exist somewhere; and so is an
express contradiction. Unless it be said, that as,
when we have proved the three angles of a triangle
equal to two right ones, that relation of the equality
of its angles to two right ones will be wherever a
triangle exists; so, when we have proved the necessary existence of a being, this being must exist
everywhere. But there is a great difference be-

tween these two things: the one being the proof
of a certain relation, upon supposition of such a
being's existence with such particular properties;
and consequently, wherever this being and these
properties exist, this relation must exist too: but
from the proof of the necessary existence of a being,
it is no evident consequence that it exists everywhere. My using the word *demonstration* instead
of *proof which leaves no room for doubt*, was through
negligence, for I never heard of strict demonstration of matter of fact.

In your answer to my second difficulty, you say,
" Whatsoever is necessarily existing, there is need
of its existence, in order to the supposal of the existence of any other thing." All the consequences
you draw from this proposition, I see proved demonstrably; and consequently, that the two propositions I thought independent are closely connected. But how, or upon what account, is there
need of the existence of whatever is necessarily
existing, in order to the existence of any other
thing ? Is it as there is need of space and duration, in order to the existence of anything; or is it
needful only as the cause of the existence of all
other things ? If the former be said, as your instance seems to intimate: I answer; space and
duration are very abstruse in their natures, and,
I think, cannot properly be called things, but are
considered rather as affections which belong, and
in the order of our thoughts are antecedently necessary, to the existence of all things. And I can
no more conceive how a necessarily existent being
can, on the same account, or in the same manner
as space and duration are, be needful in order to
the existence of any other being, than I can conceive extension attributed to a thought; that idea

no more belonging to a thing existing, than extension belongs to thought. But if the latter be said,
that there is need of the existence of whatever is a
necessary being, in order to the existence of any
other thing; only as this necessary being must be
the cause of the existence of all other things: I
think this is plainly begging the question; for it
supposes that there is no other being exists, but
what is caused, and so not necessary. And on what
other account, or in what other manner than one of
these two, there can be need of the existence of a
necessary being in order to the existence of anything else, I cannot conceive.

Thus, Sir, you see I entirely agree with you in
all the consequences you have drawn from your
suppositions, but cannot see the truth of the suppositions themselves.

I have aimed at nothing in my style, but only to
be intelligible; being sensible that it is very difficult (as you observe) to express one's self on these
sorts of subjects, especially for one who is altogether
unaccustomed to write upon them.

I have nothing at present more to add, but my
sincerest thanks for your trouble in answering my
letter, and for your professed readiness to be acquainted with any other difficulty that I may meet
with in any of your writings. I am willing to inter-
pret this, as somewhat like a promise of an answer
to what I have now written, if there be anything in
it which deserves one.

I am, Reverend Sir,

Your most obliged humble servant.

Nov. 23, 1713.

THE ANSWER.

SIR,

IT seems to me, that the reason why you do not apprehend ubiquity to be necessarily connected with self-existence, is because, in the order of your ideas, you first conceive a being, (a finite being, suppose,) and then conceive self-existence to be a property of that being; as the angles are properties of a triangle, when a triangle exists : whereas, on the contrary, necessity of existence, not being a property consequent upon the supposition of the things existing, but antecedently the cause or ground of that existence ; it is evident this necessity, being not limited to any antecedent subject, as angles are to a triangle ; but being itself original, absolute, and (in order of nature) antecedent to all existence; cannot but be everywhere, for the same reason that it is anywhere.   By applying this reasoning to the instance of space, you will find, that by consequence it belongs truly to that substance, whereof space is a *property, as duration also is.   What you say about a necessary being existing somewhere, sup- poses it to be finite ; and being finite, supposes some cause which determined that such a certain quantity of that being should exist, neither more nor less : and that cause must either be a voluntary cause ; or else such a necessary cause, the quantity of whose power must be determined and limited by some other cause.   But in original absolute necessity, antecedent (in order of nature) to the existence of anything, nothing of all this can have place : but the necessity is necessarily everywhere alike.

Or, mode of existence.

Concerning the second difficulty, I answer: That which exists necessarily, is needful to the existence of any other thing; not considered now as a cause, (for that indeed is begging the question,) but as a *sine qua non;* in the sense as space is necessary to everything, and nothing can possibly be conceived to exist, without thereby presupposing space: which therefore I apprehend to be a property or mode of the self-existent substance; and that, by being evidently necessary itself, it proves that the substance, of which it is a property, must also be necessary; necessary both in itself, and needful to the existence of anything else whatsoever. Extension indeed does not belong to thought, because thought is not a being; but there is need of extension to the existence of every being, to a being which has or has not thought, or any other quality whatsoever.

I am, Sir,

Your real friend and servant.

London, Nov. 28, 1713.

III.

Reverend Sir,

I DO not very well understand your meaning, when you say that you think, "in the order of my ideas I first conceive a being (finite suppose) to exist, and then conceive self-existence to be a property of that being." If you mean that I first suppose a finite being to exist I know not why; affirming necessity of existence to be only a consequent of its existence; and that, when I have supposed it finite, I very safely conclude it is not infinite ; I am utterly at a loss, upon what expressions in my letter this conjecture can be founded. But if you mean, that I first of all prove a being to exist from eternity, and then, from the reasons of things, prove that such a being must be eternally necessary ; I freely own it. Neither do I conceive it to be irregular or absurd ; for there is a great difference between the order in which things exist, and the order in which I prove to myself that they exist. Neither do I think my saying a necessary being exists somewhere, supposes it to be finite ; it only supposes that this being exists in space, without determining whether here, or there, or everywhere.

To my second objection, you say, " That which exists necessarily, is needful to the existence of any other thing, as a *sine qua non ;* in the sense space is necessary to everything : which is proved (you say) by this consideration, that space is a property of the self-existent substance ; and, being both necessary in itself, and needful to the existence of everything else ; consequently the substance, of which it is a property must be so too." Space, I own, is in one sense a property of the self-existent substance ; but, in the same sense, it is also a property of all other substances. The only difference is in respect to the quantity. And since every part of space, as well as the whole, is necessary ; every substance consequently must be self-existent, because it hath this self-existent property. Which since you will not admit for true ; if it directly follows from your arguments, they cannot be conclusive.

What you say under the first head proves, I think, to a very great probability, though not to me with the evidence of demonstration : but your arguments under the second I am not able to see the force of.

I am so far from being pleased that I can form objections to your arguments, that, besides the satisfaction it would have given me in my own mind, I should have thought it an honour to have entered into your reasonings, and seen the force of them. I cannot desire to trespass any more upon your better employed time ; so shall only add my hearty thanks for your trouble on my account, and that I am with the greatest respect,

Reverend Sir,

Your most obliged humble servant.

Dec. 5, 1713.

THE ANSWER.

SIR,

THOUGH, when I turn my thoughts every way, I fully persuade myself there is no defect in the argument itself; yet in my manner of expression I am satisfied there must be some want of clearness, when there remains any difficulty to a person of your abilities and sagacity. I did not mean that your saying a necessary being exists somewhere, does necessarily suppose it to be finite; but that the manner of expression is apt to excite in the mind an idea of a finite being, at the same time that you are thinking of a necessary being, without accurately attending to the nature of that necessity by which it exists. Necessity absolute, and antecedent (in order of nature) to the existence of any subject, has nothing to limit it; but, if it operates at all, (as it must needs do,) it must operate (if I may so speak) everywhere and at all times alike. Determination of a particular quantity, or particular time or place of existence of anything, cannot arise but from somewhat external to the thing itself. For example: why there should exist just such a small determinate quantity of matter, neither more nor less, interspersed in the immense vacuities of space, no reason can be given. Nor can there be anything in nature, which could have determined a thing so indifferent in itself, as is the measure of that quantity; but only the will of an intelligent and free agent. To suppose matter, or any other substance, necessarily existing in a finite determinate quantity; in an inch-cube, for instance; or in any certain number of cube-inches, and no more; it is exactly the same absurdity, as supposing it to exist necessarily, and yet for a finite duration only: which every one sees to be a plain contradiction. The argument is likewise the same, in the question about the original of motion. Motion cannot be necessarily existing; because, it being evident that all determinations of motion are equally possible in themselves, the original determination of the motion of any particular body this way rather than the contrary way, could not be necessarily in itself, but was either caused by the will of an intelligent and free agent, or else was an effect produced and determined without any cause at all; which is an express contradiction: as I have shown in my *Demonstration of the Being and Attributes of God*. [Page 14, edit. 4th and 5th; page 12, edit. 6th and 7th.]

To the second head of argument, I answer: Space is a property [or mode] of the self-existent substance; but not of any other substances. All other substances are in space, and are penetrated by it;

but the self-existent substance is not in space, nor penetrated by it, but is itself (if I may so speak) the substratum of space, the ground of the existence of space and duration itself. Which [space and duration] being evidently necessary, and yet themselves not substances, but properties or modes, shew evidently that the substance, without which these properties could not subsist, is itself, much more (if that were possible) necessary. And as space and duration are needful (*i. e. sine qua non*) to the existence of everything else; so consequently is the substance, to which these properties belong in that peculiar manner which I before mentioned.

I am, Sir,

Your affectionate friend and servant.

Dec. 10, 1713.

IV.

REVEREND SIR,

WHATEVER is the occasion of my not seeing the force of your reasonings, I cannot impute it to [what you do] the want of clearness in your expression. I am too well acquainted with myself, to think my not understanding an argument, a sufficient reason to conclude that it is either improperly expressed, or not conclusive; unless I can clearly shew the defect of it. It is with the greatest satisfaction I must tell you, that the more I reflect on your first argument, the more I am convinced of the truth of it; and it now seems to

me altogether unreasonable to suppose absolute
necessity can have any relation to one part of space
more than to another; and if so, an absolutely necessary being must exist everywhere.

I wish I was as well satisfied in respect to the
other. You say, " All substances, except the self-
existent one, are in space, and are penetrated by
it. All substances doubtless, whether body or spirit,
exist in space : but when I say that a spirit exists
in space, were I put upon telling my meaning, I
know not how I could do it any other way than by
saying, such a particular quantity of space termi-
nates the capacity of acting in finite spirits at one
and the same time ; so that they cannot act beyond
that determined quantity. Not but that I think there
is somewhat in the manner of existence of spirits in
respect of space, that more directly answers to the
manner of the existence of body ; but what that is,
or of the manner of their existence, I cannot possibly form an idea. And it seems (if possible) much
more difficult to determine what relation the self-
existent Being hath to space. To say he exists in
space, after the same manner that other substances
do, (somewhat like which I too rashly asserted in
my last,) perhaps would be placing the Creator too
much on a level with the creature ; or however, it
is not plainly and evidently true : and to say the
self-existent substance is the substratum of space,
in the common sense of the word, is scarce intelligible, or at least is not evident. Now though there
may be an hundred relations distinct from either of
these ; yet how we should come by ideas of them,
I cannot conceive. We may indeed have ideas to
the words, and not altogether depart from the common sense of them, when we say the self-existent
substance is the substratum of space, or the ground

of its existence: but I see no reason to think it
true, because space seems to me to be as absolutely
self-existent, as it is possible anything can be: so
that, make what other supposition you please, yet
we cannot help supposing immense space; because
there must be either an infinity of being, or (if you
will allow the expression) an infinite vacuity of
being. Perhaps it may be objected to this, that
though space is really necessary, yet the reason of
its being necessary is its being a property of the
self-existent substance; and that, it being so evidently necessary, and its dependence on the self-
existent evidence not so evident, we are ready to
conclude it absolutely self-existent, as well as necessary; and that this is the reason why the idea of
space forces itself on our minds, antecedent to, and
exclusive of (as to the ground of its existence) all
other things. Now this, though it is really an objection, yet is no direct answer to what I have said;
because it supposes the only thing to be proved,
viz. that the reason why space is necessary is its
being a property of a self-existent substance. And
supposing it not to be evident, that space is absolutely self-existent; yet, while it is doubtful, we
cannot argue as though the contrary were certain,
and we were sure that space was only a property of
the self-existent substance. But now, if space be
not absolutely independent, I do not see what we
can conclude is so: for it is manifestly necessary
itself, as well as antecedently needful to the existence of all other things, not excepting (as I think)
even the self-existent substance.

All your consequences, I see, follow demonstrably
from your supposition; and, were that evident, I
believe it would serve to prove several other things
as well as what you bring it for. Upon which ac-

count, I should be extremely pleased to see it proved by any one. For, as I design the search after truth as the business of my life, I shall not be ashamed to learn from any person; though, at the same time, I cannot but be sensible, that instruction from some men is like the gift of a prince, it reflects an honour on the person on whom it lays an obligation.

I am, Reverend Sir,

Your obliged servant.

Dec. 16, 1713.

THE ANSWER.

SIR,

MY being out of town most part of the month of January, and some other accidental avocations, hindered me from answering your letter sooner. The sum of the difficulties it contains is, I think, this: that "it is difficult to determine what relation the self-existent substance has to space:" that "to say it is the substratum of space, in the common sense of the word, is scarce intelligible, or, at least, is not evident:" that "space seems to be as absolutely self-existent, as it is possible anything can be:" and that "its being a property of the self-existent substance is supposing the thing that was to be proved." This is entering indeed into the very bottom of the matter; and I will endeavour to give you as brief and clear an answer as I can.

That the self-existent substance is the substratum of space, or space a property of the self-existent substance, are not perhaps very proper expressions; nor is it easy to find such. But what I mean is this: The idea of space (as also of time or duration) is an abstract or partial idea; an idea of a certain quality or relation, which we evidently see to be necessarily existing; and yet which (not being itself a substance) at the same time necessarily pre-supposes a substance, without which it could not exist; which substance consequently must be itself (much more, if possible) necessarily existing. I know not how to explain this so well as by the following similitude. A blind man, when he tries to frame to himself the idea of body, his idea is nothing but that of hardness. A man that had eyes, but no power of motion, or sense of feeling at all; when he tried to frame to himself the idea of body, his idea would be nothing but that of colour. Now as, in these cases, hardness is not body, and colour is not body; but yet, to the understanding of these persons, those properties necessarily infer the being of a substance, of which substance itself the persons have no idea: so space to us is not itself substance, but it necessarily infers the being of a substance, which affects none of. our present senses; and, being itself necessary, it follows, that the substance, which it infers, is (much more) necessary.

I am, Sir,

Your affectionate friend and servant.

Jan. 29, 1713.

V.

REVEREND SIR,

YOU have very comprehensively expressed, in six or seven lines, all the difficulties of my letter; which I should have endeavoured to have made shorter, had I not been afraid an improper expression might possibly occasion a mistake of my meaning. I am very glad the debate is come into so narrow a compass; for I think now it entirely turns upon this, whether our ideas of space and duration are partial, so as to presuppose the existence of some other thing. Your similitude of the blind man is very apt, to explain your meaning, (which I think I fully understand,) but does not seem to come entirely up to the matter. For what is the reason that the blind man concludes there must be somewhat external, to give him that idea of hardness? It is because he supposes it impossible for him to be thus affected, unless there were some cause of it; which cause, should it be removed, the effect would immediately cease too; and he would no more have the idea of hardness, but by remembrance. Now to apply this to the instance of space and duration: Since a man, from his having these ideas, very justly concludes that there must be somewhat external, which is the cause of them; consequently, should this cause (whatever it is) be taken away, his ideas would be so too: therefore, if what is supposed to be the cause be removed, and yet the idea remains, that supposed cause cannot be the real one. Now,

granting the self-existent substance to be the substratum of these ideas, could we make the supposition of its ceasing to be, yet space and duration
would still remain unaltered : which seems to shew,
that the self-existent substance is not the substratum of space and duration. Nor would it be an
answer to the difficulty, to say that every property
of the self-existent substance is as necessary as the
substance itself; since that will only hold, while the
substance itself exists; for there is implied, in the
idea of a property, an impossibility of subsisting
without its substratum. I grant, the supposition is
absurd : but how otherwise can we know whether
anything be a property of such a substance, but by
examining whether it would cease to be, if its supposed substance should do so? Notwithstanding
what I have now said, I cannot say that I believe
your argument not conclusive; for I must own my
ignorance, and that I am really at a loss about the
nature of space and duration. But did it plainly
appear that they were properties of a substance, we
should have an easy way with the atheists: for it
would at once prove demonstrably an eternal, necessary, self-existent Being; that there is but one
such; and that he is needful in order to the existence
of all other things. Which makes me think, that
though it may be true, yet it is not obvious to every
capacity: otherwise it would have been generally
used, as a fundamental argument to prove the being
of God.

I must add one thing more; that your argument
for the omnipresence of God seemed always to me
very probable. But being very desirous to have it
appear demonstrably conclusive, I was sometimes
forced to say what was not altogether my opinion:
not that I did this for the sake of disputing, (for,

B B

besides the particular disagreeableness of this to my
own temper, I should surely have chosen another
person to have trifled with;) but I did it to set off
the objection to advantage, that it might be more
fully answered. I heartily wish you as fair treatment from your opponents in print, as I have had
from you; though, I must own, I cannot see, in
those that I have read, that unprejudiced search
after truth, which I would have hoped for.

I am, Reverend Sir,

Your most humble servant.

Feb. 3, 1713.

THE ANSWER.

SIR,

IN a multitude of business, I mislaid your last
letter, and could not answer it, till it came again
to my hands by chance. We seem to have pushed
the matter in question between us as far as it will
go ; and, upon the whole, I cannot but take notice,
I have very seldom met with persons so reasonable
and unprejudiced as yourself, in such debates as
these.

I think all I need say, in answer to the reasoning
in your letter, is, that your granting the absurdity
of the supposition you were endeavouring to make,
is consequently granting the necessary truth of my
argument. If[5] space and duration necessarily re-

[5] Ut partium temporis ordo est immutabilis, sic etiam ordo
partium spatii. Moveantur hæ de locis suis, et movebuntur
(ut ita dicam) de seipsis. *Newton, Princip. Mathemat. Schol. ad
definit.* 8.

main, even after they are supposed to be taken
away; and be not (as it is plain they are not)
themselves substances; then the[6] substance, on
whose existence they depend, will necessarily remain likewise, even after it is supposed to be taken
away: which shews that supposition to be impossible and contradictory.

As to your observation at the end of your letter;
that the argument I have insisted on, if it were
obvious to every capacity, should have more frequently been used as a fundamental argument for a
proof of the being of God: the true cause why it
has been seldom urged, is, I think, this; that the
universal prevalency of Cartes's absurd notions
(teaching that[7] matter is necessarily infinite and
necessarily eternal, and ascribing all things to mere
mechanic laws of motion, exclusive of final causes,
and of all will and intelligence and divine Providence
from the government of the world) hath incredibly
blinded the eyes of common reason, and prevented
men from discerning *him in whom they live, and
move, and have their being.* The like has happened
in some other instances. How universally have men
for many ages believed, that eternity is no duration

[6] Deus non est æternitas vel infinitas, sed æternus et in-
finitus; non est duratio vel spatium, sed durat et adest. Durat
semper, et adest ubique; et existendo semper et ubique, dura-
tionem et spatium, æternitatem et infinitatem, constituit. Cum
unaquæque spitii particula sit semper; et unumquodque du-
rationis indivisibile momentum ubique; certe rerum omnium
Fabricator ac Dominus non erit nunquam nusquam. Omni-
præsens est, non per virtutem solam, sed etiam per substantiam:
nam virtus sine substantia subsistere non potest   In ipso con-
tinentur et moventur universa, &c. *Newton, Princip. Mathemat. Schol. general. sub finem.*

[7] Puto implicare contradictionem, ut mundus [meaning the
material world] sit finitus. *Cartes, Epist. 69. Partis primæ.*

at all, and infinity no amplitude! Something of the
like kind has happened in the matter of transub-
stantiation, and, I think, in the scholastic notion of
the Trinity, &c.

> I am, Sir,

> > Your affectionate friend and servant.

April 8, 1713.

VI.

[*From a Copy formerly belonging to Dr. Birch, and
now in the library at the British Museum.* Add.
MS. 4370.]

REVEREND DR.

'TWAS but last night I received your letter from
Gloucester, having left that place three weeks
since.   It revived in my mind some very melancholy
thoughts I had upon my being obliged to quit those
studies, that had a direct tendency to divinity, that
being what I should chuse for the business of my
life, it being, I think, of all other studies the most
suitable to a reasonable nature.   I say my being
obliged, for there is every encouragement (whether
one regards interest or usefulness) now-a-days for
any to enter that profession, who has not got a way
of commanding his assent to received opinions
without examination.

I had some thoughts, Sir, of paying you my ac-
knowledgments in person for that surprising air of
candour and affability with which you have treated

me in the Letters that have passed between us. But really I could not put on so bold a face, as to intrude into a gentleman's company with no other excuse but that of having received an obligation from him. I have not the least prospect of ever being in a capacity of giving any more than a verbal declaration of my gratitude : so I hope you'l accept that, and believe it's with the utmost sincerity I subscribe myself,

Sir,

Your most obliged, most obedient humble servant.

Hamlin's Coffee-house,
Tuesday Morning.

VII.

[From the European Magazine, vol. xli. p. 9.
Jan. 1802.]

SIR,

WHEN I was in town I mentioned somewhat to you of going to Cambridge to take degrees in laws; you did not disapprove of it; upon which I resolved to remove thither as soon as I could get my father's consent, which I now have, and therefore desire your advice concerning a college and tutor there; for not having taken any degree, I suppose I must enter under some particular man. When I had some thoughts formerly of going to Cambridge, as I remember, you recommended a tutor to me; but I have quite forgot his name. We

are obliged to mis-spend so much time here in
attending frivolous lectures and unintelligible dis-
putations, that I am quite tired out with such a
disagreeable way of trifling; so that if I can't be
excused from these things at Cambridge, I shall
only just keep term there.

Since I am obliged to write to you, and am not
certain when I shall be in London, I must beg leave
to trouble you with a difficulty in relation to Freedom, which very much perplexes me.

Upon reading what you last published[8] upon that
subject, I see great reason to be satisfied that *Freedom* and *Action* are *identical ideas*, and that man is,
properly speaking, an *Agent* or a *Free Being*. But
as the question concerning Freedom *is or is not* of
consequence just as it affects the purposes of Religion, my not being able clearly to make out how
Freedom renders us capable of Moral Government
perplexes me as much as tho' I was in doubt concerning Freedom itself. I am satisfied that it is in
our power to *act or not to act* in any given case,
yet I do not see that it follows from thence that it
is in our power to *act virtuously*, because the *physical* and the *moral* nature of an action comes under
quite two *different* considerations. Virtue does not
consist *barely in acting*, but in acting *upon such
motives*, and *to such ends;* and *acting upon such
motives*, &c. evidently supposes *a disposition in
our nature to be influenced by those motives*, which
disposition not being an *action*, does not depend
upon *us*, but, like the rest of our affections, seems
to proceed from our *original frame and constitution*. For instance; It is a virtue to relieve the

[8] Letters to Leibnitz, with remarks on a book entitled "A
Philofophical Enquiry concerning Human Liberty." London, 1717.

poor, *upon this account* (suppose) that it is the will of God, and tho' the action be done, yet *if it be not done upon this account,* it is not a virtuous action. I own it's in my power to relieve the poor (*i. e.* to *do the physical action*); but I don't see that it's in my power to do it upon the account, that it's the will of God (*i. e.* to *do the moral action*), unless I have a disposition in my nature to be influenced by this motive; therefore this disposition may be considered as a *sine quâ non* to the performance of every duty. Now that we have not this disposition when we neglect our duty is evident from this, that if we always had it, we should always *certainly, though not necessarily,* do our duty. How then can we be accountable for neglecting the practice of any virtue, when at what time soever we did neglect it we wanted that which was a *sine quâ non,* or absolutely necessary to the performance of it, viz. a disposition to be influenced by the proper motive?

Thus the case seems to stand as to Virtue; it's somewhat different in respect to *Vice,* or *the positive breach of God's Law,* because *here* must be *action,* and it's always in our power *not to act ;* but in this case also there is a very great difficulty; for the reason why it's expected that we should avoid Vice is, because there are *stronger motives against it* than for committing it; but then motives are *nothing* to one who is *indifferent* to them, and every man is at least indifferent to them who is not influenced by them in his actions, because if he was not indifferent, or, which is more, had not stronger dispositions to be influenced by contrary motives, it's morally certain that he would not act contrary to these. So that tho' a man can avoid Vice, yet (according to this) *he cannot avoid it upon that account,* or *for that reason*, which is the *only reason* why he ought to avoid it.

Upon the whole such is the imperfection of our nature, that it seems impossible for us to perform any one more virtuous action than we do perform; and tho' we may always avoid Vice, yet if we are indifferent to that which is the only proper motive why we should avoid it (*i. e.* cannot avoid it upon that motive), a *bare possibility* of avoiding Vice does not seem a sufficient reason for the punishment of it from a good and equitable Governor. Tho' all that I have here said should be true, I don't think the foundation of Religion would be at all removed, for there would certainly, notwithstanding, remain reasons of infinite weight to confirm the truth and enforce the practice of it; but upon another account I have cause to think that I am guilty of some mistake in this matter, viz. that I am conscious of somewhat in myself, and discern the same in others, which seems directly to contradict the foregoing objections; but I am not able at present to see where the weakness of them lies, and our people here never had any doubt in their lives concerning a received opinion; so that I cannot mention a difficulty to them. Upon which account, since it's a matter of great consequence, I hope for your excuse and assistance in it, both which I have formerly had to my great satisfaction in others.

I am, honoured Sir,

Your most obliged humble Servant.

Oriel Coll., Sept. 30.

THE ANSWER. Oct. 3, 1717.

IF I apprehend your difficulty right, I think it may be cleared by the following consideration. *A disposition in our nature* (which disposition is no *action*, nor in our *power* any further than as 'tis affected by habits) *to be influenced by right motives,* is certainly a *sine quâ non* to virtuous actions. In God, the disposition is *essential* and *invariable.* In *Angels and Saints in Heaven* 'tis *constantly effectual,* but not essentially so. In *men* 'tis that which we call *Rationality,* or the *faculty of reason,* which makes them capable of rewards or punishments, to be determined by the proportion or degree of every man's *rationality* (which is the *talent* God has given him) ——[9] with the degree of his use of that *talent in acting.*

To apply this to your instance:—*'Tis the will of God* that I should *relieve the poor.* Being a *rational creature* is having a *disposition to act upon this motive* (and therefore you wrongly suppose that any men naturally, and without very corrupt habits, can be without *that disposition*). If I relieve the poor merely out of *natural compassion,* or any other motive that is not vicious, this is still *freely obeying the will of God* as made known by the *Law of Nature.* And it *then only ceases* to be a virtuous action when I do it upon a vicious motive, and without that vicious motive would *not have done it,* that is, would, by the use of my *liberty,* have overruled my *Rationality,* or *natural disposition* to have obeyed

---

[9] There is a word here indecipherable, perhaps " coupled."

the *will of God*, made known either by *Nature*, or *Revelation*, or both. If I have either mistaken, or not satisfied your difficulty, you will let me hear from you again.

VIII.

[The original of this Letter with the answer, which is roughly written on the blank leaf, is, I believe, now in the library of Oriel College, Oxford. I am indebted for my copy to the kindness of the Rev. J. H. Newman, D. D., formerly of that College.]

REVEREND SIR,

I HAD long resisted an Inclination to desire your Thoughts upon the difficulty mentioned in my last, till I considered that the trouble in answering it would be only carrying on the general purpose of your Life, and that I might claim the same right to your Instructions with others; notwithstanding which I should not have mentioned it to you had I not thought (which is natural when one fancies one sees a thing clearly) that I could easily express it with clearness to others. However, I should by no means have given you a second trouble upon the subject had I not had your particular leave. I thought proper just to mention these things that you might not suspect me to take advantage from your Civility to trouble you with anything, but only such objections as seem to me of Weight, and which I cannot get rid of any other way. A disposition in our natures to be influenced by right motives is as absolutely necessary to render us moral Agents, as a Capacity to discern right motives is. These two are I think quite *distinct* perceptions, the *former* proceeding from a desire inseparable from a Conscious Being of its own happiness, the *latter* being only our Understanding, or Faculty of seeing Truth. Since a *disposition* to be influenced by right motives is a *sine quá non* to Virtuous Actions, an Indifferency to right motives must *incapacitate* us for Virtuous Actions, or render us, in that particular, not moral agents. I do indeed think that no Rational Creature is, *strictly speaking, Indifferent* to Right Motives, but yet there seems to be somewhat which to all intents of the present question is the same, viz. *a stronger disposition to be influenced by contrary or wrong motives,* and this I take to be always the Case when any vice is committed. But since it may be said, as you hint, that this stronger disposition to be influenced by Vicious Motives may have been contracted by repeated Acts of Wickedness, we will pitch upon the *first Vicious Action* any one is guilty of. No man would have committed this first Vicious Action if he had not had a *stronger* (at least as strong) *disposition* in him to be influenced by the *Motives of the Vicious Action,* than by the *motives of the contrary Virtuous Action;* from whence I infallibly conclude, that since every man has committed some first Vice, every man had, *antecedent* to the commission of it, a *stronger disposition* to be influenced by the *Vicious* than the *Virtuous* motive. My difficulty upon this is, that a *stronger natural disposition* to be influenced by the Vicious than the Virtuous Motive (which every one has antecedent to his first vice), seems, to all purposes of the present question, to put the Man in the same condition as though he was *indifferent to the Virtuous Motive ;* and since an *indifferency to the Virtuous Motive* would have *incapacitated* a Man from being a *moral Agent,* or *contracting guilt,* is not a *stronger disposition* to be influenced by the *Vicious* Motive as great an *Incapacity ?*   Suppose I have two diversions offered me, *both* of which I could not enjoy, I like both of them, but yet have a *stronger* inclination to one than to the other, I am not indeed strictly *indifferent* to either, because I should be glad to *enjoy both ;* but am I not exactly *in the same case, to all intents and purposes of acting,* as though I was *absolutely indifferent* to that diversion which I have the *least* inclination to ? You suppose Man to be endued naturally with a *disposition to be influenced by Virtuous Motives,* and that *this Disposition is a sine quâ non to Virtuous Actions,* both which I fully believe ; but then you *omit* to consider the natural Inclination to be influenced by Vicious Motives, which, *whenever a Vice is committed,* is at least *equally strong* with the other, and in the first Vice *is not affected by Habits,* but is as *natural,* and as much *out of a man's power* as the other.   I am much obliged to your offer of writing to Mr. Laughton, which I shall very thankfully accept of, but, am not certain when I shall go to Cambridge ; however, I believe it will be about the middle of the next month.

I am, Rev. Sir,

Your most obliged humble Servant.

Oriel, Oct. the 6th.

THE ANSWER.

YOUR objection seems indeed very dexterous, and yet I really think that there is at bottom nothing in it. But of this you are to judge, not from my assertion, but from the reason I shall endeavour to give to it.

I think, then, that a *disposition to be influenced by right motives* being what we call *rationality*, there cannot be on the contrary (properly speaking) any such thing naturally in rational creatures as a *disposition to be influenced by wrong motives.* This can be nothing but mere *perverseness of will ;* and whether even that can be said to amount to a disposition to be influenced by wrong motives, *formally*, and as such, may (I think) well be doubted. Men have by nature strong inclinations to certain objects. None of these inclinations are vicious, but vice consists in pursuing the inclination towards any object in certain circumstances, notwithstanding *reason*, or the natural disposition to be influenced by right motives, declares to the man's conscience at the same time (or would do, if he attended to it) that the object ought not to be pursued in those circumstances. Nevertheless, where the man commits the crime, the *natural disposition* was only towards the *object*, not formally towards the doing it upon wrong motives; and generally the very essence of the crime consists in the liberty of the will forcibly overruling the *actual disposition towards being influenced by right motives*, and not at all (as you suppose) in the man's having any *natural disposition to be influenced by wrong motives*, as such.

IX.

[*From the original, now in the library at the British Museum.* Add. MS. 12,101.]

REV. SIR,

I HAD the honour of your kind letter yesterday, and must own that I do now see a *difference* between the nature of *that disposition which we have to be influenced by virtuous motives*, and *that contrary disposition*, (or whatever else it may *properly* be called,) which is the *occasion* of our committing *sin;* and hope in time to get a thorough insight into this Subject by means of those helps you have been pleased to afford me. I find it necessary to consider such very abstruse questions at different times and in different dispositions; and have found particular use of this method upon that abstract subject of *Necessity:* for tho' I did not see the force of your argument for the *unity of the Divine Nature* when I had done writing to you upon that subject, I am now *fully satisfied* that it is conclusive. I will only just add that I suppose somewhat in my last letter was not clearly expressed, for I did not at all *design* to say, that *the essence of any crime consisted in the man's having a natural disposition to be influenced by wrong motives.*

I was fully resolved to have went to Cambridge
some time in this Term, not in the least expecting
but that I might have the Terms allowed there
which I have kept here, but I am informed by one
who has been there that it is not at all to be depended upon; but that it's more likely to be refused
than granted me. My design was this; when I
had taken the degree of Batchelor of Arts at Cambridge, (which I would have done to have the Pri-
viledge of that Gown,) to take that of Batchelor of
Law a year afterwards, but if I cannot have the
Terms I have kept for Batchelor of Arts allowed
there, it will be highly proper for me to stay at
Oxford to take that degree here, before I go to
Cambridge to take Batchelor of Law. I will inquire
concerning the truth of what the gentleman told
me, and if I find he is mistaken, and that I can take
the degree of Batchelor of Arts at Cambridge next
June, which is the time I shall be standing for it,
and Batchelor of Law a year after that; I will make
bold to accept of your kind offer to write to Mr.
Laughton, and will acquaint you with it as soon as
I am satisfied, otherwise I will give you no further
trouble in the matter; and indeed I am sorry I
should have given you any already upon it, but I
thought I had sufficient reason to be satisfied, and
had not the least suspicion in the world that there
was any uncertainty about getting the Terms allowed,
so I hope you will excuse it.

I am, with the greatest respect and gratitude for
all your favours,

Reverend Sir,

Your most obedient humble Servant.

Oriel Coll., Oct. 10, 1717.

I should have written yesterday, to prevent your trouble of writing to Mr. Laughton, but I was not informed of what I have mentioned before last night.[10]

[10] [The three last Letters appear to have been intended by Dr. Clarke for publication, as the passages relating to private matters have been struck through, and on the back of this last is written, "These to be added to the next edition of Leibnitz's Letters." I believe those Letters never reached a second edition.]

INDEX OF SCRIPTURE TEXTS CITED
OR REFERRED TO.

c c

INDEX OF WORDS AND THINGS.

Bath Hospital, referred to, 243, n.

Beauty, harmony, and proportion as real as truth, 150.

Begging in the streets to be discouraged, 241.

BENEVOLENCE. See *Covetousness, Hobbes, Good-will, Affection, Good-humour, Love.*

whether it is in man is a mere question of fact, 5, n.

is not love of power, 4, n. 343.

but sometimes love of power to be used in doing good, 343.

ambition is often like it, 5, n.

is only the sum of virtue when directed by reason and reflection, 165.

common virtues may be traced up to it, or the want of it, 167.

its exercise should be directed by reason, 165.

reasonable good-will and right behaviour in a manner the same, 167.

its effects upon us, 155.

source of our obligations to it, 109.

resentment not inconsistent with it, 108.

vice or injury may lessen but not destroy it. 109, 305.

nor does the peculiar regard due to ourselves, 109.

may be very great and yet be overruled by other principles, 158.

is to society what self-love is to the individual, 4.

suspected of being contrary to self-love, 134.

the course of action it leads to is not peculiarly contrary to self-love, 142.

it is not contrary to self-love because different from it, 140.

is no more distant from self-love than hatred is, 141.

sometimes interferes with self-love, but not oftener than other affections, 147.

the interest others have in this affection does not lessen our enjoyment, 148.

it relates more to the materials of enjoyment than to enjoyment itself, 147.

persons in all ages have found pleasure in it, 144.

has gratifications as a *virtuous principle*, and as a *natural affection*, 146.

its gratification leads to our own gratification, 143.

is in a degree its own gratification, 143, 149.

is really coincident with self-love, 6, 52.

is more advantageous than other pursuits if disappointed, 143.

BENEVOLENCE (*continued*).

the temper it forms in us is peculiarly a happy one, 144.
it rises into the love of GOD, 169.

BODY.

relation of its parts analogous to our relations in society, 3.
men are very much one body, 12.
our being one body in Christ, a motive to Christian
duties, 2.
felt most in the first ages, 2.

BRISTOL, Fragment of a Charge to the Clergy of, 338.

BRISTOL INFIRMARY.

deserving of support, 243.
Mr. Tucker's sermon for it referred to, 308.

BRUTE CREATURES.

actions natural in them, not so in us, 24.
to be entirely governed by our affections would sink us
almost to them, 57.
man is not left to live at random like them, 32.

BRUTUS.

what is said of his reading true of very few, 120.
what is said of his strength of will, 343.

C ANONS.

the 61st quoted, 334,
the 67th referred to, 338.

Cambridge, Butler's intention of going there, 373, 380, 383-4.

Carelessness, generally considered faulty, 96, 236.

CARTES (Des), *Ep.* 69, *partis primæ*, cited, 371.

CASAUBON, *in Athenæum*, cited, 331.

CATO, his saying that he never forgave faults in himself, 113.

CHARACTER.

determined by the proportion of our qualities, 157.
a just way of trying one's own, 163.
affections toward good characters, 172.
we may imagine one absolutely good and perfect, 176.
how the contemplation of it would affect us, 177.
giving of characters dangerous talk, 48.
some reason needed beside mere truth, 50.
how to be conducted when necessary, 49.

CHARITY. See *Benevolence, Love, Poor, Rich, Associations.*

what it is, 300.
how described by St. Paul, 162.

CLERGY. See *Affectation, Sermons, Bristol, Durham.*
 often reproached for what is not their fault, 336.
 should give themselves wholly to their work, 336.
 how to revive a spirit of religion, 324, 337.
 have promised to visit the sick, 338.
 private intercourse with their parishioners, 278, 308, 334.
 should take advantages of opportunities to speak of religion, 333.
 instances of such opportunities, 333.
 their general behaviour with unbelievers, 320-324.
 should keep their chancels in good order, 328.
Cloak, required by wrong doing, 252, 260.

COLONIES. See *Slaves, Natives.*
 we are bound to keep up Christianity in them, 221.
 or they may sink into stupid Atheism, 226.

COMMERCE.
 promoted by the invention of money, 232.
 good effects of its increase, 233.
 frugality and diligence peculiarly become those engaged in it, 313.
 should be consecrated to religion, 221, 222.

COMMON PEOPLE. See *Poor.*
 not to be influenced against measures they are not judges of, 297.
Communion, rubric as to giving notice, 335.

COMPASSION. See *Sympathy, Fellow-feeling, Tyranny.*
 SERMONS V. and VI, 52, 66.
 its final causes, 68.
 belongs to us in our public or social capacity, 52.
 its object is not ourselves, but another in distress, 53, n.
 distinguished from two other effects of the sight of distress, 55, n.
 is greater towards our friends than to others, 54, n.
 why more necessary than sympathy in prosperity, 56, 67.
 is much stronger, and felt more generally than delight at the good of others, 56, 67.
 there are instances of it in nature, 69, 306.
 men would be more cruel without it, 61, 68.
 it gives the indigent access to us, 62.
 is a call of nature to relieve the unhappy, 70.
 makes us merciful rather than merely liberal, 70.

COMPASSION (*continued*).

    may be carried too far, but insensibility is far more common, 72.

    resentment is a balance to it, 99.

    a man is compassionate or resentful according to the proportion and influence of other principles, 158.

    it causes more good and delight than sorrow and evil, 59-60.

    to the sufferer and to the compassionate also, 60.

    perhaps in the judicial capacity the affection should not be heard, 63.

    all evil-doers properly objects of it, 114.

    when it will be lost, 76.

Competent provision, a thing really limited though hard to determine, 160.

Confirmation, a good time for private instruction, 334.

Congratulation and Condolence, scarcely signify an inward feeling, 56.

CONSCIENCE. See *Witness, Judgment, Reflection.*

    is the principle which approves and disapproves, 10.

    its existence is not to be denied, 10.

    is not to be omitted in any argument from man's nature, 17.

    reflection is manifestly superior to passions and appetites, 27.

    its being a law of our nature implies an obligation to obey it, 33.

    the natural superiority of one faculty over another is part of the idea of it, 26.

    presiding and governing are part of the idea of it, 27.

    man's violating it does not affect its *natural right and office*, 28.

    not to allow its natural supremacy leads to gross absurdities, 28.

    it makes a man a moral agent and a law to himself, 24, 381.

    leads us to do good to others, 10.

    there are small diversities in regard of it, 18.

    may be laid asleep by half-deceits, 85.

    corrupted by self-deceit, 132.

CONSTITUTION. See *System, Nature, England, Establishment, King, Government, Liberty.*

    implies subordination under a supreme authority, 30.

    that of man compared with that of a civil government, 30, 31, n.

CONSTITUTION (*continued*).

that of Society is visibly moral, 253, 288.

the English Constitution overthrown by the great rebellion, 256-259.

ought to be greatly respected although not perfect, 259.

how liberty affects our Ecclesiastical Constitution, 291.

why we should value and how use it, 298.

Conveniences, somewhat *ornamental* and for *entertainment,* soon begin to be sought for by rich persons, 231.

CONVERSATION. See *Tongue.*

good in itself, 44.

implies mutual discourse, 46.

a wise man would make it instructive, 48.

Corrections. See *Punishment.*

COVETOUSNESS.

temptations to it from the use of money, 232.

has as little to do with self-love as benevolence has, 146.

means sometimes more than the mere love of riches, 146.

it then includes self-love and is called selfishness, 147.

it is directly contrary to charity in its temper, 233.

CREATION. See GOD.

incomprehensible but certain, 198.

wickedness and wrong its only deformity, 101.

the Creator must be superior to His works, 193.

Creatures of some orders may understand the designs of providence, 208.

CRUELTY. See *Love of injustice.*

on HOBBES' principles the same as benevolence, 5, n.

prevented by compassion, 61, 62.

resentment is adapted to prevent it and injustice, 96.

CUDWORTH, *on the Lord's Supper,* cited, 331.

DANIEL.

his prophecy of God's kingdom, 214.

DAVID, not hard hearted, 124.

his self-deceit, 118, 125, 131.

his language in the Psalms most applicable to the wants and hopes of good men, 195.

Day-dreams, not to be indulged in, 345.

DEATH. See *Executions.*

should be received as the penalty of sin, 339.

FACE, its beauty determined as moral character is by the proportion of its features, 157.

Fact, the existence of goodwill between men a fact, 5, n.

Faction is tyranny out of power, 255.

Faculties naturally give delight as well as being useful, 43.

FAITH, how a virtue, 202.

" faith in Christ," what it means, 271.

Family Prayers, desirable, 330.

Faults of good men are generally what make them disliked, 344.

FEAR.

confounded with compassion by Hobbes, 53, n.

" Fear of God," its effect in religious discussions, 323.

what it means in the Bible, 271.

servile fear not due to God, 172.

FEELINGS.   See *Affections*.

inward, are real and may be argued from, 18.

Fellow-creatures, respect to them natural, 12.

FELLOW-FEELING.   See *Delight, Compassion, Sympathy*.

those who have got over it, insensible to many satisfactions, 61, 63.

indignation at vice is a fellow-feeling for the whole species, 95.

FINAL CAUSES.

tell us something of the designs of Providence, 199.

those in regard to man's inward principles, 18, 66.

of compassion, 68.

First thoughts, why often best, 87.

Fitness of actions, as real as truth itself, 150.

FLEETWOOD, *Bishop of St. Asaph*, his observation on repairing churches, 329.

Folly, a subject of pity and laughter, 72.

Forgetfulness of themselves and their true state, the condition of most men, 74.

FORGIVENESS OF INJURIES.   SERM. IX, 102.

of ENEMIES, see *Enemies*.

shows greatness of mind, as in our Lord's example, 114.

a forgiving spirit can alone give us a hope of mercy, 114-16.

Form of godliness to be kept up as well as the *power* of it, 332.

FRAME. See *Constitution.*

INWARD FRAME OF MAN includes conscience, 11.
> answers in a peculiar manner to his condition and circumstances, 66.
> moral obligation may be proved from it, 16.
> is a constitution how ruled and how impaired, 31, n.
> we understand something real by it, 18.

FREEDOM. See *Liberty, Government, England, Love of* GOD.
freedom and action are identical ideas, 374.
> but virtue cannot exist without a disposition in our nature to do the action on a virtuous motive, are we accountable for want of this? 374.
> can vice exist without a disposition to be influenced by motives contrary to virtue so strong as to be practically conclusive? 375.

ANS. The disposition to be influenced by right motives is rationality, which may be overruled by the use of our freedom of action, 377, 29.

But is there not before every first vice a stronger natural disposition to be swayed by wrong motives, which negatives the other? 379.

ANS. There is no such thing as a disposition to be influenced by wrong motives, but only a perverseness of will, following an object, good in itself, against what reason declares to the conscience to be right under the circumstances, 381. See *Love of Injustice.*

FRIENDSHIP.
a disposition to it is benevolence, 5-6.
friendship and natural relations bias us as self-deceit does, 120, 129.
what it is from a perfect being to ourselves, 177.

GAIN. See *Interest.*
GEORGE II. his praises, 265, 289, 291, 294, 297.

GOD. See *Goodness, Ignorance, Love, Presence, Unity.*
though He is One we cannot but consider Him in different views, 183.
the argument from final causes proves His wisdom and design, 66.
cannot approve of anything but what is right, fit, and just, 341.

GOD (*continued*).

His plans and reasons not to be too curiously inquired into, 91.

His dealings with man cannot be fully judged of by what we see, 200.

we have no clear conception of any moral attribute that may not be resolved into goodness, 169.

words cannot express how all beauty and order meet in Him, 192.

His perfect goodness the principle whence the world was brought into being, 90.

He loves the whole universe, 153.

is unmoved by passion or affection, 57.

foresaw and provided against irregularities and disorders, 102.

our particular affections are instance of His care and love for us, 9.

has provided mitigations and reliefs for our afflictions and frailties, 69, 306.

His goodness is shown in making the use of our faculties give us pleasure, 43.

the wisdom of Providence is shown in bringing good out of evil, 108, 278.

pain and resentment are instances of His goodness, 101.

His government does what civil government never can do, 266, 289.

the affections which naturally rest in Him, 172, 179.

those which are due from us, 184.

love of GOD is an example of benevolence, 169.

the affections due to a perfect creature are due also to Him, 179.

our senses not perceiving Him does not remove them, 180.

we may hereafter see those qualities we now only see the effects of, 192.

and GOD's own Nature is something still beyond, 192.

He must be in all senses and in every respect the highest object to the mind, 192.

He is revealed to us as our happiness in a future state, 195.

approving ourselves to His judgment, a source of pleasure, 145, 181.

we should accept His will without murmuring, 344.

to " walk with GOD" is to give up our will to His, 187, 185

GOD (*continued*).

carelessness or conceited confidence about His worship unspeakable presumption, 342.

the trespasses of others against us should remind us of ours against Him, 114.

we must not "*charge* GOD *foolishly,*" 101.

" For GOD's sake," its use and meaning, 247.

the leave given to Balaam was given *in His anger*, 81.

GOOD. See GOD, *Just.*

cannot be done and not approved of, 10.

generally easy to distinguish from evil, 64, 87.

possible exceptions, 32.

it is very dangerous to discountenance what is good, because it might be better, 228, 284.

a good man is a general blessing, 163.

is unsuspicious and willing to forgo his own, 162.

is ready to say good and reluctant to tell evil of others, 49.

GOOD-HUMOUR is not charity, 301.

is benevolence while it lasts, 144.

GOOD-WILL. See *Benevolence, Virtue.*

the cultivation and exercise of it is virtue and religion, 6, n.

sometimes blinds, sometimes opens our eyes to faults, 122, n.

GOODNESS. See GOD, *Benevolence, Virtue.*

is the moral quality which is the immediate object of love, 176.

implies the love of itself, 169, 175, 181.

our hearts must be formed to a love and liking of it, 156.

the perfection of goodness consists in love of the whole universe, 153.

perfect goodness may satisfy all our affections, 194.

GOSPEL. See *Christianity, Missions, Miracles.*

was given when Infinite Wisdom saw proper, 214.

is a witness and warning to all, 217.

is sure to have its genuine effect on some, 223.

conditions of the Gospel covenant, 332.

GOVERNMENT. See *Authority, Constitution, Liberty, Moral.*

is a Divine appointment, 264.

how different from mere power, 261.

cannot be free without general stated laws, 263.

JEWS, designed as a witness to other nations, 214.
    had fixed times for private prayer, 330.
    offered sacrifices, &c. for kings, 295.
    their laws as to persecution no guide to us, 293.
JOB, his account of wisdom, 207.
JUDGMENT. See *Conscience, Reflection.*
    influenced by our passions and pursuits, 123.
    equity of the last judgment, 115.
Judicial capacity, perhaps men ought in it to be deaf to af-
    fection, 63.
Just, right, and good, the pursuit of what is so a source of plea-
    sure, 144, 341.
Justice, resentment a great safeguard to it, 100.

KINGS. See CHARLES I, GEORGE II.
    our duty to pray for them, 295.
    the respect due to them, 296.
" *Know thyself,*" why insisted on as a precept, 119.
KNOWLEDGE. See *Attention, Ignorance.*
    not the chief good of man, 193.
    not our proper happiness, 206.
    to know everything as well as we know anything would
    be too little, 199.
    knowledge is of avail only as it teaches us to do our
    duty, 208.

LANGUAGE, something analogous to the use of money,
    232.
LAW. See *Witness.*
LAWS. See *Government.*
    cannot comprehend every case, 263.
    the fundamental laws of all governments are moral, 252.
LIBERTY. See *Freedom, England, Licentiousness.*
    what it signifies in the New Testament, 250.
    what in 1 Pet. II. 16, 251.
    liable to degenerate into licentiousness, 260.
    a cloak for many evil designs, 256.
    those who pretended to love it opposed charity schools,
    276.
    it is no recommendation of any kind of liberty that it
    enables us to do ill, 297.

LOVE of our NEIGHBOUR.   See *Benevolence, Good-will.*
  Sermons XI. and XII, 133 and 152.
  its objects and extent, 152.
  the temper it leads to, 162.
  includes in it all virtues, 164, 167.
  would make a man better in all the relations of life, 163.
  love and good-will cause meekness and easiness of
    temper, 162.
  moderate resentment and prevent strife and enmity, 164.
  imply temperance, sobriety, and self-restraint, 167.
  who is our neighbour, 153, 154, 314.
  in what sense to be loved *as ourselves*, 154.
      with the same kind of affection, 154.
      in some proportion to our self-love, 156-59.
      perhaps with an equality of affection, 160-62.
      the more care, thought, and riches we employ about
        our neighbour the nearer we come up to it, 160.
      we can never have the same perception of our
        neighbours' wants as of our own, 161.

LUXURY.   See *Poverty.*
  how it came into the world, 231.
  easily restrained by rich men, 232.

MACHINES are not so high an object as the mind of
    the artificer, 193.
Mahometans, their short daily devotions, 326.
Malice. See *Resentment.*

MAN. See *Character, Frame, Ignorance, Nature, Human, Good.*
  is a free being, 374, &c.
  insufficient for his own happiness, 189.
  men are imperfect and continually dependent, 57.
  made for society, 11.
  men are very much one body, 12.
  the latitude and compass of man's actions, 28.
  is so constituted as to rest content without what does
    not belong to his condition of being, 185.
  has sufficient capacities for the business assigned to him,
    203.
  what course of life he was made for, 28.
  his province is virtue and religion, life and manners, 208.
  his inward frame is a constitution or system, and how
    ordered, 31, n.
  his nature must not be judged of by rare exceptions, 14.

MAN (*continued*).

    he has a rule of right within, 32.

    vice is his misery, 89.

    what makes him capable of moral government, 377.

    often violates his own nature, 16, 25.

    as rarely obtains the greatest possible happiness as the greatest possible good, 14.

    ill men profess the law of virtue which condemns them, 256. See *Cloak*.

    the whole system of affections stronger in some than in others, 158.

    the right proportion of our affections determined by our nature and condition, 159.

    source of his obligations to good-will, 109.

    seeks naturally for grounds of acquaintance and friendship, 12.

    must confine the object of his benevolence, 153.

    ought not to make others too dependent on himself, 343.

    is mankind equally vicious in all ages? 133.

    one generation depends very much on those before it, 268.

    riches, honours, and sensual gratifications leave a want still, 190.

    man's love of order and harmony as real as of sensual pleasures, 192.

    his wants will remain after death, 191.

    an Infinite Being may supply them all, 190.

Meanness, 168, n.

Medicines, a natural provision made by GOD for man, 302.

MICAH VI. 8, reason for saying *do* justly and *love* mercy, 156

Mind, able to take a survey of itself, 9.

Miracles, not now necessary to the preaching of the Gospel, 224.

MISERY. See *Happiness, Vice, Compassion*.

    pain, sorrow, and misery have a right to our assistance, 705.

    men turn away from the sight of them, 69.

    compassion was given to make us attend, 69, 70.

    compassion in misery more necessary than sympathy in joy, 67.

    we can relieve it more easily than give happiness, 67.

    many things more cause it, 67.

    we are not capable of happiness for so long a time, 67.

    the miseries of life tend to make us moderate, humble, and sober, 74.

MISERY (*continued*).

 they tell us this world is not our home, 75.

 how we may get the advantage without the pain, 74.

MISSIONS. See *Gospel.*

 a means of carrying on GOD's scheme, 222.

 it is to be desired that all persons should join in them, 225.

Misunderstanding, universal when we feel offended, 111, 112.

Money, its origin and use, 232.

MORALS. See *Laws, Constitution.*

 the sum of morals, 106.

 MORAL CONSIDERATIONS make ourselves more a care to us than others can be, 161.

 GOVERNMENT, what makes men capable of it, 374-82.

 OBLIGATIONS (see *Obligations*) run only to natural possibilities, 161.

 may be proved from the adaptation of nature, 17.

 often evaded by refinements, 87.

 the observance of the decencies of behaviour are obligations of morality, 46, 168, n.

 REFLECTIONS seldom applied to ourselves, 120.

Motives to piety and virtue, 2.

NATHAN.

 his parable to David, 117.

Natives of our colonies ought to be taught Christianity, 221.

NATURE. See *Unnatural.*

 OF MAN. See *Man, Human, Frame, Feelings, Affections,* &c.

 " nature " used in three senses, 21, 22.

 man's nature and circumstances ought to be argued upon as they are, 64, 90.

 the argument as to what is natural to man summed up, 36, 37.

 doing as we please is not following nature, 21.

 man may act in a manner disproportionate to it, 24.

 his abuses of his nature not to be charged upon it, 101.

 it may be changed by habits, 97.

 it is not followed in violating known rules of justice and honesty, 21.

 our passions as well as our senses are supplies for its imperfections, 58.

 it is a constitution violated when passion prevails over conscience, 30.

OBJECTIONS CONSIDERED (*continued*).

delight in order and proportion is mere enthusiasm, 191.

preaching the Gospel has little success, 223.

you can do nothing unless you could work miracles, 224.

the converts there are Christians without evidence, 225.

charity-school children should be taught to work, 244, 278.

children may learn superstition under the notion of religion, 272.

poor people will only pervert what they learn, 275.

charity schools have not reformed the world, 282.

how can charity cover a multitude of sins? 300.

the poor do not deserve to be helped, 303.

we are too indulgent to them, 304.

hospitals are largely enough supported already, 309.

formal recommendations of them at church might well be spared, 309.

the disabled poor are enough provided for already, 310.

there is no need to be anxious how we serve God if we are sincere, 342.

OBLIGATIONS.   See *Morals.*

are not absolute and without exception, 264.

general and more enlarged destroy particular and confined ones, 109.

the general obligations to charity are appropriated by circumstances, 222.

source of our obligations to benevolence, 109.

Obstinacy and wilfulness, how to be cured, 75.

OMNIPRESENCE.

whether it follows from necessary existence, 347, 363.

OBJ. May not a necessary being be absent from some place though not from all? 348.

ANS. But whatever is necessary at all is necessary everywhere, 352.

OBJ. Is this true of things, or of relations only? 355.

ANS. Of things, because there can be no limit of time, or space, or relation to an original necessity, 358.

OBJ. Does a being's existing somewhere suppose it finite? 360.

ANS. Nothing limited in any way can be absolutely necessary, 362.

Opposition, if fair, always allowable under a free government, 296.

Oppression, very detestable, but hard to define, 125.

Order, harmony, proportion, beauty, nonsensual ideas, 190.

PLEASURE. See *Happiness, Self-love, Misery*.
disengagement necessary to it, 138.
could not exist without particular affections, 135.
benevolence and pleasing GOD sources of it, 144, 145.
is always greater from an assurance it will end well, 145.
riches, honours, and sensuality do not complete the greatest pleasure we are capable of, 144.
the materials of enjoyment may be parted with without lessening pleasure, 148.
to make pleasure our business a most romantic scheme of life, 73.
men of pleasure, their hardness of heart is a loss to them, 61, 63.

POOR. See *Charity Schools, Rich, Superiors*.
the ordinary life and behaviour of the poor, 234.
they ought to be attended to rather than the rich, 71.
their faults ought to be judged of mildly and favourably, 305.
the ill desert of some is no reason against providing for them in sickness, 303.
is our common fault against them harshness or laxity? 304.
their English liberty will not be a blessing without some principle to prevent its abuse, 245.
they are put by GOD under the superintendence and patronage of the rich, 237.
but ought not to imitate the rich in wrong doing, 239, 277.
the poor law was a new thing in Queen Elizabeth's time, 273.
the education of poor children needed some provision, 274, 276, 285.

POVERTY.
increases most in times of profusion and debauchery, 303.
far from the worst evil attending on luxury, 231.

POWER. See *Authority, Tyranny*.
distinguished from authority in regard to conscience and passion, 27.
the love of it will not account for benevolence, 4, n. 343.

PRAYER. See *Devotion*.
frequent secret prayer recommended, 330.
a prayer for the love of GOD and for our neighbour, 170.

E E

PRAYER (*continued*).
    one for the children in charity-schools, 286.
Prerogative of conscience, 24.
PRESENCE. See *Omnipresence*.
    the presence of a friend compared with that of GOD, 145,
      180, 194.
Pretences, always used to cover wrong designs, 256, 252, &c.
PRETENDER, the rebellion of 1745 referred to, 295.
PRINCIPLES. See *Particular Affections*.
    do not singly form a man's character, 157.
    sometimes contradict one another, 22.
    some have a superior nature to others, 26, 28.
    this is part of the idea of conscience, 26.
    one approved and loved for itself will be so in all men,
      176.
Printing, the time of its invention and its effects, 276.
Prisons, possible improvements in them, 244.
Profane swearing, what it implies, 29.
Profaneness. See *Atheism, Impiety*.
PROPERTY. See *Rich*.
    is not happiness, 148, 149, 190.
    riches and time may be given away without loss of en-
      joyment, 148.
    the word excludes the interest of other people, 140.
    the notion of it wrongly brought into that of self-love,
      140.
PROPORTION. See *Order*.
    the proportion of particular affections determines cha-
      racter, 157.
    the right proportion between benevolence and self-love,
      159.
ROVIDENCE. See GOD, *Charity*.
    brings good out of evil, 108, 278.
    men are instruments in its hands, 9.
    gives us the care of particular persons, &c., 165.
PRUDENCE. See *Competent*.
    we are responsible for the good want of prudence prevents
      our doing, 312.
    we are liable to mistakes in prudence as in religion, 272.
PUBLIC GOOD. See *Benevolence*.
    passions which lead to it, 8.
    not inconsistent with private good, 3, 52.
    private good as often contravened, 14.

Public spirit, not strong enough to enable us to do without
compassion, &c. 62.

PUNISHMENT. See *Execution, Death.*
easily becomes excessive, 307.
may and should be relieved, 306.
objects of the punishment of criminals, 244, 109.
punishment is sure to all vice, but proportioned to its
guilt, 240.

R *ANT,* love of enemies not a rant, 110.
Rationality consists in a disposition to be influenced
by right motives, 381. See *Freedom.*

REASON. See *World.*
distinguished from affection, 173.
is sometimes overcome by strong passions, 84.
is not sufficient alone as a motive to virtue, 57.
nor indeed to the care of our bodies, 61.
compassion and fellow-feeling helps to it, 58.
its effects in directing benevolence, 165, 241.
what it tells us is as directly from GOD as revelation is,
220
it is the candle of the LORD within us, 132.
could not have discovered the doctrine of repentance or
of a mediator, 214.
" *Reasonable" Religion,* 171.
Refinements in morals and religion to be avoided, 64, 87.

REFLECTION. See *Conscience, Mind.*
how it gives pleasure, 174.
distinguishes and judges actions, 9.
is conscience, 10.

RELIGION. See *Virtue, Natural Religion, Christianity,
Revelation.*
is in general a practical thing, 325.
the religious affections suitable to our mortal state, 184.
needs the exercise of the affections to assist its influence, 58.
does not demand new affections, but the right use of
those we have, 181.
does not disown, but appeals to self-love, 149.
its sanctions are our security in temptation, 156.
its general decay, 319.
how many who make great pretensions to it allow themselves in unjustifiable courses, 86.

RELIGION (*continued*).

Balaam had a true sense of it and yet chose wickedness, 83, 85.

the want of it is not generally owing to speculative disbelief, 325.

its evidence is complex and various, 322.

it is not to be discussed for amusement, 321.

is not to be spoken of as a doubtful thing, 324.

we must not seem to acquiesce in what is said against it, 323.

its general doctrine was revealed and left to men to preserve, 213.

children ought to be instructed in it, 271.

like common prudence, our mistakes in it should not hinder our teaching it, 272.

like it, it does not consist in mere knowledge and belief, 271.

the substance cannot be preserved without the form, 326.

external religion is to be insisted upon, 328, 332.

how to treat its professed enemies, 320.

no Christian can despair of it, 319.

RELIGIOUS ASSOCIATIONS of Butler's time, 227.

(these were particularly the Society for Promoting Christian Knowledge, the Society for the Propagation of the Gospel in Foreign Parts, the Societies for the Reformation of Manners, and the Society for Promoting Schools in Ireland.)

RELIGIOUS INSTRUCTION. See *Charity Schools*.

in prisons, 244.

in hospitals, 308.

REPENTANCE. See *Reason*.

anything that can be called so is better than impenitence, 340.

a right frame of mind for it, 75.

RESENTMENT. See *Revenge*.

SERMON VIII, 90.

is exceedingly different from all other passions, 107.

is a secondary passion and evil if taken absolutely, 107.

is not evil, 13, 92.

its object is to prevent injury, injustice, and cruelty, 96.

is a generous movement of the mind, 101.

procures the punishment of evil-doers, 100.

RESENTMENT (*continued*).

   it is a balance to the weakness of pity, 99.

   not merely a reasonable concern for our safety, 6, n.

   compassion is a restraint upon it, 68.

   its abuses, 98.

   malice and revenge are abuses of it, 91.

   it is of two kinds, sudden and settled, or deliberate, 92.

   how distinguished from sudden anger, 97.

   sudden resentment is ANGER, which *see*.

   deliberate anger or resentment has wrong and not harm for its object, 94.

      is heightened or lessened by what heightens or lessens the fault, 95.

      injury intended rouses indignation even though prevented, 94.

      it varies as the deliberation, the evil designed and the evil done, 96.

      this indignation is not malice, 94.

   it cannot be right to hate our enemies as we love our friends, 91.

   resentment is a painful remedy, and, therefore, to be used sparingly, 105.

   it must either serve its end or altogether contradict it, 107.

   where it entirely destroys benevolence it is excessive, 108.

   obstinate misconception generally attends excessive resentment, 99.

   it ought not to change our view of other parts of a man's character, 112.

RESIGNATION. See *Submission*.

   grounds of it, 186, 344.

   clears away many cares, 186, 187.

   devotion and worship are this temper in act, 187.

   resignation to the will of GOD is the whole of piety, 185, 187, 202.

   it is perfect where our will is lost in GOD'S, 186.

   will be exalted into love by seeing Him as He is, 188.

Restrictions and limitations implied in almost everything we say, 165.

Retaliation. See *Revenge*.

REVELATION. See *Christianity, Religion*.

   lays us under peculiar obligations, 220.

   what we know by reason comes equally directly from GOD, 220.

REVENGE. See *Resentment.*
  revenge and retaliation are absolutely unlawful, 104.
  propagate themselves in a peculiar manner, 104.
  make a man judge in his own cause, 105.
  invite GOD's judgment upon us, 115.
  the good effects they may have, no justification of them,
    108.

RICH. See *Riches, Conveniences, Poor.*
  relations between the rich and poor in primitive ages,
    236.
  the same obligations exist now, 237.
  relations of the rich to the poor and their duties, 234,
    235, 238, 277, 314, 336.
  their power is a trust and privilege, 236, 237, 238.
  their power may lead to greater rewards or greater
    penalties, 238.
  dissolute persons of fortune greatly increase want and
    misery, 246, 303.
  charity schools to make the rich good, useful, and con-
    tented, greatly wanted, 279.
  rich people as likely to make a bad use of education as
    poor ones, 276.
  middle class people are rich by comparison, 233.

RICHES. See *Property, Money.*
  their first origin in the world, 230.
  effects of the use of money, 232.
  riches, honours, and sensual gratifications falsely reckoned
    the greatest happiness of life, 15, 190.
  they are so only in a moderate degree, 15.
  riches and time may be given away without loss of en-
    joyment, 148.
  what superiority riches give to those who have them
    235, 336
  the abuse of this blameable, 236.
  the prerogative of riches is the power they give of doing
    good, 317.
  how unhappy those are who neglect it, 318.
  the generality of mankind have cause to be thankful
    they have them not, 313.

RIGHT. See *Good.*
" *Righteous,*" what Balaam understood by the word, 79.
Rivalship more common among men than is suspected, 48.
ROMAN CATHOLICS. See *Persecution.*
  their holidays and frequent devotions, 326.

ROMAN CATHOLICS (*continued*).

    lay too much stress on what is done at the moment of death, 338.

    their Church compared with that established in England, 292.

ROMANS, had public officers to curse their enemies, 78.

*S*ALVATION, peculiarly our own concern, 219.

    Saviour. See CHRIST.

    Scales moved by comparative weights as man by the comparative power of his affections, 159.

SCEPTICISM. See *Doubtfulness.*

    should lead to virtue, 204, 321, 322.

    should make men careful and circumspect, 343.

SCRIPTURE. See *Revelation.*

    cannot be preserved as a revelation without Christian Churches, 225.

    has been preserved by very corrupt Churches, 216.

    is not a book of theory, 153.

    its teaching in regard to civil government, 264.

    upon the various kinds of hypocrisy, 249, n

    how it recommends almsgiving, 317.

SELF-DECEIT. See BALAAM, *Suspicion.*

    SERMON X, 117.

    great power we have of self-deceit, 120.

    its fearful effects, 132.

    it is essentially vicious, 126.

    it is common with even the better sort of men, 254.

    few go on very badly without it, 254.

    many operations of the mind are never reflected on, 88.

    generally men have no doubt or distrust of themselves, 119.

    caution from the effect of friendship upon the judgment, 120, 129.

    those who have never suspected themselves are generally its victims, 168.

    it fortifies against conviction, 126.

    the prevalence of wickedness proves the prevalence of self-deceit, 88.

    degrees of self-ignorance and self-partiality, 118, 121.

    there is such a thing as putting half deceits upon one-self, 85.

    Balaam an instance of this, 85.

    it has great scope in vices that cannot be exactly defined, 124, 156.

SELF-DECEIT (*continued*).

and in the circumstances of wicked acts, 125.
it makes no difference in the real nature of things, 89.
neglect of self-examination is no excuse, 128.
we may guard against it by considering what the world
would believe against us, 130.
and by doing as we would be done by, 130.

Self-enjoyment and home satisfaction, rules for it, 128.
Self-examination may grow into the most commendable turn
of mind possible, 122, n. 74, 114.
Self-existence. See *Unity, Omnipresence.*
Self-hatred, does not exist, 13.
Self-ignorance. See *Self-deceit, Forgetfulness.*

SELF-LOVE. See *Benevolence, Proportion, Unnatural.*

its nature and objects, 134, 137, 140.
is not disowned by religion, 149.
generally coincides with virtue, 36, 140.
does not exclude good-will, 140.
is a security of our right behaviour, 6.
would lead us to get over inordinate regard to ourselves,
139.
is distinct from particular passions and affections, 7, n. 136.
appetites and passions are given as helps to it, 61.
it does not make this or that our interest only impels us
to it, 138.
it seeks things external only as a means of happiness, 135.
helps those in misery by setting them to remove its
causes, 137.
cautions concerning it, 113.
is not generally cool and reasonable enough, 15.
men often contradict it by giving themselves up to some
passion, 147.
most men are indulgent to self, implacable to others, 114.
partial false self-love the weakness of our nature, 111.
whether it may not disappoint itself, 134, 138, 139, 145.
when in excess is often downright pain and misery, 139.
it magnifies the faults of others and lessens our own, 112.
only those blinded by it will not own the duty of forgiveness, 110.
an equal affection to others as to ourselves would leave
ourselves our chief care, 160
persons do not, as the world goes, forget what is due to
themselves, 160.

Self-partiality in excess alone can hinder our forgiving injuries, 110.

Self-regard makes us sometimes partial, sometimes severe to ourselves, 122, n.

SELFISHNESS, 147.
　　includes more than self-love, 140.
　　averse to happiness, 138.

Sermons, should avoid an air of controversy, 324.

Shame, its natural object good though sometimes it leads to evil, 14.

Sickness, some of its uses, 338.

SILENCE. See *Tongue.*
　　when to be observed, 45, 47.
　　sometimes very expressive, 323.

SIMPLICITY of MIND.
　　recommended by our Saviour, 88, 126.
　　the absence of it evil and vicious, 126.

Sincerity, not consistent with carelessness how we worship GOD, 342.

SLAVERY.
　　legally abolished in Great Britain in Butler's time, 290.
　　law cannot abolish voluntary slavery, 290.

Slaves, ought to be instructed in Christianity, 221.

Societies. See *Religious Associations.*

SOCIETY. See *Benevolence, Man, Constitution.*
　　its constitution plainly moral, 253.
　　men are led to it as they are not led to evil, 19.
　　they are made for it as they are for self, 11.
　　they contradict their nature as often in one respect as in the other, 14.

SOCIETY for the Promotion of Christian Knowledge.
　　its work in distributing books (to the number of 32,915 in 1744; in this year they printed an edition of 15,000 Bibles and Prayer-books in Welch, towards which Bp. Butler gave £10 10s.), 278.
　　in founding Charity Schools (there were, in 1744, 146 in London, educating 5,475 children, 1329 in the country, educating 23,421, and 74 in Wales, with 4,253 children, in all 1,549 schools and 33,149 scholars), 274.

SOCRATES, his teaching anticipated by Moses, Job, and Solomon, 208.

SOLOMON. See ECCLESIASTES.
　　wrote chiefly of human life and nature, 197.
　　says the rich ruleth over the poor, 234.

SOLOMON (*continued*).
    what he meant by training up a child in the way he should go, 269.
Space. See *Unity, Omnipresence.*
Speculation in morals and religion often leads to absurdities, 64.

SPEECH. See *Tongue.*
    the objects for which it was given to us, 43
    its abuses, 44.
    may be the instrument of many vices, 41.
STOICS, their apathy morbid, 62.

SUBMISSION. See *Resignation, Authority.*
    there is a general principle of it in our nature, 185.
    is taught us by our ignorance, 209.
    is due to civil government, 264.
    our state here is a school of it, 202.
Superfluities, their origin and production, 231.
Superior excellence excites awe and reverence, 177.

SUPERIORS. See *Rich.*
    their power over the lives of the poor, 235, 277, 336.
    their vices tend to destroy all reverence for authority, 262.

SUPERSTITION.
    is an evil that can never be out of sight, 226.
    abates the force of religion, 298.
    hinders the discernment of good and evil, 32.
    how wickedness is made to sit easy by the superstitious, 87, 88.
    atheism and profaneness bring it in, 227.
    advice for avoiding it, 65, 227.

SUSPICION THAT ALL IS NOT WELL.
    common with self-deceivers, 126.
    sometimes makes them refuse to examine themselves, 127.

SYMPATHY. See *Delight, Compassion, Fellow-feeling.*
    proved by Hobbes' account of pity, 55, n.

SYSTEM. See *Constitution.*
    its perfection consists in its adaptation to its end, 205, n.
    can only be judged of by reference to its object, 205.
    what appears right probably intended, what appears wrong probably not, 206, n.
    the universe is a system, 200.

TALKATIVENESS. See *Tongue, Silence.*
  is not a light matter, 39.
  is a vice, 39, 47.
  exists without other evil intention, 41.
  what it leads to, 40.
  is like a torrent or a fire, 41.
  leads to many faults and follies, 42.
  makes people insignificant, 46.
Temper, proper temper for inquiring into religious things, 203.

TEMPTATIONS.
  a way to become proof against them, 75
  future sanctions of religion a safeguard to us, 156.

TIME. See *Unity, Omnipresence.*
  greatly relieves sorrow, &c. 69.

TONGUE. See *Conversation, Speech, Talkativeness, Silence.*
  its government. SERMON IV, 38.
  what is meant by bridling the tongue, 39, 43.
  dangers and cautions in regard to the use of the tongue, 44, 50.
    in talking of indifferent matters, 47.
    in giving of characters, 48.
  precepts and reflections from Ecclesiastes, 50.
Trade. See *Commerce.*

TRUTH.
  truth and right are real and not to be judged by their abuses, 171.
  truth, good sense, and integrity carry with them a consciousness of right, 127.
  men cannot join in wicked things without a pretence of these, 255.
TUCKER, *Rev. S.* his Sermon for the Bristol Infirmary referred to, 308.
Twilight, analogous to imperfect evidence, 204.

TYRANNY. See *Oppression.*
  the nearest and most dangerous is that of our passions, 298.
  it is carried on with pretences of truth, right, &c. 255.
  what makes us withstand it should make us reverence authority, 260.
  faction is tyranny out of power, 255.
  a Church establishment without toleration is and leads to it, 291.
  tyrants are kept in awe by compassion in other men, 62.

UNITY.
   whether it follows from self-existence, 348, 382.
   OBJ. May not two beings exist without mutual depen-
      dence? 349.
   to take existing alone to exclude this seems begging
      the question, 350.
   ANS. Whatever exists necessarily is necessary to every-
      thing else, 353.
   OBJ. How can this be unless as *space* and *time* are ne-
      cessary and they are not things, 356.
   ANS. Space is a property of the necessary Being, and
      therefore that Being is a *sine quâ non* to all else, 359.
   OBJ. Is not space a property of all substances? 360.
   ANS. Space is not a property of things contained in it,
      363.
   OBJ. Quære as to the relations of spirits and of the self-
      existent Being to space? Is not space itself necessarily
      self-existent? 365.
   ANS. The idea of space is abstract or partial, like that of
      hardness, and supposes the necessary Being, as hard-
      ness does a hard substance, 367.
   OBJ. But one sees the hardness would cease without
      the substance and cannot conceive of space ceasing,
      368.
   ANS. That fact proves the substance it depends on can-
      not be ever supposed away, q. e. d. 371.
Universe is a system, 200.
UNNATURAL.
   means disproportionate to man's nature, 25.
   does not consist in going against *any* inward principle,
      25.
   but does in going against cool self-love, 26.

VAGABONDS, not to be helped, 241.
   VICE. See *Cloak, Punishment.*
   vice and folly take different turns in different ages, 133.
   in numberless cases it cannot be exactly defined, 124.
   consists in an unreasonable regard to ourselves, 122.
   when it consists in excess is peculiarly contrary to the
      virtue it is an excess of, 260.
   there is great viciousness of mind implied in talkative-
      ness, 43.
   vice is of ill desert, 100, 239.

VICE (*continued*).
    a subject of pity and indignation, 72.
    it causes disturbance and implicit dissatisfaction, 89.
    none ever did designed injury to another without doing more to himself, 114.
    it is not free from restraint and confinement, 34.
    the restraints upon it, 35, 36.
    seeing examples takes away our horror of it, 321.

VIRTUE. See *Morals, Good.*
    false professions of it, their commonness and origin, 253.
    is always professed a great deal more than practised, 256.
    man's nature leads to it, 16, 254.
    it is affection to and pursuit of what is right and good as such, 150.
    virtue and religion are the cultivation and exercise of good-will, 6, n.
    their business is to procure universal good-will, trust, and friendship, 59.
    it is in a degree its own reward, 143.
    virtue and a good mind give greater satisfaction than covetousness and ambition, 35, 143.
    to get over what leads on the whole to inconvenience is generally to follow virtue, 35.
    the restraints it puts us under soon become delights, 36.
    it is no more disinterested than many vices and all common affections, 141.
    it is justified to ourselves by being for our advantage, 150.
    and this secures the theory of it from scorn, 150.
    the government of the tongue is required by it, 39.

W*INGS*, why not given to us, 203.
    WITNESS. See *Gospel.*
    what the Scripture speaks of as witnesses, 218, 283.
    how possibly the *witness of conscience* may be distinguished —*the works of the law written in our hearts*, 23.
Words taken from sensible things must be used in speaking of others, 106, 232.

WORLD.   See *System.*
  reason can give no account of men's love of the world,
    84.
WRONG.   See *Vice.*
  requires some cloak to hide it, 252.
  is the peculiar object of settled resentment, 94.

Z EAL, for nothing, 319.

FINIS.

CHISWICK PRESS:—PRINTED BY WHITTINGHAM AND WILKINS,
TOOKS COURT, CHANCERY LANE.